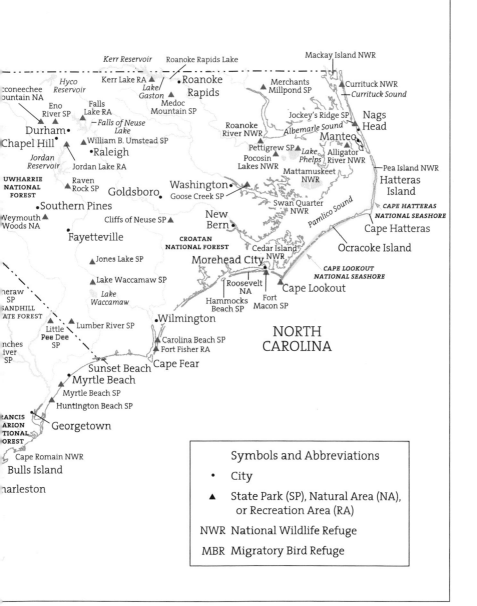

P9-DUP-446

Kerr Reservoir   Roanoke Rapids Lake   Mackay Island NWR

Hyco Reservoir   Kerr Lake RA   •Roanoke   Merchants Millpond SP   ▲Currituck NWR
cconeechee   Lake Gaston ▲   Rapids   —Currituck Sound
ountain NA
Eno   Falls   Medoc
River SP   Lake RA   Mountain SP   Jockey's Ridge SP   Nags
Durham•   —Falls of Neuse   Roanoke   Albemarle Sound   Head
Chapel Hill•   Lake   River NWR   Manteo
        ▲William B. Umstead SP   Pettigrew SP▲Lake Alligator
Jordan   •Raleigh   Pocosin   Phelps River NWR
Reservoir   Jordan Lake RA   Lakes NWR   Mattamuskeet   —Pea Island NWR
UWHARRIE   Raven   NWR   Hatteras
NATIONAL   ▲Rock SP   Washington•   Island
FOREST   Goldsboro•   Goose Creek SP•   Swan Quarter   CAPE HATTERAS
•Southern Pines   NWR   NATIONAL SEASHORE
Weymouth▲   Cliffs of Neuse SP▲   New   Pamlico Sound   Cape Hatteras
Woods NA   Fayetteville   Bern•
            CROATAN   Cedar Island   Ocracoke Island
            NATIONAL FOREST   NWR
        ▲Jones Lake SP   Morehead City•
            CAPE LOOKOUT
        ▲Lake Waccamaw SP   Roosevelt   NATIONAL SEASHORE
heraw   Lake   NA   Cape Lookout
SP   Waccamaw   Hammocks   Fort
SANDHILL   Beach SP   Macon SP
ATE FOREST   ▲Lumber River SP   •Wilmington
Little
Pee Dee   NORTH
nches   SP   ▲Carolina Beach SP   CAROLINA
iver   ▲Fort Fisher RA
SP   Sunset Beach Cape Fear
•Myrtle Beach
Myrtle Beach SP
Huntington Beach SP

RANCIS
ARION   Georgetown
TIONAL
OREST

Cape Romain NWR
Bulls Island
harleston

Symbols and Abbreviations

• City

▲ State Park (SP), Natural Area (NA), or Recreation Area (RA)

NWR National Wildlife Refuge

MBR Migratory Bird Refuge

ELOISE F. POTTER

JAMES F. PARNELL

ROBERT P. TEULINGS

RICKY DAVIS

Birds of the

SECOND EDITION

Carolinas

THE UNIVERSITY OF NORTH CAROLINA PRESS Chapel Hill

2006 The University of North Carolina Press
Set in The Serif types
by Eric M. Brooks

Manufactured in England

The paper in this book meets the guidelines for
permanence and durability of the Committee on
Production Guidelines for Book Longevity of the
Council on Library Resources.

Library of Congress
Cataloging-in-Publication Data
Potter, Eloise F., 1931–
Birds of the Carolinas / by Eloise F. Potter, James F. Parnell,
Robert P. Teulings.—2nd ed.
    p. cm.
Includes bibliographical references and index.
ISBN-13: 978-0-8078-2999-8 (cloth: alk. paper)
ISBN-10: 0-8078-2999-4 (cloth: alk. paper)
ISBN-13: 978-0-8078-5671-0 (pbk.: alk. paper)
ISBN-10: 0-8078-5671-1 (pbk.: alk. paper)
1. Birds—North Carolina. 2. Birds—South Carolina.
3. Bird watching—North Carolina. 4. Bird watching—South
Carolina. I. Parnell, James F. II. Teulings, Robert P., 1934–
III. Title.
QL684.N8P67   2006
598'.09756—dc22   2005022837

cloth   10 09 08 07 06   5 4 3 2 1
paper   10 09 08 07 06   5 4 3 2 1

In memory of
Beatrice Gladys Baker
(1906–2001),
who introduced me to
bird study
—EFP

In honor of
Thomas L. Quay,
teacher, mentor, and friend
—JFP

In memory of
Robert J. (Bob) Hader
(1919–2003)
—RPT

In honor of
my father, who endured
many hours in a cold car and
waged war against hordes of
mosquitoes on trips to Pea
Island during my formative
years as a bird-watcher
—RD

BIRDS OF THE CAROLINAS

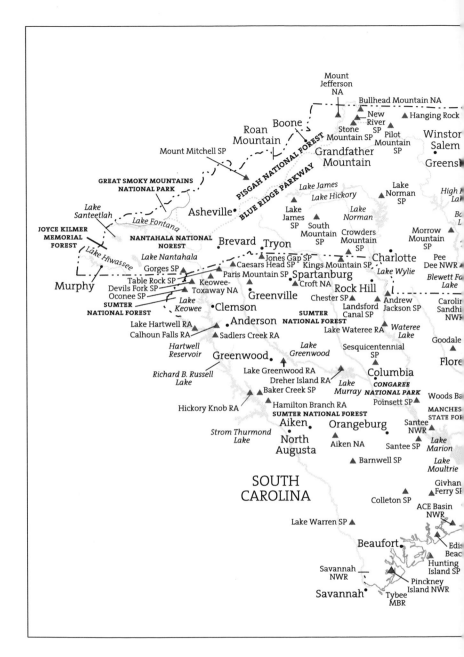

CONTENTS

Many changes have occurred in the bird life of the Carolinas during the past 25 years. The present species accounts provide information on more than 60 species that were not known to occur in the region in 1980. Some of the birds that are new to the Carolinas traveled thousands of miles to reach our fields, woodlands, bird feeders, lakes, beaches, and offshore waters. A few are familiar birds now considered two species instead of one, as a result of DNA research. Birds such as the House Finch are far more plentiful than they used to be. Others, unfortunately, are now less abundant than they were in 1980 and may even be considered threatened or endangered.

As the human population of the Carolinas has increased in recent years, so has the number of residents who provide food for the birds. Hummingbird feeders have become extremely popular. Consequently, several of the species new to the Carolinas are hummingbirds, brilliantly colored visitors from the western United States or the tropics. The number of bird-watchers participating in offshore trips, especially those bound for the Gulf Stream, has increased greatly, resulting in numerous sightings of rare pelagic birds. Thanks to the Blue Ridge Parkway, the Cape Hatteras National Seashore, the Cape Romain National Wildlife Refuge, Francis Marion National Forest, and numerous other state and national forests, parks, and refuges, the Carolinas have become a destination of choice, attracting casual bird-watchers and experienced bird-watchers from all parts of the United States and from many other countries.

Today's image of a bird-watcher is nothing like the long-ridiculed "little old lady in tennis shoes." The current image is that of men and women riding in a four-wheel-drive vehicle while dressed in appropriate field attire and equipped with an impressive assortment of field guides, binoculars, telescopes, cell phones, digital cameras, videocameras, and perhaps even a global positioning system.

Fortunately, the latest equipment is not required for the enjoyment of birds. The truly wonderful thing about bird study is that seeing a species for the first time is exciting even if the bird is an abundant one found in your own yard. Whether you carry all the latest optical equipment or just a forty-year-old binocular, identifying a bird provides a sense of satisfaction. If the bird happens to be a rare species or a common one behaving in an unusual manner, so much the better. The point of bird-watching is to enjoy it and to share that enjoyment with others.

Acknowledgments

Much of the success enjoyed by the first edition of *Birds of the Carolinas* was a result of the teamwork that went into writing the species accounts and the willingness of photographers to donate one-time use of their bird pictures. In recognition of that generosity, Carolina Bird Club, Inc., received a percentage of the royalties paid by the publisher. A portion of the club's royalty income was set aside to make awards supporting students conducting ornithological research while enrolled at colleges and universities in the Carolinas. Results of some of those research projects were published in the Carolina Bird Club's quarterly journal, *The Chat*, and provided information useful in revising a few of the species accounts for the present work.

The authors are grateful to everyone who contributed papers, notes, and miscellaneous sightings for publication in *The Chat*, and to the editors of the journal. Susan Campbell, John A. Gerwin, David S. Lee, Norma Siebenheller, and Marcus B. Simpson Jr. reviewed accounts for species of particular interest to them. Special thanks go to Nell P. Barkley, the birdwatching librarian who compiled the list of suggested reading.

Photographers who submitted materials for consideration are William C. Alexander, Reg Daves, Jack F. Dermid, Bill Duyck, Walker Golder, Gilbert S. Grant, E. Wayne Irvin, Jeff Lewis, Chris Marsh, Brian Patteson, the late Hollis J. Rogers (courtesy of his family), Michael P. Schultz, Harry D. Sell, and Garland L. Smith Jr. Along with their beautiful photographs, they sent us encouragement and good wishes, for which we are sincerely grateful. Individual photo credits are given on page 391.

Others who provided assistance include Charlotte Goedsche, Jim and Ramona Hendrix, Charles A. Horton, Charles D. Peterson, David T. Potter, Bill Sanderson, Curtis Smalling, and staff members of the U.S. Army Corps of Engineers and the North Carolina Wildlife Resources Commission.

During three days of intense effort to select the best photographs available and tie up the loose ends in the text, Frances Parnell was our cheerful and gracious hostess, helping us turn what could have become a stressful process into a most enjoyable experience.

We are indebted to the many photographers who submitted color transparencies for our consideration. Their generous cooperation made possible the publication of this book. Most of the donors are members of Carolina Bird Club, but a few are friends from distant states. A credit line appears with each picture.

References used in preparing the species accounts are *South Carolina Bird Life* by Alexander Sprunt Jr. and E. Burnham Chamberlain (1949, revised by E. Milby Burton 1970); *Birds of North Carolina* by T. Gilbert Pearson, C. S. Brimley, and H. H. Brimley (1942, revised by David L. Wray and Harry T. Davis 1959); *Notes on the Birds of the Great Smoky Mountains National Park* by Arthur Stupka (1963); *Birds of the AEC Savannah River Plant Area* by Robert A. Norris (1963); *South Carolina Birds of the Foothills* by Jay Shuler (1966); A. C. Bent's *Life Histories of North American Birds* (20 volumes, 1919–1968); *Chat*, volumes 1–43 (1937–1979); *American Birds* (formerly *Audubon Field Notes*) volumes 17–31 (1963–1977); "The Fall Migration of Land Birds Along the Bodie Island–Pea Island Region of Northeastern North Carolina" by Paul W. Sykes Jr. (Master's thesis, Department of Zoology, North Carolina State University, 1967); "Spring Migration Routes and Patterns of the Parulidae in North Carolina and the Southeastern United States" by Harry E. LeGrand Jr. (Master's thesis, Department of Zoology, North Carolina State University, 1973); *Birds of Charlotte and Mecklenburg County, North Carolina* by Elizabeth B. Clarkson (privately printed, Charlotte, N.C., 1970); *Endangered and Threatened Plants and Animals of North Carolina* by John E. Cooper, Sarah S. Robinson, and John B. Funderburg (North Carolina State Museum, Raleigh, N.C., 1977); and *Atlas of Colonial Waterbirds in North Carolina Estuaries* by James F. Parnell and Robert F. Soots Jr. (North Carolina Sea Grant Program, Raleigh, N.C., 1979). *Birds of the World* by Oliver L. Austin Jr. (1961) was a valuable source of information on the orders and families of birds.

J. H. Carter III, David S. Lee, and Harry E. LeGrand Jr. reviewed the manuscript and added significant unpublished data on current ranges, relative abundance, and habitat preferences. Gladys Baker, Dr. Paul Hosier, Dr. Donald A. McCrimmon, Dr. Thomas L. Quay, Dr. Marcus B. Simpson Jr., and Elizabeth P. Teulings also read the manuscript and made many constructive suggestions. John O. Fussell III, J. Merrill Lynch, Chris Marsh, Wendell P. Smith, and Michael Tove gave us the benefit of their field experience and unpublished distributional data. Roxie C. Laybourne provided guidance and comment concerning our arrangement of the species accounts. The bird topography illustration (page 381) was prepared by Nikki Bane.

Many friends, whether they could offer us bird pictures and field data or not, gave us something very special—encouragement. Foremost among those very important people is Frances Parnell, who was our gracious hostess during the weekends spent evaluating slides and revising the manuscript. Faced with a multitude of decisions, authors must not underestimate the value of a pleasant place to work, a delicious meal, and a cheerful conversation, all of which Frances unfailingly provided according to our needs.

Few regions in North America have a richer bird life than the Carolinas. North and South Carolina offer great diversity of land form, climate, and vegetation, resulting in habitat suitable for a remarkable diversity of birds. The two states stretch from the high mountain forests of western North Carolina to the semitropical islands of the South Carolina low country. Within the borders of these two states occur most of the major plant communities of eastern North America. On the high mountain peaks, birds characteristic of the spruce-fir forests of Canada are found. In the low country of southeastern South Carolina, birds more commonly associated with Florida occur regularly. In regions between the two extremes, one may see most of the species found in eastern North America. Carolina offshore waters, especially the Gulf Stream, attract numerous seabirds that breed from the Arctic region to Antarctica and on many of the islands and shorelines of the western Atlantic Ocean.

Our richness of bird life has led to a very rich history of ornithological exploration in the Carolinas. Arthur T. Wayne, an early Carolina ornithologist, commented that more birds were made known to science from South Carolina than from any other state. Many well-known naturalists spent time in the Carolinas. John James Audubon, Mark Catesby, and Alexander Wilson all wrote of the Carolinas, and Dr. John Bachman (a clergyman), William Brewster, J. S. Cairns, M. A. Curtis (another clergyman),

and Wayne added much to our early knowledge of Carolina bird life.

The first book devoted exclusively to the birds of the region was Wayne's *Birds of South Carolina*, which was published as a contribution of the Charleston Museum in 1910. His work was followed in 1919 by the appearance of *Birds of North Carolina*, by T. Gilbert Pearson, C. S. Brimley, and H. H. Brimley, as part of the North Carolina Geological and Economic Survey. In 1942 a second edition of *Birds of North Carolina* was prepared by the same authors and published by the North Carolina State Museum through the state Department of Agriculture. In 1959 David L. Wray and Harry T. Davis revised the 1942 edition.

In 1949 *South Carolina Bird Life*, written by Alexander Sprunt Jr. and E. Burnham Chamberlain, was published by the University of South Carolina Press. It was revised in 1970 by E. Milby Burton.

In addition to those major works, several other regional books have been published in recent years. *Birds of the Blue Ridge Mountains*, by Marcus B. Simpson Jr. (University of North Carolina Press, 1992), and *A Birder's Guide to Coastal North Carolina*, by John O. Fussell III (University of North Carolina Press, 1994), are important references pertaining to the mountains and coastal plain of North Carolina. *Finding Birds in South Carolina*, by Robin Carter (University of South Carolina Press, 1993), adds much detail to our knowledge of South Carolina bird life.

Many works having a broad geographic scope are helpful to residents of the Carolinas and visitors to the region. See the list of suggested reading for further information.

Birds of the Carolinas is designed to introduce you to the remarkably diverse avifauna of the region and to stimulate your curiosity about how birds live. Whether your primary interest is in the birds coming to your feeders or in the ones you see during your travels, information in this book will increase your understanding of when, where, and why the various species occur in our region. *Birds of the Carolinas* is best used as a supplement to a good guide to field identification, which should illustrate all of the species likely to occur in the Carolinas and provide range maps for eastern North America or for most of the continent. Field guides generally fit comfortably in a jacket pocket. A convenient abbreviated index can be purchased and mounted inside the back cover of some editions to help users find the right page in a hurry.

It is natural to want to learn to identify birds, as we regularly come in contact with them at home and everywhere we go. Most people feel a real closeness to wildlife, and birds are the most accessible and colorful of the animals we normally see. As any experienced birder knows, however, it is not always easy to identify birds in the field. Achieving competence in the skill of species identification requires both patience and practice.

A major problem involves plumage differences within a species. Often males and females are quite different in appearance. Females are usually cryptically colored, an advantage during incubation of eggs. If males assist with incubation, they may also be protectively colored. If the male does not assist with incubation, he is often brightly colored. Bright plumage has an advantage during courtship, serving to attract females and to repel other males. Cardinals and most warblers are examples of species that have brightly colored males and relatively inconspicuous females.

To further complicate identification, males may lose their bright colors in the fall, and until the following spring they may look like the females. In other cases immature birds may appear quite different from adults. For example, the Herring Gull's plumage is different during each of its first three years. Thus, you may have to learn several color patterns to be able to identify members of a single species. With a little effort, however, you can learn to identify both sexes of those species that come to your feeders or nest in your yard. Each time you become thoroughly familiar with one species, a new one becomes a little easier to identify.

Although plumages may differ considerably within some species, other external characteristics are less variable. Bills and feet are particularly useful in identification. Bill size and shape relate very closely to food habits and are usually relatively constant for both sexes and all ages. However, bill color changes with attainment of sexual maturity. The short, powerful bills of cardinals and sparrows are designed for crushing seeds, while the slender bills of warblers are adapted for catching insects. Similarly, the long legs of wading birds are good field characteristics, and differences in leg color are helpful in identifying many species.

The behavior of birds is also a great help in making identifications. Each species goes about its daily activities in characteristic ways. You can probably recognize most of your friends by their ways of walking, talking, or gesturing. Birds are just as easy. Look for differences in behavior among species. Do they feed by searching for insects at the tips of branches, or do they dart out from exposed perches to catch insects in midair? Do they walk or hop? Are they calm or fidgety? With a little practice you will find that you can recognize many species by their actions without ever seeing plumage patterns or colors. The advanced birder who identifies a bird by a mere flicker of movement in a thicket is using such information.

There are many such clues to the identity of birds. The secret is to become familiar with as many aspects of their lives as possible and to notice birds wherever you go. Daily contact will add to your knowledge, and soon you will find that you know a great deal more than you suspected. You may even be startled to realize that you have passed, without thought, from bird identification to bird study and have begun an avocation that will give you much pleasure throughout life.

Several aids can make identifying birds relatively easy. First, obtain a good pair of binoculars. Buy the best pair you can afford. With proper care, good binoculars will last a lifetime and add a whole new dimension to your activities. Seven- or eight-power glasses (with the large lens at least five times the size of the small one, e.g., 7 x 35 or 8 x 50) are generally considered best for bird identification. The lighter the weight, the easier binoculars are to use. A spotting scope will provide more magnification, but using it requires a tripod. Spotting scopes are great if your house overlooks a large body of water or if you regularly travel to watch birds over open habitats such as grasslands, lakes, or the ocean.

Next, purchase a good field guide to the birds of your region. Several are listed in the Suggested Reading section of this book. If there is a bird club in your area, by all means join. Most bird clubs have programs and field trips that help inexperienced bird-watchers develop confidence in their ability to identify birds. Carolina Bird Club, Inc. (mailing address: 11 W. Jones St., Raleigh, NC 27601-1029), serves residents of North and South Carolina. The organization publishes a bimonthly newsletter and a quarterly journal, *The Chat*. Further information is available at <www.carolinabirdclub. org>.

One of the joys of bird-watching is to discover an unexpected bird, one outside the region generally accepted as its normal range. Most species, however, have definite breeding ranges, migratory pathways, and winter homes. Use knowledge of normal range to your advantage. When you first identify a new bird, look immediately to see if it belongs where you have found it. *Birds of the Carolinas* gives the residence status and range in the Carolinas for all species that have been recorded here since 1900. If the range or season of occurrence does not fit, check to see if a similar species should be present. Chances are that the bird in question was a species that is supposed to be present rather than a wanderer from another region. If a videocamera is handy, try to document the occurrence right away, just in case the bird is a rare species or a common one in unusual plumage.

If, after a careful check, the bird still appears to be something rare for the region, have a friend verify your identification. Even experts try to have their unusual sightings corroborated by another experienced observer. Once you are confident that the bird is rare for the region, immediately notify the resident "bird expert" at the nearest museum of natural history, college or university biology department, or local bird club. People at those places are accustomed to requests for assistance, and they will be interested in learning about your find. Should your rare bird linger long enough, a photographer or a bird-bander may help you document the occurrence.

Each fall millions of birds travel from their breeding grounds in the northern United States and Canada to wintering areas in the southern United States, Central America, or South America. The Carolinas are located along the migratory routes of many such birds and twice yearly are flooded with transients. Migration adds much excitement to bird study.

Most small, weak-flying birds (e.g., warblers and sparrows) migrate by night, often departing just after dark and flying for several hours before landing prior to dawn to rest and feed during daylight hours. Strong fliers, including swallows and hawks, are usually daytime migrants. Their passage is often visible, especially along corridors such as the Outer Banks of North Carolina in autumn or the crest of the Blue Ridge Mountains in both spring and fall. Some strong fliers (e.g., American Golden-Plover) migrate nonstop over a long distance, thus being in flight both day and night.

The timing of the passage through a given area is often closely associated with the weather. In the eastern United States autumn is a time of cold fronts and prevailing northerly or northwesterly winds. Most fall migrants, especially small land birds, follow tail winds southward. Northwesterly winds tend to push birds eastward, often creating a massive buildup of birds along the coast. Because the Outer Banks of North Carolina act as a natural funnel, birding there in fall is often spectacular. At dawn many nocturnal migrants may be seen flying in off the ocean and seeking shelter in the first available grass or shrub. Sometimes, exhausted migrating passerines stop to rest on railings of offshore fishing boats.

In spring, warm fronts followed by southerly winds alternate with cold fronts followed by northerly winds. Most small land birds move northward on the tail winds associated with warm fronts. As cold fronts pass and northerly winds prevail, the migratory movement is temporarily halted, perhaps even reversed. Birds pause to feed and rest until conditions are again favorable for migration. Consequently, the best time to find large numbers of migrant land birds in spring is shortly after the passage of a cold front, when thickets and forests are often filled with colorful transients. In contrast to events in the fall, spring wind patterns do not push migrating birds to the coast. As a result, the passage of land birds northward is much more spectacular in the piedmont and mountains than toward the coast.

Food supply is another factor in the westward displacement of spring migrants. The coastal plain is primarily an evergreen area, whereas the piedmont and mountains have an abundance of deciduous vegetation. As new leaves burst forth in spring, there is a corresponding sudden emergence of defoliating insects in deciduous forests. The northward movement of insectivorous birds coincides with the emergence of the bountiful food supply.

Although migrations of small

land birds are greatly influenced by weather and food supply, movements of large, strong-flying birds such as shorebirds and waterfowl appear less closely related to seasonal variables. For example, the arrival of large numbers of wintering Tundra Swans at Lake Mattamuskeet usually occurs in early November regardless of the weather.

Most shorebirds and many waterbirds such as scoters generally migrate along the coast. However, in years of low water levels, when extensive mudflats appear around inland lakes, or when heavy rains flood low-lying fields, migrating shorebirds are often found far inland in considerable numbers. Heavy rains in late summer and early fall may result in the formation of temporary marshes. Waterfowl may use such sites in passage. Although major passageways are recognized, birds migrate over every portion of the Carolinas. Timely occurrences of suitable weather and habitat conditions may result in stopovers in unexpected places. Bird-watchers can use knowledge of weather and habitat conditions to good advantage.

There are predictable differences between the two Carolinas in the times of appearance of migrants. Spring migrants may reach southeastern South Carolina as much as a month before the same species can be found above 4,000 feet (1,200 m) in the southern Appalachian Mountains. Fall migrants generally arrive in North Carolina a little earlier than in South Carolina. Arrival and departure dates given in this book, unless otherwise stated, are approximations based on average dates from widely separated points. The reader should expect to notice many local and seasonal variations during several years of bird-watching.

In late winter, inner physiological changes are initiated that prepare birds for both migration and reproduction. Migrant species in their winter habitats become restless, and by April and May migration is at a peak in the Carolinas. Permanent residents may nest in the same vicinity where they spend the winter, and some will begin nesting while the weather is still quite cold. The Great Horned Owl may begin laying eggs in December, and by January the American Woodcock may have begun its spectacular courtship flights. By early April many permanent residents will have begun nesting. Migrants arriving from farther south may not begin nesting until much later, perhaps as late as June in our highest mountain habitats.

Courtship and Nesting

As the urge to begin the reproductive process takes hold, males of many species establish territories, areas from which other reproductively active males of their species are excluded. Small land birds usually advertise territory ownership by singing. The song has a dual function: It warns other breeding males away from the territory and attracts prospective mates. Most small land birds have territories large enough to provide all the necessities for raising a brood. Birds such as herons and egrets may have very small territories, restricted to the distance members of a pair can reach while standing on

the nest. Males may use display to advertise territorial ownership and to attract females. Herons and other colonial waterbirds must forage outside their territories, often a considerable distance from the nesting site.

Females attracted to a territory are courted vigorously by the resident breeding male. He may sing, perform plumage displays, dance, or make acrobatic flights, all in an effort to attract the female. If she crouches and flutters her wings like a baby bird, the male may respond by offering her a bit of food, an act called "courtship feeding." The final choice of mate appears to be up to the female. Pair formation is usually for a season but may be for only a single brood. In some species, including the Canada Goose, the bond usually is for life.

One mate at a time, monogamy, is the rule among birds, but polygamy, the situation in which an individual may have more than one mate at the same time, is not uncommon. In gallinaceous birds, such as the Wild Turkey, one male may mate with several females, each of which then raises a brood of young. In some shorebirds, such as the Spotted Sandpiper, the role of the sexes may be reversed. In that case, one female may mate with several males. She provides each male with a clutch of eggs. He incubates the eggs and also tends the young, which are able to leave the nest very soon after hatching but are not yet able to fly.

In most species, pair formation is

followed by copulation, nest construction, egg laying, incubation, hatching, care of young in the nest, and care of young after fledging. Incubation may begin with the laying of the first egg or may be delayed until the clutch is nearly complete. Consequently, the entire clutch may hatch almost at once, as in ducks, or individual eggs may hatch on several consecutive days, as in many songbirds, including Eastern Bluebirds and Carolina Wrens.

The condition of the young at hatching is often correlated with the nature of the nest. Birds whose offspring are precocial (covered with down and able to follow parents almost immediately after hatching) often lay their eggs in simple depressions in the ground and usually begin incubation with the laying of the last egg. Their eggs will all hatch about the same time, as is the case with the Spotted Sandpiper.

Birds whose offspring are altricial (hatched naked, blind, and helpless) usually occupy nesting cavities or carefully camouflaged nests that help keep the young safe until they are well feathered and able to move about quickly enough to hide from predators. Parents of altricial young usually begin incubation with the laying of the first egg. Hatching may take place over a period of several days, as is the case with all of our familiar songbirds. For birds that raise more than one brood, the nesting season may extend throughout the summer, but some single-brooded early nesters may have finished rearing their families by early June.

During June and July nearly all passerines breeding in the Carolinas are in molt. Young of the year are undergoing the postjuvenal molt, and adults are undergoing the postnuptial molt. Adults sometimes begin replacing feathers while young of late broods are still in the nest.

Late summer to early autumn appears to be a leisurely time for birds. Young are on the wing, molt is largely completed, temperatures are mild, and food is usually abundant. For many species there is a renewal of song and even an occasional pursuit flight or courtship feeding. At this time of year immature birds may wander in all directions away from where they hatched. Herons and egrets, for example, often appear at inland sites far from the breeding colonies and normal migratory lanes.

Fall and Winter
Fall migration actually begins in summer for many species and extends into late November or even early winter for others. A prolonged warm spell in January may give some birds (usually Mourning Doves or American Robins) the urge to mate and lay eggs. Young hatched from such abnormal winter clutches are rarely reared to fledging.

In fall and winter, small land birds often feed in loose flocks containing several species. Eastern Bluebirds may have as their companions Downy Woodpeckers, Carolina Chickadees, Tufted Titmice, Brown-headed Nuthatches, Pine Warblers, and, occasionally, an unusual migrating warbler. Fall-migrant warblers are also attracted to the spray of a garden hose. They sometimes bathe in water dripping from the leaves of shrubbery or in a temporary pool that may form in a shallow depression on bare ground beneath a sprinkler.

Normally, winter is a time of intense feeding activity because birds require great amounts of energy to counteract severely cold weather. As the days begin to lengthen in late winter, the reproductive urge again takes precedence, and the annual cycle begins anew.

Feathers are a unique characteristic of birds. Feathers provide a lightweight covering that sheds water, helps the bird regulate its body temperature, and makes flight possible. During summer and early autumn, most Carolina birds, both adults and young of the year, renew all or part of their plumage in a process called molting. Adults have a postnuptial molt, and young of the year have a postjuvenal molt. Some species also undergo a partial or complete prenuptial molt in late winter and early spring. Others acquire their bright breeding colors by gradual feather wear.

Healthy birds keep their plumage neatly arranged and well cared for at all seasons, but during the molting period they devote a great deal of time to grooming. Then even casual bird-watchers are likely to see birds water-bathing, preening, bill-wiping, scratching themselves, shaking themselves to settle feathers, and stretching the wings and tail—either one side at a time or both sides simultaneously.

Normally, only a few feathers drop out at a time, and new ones encased in a protective sheath (pinfeathers) quickly emerge from the underlying feather follicles. Only the keenest observer can detect the subtle day-to-day changes in the plumage. Sometimes, particularly after sudden heavy rainfall during the molting period, birds drop all of their loose feathers at once. For a week or so birds with bald heads, gaps in the flight feathers of the wings, or only a few crooked tail feathers can be seen everywhere (Fig. 1). Many new feathers emerge simultaneously, and the birds soon look normal again.

During periods of heavy feather growth, birds are likely to practice two kinds of behavior that have long been assumed to be means of ridding themselves of ectoparasites: anting and sunning. There are two forms of anting. During active anting, the bird seizes ants in its beak and inserts them among the feathers. It may eat the crushed ants or cast them aside. During passive anting, the bird lies prostrate upon an anthill or in the path of marching ants and allows them to crawl into its plumage. Some of the positions assumed during passive anting are much like those adopted by birds that are sunbathing: sprawling flat on the ground with both wings spread wide open, lying on one side with the opposite wing raised vertically, or standing facing the sun with wing tips and the tip of the tail touching the ground. In all sunning positions, the bird raises some or all of the small feathers covering the head and body (contour feathers).

In 1974 Eloise F. Potter and the late Doris C. Hauser published a paper in *The Auk* (91:537–563) stating that anting and sunning behavior peak during the time of the postnuptial and postjuvenal molts of passerines. They found that anting behavior is correlated with the rapid replacement of feathers emerging from certain parts of the body (feather tracts) that can be reached by the bill (wings, tail,

FIGURE 1. *Northern Cardinal in heavy molt*

chemicals can dissipate rapidly, as they must in nature to function effectively as pheromones and allomones, most of the presumed ectoparasites survive treatment with formic acid. Furthermore, there is now good evidence that feather mites actually clean the feathers by feeding on stale preen oil and various microbes trapped by the plumage. Therefore, feather mites are not parasites at all, but helpful commensals or perhaps even mutualists.

lower breast, and belly). Sunning, they concluded, occurs most frequently when birds are molting feather tracts that are not accessible to the bill (head, neck, and upper breast).

Although formic acid applied to mites or lice placed on a feather kills most such organisms in a covered petri dish, recent unpublished experiments indicate that the substance is not particularly harmful to mites and lice in an uncovered dish. If the ant

The role of dusting and passive anting in feather care remains unclear. At the present time both appear to be, like active anting and sunning, primarily a means of applying heat (or the soothing sensation of heat) to the feather tracts. Only a few species of wild birds are known to dust in the Carolinas, and those that do so tend to be large or fairly large (e.g., Wild Turkey, Northern Bobwhite, Great Crested Flycatcher, and Brown Thrasher) or small ones that feed primarily on the ground (e.g., Chipping Sparrow).

Birds have tremendous potential for travel. Because they can fly, birds easily traverse barriers that are impassable to most animals. Yet we do not find Ruffed Grouse along the coast, but in the mountains. We do not typically find Brown Pelicans in mountain forests but, rather, along coastal waterways. Although birds have a potential for far-ranging movement, they are generally found only in those regions and habitats where they can best live and reproduce. Thus we know that the Ruffed Grouse is a forest bird, the Killdeer is a bird of open fields, and the Canvasback is a duck of open waters. The key to the abundance and diversity of birds in the Carolinas lies in the diversity of the landscape.

Mount Mitchell, in western North Carolina, rises to 6,684 feet (2,025.7 m) and is the highest point in eastern North America. On Mount Mitchell and other peaks of the southern Appalachian Mountains, there are spruce-fir forests similar to those found in Canada. In the coastal counties of the Carolinas, there are vast swamplands and estuaries reminiscent of some tropical regions. At Mount Mitchell winter temperatures may remain below freezing for weeks at a time, while at Charleston temperatures seldom drop to the freezing point. Between those extremes lie oak-hickory forests, pine forests, floodplain forests, lakes, ponds, bogs, backyards, pastures, old fields, and many other plant communities. Each community has its characteristic birds—birds that function best in the complex set of circumstances that make up a particular habitat, birds that, in spite of their mobility, will usually be found in the habitat for which they are best fitted.

Mountain Habitats

The western counties of both Carolinas rise into the Blue Ridge Mountains. In extreme western North Carolina lie the Great Smoky Mountains. Mountain forests add much to the diversity of bird habitats in the Carolinas, and here many birds characteristic of northern forests reach their southern limits.

At the highest elevations, southern extensions of the great northern coniferous forests are found (Fig. 2). These forests are generally isolated units at elevations above 4,500 feet (1,380 m). Dominant trees are Fraser fir and red spruce. In such forests occur several nesting birds usually found in the forests of the northeastern United States and adjacent Canada. For example, the Golden-crowned Kinglet, Red-breasted Nuthatch, and Black-capped Chickadee reach the southern limit of their breeding range in the high-elevation spruce-fir forests.

Dense shrub thickets called rhododendron balds, or heath balds, develop on many mountain peaks. These distinct mountain communities are known primarily for dazzling summer displays of rhododendron flowers. They are also excellent places to observe such characteristic mountain nesting birds as the Canada, Black-

FIGURE 3. *Mixed oak forest in Blue Ridge Mountains of western North Carolina*

FIGURE 2. *Northern coniferous forest in western North Carolina*

throated Blue, and Chestnut-sided Warblers and the Carolina race of the Dark-eyed Junco.

Deciduous forests dominate all except the driest and most southerly mountain slopes. Although oaks dominate, this general forest type is highly variable depending on altitude, slope direction, moisture, and substrate. Magnificent oak-chestnut forests once occurred on the higher slopes, but the chestnut is now essentially gone, having been destroyed by blight. Present-day oak forests, however, remain important and extensive (Fig. 3). Characteristic breeding birds of the more elevated, moist slopes covered with deciduous forests are the Blue-headed Vireo, Black-throated Blue Warbler, and Rose-breasted Grosbeak. The lower and drier oak-dominated forests are the summer homes for a host of small land birds that we associate with

piedmont deciduous forests. Carolina Chickadees, Tufted Titmice, Red-eyed Vireos, Black-and-white Warblers, and Scarlet Tanagers are usually common.

In moist, fertile coves throughout the mountains, beautiful cove forests develop. Here a great diversity of deciduous trees occurs. It is in this habitat that mountain herbaceous wildflowers reach their peak of development. Coves are the summer homes for many birds, including Scarlet Tanagers and Black-and-white Warblers.

Whenever forests are timbered or burned, characteristic patterns of plant succession occur that eventually lead to a redevelopment of the mature forest. Each stage of succession will have characteristic birds. Of particular interest in the mountains are the dense thickets of shrubs and saplings typical of cutover forests. Here such interesting mountain species as Canada and Golden-winged Warblers find conditions suitable for nesting. As the forests mature, those species will move into other cutover or otherwise disturbed areas. Because the locations of such habitat are determined by human activity, the observer must seek them out and be prepared to find new locations every few years.

Small, cool streams characterized by pools and rapids drain the high mountains, flowing through mountain valleys and into the piedmont. Such streams are often lined with characteristic streamside forests (Fig. 4). Hemlocks are usually the dominant overstory tree associated with a dense understory of rhododendron and mountain laurel. Nesting species include Blackburnian Warbler, Canada Warbler, and the southern Appalachian population of Swainson's Warbler. On dry slopes with thin soils, shortleaf and Virginia pine may be dominant. Here bird life is quite similar to that of piedmont pine forests. Typical birds are Blue Jays, Carolina Chickadees, and Blue-headed Vireos.

Of particular interest are the high, rocky cliff faces such as those at Whiteside Mountain, Mount Mitchell, Chimney Rock, and Table Rock. There and at other such high, rocky outcrops one may find scattered groups of Common Ravens. Although they apparently breed regularly in the mountains, nests are difficult to find and actual reports of nesting are few. Peregrine Falcons have also been reintroduced to some of those sites and are nesting successfully at a few places.

Many of our highest mountain peaks are in the Great Smoky Mountains National Park, along the border between North Carolina and Ten-

FIGURE 4. Hemlock forest adjacent to mountain stream

nessee. All major mountain habitats occur within the Smokies, and all of the characteristic mountain birds may be found there.

A popular approach to mountain bird-watching is to travel the Blue Ridge Parkway, which extends across North Carolina from Virginia to the Great Smoky Mountains. This scenic highway passes through most mountain habitats. Overlooks, picnic areas, and campgrounds provide easy access to excellent birding sites. Details regarding bird life and facilities can be found in *Birds of the Blue Ridge Mountains*, by M. B. Simpson Jr. (University of North Carolina Press, 1992).

At 3,560 feet (1,095 m) Sassafras Mountain is the highest point in South Carolina. Here and at nearby Table Rock State Park some birds characteristic of the taller peaks in the Blue Ridge Mountains can be found. A number of other parks and national forests in the mountains of North and South Carolina offer undisturbed mountain habitats, trails to remote areas, and generally exciting birding opportunities.

It is through the deciduous forests of the piedmont and mountains that most small land birds pour northward during the spring migration. Birding is often spectacular in spring, the time of year when bird-watchers are most strongly attracted to the mountains. As summer arrives, the spectacular passage wanes, but the forests still contain many interesting birds. For example, 23 species of warblers have been recorded nesting in the Great Smoky Mountains National Park. In the Carolinas many of those warblers nest only in mountain forests.

Autumn brings a southward movement that is not as spectacular as spring in the mountains because fall migrants travel mostly along the coast. In fall, however, migration may be exciting, especially when large numbers of hawks move southward. Hawk-watchers often gather at favored locations such as Pores Knob in the Brushy Mountains, Pilot Mountain State Park, and Mount Pisgah, in North Carolina, or Caesar's Head, in South Carolina, to view the passage and record the number of each species seen.

Even in winter there is interest. People hardy enough to brave the wind and cold may find Snow Buntings on a mountain bald or a flock of White-winged Crossbills feeding in conifers. Mountain bird feeders often attract large numbers of finches that sometimes pour out of the northern forests into all parts of our region, even to the coast.

Piedmont Habitats

Although parts of the mountains are farmed, and pastures and open fields are common, the mountain slopes are generally forested, and the bird life is usually that of the forest type. As one moves down the slopes into the foothills and rolling country of the piedmont, the forests become increasingly broken and the influence of human activity is generally evident (Fig. 5). From the air this portion of the Carolinas looks like a great patchwork quilt, with cultivated land, brushy overgrown fields, pastures, and wood-lots mixed without apparent order. That pattern persists eastward to the extensive swamp forests and open agricultural lands of the coastal plain.

The piedmont offers a range and abundance of bird life that parallels the diversity of the habitat. Farm ponds provide shelter for small numbers of waterfowl and shorebirds; fields are populated by sparrows, quail, and other ground birds; and each stage in the successional pattern from abandoned field to mature deciduous forest has its characteristic complement of birds.

Most of the central portion of the Carolinas has been heavily modified by human activity. Only the flood-plains of rivers flowing out of the mountains and down to the ocean have retained a semblance of their original wildness (Fig. 6), and often these are the most significant blocks of mature forests remaining. Flood-plains, such as those associated with the Wateree, Pee Dee, Cape Fear, and Roanoke Rivers, usually provide excellent opportunities to observe many kinds of birds.

The original forest of the piedmont was dominated by various oaks and

FIGURE 5. *Piedmont woodlot and plowed field*

FIGURE 6. *Floodplain of Cape Fear River in Raven Rock State Park, North Carolina*

hickories, but only scattered stands of that forest type remain. The best examples are generally found in state parks, such as Umstead State Park near Raleigh, North Carolina. Much of the original deciduous forest has been cleared and converted to farmland. A more recent trend has been the replanting of abandoned farmland to forests, primarily loblolly pine. The change from deciduous to coniferous forests has undoubtedly resulted in shifts in the relative abundance of many piedmont birds.

The Carolina sandhills, which are situated along the border between the coastal plain and the piedmont, overlap the two Carolinas. Here the soil is poor, and until recently, vast stands of longleaf pine and scrub oak dominated. That forest type provides important habitat for birds such as Bachman's Sparrow and the endangered Red-cockaded Woodpecker. Large acreages of longleaf pines are preserved in the Fort Bragg Military Reservation (Fig. 7) as well as in national forests, state forests, wildlife refuges, and nature preserves in both Carolinas.

A number of large reservoirs have

FIGURE 7. *Longleaf pine forest in Carolina sandhills*

been built in the foothills, piedmont, and upper coastal plain. Although the resulting impoundments destroyed large acreages of forests, they now provide excellent habitat for waterbirds where little existed before (Fig. 8). In recent years, observations of ducks, geese, and other more typically coastal waterbirds have greatly increased in the interior. Of particular interest has been the establishment of colonies of Cliff Swallows nesting on dams and bridges at several large man-made lakes in the piedmont, notably Lake Hartwell in western South Carolina and Kerr Lake in

FIGURE 8. *Man-made impoundment in piedmont*

FIGURE 10. *Gum swamp in coastal plain near Florence, South Carolina*

FIGURE 9. *Aerial view of farmland in coastal plain*

northeastern North Carolina. Cliff Swallows were not known to nest in the Carolinas prior to the establishment of those large reservoirs. Now the species can be found nesting in the Carolinas almost everywhere suitable habitat is available.

Coastal-Plain Habitats

The coastal plain of the Carolinas is a land of rivers, floodplain forests, swamps, extensive bays or pocosins, pine forests, and large cultivated fields. Much land has been cleared, and farming is important to the economy; but vast areas remain heavily wooded, and the harvesting of trees for use in the manufacture of plywood and paper products is a major industry. When the coastal plain is viewed from the air, forests remain an important feature, but large areas have been cleared in recent years for agriculture (Fig. 9).

Habitats in the coastal plain are diverse, and birds abound. In the lowland swamps and forests one may still find conditions approaching wilderness. Here travel on foot is often difficult, and myriad insects add to the discomfort. Nevertheless, the rewards of a visit may be great. The bird life is often spectacular but still sometimes poorly known.

The swamp forests of eastern Carolina consist primarily of stands of cypress and gums (Fig. 10). Usually flooded for most of the year, those forests are important wintering grounds for waterfowl, especially Wood Ducks and Mallards. Wood Ducks also nest extensively in swamp forests.

Floodplains are closely associated with swamps, and at certain times of the year the two are difficult to separate. Swamps are usually under water during the growing season and often for most of the year, whereas flood-plain forests are usually not flooded during the growing season and are most likely to be wet in winter. Floodplains and swamps generally support a great diversity of bird life. They are summer homes for many insectivorous birds such as the Prothonotary Warbler and the coastal-plain population of Swainson's Warbler. Inland freshwater marshes are not abundant in North Carolina but are relatively extensive in coastal South Carolina as remnants of the earlier rice-growing industry. Such marshes (Fig. 11) are highly productive, and they usually sustain large and diverse bird populations at all seasons. During fall and winter, these marshes are of major importance to waterbirds such as puddle ducks, American Coots, and Pied-billed Grebes. In summer they are occupied by Red-winged Blackbirds, various herons and egrets, gallinules, and small insectivorous birds.

There are few natural lakes in the coastal plain, but several large man-made systems, such as the Santee-Cooper Reservoir in South Carolina, augment natural ones, including Lake Waccamaw (Fig. 12) and Lake Mattamuskeet in North Carolina. Large lakes have significant value as wintering areas for waterfowl, especially if, as at Lake Mattamuskeet, there are associated freshwater marshes. In summer, large lakes may be important feeding or nesting areas for birds such as the Osprey and the Great Blue Heron.

In addition to the large bodies of water, there are many smaller lakes and ponds scattered throughout the coastal plain. Old mill ponds, municipal water reservoirs, and wastewater

FIGURE 11. *Freshwater marsh near Georgetown, South Carolina*

FIGURE 12. *Lake Waccamaw in southeastern North Carolina*

treatment plants provide valuable habitat and excellent birding. Farm ponds are generally numerous and, especially when surrounded by pastures, regularly attract waterfowl, long-legged waders, and shorebirds.

There are two basic types of pine-dominated upland forest in the coastal plain. On dry, sandy soils along the coast, extensively in South Carolina and into the southern edge of North Carolina, occur stands of longleaf pine, turkey oak, and wiregrass. Those open forests, historically maintained by periodic fires, have an avifauna characterized by the Red-cockaded Woodpecker, Bachman's Sparrow, and Brown-headed Nuthatch. Most rich soils of the coastal plain are now vegetated by forests dominated by loblolly pines, which are often quite dense with well-developed understories. They have been extensively logged and cleared to provide agricultural lands and now often remain only as woodlots. They are the homes for many familiar birds such as Pine Warblers, Tufted Titmice, Northern Cardinals, and Eastern (Rufous-sided) Towhees.

Many places in the coastal plain offer excellent birding. Three are especially impressive. Mattamuskeet National Wildlife Refuge is the winter home for thousands of Tundra Swans, Canada Geese, and ducks. The marshes also provide prime habitat for rails and long-legged waders, while adjacent loblolly pine forests and cultivated lands attract a variety of upland birds. Nesting Bald Eagles may add to the excitement.

In South Carolina, the Francis Marion National Forest, located in Charleston and Berkeley Counties, provides all of the major coastal-plain habitats. The forest is especially extensive and wild, and one may expect to see Swallow-tailed Kites. It is also the site of the last known Carolina observation of the extremely rare and perhaps extinct Bachman's Warbler.

South of Charleston, US 17 crosses three rivers important to South Carolina wildlife, the Ashepoo, the Combahee (pronounced CUM-bee), and the Edisto. The waters of those rivers flow from US 17 to the Atlantic Ocean through Colleton County and a region known as the ACE Basin. Within the ACE Basin, Bear Island Wildlife Management Area, Edisto Beach, and the

Edisto Nature Trail are three of many excellent sites for bird study.

Coastal Habitats

Coastal Carolina may be thought of as a vast intermingling of ocean and land. The mixing of warm saline waters from the Atlantic Ocean with silt-laden fresh waters from upland areas has helped to create a rich and diverse estuarine environment. Intermittent barrier islands separate the shallow estuaries from the ocean. In North Carolina the barrier islands are broken only by a series of narrow inlets, but in South Carolina the barrier is often broken by large, isolated embayments and river mouths. The upper portion of the Carolina barrier beach system, known as the Outer Banks, often reaches to within 20 to 40 miles (32 to 65 km) of the Gulf Stream; sounds and bays separate the banks from the mainland by as much as 25 miles (40 km). Farther south the barrier islands may be only a few hundred yards from the mainland.

Most of the Outer Banks of North Carolina lie within the boundaries of the Cape Hatteras and Cape Lookout National Seashores (Fig. 13). One of the largest of South Carolina's barrier islands, Bulls Island, is a part of the Cape Romain National Wildlife Refuge. Behind the barrier beaches lie shallow sounds and bays as well as extensive salt marshes. North Carolina has a series of interconnected sounds, such as Pamlico and Core, but South Carolina has a series of isolated embayments, such as historic Bulls Bay and Port Royal Sound. Along the borders of these bays occur the extensive salt marshes and flats so much a part of the estuary. Salt marshes and flats are the key to the productivity

FIGURE 13. *Cape Lookout on the Outer Banks of North Carolina*

of the estuaries. By photosynthesis they convert solar energy into huge quantities of plant tissue—food that eventually provides a source of energy for the animals of the estuary and coastal waters. Without salt marshes, the estuaries would be unable to support their vast populations of invertebrates, fish, and birds.

The coast of the Carolinas has undergone tremendous change in recent years. People have increased their use of the estuaries greatly as they have harvested seafood and waterfowl from coastal waters, constructed marinas for boats, and built commercial and residential structures on the barrier beaches or on land created by the destruction of the salt marshes. Humans have modified the very face of the barrier beaches as they have destroyed the maritime forests, built roads and bridges, and attempted to stabilize the dunes. They have even opened and closed inlets between the ocean and sounds. Such changes have been generally detrimental to the coastal wildlife, and what we see now is only a remnant of vast populations of earlier times. Conservation efforts

are ongoing, but existing programs must be strengthened and broadened if we are to retain the coastal beaches and estuaries as places of exceptional natural riches.

The coast is a very special place for bird-watchers. Here the diversity of habitat combined with a rich food supply has resulted in a wealth of bird life at all seasons. The shallow water of the Atlantic Ocean overlying the continental shelf represents the most easterly bird habitat of the Carolinas. Loons, grebes, gannets, and several species of gulls winter regularly, and such rare visitors as jaegers, alcids (puffins, murres, and dovekies), frigatebirds, and tropicbirds occur often enough to excite expectations.

Major migratory routes for many waterbirds lie off the coast. Each spring and fall thousands of shearwaters, petrels, and storm-petrels pass the Carolinas, mostly well offshore but within range of charter and sport vessels. Closer inshore and often visible from the beach, birds such as loons, scoters, and other waterfowl pass in sometimes spectacular numbers. Cape Point near Buxton, North Carolina, is perhaps the best place in the Carolinas to witness seabird migration while standing on dry land. Here pelagic birds sometimes come very close inshore as they round the point and may even pause to rest in the salt pond.

In autumn, barrier islands provide a corridor for the southward passage of large numbers of land birds. Many species of passerines can be found in the scrub thickets and maritime forests. Spectacular flights of hawks also occur. The barrier beaches in autumn are excellent places to see the uncommon and strikingly handsome

FIGURE 14. *Palms and sea oats on beach at Bulls Island, South Carolina*

Peregrine Falcon, plus a good number of the smaller falcons.

The wild and remote sandy shores of the Carolinas once teemed with bird life and provided nesting sites for thousands of terns and many shorebirds. As people and vehicles have come in increasing numbers, only a few of our beaches remain truly wild. One of them is the magnificent strand of Bulls Island (Fig. 14). On nearby Cape Island several species of terns still nest in good numbers on natural beaches. In recent years small numbers of terns have returned to nest on the beaches of both Carolinas as protection has been provided by local, state, and national conservation and management agencies.

In spite of the crowds of people, the bird life remains spectacular, as many species of shorebirds migrate southward along the beaches in the fall and back northward a few months later in the spring. A few, such as the Black-bellied Plover and the Dunlin, will make the beaches their winter home. Willets, American Oystercatchers, and Wilson's Plovers remain to nest in the sand and grasses on and just behind the foredunes.

Beaches are also favorite resting and foraging places for gulls and terns. In fall and winter, when people fishing in the surf provide bountiful food in the form of trash fish, the beaches are crowded with gulls, mostly Herring and Ring-billed. In summer they are largely replaced by the familiar black-headed Laughing Gulls and several species of terns.

The Carolinas have no extensive, naturally occurring rocky coasts, but in a few small ways people have created a facsimile of that more northern habitat. As they have attempted to protect beaches and inlets, humans have built rock jetties. Those piles of large stones extending outward from beaches or lying adjacent to inlets or ship channels are similar enough to rocky shorelines to attract birds associated with that habitat farther north. Thus one may find Purple Sandpipers wintering fairly regularly on jetties at Oregon Inlet, at Fort Macon near Atlantic Beach, at Wrightsville Beach, at Huntington Beach, and even in Charleston harbor. Various waterbirds, including an occasional eider or alcid, may be found diving in the rough waters adjacent to such jetties.

Mudflats and sandflats are especially important coastal bird habitats (Fig. 15). Sandflats are usually associated with inlets or with overwash zones where wind and tide have moved beach sands to the rear of the barrier islands. Mudflats are usually associated with quieter portions of the estuary where fine sediments are being deposited. Such flats are often intertidal and are exposed to use by birds for only part of each day. When these flats are exposed by the falling tide, a bounteous food supply is made available, and many species

FIGURE 15. *Mudflats in the Cape Romain National Wildlife Refuge near McClellanville, South Carolina*

FIGURE 16. *Regularly flooded salt marsh at Smith Island, North Carolina*

of shorebirds and long-legged waders find sustenance here. As the returning tide covers the food supply, the birds retreat to the sandflats, which are often above high tide, to rest until the next feeding period.

During the spring and fall migrations, when shorebirds are most numerous in the Carolinas, it is possible to find thousands of individuals of several species feeding actively on favored flats, such as those just south of North Pond at the Pea Island National Wildlife Refuge or between the mainland and Bulls Island at the Cape Romain National Wildlife Refuge.

Along the inside of the barrier islands, adjacent to the mainland, and in fact wherever water is shallow and well protected, marshes develop. We generally think of the vast acreages of smooth cordgrass when we think of salt marshes in the Carolinas (Fig. 16). This is the species that dominates most of the areas twice flooded and twice exposed by the daily tidal rhythm. Salt marshes are of primary importance in maintaining the abundance and diversity of estuarine life.

There are also other kinds of coastal marshes. Those flooded only by spring tides will generally be occupied by grasses such as saltmeadow cordgrass. Still less saline areas flooded only by irregular storm tides, such as the vast marshes adjacent to the mainland on the western edge of Pamlico Sound, generally will be dominated by black needlerush.

Birds use all of those grasslands. The extensive regularly flooded marshes are a very special environment, and only a few species live there. Clapper Rails are abundant all year, and Seaside Sparrows nest at scattered locations and winter throughout the marsh. Other rails are present during the migratory periods, and some winter here along with American Bitterns and both Nelson's and Saltmarsh Sharp-tailed Sparrows.

In northeastern North Carolina, Snow Geese winter in the upper portions of the marshes and on grassy upland meadows, where Canada Geese and some ducks also feed regularly. Certain shorebirds, including the Whimbrel, show an affinity for the short-grass meadows, and many species of shorebirds forage in the relatively open portions of these coastal grasslands.

The bays and sounds are places of constant change. In Pamlico Sound in northeastern North Carolina, the lunar tidal change is only a few inches, but winds may result in nonrhythmic tides of 2 feet (0.6 m). In Bulls Bay lunar tidal differences of more than 5 feet (1.5 m) are experienced. Thus, what is open water occupied by diving ducks one morning may be a mudflat or oyster bar occupied by several species of shorebirds the same afternoon.

FIGURE 17. *Ducks, geese, and swans at Mattamuskeet National Wildlife Refuge in northeastern North Carolina*

Sounds and bays are traditional wintering grounds for vast numbers of waterfowl. The lore of both Carolinas is filled with stories of the abundance of ducks and geese as recently as the early 1900s. Although we are unlikely to witness such massive flights of ducks and geese ever again, we may still see impressive remnants of those huge flocks at refuges such as the Mattamuskeet National Wildlife Refuge (Fig. 17). The shoals of Pamlico Sound still provide eelgrass for wintering Canada Geese, Brant, and many species of ducks. Charleston Harbor still winters thousands of scaup, and puddle ducks of several species still feed along the edges of the sounds and over the shallow shoals.

In summer, waterfowl are replaced by gulls, terns, and pelicans that nest on the sandy islands, both natural and man-made, and feed young on the bounty of the shallow, rich estuary. Brown Pelicans, Black Skimmers, Laughing Gulls, and at least five species of terns nest in colonies ranging from a few pairs to 10,000 to 20,000 mixed pairs (Fig. 18). On these isolated, windswept islands one may still see

FIGURE 18. *Royal Tern colony on an island formed by dredged material in the lower Cape Fear River near Southport, North Carolina*

a remnant of the grandeur of the coastal wilderness of the Carolinas.

Birds are abundant at all seasons along the coast of the Carolinas, but several places are especially significant. In South Carolina the Cape Romain National Wildlife Refuge, located opposite McClellanville, offers spectacular birding at any season. Although portions of the refuge containing the large tern colonies are closed to the public, Bulls Island, accessible by boat, is open to visitors. Throughout the refuge, extensive salt marshes, tidal creeks, fresh marshes and ponds, maritime forests, and a spectacular natural beach provide great diversity of habitat. Other birding "hot spots" in southeastern South Carolina are the Savannah River Refuge and the U.S. Corps of Engineers Savannah River Spoil Site in Jasper County.

In northeastern North Carolina, the Pea Island National Wildlife Refuge, the Cape Hatteras National Seashore, and the Cape Lookout National Seashore occupy more than 70 miles (110 km) of barrier beach, marshes, sounds, inlets, and man-made freshwater ponds. Although bird-watching is good at any season, fall, winter, and spring are better than summer. Offshore trips to the nearby Gulf Stream provide the best regional access to pelagic birds.

Altogether, the Carolina coast offers outstanding opportunities for bird-watching, indeed some of the best in the eastern United States. See *A Birder's Guide to Coastal North Carolina*, by J. O. Fussell III (University of North Carolina Press, 1994), for further details, including directions to the best spots for finding particular species in the region. *Finding Birds in South Carolina*, by R. M. Carter (University of South Carolina Press, 1993), provides similar assistance for the southern state.

Conservation is a tradition in the Carolinas, where people have participated in the nation's conservation efforts since the 1800s. Recently we have shared the rush of environmental concern and have profited greatly from this newly kindled interest. Historically, conservation interests have been expressed in several ways. The protection of certain species such as long-legged waders was an especially significant step, followed by success in management and protection of both species and habitat. Today we find ourselves concerned not only with those issues but also with the management of the increasing number of people who want to use our natural resources.

Species protection originally meant the restriction of the taking of certain birds or their nests and eggs. All migratory birds are now protected by federal law, although there are regulated hunting seasons on some species. More recently, all nonmigratory hawks and owls have been given protected status and may not be killed legally. Their protection is aided by various local rehabilitation centers with staff members skilled in the care of injured hawks and owls.

Recent federal legislation has established lists of rare and endangered plants and animals, and both North and South Carolina have state lists of rare and endangered birds. Official recognition of rare and endangered species provides additional protection and encourages further scientific study of such species and their habitat requirements. See Suggested Reading for further information on protected species.

Protection of habitat is a relatively new concept. It was first implemented in the United States with the establishment of national and state wildlife refuge systems. State and national parks and forests also provide protection, albeit often coincidental to other purposes. Only in very recent years have significant habitat units been managed specifically for nongame species. An excellent example involves the management of state and federal lands for the rare and endangered Red-cockaded Woodpecker. A new Important Bird Area program, managed by the National Audubon Society, is identifying key units of bird habitat in both Carolinas.

The problem of habitat loss and degradation remains the most serious regional conservation issue concerning birds. Each species must have an adequate amount of appropriate healthy habitat. As we humans continue to modify the landscape on an ever-increasing scale, we face the very real problem of the complete elimination of some species from the Carolinas and the severe reduction in numbers of others. Species in serious trouble are those that have the most rigid requirements (e.g., beach nesters and occupants of mature forests) or restricted habitat (e.g., spruce-fir forests of western North Carolina). Unless commitments are made to maintain suitable areas of living space, we will see our avifauna continue to diminish. Many of our birds are migrants, and while there have been reductions in the use of harmful pesticides in the Carolinas, chemicals prohibited here are still widely used in the tropics. Deforestation is also a very serious threat in the tropics, and many of our summer-resident species are finding less and less suitable habitat each winter when they return to Central and South America. Now it is even more important that we protect both quantity and quality of habitat in the Carolinas and add our voices to the call for habitat protection in the tropics.

Human population density is a major problem in the Carolinas and around the world. As our numbers increase, we continue to place severe pressures on our wild neighbors. We must slow population growth as well as increase awareness of the importance of a diverse and healthy natural environment if the Carolinas are to remain a very special place for both people and wildlife.

There are several important conservation organizations in the Carolinas that birders should support. For many years the South Carolina Fish and Game Commission and the North Carolina Wildlife Resources Commission have effectively managed and protected game species. In recent years both have increased their emphasis on protection of nongame species and habitat management favoring them.

Citizens' groups have also been important. Carolina Bird Club, formed in 1948 by combining clubs in North and South Carolina, actively promotes both conservation and bird study. The Wildlife Federations of both North Carolina and South Carolina serve as conservation arms of hunters and fishermen. Both have been important in the conservation of many species. National Audubon Society has local chapters scattered throughout the Carolinas and maintains strong sanctuary systems in both states. The society works on local, regional, and national conservation issues. Scattered across the Carolinas, land conservancies, such as the Raleigh-based Triangle Land Conservancy, are highly effective in the preservation and protection of natural habitats in specific regions of each state. Local, state, and national parks and forests in both Carolinas protect many thousands of acres of bird habitat and often have active programs that benefit birds and offer guided nature walks. Many other state and national organizations include birds in their broad conservation interests.

Of major importance is the work of civic clubs, garden clubs, and other local organizations. They respond to local conservation needs and are often instrumental in the preservation of actual habitat units such as parks and refuges. They are led by local people and work on local projects—and that is where the most effective action takes place.

There is now a growing awareness in both public and private sectors that bird-watchers are important to the economy. Many cities have specialty stores offering supplies and equipment used by birders. Hotels and restaurants near favorite birding sites benefit from the patronage of birdwatchers, especially from late fall into early spring. We encourage you to let businesses know why you have come to their area and how important habitat protection is to you and to the birds you watch. We also urge you to work at all levels from local to worldwide to protect both habitat and the quality of life for all wildlife.

Included in the species accounts are all birds reported from North Carolina or South Carolina under circumstances that leave little or no doubt as to the authenticity of the occurrence. The great majority of the species are supported by a specimen collected in the Carolinas and deposited in the Charleston Museum, the North Carolina State Museum of Natural Sciences, or the U.S. National Museum. A few species have been included on the basis of a recognizable photograph supported by a convincing published account of the occurrence. Provided a species is readily identifiable under field conditions, some birds have been listed on the basis of three or more independent sight records supported by convincing details published in a state bird book or ornithological journal.

We have omitted accidental or exotic species recorded in our region more than 100 years ago and not supported by subsequent records from the Carolinas. Obsolete common names still in general use (sometimes for a race formerly regarded as a species) are noted in parentheses following the presently adopted ones. Colloquial names are placed within quotation marks.

Nomenclature follows the American Ornithologists' Union (AOU) *Check-list of North American Birds* posted on the Internet in January 2005. As a result of DNA studies and other research, avian nomenclature is in a state of flux. Two forms previously considered separate species

may now be treated as a single species, a process informally known as lumping. Two forms previously considered races of a single species may now be recognized as genetically distinct and treated as separate species, informally known as splitting. Because revision of the AOU checklist is an ongoing process, the reader needs to be aware of it even though most of the species presently involved are not yet known to occur in the Carolinas.

Of greater concern are several major changes in the arrangement of orders and families of birds. Loons and grebes no longer come first, as they do in virtually every general work on North American birds on library shelves today. It will take a good while for North American bird students to become accustomed to having whistling-ducks, geese, swans, and ducks plus all of the fowl-like birds preceding loons and grebes. Although there are numerous other recent changes in species order, the House Sparrow still falls at the very end of the Carolina list.

The value in inches (centimeters) following the common and scientific names of each species is the approximate length of the bird as measured from the tip of the bill to the tip of the tail. For some birds with unusually long wings in proportion to body size (mostly pelagic species), the wingspan (W) is given in addition to length (L). Measurements are provided to give the reader a general idea of the relative size of the various species.

Species accounts have four principal subheadings: Range, Nesting Habits, Feeding Habits, and Description.

RANGE

Range includes statements of seasonal abundance, residence status, and distribution in the Carolinas. Data on habitat preference and seasonal abundance refer specifically to the situation in the Carolinas. Such information is based on the authors' personal knowledge, the comments of experienced field observers who reviewed the manuscript, and the current literature on Carolina bird life. Terms of residence status are defined as follows:

Permanent resident: The species is present throughout the year and breeds in the given region. Some species, particularly shorebirds, can be found in the Carolinas all 12 months of the year, but they do not breed here and therefore are not considered to be permanent residents.

Summer resident: The species arrives in the spring, breeds, and departs before winter. A few individuals may occur as winter stragglers.

Winter resident: The species arrives in late summer or autumn, remains all winter, and departs in spring.

Summer or winter visitor: The species is present only part of a given season and generally is somewhat erratic in its occurrence, although it is expected to be present with some degree of regularity. Summer visitors do not breed, not even when they are present regularly throughout the season, as is the case with some pelagic birds that breed in the Southern Hemisphere.

Spring or fall transient: The species passes through the region during migration.

Accidental: This term refers to birds found outside their normal ranges.

Straggler: This term refers to birds found during a season when the species normally is absent.

Residence status is uncertain for a few species. In such cases the period of known occurrence has been noted, but determination of status must await additional data and further analysis. Residence status may change as species shift their range boundaries or migration routes.

RELATIVE ABUNDANCE

Listed below are the terms of relative abundance used in this book. They are based on the probability of seeing a given species during several hours of active bird-watching at the proper season and in suitable habitat as well as the number of reports in the recent literature.

Abundant: Always expect to see a large number of individuals. Example: Royal Tern on coast in summer.

Very common: Always expect to see a moderate number of individuals. Example: Northern Cardinal in piedmont throughout year.

Common: Almost always expect to see a moderate number of individuals. Example: Tufted Titmouse in piedmont throughout year.

Fairly common: Usually expect to see a few individuals. Numerous reports in the literature. Example:

Ruby-throated Hummingbird in summer.

Uncommon: Expect to see a small number of individuals occasionally. Regular reports in the literature. Example: Upland Sandpiper as a fall migrant.

Rare: Expect to see no more than one individual per year. Few reports in the literature. Example: Nashville Warbler as a spring and fall migrant.

Very rare: Expect to see less than one individual every five seasons. Very few reports in the literature. Example: Kirtland's Warbler as a fall migrant.

NESTING HABITS

For birds breeding in the Carolinas, the species accounts include an outline of the reproductive process: nest construction, clutch size (number of eggs most commonly found), egg description (smooth and ovate unless otherwise stated), incubation period, and care and development of young. To emphasize important similarities, the pattern of nesting behavior may be given under the appropriate order or family heading.

When details of the reproductive cycle were not available directly from the Carolinas, data were taken from the general literature, principally Bent's *Life Histories of North American Birds.* A recent work of similar scope is *The Birds of North America: Life Histories for the 21st Century,* edited by A. Poole and F. Gill. On the Internet, individual species accounts can be downloaded for a fee. Many libraries subscribe to this service. For more information, visit <www.buteobooks.com>.

We hope that *Birds of the Carolinas* will encourage readers to watch closely those species whose habits are poorly known and to investigate an occurrence or behavior that appears to be unusual. The chief purpose of *The Chat,* the quarterly journal of Carolina Bird Club, is to help local bird-watchers and professional biologists communicate with one another. Ornithology remains a field of science in which the contributions of informed amateurs are both needed and appreciated.

FEEDING HABITS

Major foods are listed for each species, but other foods probably are consumed. Food resources in the Carolinas may differ from those available elsewhere in the species' range. Feeding methods also are given. Often feeding habits are essentially the same for all birds in a family or order. In such cases the reader is referred to the appropriate heading.

DESCRIPTION

Descriptions are designed to supplement the photographs, which cannot possibly illustrate all plumages for the more than 400 species found in the Carolinas. Descriptions emphasize characteristics that separate similar species, but such descriptions are not always adequate for positive identification of some birds. Field guides and more detailed works such as some mentioned in the Suggested Reading section of this book should be consulted.

If an unidentified bird remains at one location long enough, invite an experienced bird student to look at it. Sometimes an unusual plumage variation can turn something as familiar as a Northern Mockingbird into a mystery bird. Because asking for help is a sign of eagerness to learn, most experienced birders welcome an opportunity to share their knowledge. Bird study is at its best when adding a new species to one's life list also marks the beginning of a new friendship.

BIRDS OF THE CAROLINAS

All species in this superorder have a primitive structure of the palate.

Order ANSERIFORMES: Whistling-Ducks, Geese, Swans, and Ducks

Anseriformes are web-footed aquatic birds that have flattened bills with serrated edges, or lamellae, which serve as strainers, permitting ejection of water and mud from the mouth during feeding.

Whistling-ducks, swans, and geese feed primarily on vegetable matter obtained mostly by grubbing or grazing. Puddle ducks (e.g., Mallard, teals, wigeons) feed mostly on vegetable matter obtained by dabbling and tipping in shallow water. Bay ducks (e.g., Canvasback, scaups) feed by diving from the surface and swimming underwater. In general they take more animal food than do surface-feeding species. Sea ducks (e.g., scoters, eiders) also are diving birds, feeding mostly on mollusks.

Waterfowl have bodies well insulated with down, which is used commercially to fill pillows, sleeping bags, comforters, and winter clothing. Most ducks, geese, and swans breed in the northern and western portions of North America, from the potholes of the Dakotas to the Arctic Circle. A few, most notably the Wood Duck and the growing population of nonmigratory Canada Geese, nest throughout the Carolinas. Large clutches of 8 to 14 unspotted pale greenish or creamy buff eggs are laid in nests lined with down the female plucked from her own body. Eggs are covered with down when they are left unattended.

Nests may be bulky mounds of plant materials and debris, in the case of swans; depressions in the ground, well lined with plant materials and concealed by natural vegetation, as with Mallards; or beds of moss, decaying wood chips, and other debris in natural cavities or man-made nest boxes, as with Wood Ducks. Incubation requires about a month for most waterfowl. The downy young chicks are precocial, being able to walk and swim within a few hours after hatching.

On the secondary flight feathers of each wing, some ducks have a well-marked rectangle of color, the speculum. Often ducks can be recognized in flight at considerable distances because of their distinctive wing patterns. In summer male ducks assume a drab eclipse plumage, which aids in concealing them during the period of about 2 to 4 weeks when they are flightless after having dropped their wing quills almost simultaneously. A second molt of the contour feathers prior to fall migration restores the colorful plumage after the flight feathers have been replaced. Females molt their flight feathers later in the summer than do the males, after the young are fully independent.

Migration patterns of the goose-like whistling-ducks that occur in eastern North America are unlike those of the other waterfowl found in the Carolinas. Following the breeding season, whistling-ducks disperse northward from southern Florida, the Mississippi Delta area, southern Texas, or Mexico. They migrate southward in spring.

Family ANATIDAE: Whistling-Ducks, Geese, Swans, and Ducks

Members of this family live over much of the world. Ranging from large swans to small ducks, they are gregarious birds that feed mostly on plants and animals living in water.

Subfamily Dendrocygninae: Whistling-Ducks

These long-necked, long-legged, goose-like waterfowl are named for their whistling calls. Their wingbeat is slower than that of most ducks but faster than that of a goose. Whistling-ducks are primarily tropical and subtropical species. However, several species are kept in captivity at various places in the Southeast. A few escape from time to time, and some now breed in the wild in Florida and perhaps elsewhere in the region. Listing a waterfowl species as one known to have been seen in the wild in the Carolinas does not eliminate the possibility that some birds might have escaped from captivity.

White-faced Whistling-Duck
Dendrocygna viduata
17 in. (43 cm)

Range: One photographed near Duck in Currituck County, N.C., in April 1998 showed no signs of having been kept in captivity and may have been a naturally occurring vagrant. It was accompanied by a Black-bellied Whistling-Duck. In the Western Hemisphere, the White-faced Whistling-Duck is essentially resident from Costa Rica south to central Peru, Bolivia, northern Argentina, and Uruguay. It occurs casually in the Greater Antilles and could conceivably have been displaced northward by a tropical storm.

Feeding habits: This species feeds in rice fields and on mudflats, often in company with Fulvous and Black-bellied Whistling-Ducks.

Description: The face and foreneck are white, the rest of the neck and the back of the head are black, the back is reddish brown, and the breast is rufous chestnut.

Black-bellied Whistling-Duck
Dendrocygna autumnalis
19–21 in. (48–53 cm)

Range: Although the individual collected in Carteret County, N.C., in February 1968 was assumed to have escaped from captivity, that may not have been the case. An adult in fresh plumage, it showed no signs of recent captivity. The bird may have come from the established population in southern Texas and northern Mexico. Although some Black-bellied Whistling-Ducks found in eastern North Carolina in the winter of 1998–1999 are believed to have been lost by a hunting club, the ongoing occurrences in the Carolinas, including a group of five in Tyrrell County, N.C., in May 2004, may represent wanderers from the established and growing population of formerly captive birds now nesting in the wild in Florida. The first known nesting by non-captive birds in South Carolina occurred at the Donnelley Wildlife Management Area in the summer of 2003. No nest was found, but a male and a female were seen with a brood of ducklings. On July 24, 2004, the Donnelley wildlife manager saw a pair with a brood of 10 ducklings.

Nesting habits: Although Black-bellied Whistling-Ducks will nest on the ground, they generally prefer a cavity (natural or a nest box) in the vicinity of shallow freshwater lakes and ponds having emergent vegetation such as cattails and water lilies. There is no evidence to date of their occupying nest boxes erected for Wood Ducks in the Carolinas.

Feeding habits: The Black-bellied Whistling-Duck often feeds at night and does not dive. It eats corn, acorns, and various other seeds as well as some insects and mollusks, primarily snails.

Description: Adults of this goose-like species are marked by a red bill, gray face, reddish-brown body, black belly, and a prominent white stripe running the length of the wing. The juvenile is a drab bird with a white wing stripe visible both perched and in flight.

Fulvous Whistling-Duck
Dendrocygna bicolor
20 in. (51 cm)

Range: Since the 1950s the Fulvous Whistling-Duck has been an uncommon and erratic winter visitor in freshwater marshes and impoundments along the Carolina coast. Inland sightings are rare and occur mostly in spring. Although individual birds may linger into June, there is no evidence of breeding by this essentially Central and South American species.

Fulvous Whistling-Duck

Feeding habits: The Fulvous Whistling-Duck feeds at night and does not dive. It eats corn, acorns, and various seeds. Where rice is grown, it consumes many seeds of weeds that invade the plantings of that crop.

Description: This tawny-brown goose-like duck has a dark bill, bluish feet, and white marks on the sides and rump. Its call is a shrill whistle.

Subfamily Anserinae:
Geese and Swans

Although geese and swans feed in water, they are frequently found grazing on land.

Greater White-fronted Goose
Anser albifrons
26–30 in. (66–76 cm)

Range: In North America, the Greater White-fronted Goose breeds in Alaska and northern Canada and winters primarily west of the Rocky Mountains, in Mexico, and along the Gulf Coast of Texas or Louisiana. A generally rare but increasingly regular winter visitor to the Carolinas, the Greater White-fronted Goose can be found from early

Greater White-fronted Goose

Greater Snow Goose (white phase)

Greater Snow Goose (blue phase)

November to February and rarely even as late as May. Look for White-fronteds among the large numbers of waterfowl that congregate at wildlife refuges.

Feeding habits: See Canada Goose.

Description: This is a mostly gray goose. Adults have a narrow band of white feathers completely encircling the base of the pink bill and irregular black bands across the underparts. Young of the year, with a yellowish bill and pinkish legs, are easily mistaken for members of the race *A. a. flavirostris*, which nests in Greenland and generally winters in the British Isles but has been observed in North Carolina several times. Inexperienced observers should also be careful not to mistake a domesticated, yellow-legged Graylag Goose (*Anser anser*) for the orange-legged White-fronted Goose.

Snow Goose
Chen caerulescens
23–38 in. (58–96 cm)

Range: From early November to February or March, large numbers of Snow Geese winter at Lake Mattamuskeet, around Currituck Sound, and in the Bodie–Pea Island area of North Carolina. Inland and south of Pea Island, the species becomes rare, but small numbers may occur sporadically throughout the region, even in the mountains.

Feeding habits: Wintering Snow Geese prefer the roots and tubers of coastal marsh plants.

Description: Snow Geese wintering in the Carolinas occur in two color phases and two subspecies. The dark phase, formerly called the Blue Goose, is less common than the white phase. Dark-phase juveniles are an almost solid dark gray. White-phase juveniles are mostly pale gray above and dingy white below. All juveniles have black bills and legs. The adult dark phase has a white head. The adult white phase is white except for black primary wing feathers. All adults have pink bills and legs.

Subspecies: The Lesser Snow Goose (*C. c. caerulescens*) is, as the name implies, smaller in overall size than the Greater Snow Goose (*C. c. atlanticus*). In addition, the bill length of the Greater averages 20% longer than that of the Lesser, making the head more strongly wedge shaped and increasing the prominence of the "grin patch" on each side of the bill. Dark-phase birds are common in the eastern population of the Lesser Snow Goose but rare in the Greater Snow Goose population. In recent years the Greater Snow Goose population at Pea Island has declined in numbers, but Lesser Snow Geese continue to be present in impressive numbers at Pungo Lake in the Pocosin Lakes National Wildlife Refuge, Lake Mattamuskeet, and Currituck Sound.

Ross's Goose
Chen rossii
23 in. (58 cm)

Range: The smallest and probably still the least abundant of our North American geese, Ross's Goose breeds in the Arctic and winters primarily in the interior valleys of California. A relatively small number winter regularly on the Gulf Coast of Texas and Louisiana. The species was considered endangered prior to a population explosion in the 1960s and development of improved census techniques, but it remains susceptible to almost total nesting failure in some years, owing to adverse weather conditions on its relatively small breeding grounds.

The first known Ross's Goose on the Atlantic Coast occurred in December 1967, when a bird with a crippled leg appeared in North Carolina at Pea Island National Wildlife Refuge. The gimpy bird and at least one other Ross's Goose appeared in subsequent winters, once having lingered until early April. Singles and small flocks continue to appear each winter at various places in the coastal plain of North Carolina. The first record in the mountains occurred in January 1994, and one bird was photographed in Laurens County, S.C., where it remained at a horse farm from November 1995 until February 1996.

Feeding habits: See Snow Goose.

Description: Ross's Goose is similar to a white-phase Snow Goose. Look for Ross's smaller size, its stubby bill, and the absence of the "grin patch," a dark streak made by the lamellae on the bill of the Snow Goose. When seen at very close range, the adult Ross's Goose has warty protuberances at the base of its bill.

Canada Goose
Branta canadensis

Cackling Goose
Branta hutchinsii
30–43 in. (76–109 cm)

Canada Geese

Range: There are two populations of Canada Geese in the Carolinas. Though their numbers have declined greatly in recent years, wild, migratory birds are regular winter residents in eastern North Carolina south to Cape Lookout and occur elsewhere throughout the region. Some individuals may spend the summer at Pea Island and a few other refuges, but nesting does not normally take place. Inland, geese tend to congregate in winter on large man-made lakes in the piedmont and inner coastal plain.

A nonmigratory population of Canada Geese is growing rapidly and becoming increasingly unwelcome in urban, suburban, and rural areas of the Carolinas, including the Pea Island National Wildlife Refuge, and elsewhere in the eastern United States. Apparently descendants of introduced birds that escaped from captivity or were released to supplement the wild population, the nonmigratory Canadas occur primarily in suburban areas where hunting is illegal and natural enemies are not abundant enough to keep the population under control. Goose droppings foul small ponds, lawns, parks, golf courses, sidewalks, and even the porches and patios of homes. Adults defending nests are potentially dangerous to small children and persons with disabilities.

The nonmigratory population is protected by the same game laws that govern migratory birds. However, changes in regulations are occurring that may permit reduction of troublesome populations of introduced species.

Nesting habits: In general, the gander selects the territory for displaying, nesting, and some feeding, but the goose selects the nest site. Most individuals begin breeding when about 2 years old, and the pair bond, once formed, is monogamous for life. Nest construction, which is almost entirely by the goose while the gander stands by to defend the territory, begins 2 or 3 days before the first egg is laid.

The goose scrapes a bowl-shaped depression at the chosen site and lines it with vegetation gathered from the immediate vicinity. She does not carry nest material in her beak, but lifts it by stages. A goose standing near the nest site may lift a clump of vegetation and throw it over her back in the direction of the nest. About the time the third egg is laid, the goose begins adding down to the nest at intervals until the clutch is complete. Occasional additions may be made during incubation. Nests may be 2 feet (60 cm) or larger in diameter, varying with the availability of suitable materials in the immediate vicinity of the nest site. The habitat may be in the open (e.g., on a grassy dam to a pond), at the edge of a marsh, or in a thicket at the edge of a lake or pond.

In central North Carolina, nests may be found in the first week of April. Clutches frequently number four to eight eggs. The goose covers her eggs with down before leaving to fly with the gander to a feeding site. Usually, the incubation period is 27 to 28 days. Peeping can be heard within the shell 48 to 60 hours prior to appearance of the first external sign of hatching (pipping), and emergence of the chick may require an additional 8 to 36 hours. As soon as its yellow natal down is dry, the chick begins to oil its plumage. Young are led from the nest on their first or second day, but they are brooded in some secluded place for the first few days. By the time the gray juvenile plumage becomes prominent, family parties may be seen walking across open areas or swimming in a line across a pond, usually with one adult leading and the other bringing up the rear.

When several pairs nest close together, young birds of various sizes may gather in a rearing group (nursery, or creche), placing a dozen or more goslings under the care of one pair of adults. However, the family group is entirely integrated prior to the young taking flight, and it normally remains intact until the following spring, when the gander becomes territorial and will no longer tolerate the presence of his offspring. Broodmates, however, may remain in close association until they reach sexual maturity, perhaps into their second spring.

Feeding habits: Geese feed primarily on vegetable matter, including roots, tubers, and seeds of aquatic plants. They are fond of rice, corn, and other grain crops, a characteristic that sometimes makes them unpopular with farmers.

Description: This dark goose has a black head and neck marked by a broad white chin strap. Watch for flocks flying in V-formation.

The Check-list Committee of the American Ornithologists' Union has split the Canada Goose into two species. Several subspecies (all large forms) are still assigned to the Canada Goose (*B. canadensis*). The small forms are assigned to the Cackling Goose (*B. hutchinsii*). Occurrence of both species and several subspecies in the Carolinas has been documented with specimens in museum collections. Most bird students will be able to spot the smaller species in a mixed flock, but determining exactly which subspecies of the Canada Goose or the Cackling Goose are present will be very difficult (usually impossible) under field conditions. In general, the Cackling Geese are about half the size of the Canada Geese.

Brant
Branta bernicla
22–30 in. (56–76 cm)

Range: Once nearly extirpated by a blight that killed its chief source of food, the Brant appears to have made a good recovery, though it is not abundant in the Carolinas. This

Brant

small goose can be seen feeding and loafing on the tidal flats of Pamlico Sound around Hatteras Inlet and Ocracoke Inlet from November until northward migration in March or April. South of Pamlico Sound the species is a rare winter visitor.

Feeding habits: The Brant feeds chiefly on eelgrass that grows in shallow salt water.

Description: This small dark goose wears a white clerical collar. A specimen of the very dark, western subspecies, the Black Brant (*B. b. nigricans*), was taken on Core Banks in 1964. Immatures lack the white marking on the neck.

Barnacle Goose
Branta leucopsis
24–28 in. (61–71 cm)

Range: This Old World goose occurs very rarely along the Atlantic Coast

southward to the Carolinas. The Barnacle Goose is more likely to be seen in late autumn or early winter around Currituck Sound, Pea Island, or Lake Mattamuskeet than elsewhere in the region. One was seen at Santee National Wildlife Refuge on Lake Marion from November 7, 1980, until at least January 22, 1981. It showed no sign of having been in captivity (e.g., leg band) and was closely associated with a flock of wild Canada Geese. Another was at Lake Mattamuskeet from November 9 to December 29, 2003. Barnacle Geese found in the eastern United States probably originated in Greenland.

Feeding habits: See Canada Goose.

Description: This small, dark goose has a black neck with a black ridge extending upward onto the crown. The face is white. In flight the dark gray flight feathers contrast with the much lighter gray of the wing lining.

Mute Swan
Cygnus olor
54–62 in. (137–157 cm)

Range: A European species frequently stocked in urban parks, the Mute Swan has a well-established non-captive breeding population from Long Island, New York, south along the coast to southeastern Virginia. The species is a rare vagrant in coastal North and South Carolina, but it appears to be just a matter of time until the first nest is found in the wild within the region. The species staged a major invasion of North Carolina in the fall of 1993. Some birds remained well into 1994. Since then there have been

Mute Swans

Tundra Swans

numerous fall, winter, and summer reports of apparently feral Mute Swans in the Carolinas, including visitors to lakes as far inland as Winston-Salem. Five Mute Swans were seen at Pea Island National Wildlife Refuge in June 2003. Two lingered in that vicinity, but there was no evidence of local breeding. About that same time, a pair of apparently feral birds attempted to nest in the wild near Wilmington.

Feeding habits: In the wild, Mute Swans consume great quantities of aquatic vegetation, feeding mostly during the day but, apparently, sometimes on moonlit nights. Free-flying birds readily become semi-domesticated when offered grain.

Description: Swans are large, long-necked waterfowl easily recognized by the white plumage of the adults. The wingspan of the Mute and Trumpeter swans is 7 feet or greater (more than 2 m). The smaller Tundra Swan has a wingspan of more than 5 feet (1.5 m). Adults of the three species that occur in the wild in the eastern United States are best separated by the appearance of the bill. The adult Mute has an orange bill with black at the base, including a knob at the top.

Adult Trumpeter and Tundra swans have bills that are mostly black, with variable amounts of yellow near the eyes of the Tundra. Some individuals have completely black bills. The border between the crown and the bill is pointed in the Trumpeter and rounded in the Tundra. Mute Swans are greatly admired for the graceful curve of the neck and their distinctive aggressive posture with wings raised and arched over the back but not extended (busking). Contrary to its name, the Mute Swan is capable of making sounds, particularly when provoked.

Trumpeter Swan
Cygnus buccinator
59–60 in. (150–152 cm)

Range: Since the Trumpeter Swan was successfully reintroduced on the Upper Peninsula of Michigan, there have been numerous sightings in the Mississippi Valley and the northeastern states. One bird was reported from Charleston Harbor

in 1998. Four were trapped and photographed at the Pungo Unit of Pocosin Lakes National Wildlife Refuge, February 25–28, 2004.
Feeding habits: Food of adult birds consists almost entirely of stems, leaves, seeds, rootstalks, and tubers of freshwater aquatic plants.
Description: See Mute Swan.

Tundra Swan (Whistling Swan)
Cygnus columbianus
47–54 in. (119–137 cm)

Range: In North America the Tundra Swan breeds in coastal Alaska and northern Canada. It winters primarily in the western United States (Washington, Oregon, and California) and on the East Coast from the Chesapeake Bay south to northeastern North Carolina. When not breeding or molting, these gregarious birds are restless, active, and noisy. Large flocks of wintering Tundra Swans occur in and around wildlife refuges in Hyde, Tyrrell, and Dare Counties.
Feeding habits: Tundra Swans gather submerged vegetation by upending if depth of water is suitable or by gleaning plant materials from tidal flats or ashore, where they are grazers as well as grubbers. In Hyde and Tyrrell Counties swans regularly graze in fields of winter wheat, usually removing leaves instead of pulling up the entire plant. Their underwater grubbing creates pits or "swan holes," which are a hazard to anyone wading through the area. Various ducks may swim among the feeding swans to gather dropped fragments of uprooted plants.
Description: See Mute Swan.

Tundra Swans

Subfamily Anatinae: Ducks

This large, worldwide subfamily is divided informally into several distinctive groups. *Perching ducks*, the Wood Duck and the Muscovy Duck, have sharp claws for perching in trees. They nest in cavities in trees or in nest boxes. *Dabbling ducks* are surface-feeding members of the genus *Anas*, including the familiar Mallard. *Pochards* are diving members of the genus *Aythya*, including the familiar Canvasback. *Eiders* are large sea ducks famous for their dense down often used in making comforters and insulated clothing. *Sea ducks* are stocky, short-necked divers. Most sea ducks migrate and spend the winter in large flocks. *Mergansers* are divers with long, thin, serrated bills, which help them capture fish, crustaceans, and aquatic insects. *Stiff-tails* include only one species commonly found in the Carolinas, the Ruddy Duck, which is easily recognized by its long, stiff tail feathers that serve as a rudder during dives and often point upward when the bird is resting on the surface.

Wood Duck
Aix sponsa
17–21 in. (43–53 cm)

Wood Duck (male)

Range: A fairly common to common permanent resident throughout the Carolinas, the Wood Duck is more common in the swamps and wooded ponds and river bottoms of the coastal plain than in the western counties. The species is less numerous in winter than at other seasons.

Nesting habits: Mating takes place about midwinter, and the female usually builds her nest in a natural cavity in a dead or living tree standing in or near water. Nest boxes and abandoned chimneys may be used, and sometimes the nest is a considerable distance from water. Eggs, creamy white and usually numbering 9 to 14, are laid from February to April, with the peak period of hatching in April and early May. A few second broods have been recorded. "Dump nests" may contain up to 40 eggs deposited by more than one female.

Only the hen incubates, but the strikingly colored drake remains more or less in attendance until the time to molt into eclipse plumage. Then the male becomes inconspicuous and flightless, having lost all flight feathers simultaneously.

Usually on the morning of the day after hatching, the downy chicks respond to coaxing calls from the parent waiting below, claw their way to the entrance hole, and flutter down to the water or soft ground. Although the young can fly at 8 to 9 weeks, they hide and feed in emergent vegetation into August. By then the brood is strong upon the wing and ready to flock with other families.

Feeding habits: Vegetable matter constitutes about 90% of the Wood Duck's diet. Favored items are cypress cones and galls, wild rice, pondweeds, water lily seeds, wild grapes, duckweed, water elm seeds, acorns, beechnuts, and water hickory nuts. Animal food is nearly always insects.

Description: This is our only native duck with a long, smoothed-down crest. The male Wood Duck has an irregular white marking extending from his chin and throat toward the eye and nape. The female has a white eye ring and a restricted white patch on her chin.

Gadwall
Anas strepera
19–23 in. (48–58 cm)

Range: An uncommon to fairly common winter resident, the Gadwall is found throughout the Carolinas, though it tends to be localized in distribution. The species has been nesting at Pea Island National Wildlife Refuge since 1939.

Gadwall (male)

Gadwall (female)

Gadwalls (pair in flight)

Nesting habits: Nests are often placed in dense grasses along impoundment dikes, on small islands in the impoundments at Pea Island, or on islands of dredged material in Pamlico Sound.

Feeding habits: Although the diet of the Gadwall is nearly 98% vegetable, the species dives much more frequently than do other surface-feeding ducks.

Description: This gray-brown duck has a dark bill and yellow feet. Its speculum is brown, black, and white, with the white patch nearest the body.

Eurasian Wigeon
Anas penelope
17–21 in. (43–53 cm)

Range: A few of these Old World ducks appear along the Atlantic Coast of North America every fall. From October to mid-April, the species has been recorded in the Carolinas as far south as the Combahee River and as far west as Greenville, S.C.

Feeding habits: See American Wigeon.

Description: Similar to the American Wigeon, the male Eurasian has a rusty head with a buffy or cinnamon forehead and crown that fade to white. The female Eurasian has a brownish head with a dark cap. Some male American Wigeons may show a buffy crown, but they have a prominent green eye patch not found on the Eurasian birds.

American Wigeon (Baldpate)
Anas americana
18–23 in. (45–58 cm)

Range: A common winter resident that is more abundant along the coast than inland, the American

*American Wigeons
(female left, male right)*

American Black Ducks (male in foreground)

Wigeon is generally present from October to April. Despite numerous June records from South Carolina, there is no evidence of breeding in the Carolinas.

Feeding habits: Wigeons are primarily plant-eaters, with small mollusks and insects composing less than 10% of their diet. Coastal birds sometimes feed heavily on certain kinds of green algae found in the intertidal zone. Those birds take on a strong repugnant odor and are generally considered unpalatable.

Description: This brownish duck has a large white patch on the leading portion of each wing. Males have a light head with a green mask extending from one eye to the other around the back of the head. Females have a gray head. Both sexes have a blue bill that distinguishes this species from the dark-billed Gadwall.

American Black Duck
Anas rubripes
20–26 in. (51–66 cm)

Range: The American Black Duck is a fairly common winter resident throughout the Carolinas, but it is far more numerous toward the coast than inland. There is justifiable concern regarding the declining populations of Black Ducks. The species breeds regularly in northeastern North Carolina and to an unknown extent southward at least to the vicinity of Cape Romain National Wildlife Refuge in South Carolina and locally inland to the mountains. Individuals are known to hybridize with Mallards.

Nesting habits: Nests are on the ground near water, and young leave the nest about mid-June.

Feeding habits: American Black Ducks eat vegetable matter, snails, crustaceans, and insects.

Description: The American Black Duck has a dark body, a light head, and a violet speculum that has no white border. In flight, white wing linings contrast with the dark body. The male has a yellow bill; the female, a mottled greenish one.

Mallards (male left, female right)

Mallard
Anas platyrhynchos
21–27 in. (53–68 cm)

Range: A common winter resident of freshwater habitats throughout the region, the Mallard breeds locally in all sections of the Carolinas. Most of the nesting birds probably have reverted to the wild from introduced stock. The British name for the Mallard is Stock Duck, a reference to the many domesticated strains derived from it.

Nesting habits: Nests are depressions in the ground, well lined with plant materials and concealed by natural vegetation. Newly hatched ducklings are not fed in the nest. They usually follow the female to water about 12 hours after hatching and begin feeding soon afterward. The ducklings remain together as a brood whether the adult stays in attendance or deserts them. Age at first flight is variable, but most are on the wing before they are 60 days old.

Feeding habits: Mallards and other puddle ducks feed mostly on vegetable matter obtained by tipping up in shallow water.

Description: The Mallard has a blue speculum bordered by white. The adult male has a yellow bill, green head, and white neck band. The female is mottled brown.

Mottled Duck
Anas fulvigula
22 in. (56 cm)

Range: The population of this introduced species appears to be increasing along the South Carolina coast northward to the vicinity of Litchfield Beach and Pawleys Island. The species is well established in Florida and along portions of the Gulf Coast from the Mississippi Delta into Mexico.

Nesting habits: See comments on order. Mottled Ducks begin courtship in January or February, prior to departure of the majority of Mallards and American Black Ducks. That overlap presents a disturbing possibility of hybridization with the latter species, which seems to be having difficulty maintaining its numbers at the southern edge of its breeding range.

Feeding habits: See comments on Mallard.

Description: The Mottled Duck, considered by some authorities to be a subspecies of the Mallard, averages slightly smaller than the Mallard. Color is slightly darker than a female or juvenile Mallard and lighter than the American Black Duck in all plumages. Wing linings are white. The adult male Mottled Duck has a bright yellow bill and an unstreaked buffy throat. His blue-green speculum has a very narrow white border.

Blue-winged Teals (pair)

Blue-winged Teal
Anas discors
14–16 in. (36–40 cm)

Range: Primarily a transient in most parts of the Carolinas, the Blue-winged Teal is fairly common inland and common along the coast, where small numbers remain throughout the winter. The species has been breeding at Pea Island since 1938, occasionally at Cape Romain since 1960, and in North Carolina's Onslow and Pamlico Counties since 1969.
Nesting habits: Nests are on the ground, and young leave them in June. The incubation period for this teal is only about 3 weeks, slightly shorter than average for larger waterfowl.
Feeding habits: Food is about 70% seeds, with the animal matter being primarily snails, insects, and crustaceans.
Description: Both sexes have a green speculum and a large pale blue patch on the leading portion of each wing. The male has a white crescent on his face.

Cinnamon Teal
Anas cyanoptera
15–17 (38–43)

Range: Although common in the western United States, the Cinnamon Teal is a rare accidental in the Carolinas, usually found along the coast in winter or early spring.
Feeding habits: Cinnamon Teals have feeding habits similar to those of the Blue-winged.
Description: The male Cinnamon Teal is solid cinnamon-red on the head and underparts. Otherwise, plumages of this species are almost identical to those of the Blue-winged Teal.

Northern Shoveler
Anas clypeata
17–22 in. (43–56 cm)

Range: A locally common winter resident along the coast, the Northern Shoveler occurs inland chiefly as an uncommon migrant. Mostly present from September through April, shovelers may linger into June, but there is no evidence of breeding in the Carolinas.
Feeding habits: All surface-feeding ducks have comblike lamellae along the edges of their bills, but in the shoveler those structures reach their highest development. A shoveler usually feeds in very shallow water by digging into soft mud while swimming along with the head partly or completely submerged. The tongue, roof of the mouth, and soft edges of the bill have many nerves sensitive to touch and taste. Those nerves, along with the lamellae, enable shovelers to filter out water, mud, and inedible items so they can feed

Northern Shoveler (male)

Northern Pintail (male)

on desirable mollusks, crustaceans, insects, and seeds.

Description: The greatly elongated bill is diagnostic. The male shoveler has a green head, and the female is mottled with brown. In flight both sexes show a large blue patch on the leading edge of each wing, but the large bill and the large amount of white on the male's body prevent confusion with the smaller Blue-winged Teal.

Northern Pintail
Anas acuta
21–30 in. (53–76 cm)

Range: Pintails are common to abundant winter residents in northeastern North Carolina from September through April. The species becomes less common southward along the coast, and inland it is primarily an uncommon migrant. Although a pair nested successfully in Guilford County, N.C., in 1950, there is no established breeding population in the Carolinas.

Feeding habits: Pintails eat mostly aquatic plants and their seeds plus a few crustaceans and insects.

Northern Pintail (female)

Description: The name "pintail" refers to the greatly elongated central tail feathers, which in some males may be 10 inches (25 cm) long. These are long-necked, slender, agile ducks. The male has a brown head and neck with white underparts extending up the neck to a point behind the eye. The female is mottled brown. Both sexes have a metallic brown speculum with a white border on the trailing edge of the wing.

Green-winged Teals

Green-winged Teal
Anas crecca
12–16 in. (30–40 cm)

Range: Common winter residents in coastal Carolina, Green-winged Teals sometimes arrive in August and linger until early May and, rarely, throughout the summer. The species is generally uncommon inland. Stragglers from the European population, formerly called Common Teal, are occasional visitors to coastal Carolina.

Feeding habits: Teals commonly associate with Northern Pintails, sharing a preference for fresh water and for a diet consisting chiefly of seeds from aquatic plants.

Description: This is the smallest of our surface-feeding ducks. The male Green-winged Teal has a rusty head with an oval patch of green about the eye, a white vertical bar on the side of its body, and a green speculum. The female is mottled brown with a green speculum. The European Green-winged Teal is similar, but the male has no white bar on its body.

Canvasback
Aythya valisineria
19–24 in. (48–61 cm)

Range: Once an extremely abundant winter resident in the sounds and

Canvasback (male)

Canvasback (female)

bays of North Carolina and Virginia, the Canvasback was brought almost to the point of extinction by overshooting, botulism, and drainage and drought in the breeding grounds. Closed hunting seasons and habitat restoration saved the species. In most years the Canvasback is a fairly common winter resident in coastal North and South Carolina from November to mid-April and an uncommon winter visitor inland.

Feeding habits: Canvasbacks gather in rafts to feed in fresh or brackish waters. Like the Redhead, this species dives from the surface and swims underwater to obtain food that is mostly vegetable matter.

Description: Redheads and Canvasbacks are so similar in appearance and behavior that many people are unable to tell them apart. Males of both species have cinnamon-red heads, black breasts, and mostly gray bodies. The Canvasback is generally larger with a lighter body color and a black bill. The flattened head-bill profile makes the eyes appear to be almost on top of the head. The Redhead has a rounded head and a bluish bill with a dark tip. The female Redhead greatly resembles a female Ring-necked Duck, but the Redhead's bill has no prominent white band across it. The female Canvasback is patterned much like the male, but her body and folded wings are a dingy-looking, pale gray-brown, and her brown head and neck appear faded in comparison with those of the male, whose white body and folded wings become grayish after the breeding season.

Redhead
Aythya americana
17–23 in. (43–58 cm)

Range: An uncommon winter resident in the Carolinas, the Redhead is most likely to be found in the salty or brackish waters of coastal sounds, bays, and estuaries. It is fairly common in Core Sound and the lower part of Pamlico Sound during most winters. Here Redheads gather in closely packed rafts of hundreds or even thousands. A few birds visit inland lakes and ponds, chiefly during migration.

Redhead

Feeding habits: The Redhead, like the Canvasback, dives from the surface and swims underwater to obtain food, most of which is vegetable matter.

Description: See Canvasback.

Ring-necked Duck
Aythya collaris
14–18 in. (35–45 cm)

Range: A common winter resident throughout the Carolinas from late October to April, the Ring-necked Duck prefers freshwater lakes and impoundments, and it is seldom seen in brackish and salt water.

Feeding habits: This is a diving duck with a predominantly vegetable diet.

Description: The species is named for the indistinct, difficult-to-see chestnut band encircling the neck of the adult male. The male has a solid black back and a prominent white vertical bar (or spur) between the gray sides and the black breast. The brownish female has a white eye ring. Both sexes have a black-tipped blue bill with a distinct white band separating the black from the blue. Because of the white mark on the

Ring-necked Duck (male)

Greater Scaup (male)

Ring-necked Duck (female)

Greater Scaup (female)

bill, some hunters refer to the species as the "ring-billed duck."

Greater Scaup
Aythya marila
16–21 in. (40–53 cm)

Range: Uncommon inland and even along the coast in South Carolina, the Greater Scaup is a fairly common winter resident only in Pamlico Sound and surrounding waters. The species is present in the Carolinas from October to April.

Feeding habits: Although about half of its food is vegetable, the Greater Scaup also consumes shellfish.

Description: Similar to male Ring-necked Ducks but larger, male scaup have a solid-blue bill, gray back, and whitish sides. Greater and Lesser Scaup are difficult to distinguish from each other reliably either in the water or on the wing. Greaters have a longer white stripe in the wing and a more rounded head. Female Greaters and Lessers are brownish and have white surrounding the base of the solid-blue bill.

Lesser Scaup
Aythya affinis
15–19 in. (38–48 cm)

Range: A fairly common to locally abundant winter resident and a common transient throughout the Carolinas from October to May, the Lesser Scaup is found on fresh water far more often than the Greater. Nevertheless, large rafts of Lesser Scaup often occur along the coast. Although stragglers are found in summer, the Lesser Scaup is not known to breed in the Carolinas.

Feeding habits: Like the Greater Scaup, the Lesser sometimes feeds on shellfish; at other times it consumes plants and becomes highly palatable.

Description: See Greater Scaup.

King Eider
Somateria spectabilis
19–25 in. (48–63 cm)

Range: Even rarer than the Common Eider along the Carolina coast southward to Charleston, the King Eider has been found from early October to late April. Usually a bird of the open sea, it sometimes occurs close to shore. Most King Eiders seen in the Carolinas are immature birds.

Feeding habits: King Eiders dive to submarine shoals to feed primarily on shellfish.

Description: The brown female has a stubby bill with a frontal shield that slopes more steeply than that of the Common Eider. First-spring males have a yellow bill, black head, white foreparts, and black body and wings. Adult males have white wing patches and white foreparts that contrast with the mostly black wings and body. The head is white with a blue-gray nape and an orange bill that flares broadly between the eyes.

Common Eider
Somateria mollissima
23–27 in. (58–68 cm)

Range: A rare winter visitor in salt water along the Carolina coast southward to Charleston, the Common Eider has been found from early November to late June. Most sightings appear to involve first-winter birds, which tend to wander farther south than adults.

Feeding habits: The Common Eider dives for mollusks and crustaceans.

Description: Females and first-winter males are brown with a dark bill that has a gently sloping frontal shield extending almost to the eyes. Females have a finely barred breast. Young males gradually acquire the black-and-white adult plumage, beginning well before spring migration. Adult males have a yellow bill, black crown, white cheek, and green nape.

Common Eider (female plumage)

Harlequin Ducks
(pair in breeding plumage)

Surf Scoters (two males and
one female in flight)

Harlequin Duck
Histrionicus histrionicus
15–21 in. (38–53 cm)

Range: Very rare in winter along our
coast as far south as Charleston
County, S.C., the Harlequin Duck is
usually found along rocky shores,
but in the Carolinas it must settle
for the turbulent waters near piers
and jetties. Although Harlequins
rarely associate closely with other
species of ducks, most of the few
that have been seen in the Carolinas were feeding near flocks of
Bufflehead.

Feeding habits: Harlequin Ducks feed
mostly on mussels, crustaceans, and
other small marine animals.

Description: The male Harlequin Duck
is mostly dark blue with white
patches on the back, breast, and
head. The female is mostly black
with white spots before, behind,
and below the eye.

Surf Scoter (male)

Surf Scoter
Melanitta perspicillata
17–22 in. (43–56 cm)

White-winged Scoter
Melanitta fusca
19–24 in. (48–61 cm)

Black Scoter
Melanitta nigra
17–21 in. (43–53 cm)

Range: Scoters are found along our
coast from October to May, rarely
into June. Although they may winter in sounds and bays or feed close

White-winged Scoter

Long-tailed Ducks (two males on right, one female on left)

to beaches, they are usually seen offshore, where they fly with rapid wingbeats in long skeins just above the waves, swim in rafts, and dive for shellfish. The White-winged Scoter is uncommon. Relative abundance of Surf and Black Scoters varies considerably from one season to the next and from place to place along our extensive coastline. Generally speaking, however, they are fairly common to common, becoming locally abundant in migration during October.

Little information is available on their numbers and movements. Individuals of all three scoter species may visit inland waters during migration, and they do so annually; but such occurrences remain somewhat rare.

Feeding habits: Scoters dive for shellfish.

Description: Scoters are large black sea ducks. The White-winged is easily recognized in flight by its white speculum; the male has a white eye patch and a black knob above the orange bill. The male Surf Scoter has a white patch on the forehead and the nape, and the male Black

Scoter has an orange knob above the black bill. For identification of adult females and first-winter birds of both sexes, consult a field guide.

Long-tailed Duck
Clangula hyemalis
Male 19–23 in. (48–56 cm)
Female 15–18 in. (38–45 cm)

Range: Formerly known as the Oldsquaw, the Long-tailed Duck is an uncommon winter resident of North Carolina sounds, bays, and offshore waters from November to April. The species is rare inland and in coastal South Carolina. Stragglers, probably injured birds, sometimes are found in summer adorned in full breeding plumage.

Feeding habits: A swift flier and expert diver, the Long-tailed Duck is primarily a fish-eater. Its small portion of vegetable food includes seaweed.

Description: The Long-tailed Duck is our only white-headed duck with completely dark wings. The male in winter has a dark patch surrounding the eye and extending toward the side of the neck. The female in winter has a black crown and a small dark cheek patch. Males have greatly elongated central tail feathers.

Bufflehead
Bucephala albeola
13–16 in. (33–40 cm)

Range: A fairly common to common winter resident from November through April or May, the Bufflehead is more abundant along the coast than inland. Birds of this species tend to stay in small flocks with a few individuals remaining on the surface while the others dive for food. At the beach, look for Buffleheads in the breakers near piers and jetties as well as in freshwater ponds and brackish tidal waters.
Feeding habits: Buffleheads dive for small aquatic animals.
Description: The male Bufflehead is mostly white with a dark greenish head that is marked by a white patch extending across the back of the head from eye to eye. The female is predominantly dark gray with an oval spot of white on each cheek.

Common Goldeneye (female)

Common Goldeneye (male)

Common Goldeneye
Bucephala clangula
16–23 in. (40–58 cm)

Range: An uncommon winter resident from October to April, the Common Goldeneye, formerly known as the American Goldeneye, is a coastal species that occurs inland as an uncommon migrant and rare winter arrival.
Feeding habits: Diving birds with a preference for deep water, goldeneyes often eat small mussels.
Description: The male Common Goldeneye has black-and-white wings and body. Its dark greenish

Bufflehead (male)

head is marked with a round white spot on the cheek. (Cheek spot is crescent-shaped in adult male Barrow's Goldeneye, which has never been documented as occurring in the Carolinas. First-winter males are almost identical in the two species.) Except for the head, the Common Goldeneye resembles the male Bufflehead in winter. The female Common Goldeneye has a gray body, cinnamon head, and white collar.

Hooded Merganser (male)

Hooded Merganser
Lophodytes cucullatus
16–19 in. (40–48 cm)

Range: A locally fairly common winter resident, the Hooded Merganser is most numerous along the coast, where it is found on both fresh and brackish waters. Hooded Mergansers breed at least occasionally at sites scattered throughout the Carolinas.

Nesting habits: A cavity-nesting species, the Hooded Merganser may occupy Wood Duck boxes or old Pileated Woodpecker nest sites. Laying may begin as early as 18 January and continue until mid- to late March. The 8 to 12 (average 10 per bird) eggs are almost round and glossy white in color. Reports of large clutches (e.g., 13 to 19 eggs) probably represent laying by more than one hen. Female Hooded Mergansers are also known to lay eggs in the nests of Wood Ducks. Most young leave the nest in April or May, following an incubation period of 33 days.

Feeding habits: Mergansers dive for fish.

Description: Mergansers have long,

Hooded Merganser (female)

slender serrated bills. The male Hooded has a black head with a fanlike white crest that is bordered with black. The female has a brownish head with a bushy crest.

Common Merganser
Mergus merganser
21–27 in. (53–68 cm)

Range: A rare to locally fairly common winter visitor from November to April, the Common Merganser is found primarily on fresh water in the northern half of North Carolina. Since 1990, Lake Phelps has attracted a sizable flock of Common

Mergansers, at times numbering 200 or more.

Nesting habits: The Common Merganser was extirpated as a breeding species in the southeastern United States in the late 1800s, about the same time that the beaver population was extirpated. Now that beaver ponds are commonplace in the Carolinas, suitable nest cavities should be readily available among the rotting trunks of trees drowned by the rising water level in thousands of beaver ponds statewide. At Jordan Lake, in the eastern piedmont of North Carolina, several individuals have been present sporadically during the summer months since the early 1990s, but no nesting site has been reported.

Feeding habits: Mergansers dive for fish.

Description: Mergansers have long, slender serrated bills. The male Common Merganser has a green head that contrasts sharply with the white neck and breast; the crest is seldom noticeable. Females have a cinnamon head that contrasts sharply with the white of the neck and breast; the crest is more pronounced than in the male. At close range the female shows a well-defined white throat patch.

Red-breasted Merganser
Mergus serrator
19–26 in. (48–66 cm)

Range: A common to abundant winter resident on salt water from late October to May, the Red-breasted Merganser is an uncommon transient and winter visitor inland. The species breeds at least locally and on very rare occasions along

Red-breasted Merganser (male)

the coast southward to Charleston. The numerous adults seen in summer are most likely nonbreeding individuals.

Nesting habits: On its Canadian breeding grounds, the species normally builds its nest on the ground in a place well concealed by driftwood, a fallen tree, or low overhanging branches. Sites usually are in the borders of freshwater ponds or rivers, but occasionally the birds nest on the shore of the ocean.

Feeding habits: Mergansers dive for fish and other aquatic animals.

Description: Mergansers have long, slender serrated bills. The male Red-breasted has a green head with a shaggy crest, and its white throat patch contrasts sharply with the reddish-brown breast patch. The female has a brown head with a shaggy crest, and the dark head and neck plumage gradually fades into the light breast.

Masked Duck
Nomonyx dominicus
13–15 in. (33–38 cm)

Range: This small, stiff-tailed duck was found at Lake Ellis in Craven County, N.C., February 20–27, 1982. Based on reports from elsewhere in the southeastern United States, there is a very good chance the bird was not an escaped captive. The species occurs all year in southeast Texas and has bred there. Masked Ducks found along the Atlantic Coast probably are storm-blown birds from the Caribbean population.

Feeding habits: Masked Ducks dive to obtain much of their food. Seeds predominate in a diet that includes other vegetable matter, insects, and small crustaceans found in fresh-water ponds and lakes or in salt water where mangroves grow.

Description: The adult male in breeding plumage has a mostly rusty brown neck and body, a blue-gray bill, and a black band extending from the crown to the throat. In flight, the adult male flashes a white swoosh on the upper wing surface. The adult female shows a similar, but smaller, white patch on the upper wing. Juveniles, females of all ages, and nonbreeding adult males show three black horizontal bars when the head is viewed from the side: one on the cheek, one through the eye, and one on the crown. Masked Ducks often associate with coots and grebes as well as Ruddy Ducks. Like the Ruddy, the Masked Duck often swims with its tail held erect.

Ruddy Duck
Oxyura jamaicensis
14–17 in. (35–43 cm)

Range: A common winter resident from October to May, the Ruddy Duck is more numerous along the coast than inland. Nearly extirpated by market hunters, Ruddy Ducks have made a good recovery and now can be found in large rafts in our estuaries. Evidence of breeding has been obtained from Colleton and Charleston Counties in South Carolina and from Pamlico County in North Carolina.

Nesting habits: Although Ruddy Ducks frequently appropriate an old coot or gallinule nest or lay eggs in the active nest of a grebe or another diving duck, the species is capable of building a very nice basket-like structure. Woven of reeds, rushes, flags, and other convenient marsh plants, the nest is built up 7 or 8 inches (17 to 20 cm) above water level. It is firmly attached to the surrounding living plants and usually well concealed by them. Only sparsely lined, the nest often has a sloping platform of reeds leading to

Ruddy Ducks (flock of males and females, some with tail cocked upward)

the water, which normally is about 2 or 3 feet (61 to 92 cm) deep at the nest site. Laying probably begins in April in the Carolinas. The species normally lays from five to ten eggs, with the larger clutches often deposited in two layers because the eggs are surprisingly large for the size of the hen. Decidedly rough and granular, freshly laid eggs are dull white, but they become stained during the 25 to 26 days of incubation.

Although the female does all the incubating, the male normally remains with her and helps tend the brood. Newly hatched Ruddy Ducks are very large and can dive for their food right away, unlike most other ducklings, which feed from the surface for several weeks.

Feeding habits: Ruddy Ducks dive for wild celery and other plants that grow in estuaries. When diving, Ruddies may flip forward like other river ducks or submerge vertically like a grebe.

Description: Both sexes have a black cap and white cheeks. Their long tail is fan shaped and often up-tilted. In taking flight Ruddy Ducks, like all divers, must patter along the surface of the water for a short distance. On land Ruddies, like grebes, are almost helpless.

WATERFOWL OF QUESTIONABLE ORIGIN

Geese and ducks are strong fliers capable of long migratory movements. Unfortunately for the keepers of state bird lists, many waterfowl are kept in captivity by hunting clubs, zoological parks, city parks, research institutions, and private citizens. Species found in the wild in the Carolinas and considered likely to have escaped from captivity include Muscovy Duck (*Cairina moschata*), Falcated Duck (*Anas falcata*), Ruddy Shelduck (*Tadorna ferruginea*), Garganey (*Anas querquedula*), Baikal Teal (*Anas formosa*), and Mandarin Duck (*Aix galericulata*). The preceding species are given hypothetical or provisional status on state bird lists until there is a good reason to believe that at least some individuals came from a population breeding in the wild.

Order GALLIFORMES: Fowl-like Birds

All members of this order of fowl-like scratching birds, including the many varieties of domestic chickens supposedly developed from an Asian jungle fowl, are highly esteemed on the dinner table. They are good runners and fly well for short distances.

Family PHASIANIDAE:
Pheasants, Grouse, and Turkeys

These ground-dwellers have feathered nostrils, strong short bills, and short rounded wings. They can fly strongly for short distances. Males perform elaborate courtship displays. Some species, such as the Ruffed Grouse, return annually to the same strutting ground, which is known as a "lek."

Subfamily Phasianinae:
Pheasants

Our only member of this subfamily is not native to North America.

Ring-necked Pheasant
Phasianus colchicus
Male 30 in. (76 cm)
Female 20–24 in. (51–61 cm)

Range: Many attempts have been made to introduce this handsome, long-tailed Asian game bird in various parts of the United States. Introductions in the northern and western states generally have been successful, but one of the few breeding populations in the Southeast was introduced on Hatteras Island, N.C. The birds were found nesting near Cape Hatteras in the 1930s and appeared well established as far north as Pea Island in the 1980s. However, that population was extirpated about 1990. Small numbers remain on Portsmouth Island and Core Banks. Pheasants are often reared on shooting preserves. When escapes occur, sightings give rise to occasional reports from the Outer Banks and elsewhere.

Nesting habits: Pheasants usually are polygamous, but some males have monogamous tendencies. The female deposits her 10 to 12 olive-buff eggs in a natural depression in the ground or hollows out a site for herself. The nest is lined with leaves, grasses, or weed stems and often is concealed by overhanging grass or weeds. Laying probably begins by mid-April, and the incubation period is 23 to 27 days. Although the young are brooded and remain with the female for 6 or 7 weeks, they are able to follow the hen in search of food as soon as their down is dry and can fly at 2 weeks. The male assumes no role in incubation of eggs or care of young. Crowing is most frequent in spring when males proclaim their territories, but cocks sometimes are heard in autumn and on pleasant days in winter.

Feeding habits: Pheasants eat insects, weed seeds, and wild fruits and berries. In some situations they become very destructive to cultivated crops, but at other times they destroy many mice and harmful insects.

Description: The Ring-necked Pheasant is our only large, brown, and heavy-bodied bird with a very long and slender pointed tail. The male has an iridescent head and a white neck band. Colorful head markings are absent on the female.

Subfamily Tetraoninae: Grouse

Only one species of grouse occurs in the Carolinas.

Ruffed Grouse
Bonasa umbellus
16–19 in. (40–48 cm)

Range: The Ruffed Grouse lives in the heavy woodlands of the mountains and extreme western piedmont of the Carolinas, where it is a fairly common permanent resident. Watch for grouse standing beside or crossing roads, especially along the Blue Ridge Parkway.

Nesting habits: Male Ruffed Grouse are famous for their drumming performances, which may be heard throughout the year, although they are most frequent in spring and fall. The sound may carry up to a mile (1.6 km) in calm weather. Each cock has a favorite elevated place, usually a log or stump, where he stands while rapidly beating his wings, both to attract a mate and to warn other males to stay out of his territory.

The 8 to 14 creamy or buffy eggs are generally laid in May or June, but possibly in late April. At the southern extreme of the range in Pickens County, S.C., in a nest beneath a stump near the Foothills Trail, a clutch of seven eggs was complete on May 5, 2000. Chicks could be heard peeping within the eggs, and some pipped on the morning of May 26. Eggs usually

Ruffed Grouse

hatch in 3 weeks, or perhaps a little longer in cold weather.

The female has complete responsibility for incubation of eggs and care of the precocial young, which have their eyes open at hatching and leave the nest as soon as their protectively colored down is dry. Although the chicks quickly learn to scratch for food, the hen must keep them warm and dry at night and in wet weather. Young birds can fly when 10 to 12 days old.

Feeding habits: Ruffed Grouse prefer vegetable food such as berries, nuts, acorns, and various seeds, but they consume many grasshoppers and crickets, sometimes searching for them along roadsides and in fields.

Description: This grayish- or reddish-brown bird has a heavy body, a slightly crested head, and a wide tail that is barred and broadly tipped with black. The name, often mistakenly given as "Ruffled Grouse," is derived from tufts of black feathers the bird can erect on each side of the neck. The ruff is greatly reduced or absent in the female. Displaying males erect the ruff and point the fanned tail upward. Flight is rapid and evasive.

Subfamily Meleagridinae: Turkeys

The largest game bird in North America, the Wild Turkey was proposed as the national emblem for the United States, but it lost to the majestic Bald Eagle.

Wild Turkey
Meleagris gallopavo
48–50 in. (122–127 cm)

Range: Formerly permanent residents throughout the Carolinas from the mountains to the sea, the Wild Turkey was extirpated from most of the region. However, the species is now expanding its range and increasing in numbers. Thanks to sound wildlife management practices, Wild Turkeys are once again being found throughout both Carolinas.

Nesting habits: When a hen is ready to lay, usually about mid-April, she slips away from the cock and his harem to deposit her 8 to 15 eggs on the ground in a sheltered depression lined with leaves or grass. The whitish or light buff eggs are heavily speckled with reddish brown. The hen alone incubates the eggs for 28 days and cares for her single annual brood of precocial chicks. Turkeys seldom fly and prefer to run from danger. They do fly to roosts in trees at night. Young birds can fly to a low perch when they are about 2 weeks old.

Feeding habits: Wild Turkeys feed on insects, berries, and seeds, with acorns at times making up 60% of their diet.

Wild Turkey (male)

Wild Turkey (female)

Description: Although they sound just like the domestic birds, Wild Turkeys are more slender and long legged, with chestnut-tipped tail feathers and a brilliant metallic bronze sheen to the plumage. The gobbler wears a beard of coarse, hairlike tufts protruding from the breast, a characteristic sometimes found in the hen. Rarely, a gobbler may have two beards. Weights of adult birds generally range from 12 to 25 pounds (5.5 to 11.4 kg), and gobblers very rarely reach a maximum of about 40 pounds (18 kg).

Family ODONTOPHORIDAE: New World Quail

Only recently placed in their own family, the New World quail have rounded bodies and a crest or head plumes. Only one species is native to the Carolinas.

Northern Bobwhite
Colinus virginianus
8–11 in. (20–28 cm)

Range: Formerly a common permanent resident in all parts of the Carolinas, the "quail" or "partridge" has seen its numbers greatly reduced in many parts of the Carolinas by hunting, habitat destruction, feral cats, changes in farming practices, too little or too much rain during the nesting season, and other circumstances not easily identified. In spite of the bobwhite's high reproductive rate, the population as a whole has declined significantly since the 1980s. Habitat restoration projects now under way offer hope for a population rebound in some parts of the Carolinas, but interstate highways and housing developments are rapidly replacing large tracts of the rural habitat hospitable to bobwhites.

Nesting habits: In spring the male's clearly whistled *bob-white* can be heard wherever hedgerows, overgrown fields, and open woods offer suitable habitat. The female responds with a lovely four-syllable whistle. Clutches of 12 to 20 pure white eggs are generally completed

Northern Bobwhite (male)

by late May. The eggs are sharply pointed at one end and fit snugly under the body of the incubating bird during the 23 or 24 days required for hatching.

Both adults share in nest construction and in the care of eggs and young. The nest is difficult to find because the incubating bird flushes very reluctantly. Always on the ground, the nest is a hollow lined with dead grass and usually protected by overhanging vegetation or a fence. If eggs are taken by predators, a hen may lay again and again until at least one chick survives. That explains reports of young birds seen in November.

Bobwhite chicks are precocial and ready to travel almost as soon as they are dry. In the event of danger, they will scatter and freeze while chicks and adults simultaneously utter the piping "scatter" call to confuse the intruder. Once the chicks have hidden, the parents give a monotonous alarm note with mechanical regularity until the threat has passed. Other special calls can be detected by the careful listener. Winter coveys of perhaps as many as 30 birds are based on the family group. At night the covey roosts on the ground positioned in a circle with heads pointed outward. When disturbed, quail take off in all directions at once with a whir of wings almost as startling as an explosion.

Feeding habits: The bobwhite eats a great deal of vegetable matter, including various weed seeds; but approximately 17% of its food is insects such as grasshoppers, boll weevils, cutworms, and potato beetles. Many farmers plant lespedeza to provide an abundance of wholesome food for these economically valuable birds.

Description: The Northern Bobwhite is a short-tailed, chunky brown bird. The male has a white throat patch and a white stripe over the eye. The female has a buffy throat and eye stripe.

INTRODUCED GAME BIRDS

From time to time game management personnel have attempted to improve hunting opportunities by introducing birds from other parts of the world. Introductions include smaller races of bobwhite often called "Mexican quail," the Japanese Quail (*Coturnix coturnix japonica*), and the Chukar (*Alectoris chukar*), a large European partridge that has become established in the western United States. No evidence has been found that those introduced birds have begun breeding in the Carolinas, although some of the smaller bobwhite may have interbred with the resident population.

Birds in this superorder do not have the primitive type of palate found in the Paleognathae.

Order GAVIIFORMES: Loons

Loons have webbed toes and obtain their food, primarily fish not considered suitable for table use, by diving and pursuing their prey underwater. Their legs are set so far back on their heavy body that they move on land with great difficulty, usually sliding down from shore to water much like a seal. Because they can take flight only by pattering along the surface of open water for a considerable distance, loons become stranded if they mistake wet pavement for water during night migrations.

Family GAVIIDAE: Loons

All five members of this family occur in North America, and all retain juvenile-like plumage through their first summer. Four of the five have been identified in the Carolinas.

Red-throated Loon
Gavia stellata
24–27 in. (60–68 cm)

Range: The Red-throated Loon is a fairly common to common winter resident in coastal waters from mid-October to mid-May, but it rarely occurs inland or offshore. This species is seen primarily close inshore, especially in sounds and inlets, where it generally outnumbers the Common Loon.

Red-throated Loon (in winter plumage)

Feeding habits: See comments on order.
Description: The Red-throated Loon is similar to the Common Loon but smaller, with a shorter, more slender, and slightly upturned bill. In spring the adult has a reddish throat patch.

Pacific Loon
Gavia pacifica
25 in. (64 cm)

Range: First reported in North Carolina at Cape Hatteras on May 15, 1987, and in South Carolina at Murrells Inlet in December 1992, the Pacific Loon is now an annual winter visitor to the Carolina coast. Small numbers occur alone or in flocks of Common Loons. Pacific Loons have been reported mostly from early November into March, but several individuals have been found in May and July.
Feeding habits: See comments on order.

Description: In winter plumage, the Pacific Loon is similar to the abundant Common Loon. Field marks include the small size of the Pacific, its more rounded head, and its smaller, more dagger-like bill. Dark flanks separate the Pacific from the white-flanked Arctic Loon (*Gavia arctica*), which has been reliably reported from eastern North America only a very few times, including one at Wrightsville Beach, N.C., in early January 2005.

Common Loon

Common Loon
Gavia immer
28–36 in. (70–90 cm)

Range: Common Loons begin moving southward in September and are common winter residents in Carolina coastal waters until mid-May. Small numbers of Common Loons are found regularly on large inland lakes, mostly during migration. Nonbreeding individuals occasionally remain throughout the summer in coastal sounds, bays, and estuaries or on large inland reservoirs, such as Lake Gaston, N.C., where the tremolo of their haunting cries may be heard, often when the bird is in flight.

Feeding habits: See comments on order.

Description: This diver's bill is dark, stout, and evenly tapered. Summer plumage is black with white spots arranged in bands across the back. Winter plumage is unspotted gray above and white below. The similar but larger Yellow-billed Loon (*Gavia adamsii*) is a rare accidental around the Great Lakes and on the northern portion of the East Coast, but the species has been documented only once from the southeastern states (Georgia, winter 2003–2004).

Order PODICIPEDIFORMES: Grebes

The name of the order (literally, "rump-foot") refers to the placement of the feet very far back on the body. Grebes also have rudimentary tails, short wings, and lobed toes that may be partially webbed.

Family PODICIPEDIDAE: Grebes

Seven species of this worldwide family occur in North America. Grebes are rarely seen on land or in flight. Their lobed toes make them excellent swimmers and divers, well adapted for the rapid underwater pursuit of aquatic insects and small fishes. Sometimes grebes swim with only the head and neck above the water.

Pied-billed Grebe
Podilymbus podiceps
12–15 in. (31–38 cm)

Range: Found in the Carolinas at all seasons, the Pied-billed Grebe is most abundant in fresh waters along the coast from September until May. It winters commonly on lakes and ponds throughout the inland counties. Breeding records come chiefly from the swamps, rice fields, small ponds, or bogs of the coastal region, but some nesting does occur inland, even in the mountains.

Nesting habits: Mating may take place in late February on the South Carolina coast, but a slightly later date probably is the case northward and inland. Built by both adults, the nest is a little floating island of rushes, aquatic grasses, and water-logged debris, usually anchored to

Pied-billed Grebe

emergent vegetation. Incubation of the five to seven brown-stained eggs lasts 23 to 24 days, and only one brood is raised each season. The downy young are heavily streaked on the head, back, and sides. They are able to swim shortly after hatching and often are carried on the backs of the adults even during dives.

Feeding habits: See comments on family.

Description: This species is the "water-witch," "didapper," or "hell-diver" familiar to everyone who lives near a farm pond. When disturbed, the Pied-billed Grebe almost never flies. Instead it dives, or sinks like a sub-marine, and swims underwater to a sheltered nook, where it remains hidden with only its head above water until danger has passed. That habit gives the impression that the bird dives and never returns to the surface. The Pied-billed Grebe is a brown bird with a thick bill. It frequently points its tail upward, displaying white undertail coverts. Summer adults have a black throat patch and a bold black band around the bill.

Horned Grebe
Podiceps auritus
12–15 in. (30–38 cm)

Range: Horned Grebes are uncommon to locally common winter residents of our coastal waters from late October to early May, and they may be locally common visitors on large inland lakes. A few Horned Grebes, often wearing nuptial plumage, linger into late spring, but there is no evidence of nesting in the Carolinas. However, when the ocean is calm and flat during spring migration, pairs of Horned Grebes may be seen in mutual display, with mates standing vertically on the water face to face. Sometimes the glassy surface is dotted with Horned Grebes as far a one can see in every direction, but only a few pairs are displaying.
Feeding habits: See comments on family.
Description: Winter plumage is dark gray with white face and neck.

Horned Grebe (in winter plumage)

Summer plumage is black above with cinnamon neck and underparts and conspicuous, solid yellow ear tufts extending from the eye to the nape.

Red-necked Grebe
Podiceps grisegena
17–22 in. (43–56 cm)

Range: Usually occurring from November through March, the Red-necked Grebe is a rare winter resident along the Carolina coast, where it is found mainly in salt water. It is a very rare visitor inland. The species is more likely to be found in the northern coastal plain and piedmont of North Carolina than inland elsewhere in the Carolinas.
Feeding habits: See comments on family.
Description: The Red-necked Grebe is a stocky, long-necked diver similar to the Horned Grebe but larger. Winter plumage is gray, often with a touch of cinnamon on the neck and upper breast. Summer plumage is dark above with cinnamon on the neck and upper breast. The contrast between the dark neck and the light cheek and throat patch is distinctive in all plumages.

Eared Grebe
Podiceps nigricollis
12.5–13.5 in. (31–34 cm)

Range: The Eared Grebe is a rare but regular migrant and winter visitor on the Carolina coast from mid-December to late April. This western species has been found at several large piedmont lakes and, very rarely, in the mountains. First recorded in South Carolina in January 1959 and in North Carolina in December 1964, the species seems to be increasing in numbers along our coast. Inland, Eared Grebes tend to visit wastewater treatment plants.

Feeding habits: See comments on family.

Description: The Eared Grebe is similar to the Horned Grebe and thus easily overlooked. Winter plumage is gray with a white throat and white ear patches. Look for the relatively small head, a peak in the crown over the eye, and the slender upturned bill. Summer plumage is black with cinnamon sides and wispy buffy ear tufts. The bill appears thinner than that of the Horned Grebe.

Western Grebe
Aechmophorus occidentalis
22–29 in. (56–73 cm)

Range: The Western Grebe is a rare accidental on the Carolina coast, appearing sporadically throughout the year, but has not yet been found between late June and mid-August.

The species has been reported very rarely inland to the mountains (Lake Julian, Buncombe County, N.C., December 14–15, 2002; Henderson County, N.C., January 22–25, 2003) and seems to be attracted to large reservoirs and lakes away from the coast (one at Lake Paul Wallace, Bennettsville, S.C., August 13–October 22, 1999).

Feeding habits: See comments on family.

Description: The largest of our grebes, the Western is approximately the same size as the Common Loon, but it has a longer neck and is more slender than a loon. The Western's bill is long, slender, and dingy yellow. The black crown and the white throat meet just below a dark patch surrounding the red eye. In the very similar Clark's Grebe (*A. clarkii*) there is white above and below the red eye, and the bill is bright yellow. Intermediate birds are known to occur. An apparent Clark's Grebe was seen and photographed at Cape Hatteras, N.C., March 15–19, 2003.

Order PROCELLARIIFORMES: Tube-nosed Swimmers

Tubenoses are wide-ranging birds that normally come ashore only to breed on remote islands. They include albatrosses, fulmars, shearwaters, petrels, and storm-petrels. Although some of these birds are quite numerous in our offshore waters in summer, they do not breed in the Carolinas and therefore are called summer visitors rather than summer residents.

Most of our tubenoses nest in the South Atlantic during our winter season and migrate to the North Atlantic during our summer, but individuals that have not reached sexual maturity remain at sea during the breeding season. Thus, some of these birds may occur in Carolina waters throughout the year.

Named for the tubular external nostrils on the upper mandible, tubenoses eat small fishes, squid, and crustaceans. Like many other pelagic species, tubenoses swallow much salt water in the course of feeding and preening, thus taking in more sodium chloride than their renal system can excrete. In a highly concentrated form, the surplus salt is discharged externally through nasal glands. Tubenoses also discharge through the mouth and nostrils a foul-smelling stomach oil that is rich in vitamins A and D. Fulmars are noted for using the oil to defend their nests. Sometimes those discharges tint the white plumage of the foreparts yellow.

Family DIOMEDEIDAE: Albatrosses

The largest of the seabirds, albatrosses glide tirelessly on very long and narrow wings, alighting on water only when they are becalmed or attracted to a bountiful supply of fish, squid, or refuse. Most nest on islands in the Southern Hemisphere.

Yellow-nosed Albatross
Thalassarche chlororhynchos
L 27–34 in., w 80–90 in.
(L 69–86 cm, w 203–228 cm)

Range: On April 22, 1997, two observers saw a subadult Yellow-nosed Albatross from a fourth-floor oceanfront window of a hotel at Whalebone, Dare County, N.C. The bird circled three times before sailing out of sight to the north without ever flapping its wings. The albatross was stockier through the head, neck, and body than the nearby Northern Gannets and had strikingly longer, more slender wings in proportion to body size. The upper wing surfaces and upper back of the albatross were black; head, lower back, and underparts were predominantly white except for a brownish patch of dark feathers on the side where the body meets the underwing. No black could be seen on the short tail, apparently because it was in heavy molt. The bill was long, slender, and hooked at the tip; it seemed to be all black. The short tail reduced the overall length of the albatross to approximately that of a gannet.

Since April 1997, Yellow-nosed Albatrosses were photographed off Cape Hatteras on February 15, 2000, and at Cape Hatteras Point on April 11, 2004. The species now appears to be a rare visitor to North Carolina offshore and inshore waters in winter and early spring. The bird seen off the North Carolina coast and formerly believed to have been a Black-browed Albatross (*Thalassarche melanophris*) is now best considered to have been one of an undetermined species.

Feeding habits: Most albatrosses feed by snatching small animals and carrion from water at or near the surface of the ocean.

Description: Yellow-nosed Albatrosses are large, long-winged seabirds that come to land only when breeding. Having much longer wings than a Northern Gannet, they fly with stiff wingbeats and glide without flapping in long, graceful arcs. The yellow "nose" is confined to a narrow stripe running atop the upper mandible from base to tip, a feature not likely to be seen on a bird in flight. Consult a reliable guide to seabirds for the characteristics useful in separating the albatross species known to occur in the North Atlantic Ocean.

Family PROCELLARIIDAE: Petrels and Shearwaters

Most petrels and shearwaters are rarely seen from shore. These gull-sized seabirds have nostril tubes atop their bills. Longer-winged than gulls, they alternate rapid wingbeats with periods of stiff-winged gliding. That behavior presents a distinctive flight pattern as the birds skim low over the water to snatch food from the waves.

Northern Fulmar
Fulmarus glacialis
L 19 in., W 42 in.
(L 48 cm, W 106 cm)

Range: The Northern Fulmar nests in the Arctic and around the British Isles. The species was first reported from the Carolinas during the 1970s, but its status in our offshore waters remains somewhat a mystery. Fulmars, mostly in the light phase, have been recorded in fall (October–November) and spring (February–May) off Cape Hatteras. There are records from South Carolina in November, February, and March. Those data suggest that fulmars spend December and January south of the Carolinas, but there is no documentation to support such a supposition. On January 24, 1998, more than 70 Northern Fulmars were counted off Oregon Inlet.

Perhaps the winter hiatus is an artifact of the small number of offshore trips made in winter or a result of the birds' generally feeding farther offshore in December and

Northern Fulmar

January than during the remainder of their Carolina sojourn. The only thing that seems to be certain is that the species is a regular visitor off the Carolinas, mostly in fall and spring but erratically in winter.

Feeding habits: Fulmars have a taste for waste fish thrown overboard from boats, and they regularly follow fishing boats and cannery ships.

Description: The light-phase Northern Fulmar resembles an adult Herring Gull, with a stubby yellow bill, heavy head and neck, and gray rump and tail. At close range the fulmar's nasal tubes clearly distinguish it from a gull. The white of the fulmar's head, neck, and underparts is often stained yellowish by discharged stomach oil. Flight is stiff, with alternate flapping and gliding. The long wings have light patches on the upper surface near the base of the primaries. Dark-phase birds are dusky above and below, lack the light wing patches, and generally resemble shearwaters; but the stubby yellow bill remains a good field mark when the birds come close to boats.

Herald Petrel
(Trinidade Petrel)
Pterodroma arminjoniana
L 15 in., w 38–40 in.
(L 38 cm, w 96–100 cm)

Range: First recorded in the Carolinas off Oregon Inlet, N.C., on August 20, 1978, the rare but regular Herald Petrel can be expected in North Carolina offshore waters annually from late May to late September. More than 90% of the records from the western North Atlantic are from the Gulf Stream off the Outer Banks. The species has not yet been documented for South Carolina, but individuals breeding on Trinidade Island (in the South Atlantic Ocean west of the Falkland Islands and governed by Brazil) would be expected to pass over South Carolina offshore waters en route to the Gulf Stream off North Carolina and Virginia. The predominance of dark-phase birds among the Herald Petrels seen off North Carolina supports Trinidade Island as their point of origin.

Feeding habits: See comments on order and family.

Description: Though similar in size and flight to the Black-capped Petrel, the Herald Petrel is less heavily built and has a relatively long tail. With two color phases and many intermediate individuals, plumage is highly variable and lacks easily recognized field marks. Reference to field guides on seabirds is essential.

Bermuda Petrel
Pterodroma cahow
L 15 in., w 35 in.
(L 38 cm, w 89 cm)

Range: The breeding range of this extremely rare petrel is restricted to the Bermuda Islands, where the birds were brought back from the brink of extinction by extraordinary efforts to protect nesting burrows in cliffs from potential predators. Virtually nothing is known about movements of Bermuda Petrels at sea. Photographs taken off Cape Hatteras in May and July 1996 were accepted by the N.C. Bird Records Committee, as were several sight records from May, June, July, and August. The possibility that Bermuda Petrels are of regular occurrence in waters over the outer continental shelf of North Carolina from late May to late August is an issue of major importance in regard to potential petroleum exploration in that area.

Feeding habits: See comments on order and family.

Description: The Bermuda Petrel differs from the typical Black-capped Petrel primarily in the absence of a white band across the back of its neck. However, Black-capped Petrels (*P. hasitata*) also may have an entirely dark hindneck. Some authorities believe the Bermuda Petrel can be reliably separated from a population of small, dark Black-capped Petrels *only* by examination of internal structures.

Black-capped Petrel
Pterodroma hasitata
L 14–18 in., w 35 in.
(L 36–45 cm, w 89 cm)

Range: Black-capped Petrels were first reported from South Carolina offshore waters in 1966 and from North Carolina offshore waters in 1972. Although this Caribbean species is generally considered rare off the Atlantic Coast of the United States, it is present off Cape Hatteras during all seasons of the year, being most numerous there during summer and fall. It is usually found along the western edge of the Gulf Stream. Therefore, the Black-capped Petrel is rarely reported south of Cape Lookout because the western edge of the Gulf Stream is generally 70 to 80 miles or more off southeastern North Carolina, South

Black-capped Petrel

Carolina, and Georgia. That distance is beyond the range of one-day trips offshore in search of pelagic birds.

Feeding habits: See comments on order and family.

Description: A large petrel, dark above and light below, the Black-capped has a distinctive white band across the hindneck and a broad white V at the base of the tail. A band of white also separates the black bill from the black crown. This species is easily confused with the Greater Shearwater, which has black lores and forehead. See also Bermuda Petrel.

OTHER PETRELS

Two additional species have been reported from North Carolina offshore waters. Fea's Petrel (*Pterodroma feae*), also known as the Cape Verde Petrel, and Bulwer's Petrel (*Bulweria bulwerii*) are presently of uncertain taxonomic status; therefore, species accounts are not provided. Both forms might best be described as rare and accidental off the coast of the eastern United States.

Cory's Shearwater

Greater Shearwater

Cory's Shearwater
Calonectris diomedea
L 19 in., W 44 in.
(L 48 cm, W 112 cm)

Range: Cory's Shearwaters are generally fairly common summer visitors
offshore from mid-May to early November. They are locally abundant
at the peak of spring and fall migration, when thousands may be seen
in a single day and large numbers
may pass close inshore.
Feeding habits: See comments on
order and family.
General comments on shearwaters:
Members of boating parties sometimes see large numbers of shearwaters off the Carolina coast from
May to October, but mostly in late
summer. Long-winged birds with
slender hooked bills, shearwaters
skim the troughs between waves,
seldom follow ships, and rarely visit
our beaches except after storms.
Ashore look for shearwaters at
capes and inlets, particularly along
the Outer Banks.
Description: Cory's Shearwater is dark
brown with white underparts and a
dark-tipped yellow bill.

One form of the Cory's Shearwater was recently elevated to
species status as the Cape Verde
Shearwater (*C. edwardsii*). An
individual apparently of that newly
recognized species, named for its
breeding site in the Cape Verde
Islands, was photographed off Cape
Hatteras on August 15, 2004.

Greater Shearwater
Puffinus gravis
L 18 in., W 45 in.
(L 45 cm, W 115 cm)

Range: Reported mid-April to end of
December, the Greater Shearwater
is a fairly common spring and fall
migrant and less common as a summer visitor off the Carolina coast
during June and July. Winter stragglers are very rarely reported.
Feeding habits: See comments on
order and family.
Description: Dark above and white
below with a distinct black cap and
a black bill, the Greater Shearwater
has a white band at the base of its
tail.

Sooty Shearwater
Puffinus griseus
L 16 in., w 43 in.
(L 40 cm, w 110 cm)

Range: The Sooty Shearwater is generally fairly common off the Carolina
coast from late May to mid-June,
the period of peak abundance. It is a
very rare winter straggler along the
Outer Banks.
Feeding habits: See comments on
order and family.
Description: The Sooty Shearwater is
uniform dark gray-brown above
and below except for its whitish
wing linings.

Sooty Shearwater

Manx Shearwater
Puffinus puffinus
L 13 in., w 32 in.
(L 33 cm, w 81 cm)

Range: Manx Shearwaters are rare
on the Atlantic Coast. Regular
transients (in small numbers) off
the North Carolina coast in late
spring and early summer, they are
seen occasionally in spring, fall, and
early winter from the Outer Banks
and adjacent offshore waters. There
are South Carolina records for April,
May, September, and October. Manx
Shearwater is a cold-water species
seldom present in the warm waters
of the Gulf Stream off the Carolinas.
The confusingly similar Audubon's
Shearwater is found primarily in
the Gulf Stream.
Feeding habits: See comments on
order and family.
Description: Dark upperparts and
white underparts contrast sharply
with the black crown, which extends well below the eye. The tail is
relatively short and rounded. Manx
Shearwater has a black bill and

Manx Shearwater

pink feet. Its wingbeat and flight
are relatively fast.

Audubon's Shearwater
Puffinus lherminieri
L 10–12 in., w 24–27 in.
(L 25–30 cm, w 61–69 cm)

Range: Audubon's Shearwater is
generally common off the Carolina
coast in July and August, the period
of peak abundance.
Feeding habits: See comments on
order and family.
Description: Audubon's is a small
shearwater that is dark brown
above and white below and has

no white on the rather long tail. Forehead, crown, and hindneck are brown; underparts are mostly white, with division between dark and white plumage of head usually occurring at or just below the eye. Relatively short wings, long tail, and flesh-colored feet help distinguish Audubon's from other small black-and-white shearwaters.

The species now includes, along with several other subspecies worldwide, a population of relatively small birds formerly known as the Little (Allied or Dusky) Shearwater (*P. assimilis*). Members of that population are very rare in Carolina waters, but they may be noticed because they fly with more flapping and less gliding than the slightly larger members of the species. The blue-black of the crown does not extend below the eye, and the feet are bright blue.

Family HYDROBATIDAE: Storm-Petrels

These small, mostly black birds flutter and patter across the waves, snatching plankton and small fish as they go. Some species may follow ships; others normally do not.

Wilson's Storm-Petrel
Oceanites oceanicus
L 7 in., w 16 in.
(L 17 cm, w 40 cm)

Range: Wilson's Storm-Petrels are common summer visitors off the Carolina coast from early April to late October, most frequently from mid-April to mid-September. Storm-driven individuals sometimes appear inshore and even well inland. Though not generally

Wilson's Storm-Petrels

Wilson's Storm-Petrel (in flight)

found in Carolina waters in winter, a remarkable 351 were counted off Oregon Inlet on January 21, 1987, the latest date the species has been recorded in Carolina waters.

Feeding habits: See comments on order and family. Flocks quickly gather around boats when waste fish and other foods are thrown overboard.

Description: See Leach's Storm-Petrel.

White-faced Storm-Petrel
Pelagodroma marina
L 8.0 in., w 16.5 in.
(L 20 cm, w 42 cm)

Range: This fall transient occurs in small numbers and may not be reported every year. Sightings have occurred from late June to early October, but the species is most likely to be found in August. Two White-faced Storm-Petrels were seen near Oregon Inlet on October 2, 1971, after the passage of a hurricane. All other occurrences have been well offshore.

Feeding habits: See comments on order and family.

Description: Dark above with a gray rump, this species is the only North Atlantic petrel with white underparts and a white face. Its dark legs are so long that the orange-webbed feet extend beyond the tip of the tail during its erratic, bounding flight.

Black-bellied Storm-Petrel
Fregetta tropica
L 8 in., w 19 in.
(L 20 cm, w 48 cm)

Range: One was photographed off Manteo, N.C., on May 31, 2004, for the first Atlantic Ocean report north of the equator.

Feeding habits: See comments on order.

Description: The chief difference between the Black-bellied Storm-Petrel and its sibling species, the White-bellied Storm-Petrel, is that in the former, the black of the breast extends posteriorly down the center of the white belly.

White-faced Storm-Petrel

**European Storm-Petrel
(British Storm-Petrel)**
Hydrobates pelagicus
L 5.5–6.5 in., w 14.0–15.5 in.
(L 14–17 cm, w 36–39 cm)

Range: The European Storm-Petrel breeds mainly in the eastern North Atlantic Ocean and the Mediterranean Sea. The species disperses southward in the eastern Atlantic to southern South Africa and in the western North Atlantic at least to waters off North Carolina. The first North American specimen was taken from Sable Island, Nova Scotia, in August 1970. North Carolina's only confirmed records are of at least four individuals photographed during six sightings made by participants in five boat trips offshore from the Outer Banks during the period May 30 to June 5, 2005. The only known previous sighting was a bird reported off Oregon Inlet on May 27, 2003.

Feeding habits: Like those of several closely related species.

Description: Compared with Wilson's Storm-Petrel, the European differs basically in being slightly smaller, with wings more rounded and legs short enough so feet do not project beyond tip of tail. In flight, there is a prominent diagonal white bar on the underside of each wing. On the upper wing surface, the diagonal bar is narrow and may be difficult to see.

Leach's Storm-Petrel
Oceanodroma leucorhoa
L 8 in., w 19 in.
(L 20 cm, w 48 cm)

Range: This regular but never abundant spring and fall transient is found in Carolina waters from mid-May to late October or early November. One collected from Lake Marion, S.C., on July 25, 1986, represents the first known inland record for the Carolinas. A Swinhoe's Storm-Petrel (*Oceanodroma monorhis*), which was photographed off Cape Hatteras on August 8, 1998, is considered by some authorities to be the same species as Leach's.
Feeding habits: See comments on order. Leach's Storm-Petrels appear to be largely nocturnal feeders during migration and thus are not attracted to chum in our waters.
Description: Commonly called "Mother Cary's Chickens," Leach's, Wilson's, and Band-rumped Storm-Petrels resemble Purple Martins with white rumps. Most storm-petrels flutter over the waves singly or in flocks, with their webbed

feet dangling and pattering on the surface of the water. Leach's, however, does not patter, and its flight is much like that of a Common Nighthawk, only low on the water rather than overhead. Leach's has a forked tail, prominent white rump, gray wing patch, and dark feet. Band-rumped is almost identical to Leach's, except that in flight the tail is less deeply forked and the rump patch is less clearly defined. Wilson's is similar to Leach's; but in flight the tail is rounded, and the dark feet have bright yellow webs.

Band-rumped Storm-Petrel (Harcourt's Storm-Petrel)
Oceanodroma castro
L 9 in., w 18 in.
(L 22 cm, w 45 cm)

Range: Regular in rather small numbers off the Carolinas from late May to late August or early September, Band-rumped Storm-Petrels are generally found well offshore. The first inland report from the Carolinas was that of a bird found dead at Tryon, N.C., following passage of an intense storm that moved northward from the Gulf of Mexico on August 21, 1994. On September 19, 2003, Hurricane Isabel brought a Band-rumped to Satterwhite Point on Kerr Lake, N.C.
Feeding habits: See comments on order and family.
Description: See Leach's Storm-Petrel.

Order PELECANIFORMES: Pelicans and Allies

All birds of this order are large aquatic fish-eaters with a gular pouch. These are the only birds that have all four toes connected by webs, the hind toe being turned partly forward toward the innermost front toe.

Family PHAETHONTIDAE: Tropicbirds

Adult tropicbirds are distinguished by their two extremely long central tail feathers. Usually seen far out at sea, these birds dive for fish and rest on the water with tail streamers held high.

White-tailed Tropicbird
Phaethon lepturus
L 28–32 in., W 37 in.
(L 71–81 cm, W 94 cm)

Range: An inhabitant of tropical seas, the White-tailed Tropicbird breeds as far north as Bermuda, where the "longtail" is a popular tourist attraction. The species is a regular but uncommon warm-weather visitor offshore along the Carolina coast, mid-May to mid-October. On March 23, 2003, one was extraordinarily early and unexpected in the bight at Cape Lookout. On very rare occasions storm-driven birds appear surprisingly far inland, once in Oconee County, S.C., and near Shelby, N.C.
Feeding habits: The tropicbird has a robust, dagger-like bill with a serrated edge. It dives for fish, plunging vertically from a considerable height, perhaps 50 feet (15 m), in

the manner of a gannet. Sometimes tropicbirds try to snatch bait fish from a boat.
Description: This large white bird has a yellow bill, a black eye line, and a black band running the length of the wing except where it is broken by the white primary coverts at the bend of the wing. Immatures have a yellow bill, are coarsely barred on the hind neck and back, and have black primaries contrasting with white primary coverts. Immatures lack the elongated central tail feathers that may add as much as 20 inches (50 cm) to an adult's total length.

Red-billed Tropicbird
Phaethon aethereus
L 18–19.5 in., W 39–42 in.
(L 46–50 cm, W 99–106 cm)

Range: Generally present in small numbers off the Carolina coast from May through August, the Red-billed Tropicbird has been sighted as early as March 29 and as late as October 14.
Feeding habits: See White-tailed Tropicbird.
Description: For adults, the combination of red bill, heavily barred back and nape, and white tail streamers is diagnostic. Immatures have a yellow bill and are difficult to distinguish from immature White-tailed Tropicbirds, which also have a yellow bill. Look for the juvenile bird's black primary coverts, finely barred back, and black line extending from one eye to the other across

the nape. Tail streamers may add 20 inches (50 cm) or more to an adult's total length.

Family SULIDAE:
Boobies and Gannets

Like the pelicans, boobies and gannets have air sacs beneath their skin to cushion their bodies against sudden contact with the water during dives. All sulids catch fish in spectacular plunge-dives, entering the water almost without a splash. Boobies also dive from the surface of the water. The Brown Booby often flies low over the water, fanning its tail to execute turns and making low-angle plunge-dives.

The Northern Gannet is considerably larger than the boobies and differs from them in bill structure. The gannet's feathering extends well forward of the eye above and below the bill, and a long gape line extends to the rear of the bill. Boobies have broadly rounded, almost featherless facial skin surrounding the eyes and the base of the bill. The gape line is inconspicuous.

Gannets breed along the coast of eastern Canada and northern New England. They winter along the East Coast from Massachusetts to the Gulf of Mexico. Boobies are mostly resident near their tropical and subtropical breeding grounds and do not make regular migrations; however, some individuals, principally immature Maskeds, disperse over long distances within tropical and subtropical seas and, apparently, northward in the western Atlantic Ocean along the Gulf Stream at least to the Carolinas.

Masked Booby

Masked Booby
Sula dactylatra
L 26–34 in., w 62 in.
(L 66–86 cm, w 157 cm)

Range: Birds of tropical seas, boobies rarely visit the Carolina coast. The ones that do so are often juveniles and thus somewhat difficult to identify. Masked Boobies have been found in the Carolinas from mid-June to mid-October. An adult spent the summer of 1981 in a Brown Pelican colony in the lower Cape Fear River. There was no evidence of attempted breeding. Most reports describe birds seen offshore, where they sometimes become entangled in fishing gear. A late adult followed a shrimp boat off Litchfield Beach, S.C., on November 21, 1998. A first-year female was found dead and salvaged at Folly Beach, S.C., on August 10, 2003, and another sub-adult female was found alive but unable to fly on the front beach at Sullivans Island on August 11, 2003. The latter bird died in captivity the next day. Both specimens were deposited in the Charleston Museum. The considerable increase in offshore trips by capable bird students, plus the several museum specimens from the Carolinas, warrant considering the dispersal of Masked Boobies northward from their tropical breeding grounds to be a normal, though rarely documented, event.

Feeding habits: See comments on family.

Description: Masked Boobies, both juvenile and adult, have yellow bills. Adults are predominantly white birds with a black facial mask, a black tail, and black on the trailing edge of the wings. The rump is white. In flight the black tail and black along the trailing edge of the entire wing readily separate the Masked Booby from the somewhat larger Northern Gannet. Juvenile Masked Boobies have white underparts; black on the head, tail, wings, and back; and white above only on the rump and neck.

Brown Booby
Sula leucogaster
L 26–34 in., w 57 in.
(L 66–86 cm, w 145 cm)

Range: Brown Boobies have been reported from the North Carolina coast and adjacent offshore waters during every season of the year, with more sightings in spring than any other season.

Feeding habits: See comments on family.

Description: The adult Brown Booby is a dark brown bird with bright yellow feet, pale yellow bill, and white underparts sharply separated from the dark foreparts. The juvenile has a dark bill and grayish-yellow feet. Underparts are gray with a clear demarcation of the area that will become white in the adult plumage.

Red-footed Booby
Sula sula
L 28 in., w 60 in.
(L 71 cm, w 152 cm)

Range: Resident in the Caribbean Sea, the Red-footed Booby is accidental in the Carolinas. The only record is that of a moribund bird found on July 27, 1986, at Edisto Island, Charleston County, S.C.

Feeding habits: See comments on family.

Description: At rest the adult Red-footed Booby looks very much like a Northern Gannet with red feet and too much black on the wings. In flight the black is seen to extend along the trailing edge of the wing all the way to the body. Juveniles are dark above and below with a light gray body contrasting with the completely dark underwing surface. Feet are dull reddish.

Northern Gannet
Morus bassanus
L 35–40 in., w 72 in.
(L 89–102 cm, w 183 cm)

Range: Northern Gannets are common winter residents along the Carolina coast, especially the Outer Banks, from November to April. Occasionally they appear in early October and linger into June. They are extremely rare inland. Sometimes gannets move close to the beaches or visit inlets, but most often they are found over the cold inshore waters rather than along the warm Gulf Stream. Autumn flocks usually include many dark birds, some of which might be

Northern Gannet

Family PELECANIDAE: Pelicans

Massive bills and huge throat pouches distinguish pelicans from all other birds. The pouch serves as a dip net for catching fish. In flight the pelican draws its head back on its shoulders. Pelicans, like gannets and boobies, have air sacs beneath their skin to protect their bodies from the shock of striking the water during dives.

American White Pelican
Pelecanus erythrorhynchos
50–65 in. (127–165 cm)

mistaken for boobies by an eager novice bird-watcher. The dark ones are young of the year, second-year birds, and third-year birds, which are beginning to look more or less like the adults.

Feeding habits: Folding their wings, gannets plunge headlong into the water from heights of 40 feet (12 m) or more, diving upon shoaling herring, mackerel, and menhaden. Feeding flocks often associate with whales and schools of porpoises. See also comments on family.

Description: The adult Northern Gannet is white with a long, pointed bill, pointed tail, and slender, pointed, black-tipped wings. There is a yellow wash over the head and nape. The gannet has a wingspan of 6 feet (1.8 m). Immatures are blackish, mottled with gray and white. First-, second-, and third-year birds become progressively more like the adults in appearance, but a band of white uppertail coverts is noticeable in the plumage of all subadults.

Range: American White Pelicans may appear almost anywhere in the Carolinas during any month of the year. Piedmont sightings are usually in spring or fall and most likely represent birds migrating between their winter home in Florida and their breeding grounds in the western United States and Canada. Single birds and flocks numbering as many as two dozen found during the winter months probably are wanderers from the wintering population in Florida. Pea Island and Lake Mattamuskeet in eastern North Carolina as well as Huntington Beach State Park and the Savannah Spoil Site in Jasper County, S.C., seem to be popular resorts for white pelicans. However, the largest concentration in the region can be found in the ACE (Ashepoo, Combahee, and Edisto) Basin area, south of Charleston and east of US 17, where up to 200 may congregate in winter.

In addition, a nonbreeder visited a Brown Pelican colony at Cape Romain in July 1985, and 12 white pelicans lingered from June 26, 2000, to the end of July at the Savannah

American White Pelicans (in flight)

Brown Pelicans (on nests)

Spoil Site. The flock present there throughout the summer of 2003 peaked at 101 on July 27. Summer birds may be wanderers from the breeding population found along the Gulf Coast of Texas and Louisiana. Regardless of their origin, the arrival of American White Pelicans in the Carolinas is still a surprise, but no longer as much as it used to be.

Feeding habits: The American White Pelican scoops up fish while wading or swimming in shallow water, often feeds in flocks, and does not dive.

Description: This large white bird has a yellow bill, black wing tips, and a wingspan of 8 to 9 feet (about 2.5 m). It is well known for the capacious pouch suspended from its lower mandible.

Brown Pelican
Pelecanus occidentalis
42–54 in. (107–137 cm)

Range: Once endangered by pesticide residues in some of its primary food sources, the Brown Pelican has made a remarkable recovery.

Large Brown Pelican chicks (in nest at edge of a mixed-species gull and tern colony)

The species may be more abundant in the Carolinas today than it was prior to the advent of DDT. These permanent residents may be seen resting on sandbars, gliding above the breakers, or diving for fish from heights of 10 to 30 feet (3 to 9 m). Brown Pelicans are locally fairly common to very common along the Carolina coast at all seasons. Stragglers may occur inland to the mountains, but they are rare and generally found only after the passage of a tropical storm or during the period of postbreeding wandering.

Nesting habits: Brown Pelican nesting sites in the Carolinas are on small, uninhabited coastal islands, all of which are protected by private, state, or federal conservation agencies. Nesting colonies offer one of the most spectacular sights that bird-watchers might hope to see in our region. Nests, most of which are built at ground level, are made of seaweed, marsh grass, and debris. They usually stand a foot (30 cm) or more tall. The male gathers nest materials, and the female does the building. Both parents incubate the three chalky white, bloodstained eggs, which may be laid as early as mid-March and require 28 days for hatching. At first the nestlings are naked, blind, and helpless. Their reddish skin soon turns black, and at 10 to 12 days of age they are covered with white down and have well-developed pouches. Both parents feed the young, which cannot fly until they are about 9 weeks old; they are still dependent at that stage. Only one brood is raised each year; however, if her clutch is destroyed, the female may renest.

Feeding habits: The Brown Pelican dives for small fish, plunging from the air or from the surface of the water.

Description: This large, gray-brown bird has a mostly white head that contrasts with the dark bill and gular pouch. Immatures are a dingy grayish brown. Pelicans fly with the neck and head doubled back on the shoulders. Wingspan of the Brown Pelican is 6 to 7 feet (about 2 m).

Family PHALACROCORACIDAE: Cormorants

Cormorants are dark, goose-like birds with short legs, webbed toes, a long neck, a small gular pouch, and a beak sharply hooked at the tip. Cormorants usually feed on small fish, diving from the surface of the water and outswimming their prey. Upon emerging from the water, cormorants often stand on pilings and other perches with wings extended to dry their wet feathers.

Double-crested Cormorant
Phalacrocorax auritus
22–36 in. (56.0–91.5 cm)

Range: Standing at Hatteras Inlet in winter, one may watch thousands of Double-crested Cormorants, in one black skein after another, flying from Pamlico Sound to the ocean in the morning and returning at evening. Arrival of birds from northern breeding grounds in autumn increases the coastal population of winter residents to many thousands and brings more and more cormorants to inland rivers and lakes.

The Double-crested Cormorant is present in the coastal region throughout the summer in small numbers, and it is known to nest at Lake Ellis in eastern North Carolina. Spring migration brings an increase in inland sightings in April and May. Construction of numerous large reservoirs has attracted cormorants to the piedmont region of the Carolinas, and that population continues to increase, partly as a result of successful local nesting activity. Sightings have become more frequent in the mountains, but no

Double-crested Cormorant

pendent at 10 weeks. The species is single-brooded.

Feeding habits: See comments on family.

Description: Immature Double-crested Cormorants are dull brownish in color, with the breast lighter than the belly. Adults are mostly black with a greenish or coppery sheen to some of the plumage. Double-crested Cormorants are so named because they grow a few curly filaments above and behind the eyes during the mating season. The nuptial plumes drop out soon after nesting has begun. Double-crested Cormorants often perch with wings outspread and sometimes swim with their body submerged and only the neck and head above water.

breeding has been detected in that region.

Nesting habits: Using sticks, rubbish, and a wide variety of other coarse materials, both adults participate in the building of the nest. The first year it is a flimsy affair, but after being refurbished for use in subsequent years, it becomes a substantial structure. A favored site for nesting is in stunted cypresses along the heavily forested shore of a lake. Thirty or more nests are sometimes placed in a single living tree, which may be killed by the birds' excrement. The piedmont population originally nested in standing dead trees resulting from reservoir construction. As those trees rotted and fell, the birds moved to other nearby sites.

The peak of laying in North Carolina probably is in early May, and the three or four pale bluish eggs have a soft, chalky outer layer. Both adults incubate the eggs, and the incubation period is about 4 weeks. The altricial young are fed by both parents during their 3 to 4 weeks of nestling life. Young fly at 5 to 6 weeks and become inde-

Great Cormorant
Phalacrocorax carbo
32–36 in. (81–91 cm)

Range: Among the vast numbers of Double-crested Cormorants that winter in the coastal waters of the Carolinas, keen observers occasionally find one to several Great Cormorants, usually immature birds. First noted in Dare County, N.C., in 1970, Great Cormorants have been seen with increasing frequency over the years and are now considered regular winter visitors to the Carolina coast as far south as Charleston. They occasionally visit inland lakes (Roanoke Rapids Lake, Jordan Lake, and Lake Townsend near Greensboro in North Carolina and Lake Marion in South Carolina). By 1991 a few Great Cormorants were lingering into spring or summer. As yet there is no evidence of nesting in the Carolinas.

Feeding habits: See comments on family.

Description: The adult Great Cormorant is black with a white patch at the base of its bill. White nuptial plumes appear on the flanks in spring. The yellow bill is heavier than that of the Double-crested Cormorant. Immature Great Cormorants are brownish with the belly lighter than the breast. Immature Double-cresteds are lighter on the breast than on the belly.

Anhinga

Family ANHINGIDAE: Anhingas

Like cormorants, Anhingas have water-permeable feathers and frequently perch with wings spread to let them dry. The long, slender neck and sharply pointed bill help distinguish anhingas (also known as darters) from the cormorants. In hot weather, Anhingas frequently soar in the manner of vultures. When they do so, they look like black crosses in the sky, with the outstretched neck and long tail at right angles to the outstretched wings.

Anhinga
Anhinga anhinga
32–36 in. (81–91 cm)

Range: One of the most significant ornithological events of the late twentieth century was the population explosion of the beaver (*Castor canadensis*) in the southeastern United States. In the Carolinas, busy beavers dammed creeks throughout the piedmont and upper coastal plain, creating thousands of secluded wooded ponds suitable as nesting sites for the conspicuous Great Blue Herons and the almost unnoticed Anhingas.

In 1980 the "snake bird" or "water turkey" was a fairly common permanent resident of the freshwater lakes, swamps, and rice fields of the low coastal region of South Carolina. It bred sparingly northward to Lake Ellis in Craven County, N.C. Today, Anhingas breed locally throughout the coastal plain of North Carolina, inland approximately to the I-95 corridor (near Weldon and southeast of Fayetteville). In South Carolina the species breeds inland approximately to the I-95/I-20 corridor (near Bishopville and North Augusta). Success of the range expansion can be judged primarily by increasing reports of soaring and wintering Anhingas from inland parts of the Carolinas.

Nesting habits: Breeding usually begins in April in the Carolinas. Although solitary pairs are found, Anhingas tend to nest in groups, often in association with colonial birds such as herons and ibises. The nest is a substantial structure of sticks and twigs and is often lined with green cedar or cypress foliage. It may be placed from 5 to 50 feet (1.5 to 15.0 m) or more above water.

The male brings nesting materials to the female, who does the building. The three to five pale blue eggs have an uneven chalky coating and take about 25 to 28 days to hatch. Both parents incubate eggs and feed the altricial young. Nestlings quickly sprout a thick coat of short, buffy tan down and mature rapidly. If a 2-week-old chick should fall from the nest or depart hastily to escape a predator, it can swim and dive remarkably well upon first contact with the water.

Feeding habits: Anhingas capture fish while swimming underwater. They hunt with the neck folded against the shoulders and strike to impale fish upon the sharply pointed bill. Surfacing, the successful darter tosses the fish into the air, catches it headfirst, and swallows it whole.

Description: The Anhinga's slender pointed bill, long wide tail, and shawl of predominantly white feathers readily separate it from the cormorant, which also has water-permeable flight feathers and "hangs itself out to dry." Females are black with a brown head, neck, and upper breast. Adult males are black except for the white on some plumes on the wings and back. Anhingas, like Double-crested Cormorants, often swim with only the head and neck above water.

Family FREGATIDAE:
Frigatebirds

These large, dark, long-winged seabirds have, in proportion to weight, the longest wingspan of all birds.

Magnificent Frigatebird

Magnificent Frigatebird
Fregata magnificens
37–45 in. (94–115 cm)

Range: The subtropical frigatebird is a rare but annual summer visitor along the coast of the Carolinas, having been seen from early May to early September. The species is very rare in winter.

Feeding habits: The Magnificent Frigatebird spends most of its time at sea, feeding by snatching fish from the waves or by forcing weaker birds to disgorge their latest meal, which the robber then promptly devours.

Description: Easily recognized by its dark plumage and deeply forked tail, the frigatebird has crooked wings spanning 7 to 8 feet (2.0 to 2.5 m). Juveniles have variable amounts of white on the head and underparts. Adult females are blackish brown with white on the lower underparts. Adult males are entirely black except for an orangish gular pouch, which becomes bright red when inflated during courtship displays.

Order CICONIIFORMES: Long-legged Waders

Birds in this order have long necks and long legs adapted for wading in the shallow waters where they feed on aquatic animals. Long-legged waders generally nest in colonies, with both adults sharing in construction of the nest, incubation of eggs, and feeding of altricial young. Exceptions are noted in the species accounts. Usually the male selects a territory, often a site containing the remains of a nest used the previous year, and he may initiate construction as part of the mating ritual.

After pair formation, the female usually shapes the nest while the male gathers material for her to use. Building may continue even after incubation is well under way. Many pairs perform elaborate ceremonies when one member relieves the other at the nest. Little or no effort is made to keep the nest clean.

The downy young have their eyes open at hatching but are unable to leave the nest. For most species accurate data are not available on the length of time chicks remain in the nest or their age at first flight. Young begin clambering about the nest trees almost as soon as the pinfeathers sprout, generally when only 10 to 20 days old. Most young waders probably can follow their parents on flights to the feeding grounds at 6 to 8 weeks of age. Although long-legged waders normally are single-brooded, females will lay replacement clutches if first sets of eggs are destroyed.

Family ARDEIDAE: Bitterns and Herons

Bitterns are secretive marsh dwellers that are rarely seen or heard. Herons, on the other hand, are familiar to everyone who visits lakes or beaches.

Often mistakenly called "cranes," herons have 15 to 17 vertebrae in their long necks. The bones are arranged so the neck readily assumes an S-shaped curve. Although a heron extends its neck when taking flight and landing, the airborne bird (unlike storks, ibises, cranes, and flamingos) holds its head near the body, thus appearing to have a short neck.

Although found in many other families of birds, powder-down reaches its highest development in the herons and is used by some authorities as the basis for determining relationships of the various species within the family. Powder-downs are specialized feathers that grow from certain spots on the breast, rump, and flanks of herons and bitterns. Those feathers fray continually at the tip and provide powder used for dressing the other plumage. Once the powder-down has soaked up oil, grease, and slime, it is combed from the feathers by scratching with the serrated nail of the middle toe. After each cleaning, the plumage is waterproofed with oil from the preen gland (uropygial gland).

The breeding plumes of many herons were used to decorate women's hats in the late 1800s. That practice resulted in massive systematic slaughter of nesting birds, and several species were approaching extinction before protective laws were passed in the early 1900s. Action was taken in time to save the birds, and populations of most species have made an excellent recovery.

American Bittern
Botaurus lentiginosus
24–34 in. (61–78 cm)

Range: Although known mostly as an uncommon to fairly common winter resident, more numerous toward the coast than inland, the American Bittern may appear in marshes anywhere in the Carolinas during migration and postbreeding dispersal. The species nests at least locally near the coast; but its breeding range is not well known, and very few nests have been found. In fact, very little is known about the basic biology of the species anywhere within its range at any time past or present. It is possible that the species was more abundant during the 1700s and 1800s than it is today in the Carolinas. At that time rice was a major crop from the lower Cape Fear River southward near the coast to the Altamaha River in Georgia.

Nesting habits: Breeding birds appear to require shallow, freshwater wetlands with a dense growth of emergent vegetation. The female alone builds the nest of rushes and marsh grasses on the ground in a marsh or meadow. The olive-buff eggs number three to five, and the incubation period is about 24 days. While the female is incubating eggs and caring for young, the male remains nearby, but the extent of his participation in the raising of the brood is unknown. Reports from

American Bittern

other states suggest the possibility of polygamy.

Feeding habits: See comments on order.

Description: The American Bittern is predominantly brown with a yellow bill, greenish legs, and a bold black mark on the side of the neck. Blackish primaries and secondaries separate flying birds from similar species. Bitterns are noted for their habit of freezing with the bill pointed skyward and even swaying in the breeze to enhance their appearance as just another clump of brown marsh grass.

Weird pumping calls of American Bitterns have given them the local names "stake-driver" and "thunder-pumper." In late April, listen for their calls at dawn and dusk in the marshes around Lake Phelps and Lake Mattamuskeet in eastern North Carolina, around the freshwater ponds on Bulls Island in South Carolina, and around ponds on other barrier islands in both states. Although pumping suggests local breeding, such calls may be made at stops along the migratory route.

Least Bittern
Ixobrychus exilis
11–14 in. (28–35 cm)

Least Bittern

Range: A fairly common to common summer resident of freshwater and brackish marshes of coastal Carolina, the Least Bittern also breeds in small numbers inland where extensive marshes are found. The species is a rare winter straggler near the South Carolina coast.

Nesting habits: Adults may return to breeding sites as early as March in South Carolina. Pairs may nest alone or in loosely associated groups. The nest is a platform of dried and living plants attached about a foot (30 cm) above shallow water, but near open water, to an upright stem of a cattail or aquatic reed. Apparently both the male and the female shape the nest. The four or five bluish-white eggs are laid in late April or early May, and incubation requires about 17 days. Young may leave the nest, at least temporarily, as early as the fifth day. The species appears to be single-brooded, with late clutches being replacements following a failed nesting attempt.

Feeding habits: Least Bitterns feed mostly on small fish, crustaceans, and insects. During periods of drought in late summer, family parties may visit small pools of water remaining on exposed mudflats near coastal marshes.

Description: This diminutive heron is among our most secretive and well-camouflaged species. When alarmed, the Least Bittern will, like the larger American Bittern, freeze with its bill pointed skyward. Both sexes are dark above and light below with large buff and cinnamon wing patches. Immatures are similar, but the plumage pattern is less distinct. If you see a piece of trash clinging to marsh vegetation and it flies away, that was a Least Bittern.

Great Blue Heron
Ardea herodias
45–54 in. (115–137 cm)

Range: Fairly common to common in the Carolinas at all seasons, inland as well as along the coast, the Great Blue Heron is most abundant where it nests in heavily wooded swamps and river bottoms. The return of beavers to the piedmont and inner coastal plain during the late twentieth century created an abundance

Great Blue Heron

may take wing in late August or early September.

Four unmarked, pale greenish-blue eggs usually are laid, and the incubation period is about 28 days. When parents change places on the nest, they face each other and conduct a dance-like ritual. The naked altricial hatchlings are soon covered with down. By the time they leave the nest, juveniles are as large as their parents and sport plumage very much like that of the adults. Young herons of this and other species will use their sharp beaks to strike at curious naturalists and disgorge foul-smelling, partly digested food upon intruders. Juveniles still in the nest may sunbathe the underparts the same way the older birds do, in the delta-wing position. The sunbather stands facing the sun and lifts both wings away from the body, keeping them bent at the wrist so the wing tips touch the rump or tail.

Feeding habits: The Great Blue Heron feeds mostly on fish and other animals that live in or near water and hunts either by wading slowly through shallow water or by standing with neck folded and waiting to strike passing prey. A good-sized snake may be swallowed head first, like someone sucking on a strand of cooked spaghetti.

Description: The Great Blue Heron stands about 4 feet (1.2 m) tall and flies with slow, deliberate strokes of wings that spread to 7 feet (2 m). The bill measures about 6 inches (15 cm). From a distance the birds appear completely gray, but very light on the head and neck. The Ward's Heron (*A. h. wardi*) is a

of nest sites suitable for this species along almost every creek. Nesting has been reported as far inland as Bass Lake in Watauga County, N.C., and Greer in Greenville County, S.C. Postbreeding dispersal takes Great Blues into areas where breeding has not yet been recorded. Some birds remain near nesting sites throughout the winter, even when small ponds freeze over.

Nesting habits: Usually, but not always, colonial in the breeding season, Great Blue Herons may begin nesting activities in March. Nests are crude platforms of dead sticks most likely placed near or over water in the tops of tall trees, often pines or cypresses. Sometimes there are several nests in a single tree. Standing dead trees are often used by pairs nesting at beaver ponds. Some eggs hatch by mid-April, and the last young of the year race of the Great Blue that nests northward to southeastern South Carolina. Larger and paler than Great Blues breeding elsewhere in the Carolinas, individuals of this form occasionally wander north of the normal range.

Formerly considered a separate species, the Great White Heron (*A. h. occidentalis*) is now classified as a white morph of the Great Blue Heron. Breeding in extreme southern Florida, white morphs sometimes wander northward into the Carolinas. This form is our only completely white heron with yellow bill and legs. Immature birds may have yellowish-gray legs.

Great Egret (chicks in nest)

Great Egret
Ardea alba
37–41 in. (94–104 cm)

Range: The Great Egret is a common permanent resident of shallow waters along the coast, breeding in most heronries in the coastal plain and wandering throughout the piedmont and mountains in postbreeding dispersal, mostly from July through September. Because Great Egrets nest in the same colonies with Great Blue Herons in the coastal plain, it would not be surprising for them to begin nesting in the piedmont. To date there is no documentation for Great Egret nests in piedmont Great Blue Heron colonies, where a few Great Egrets have been seen as visitors in late summer.

Nesting habits: Nests and eggs are similar to those of the Great Blue Heron, but smaller. Nesting usually begins in late March or April, and the incubation period is about 25

Great Egret (in courtship display)

days. Once nearly extirpated by plume hunters for the millinery trade, the Great Egret has made an excellent recovery, as evidenced by the increase in the number of these birds wintering and nesting in the Carolinas.

Feeding habits: See comments on order.

Description: This is the largest white heron that occurs regularly in our area. Watch for the combination of yellow bill with black legs and feet.

Snowy Egret
Egretta thula
22–26 in. (56–66 cm)

Range: The Snowy Egret is a common permanent resident along the coast, becoming less numerous in winter. Inland it is an uncommon visitor during postbreeding dispersal. In the Carolinas, breeding outside the coastal area has been documented only at Green (Bird) Island on Lake Marion, Berkeley County, S.C.

Nesting habits: The frail platform of sticks and twigs is placed in a bush or tree 1 to 30 feet (0.39 to 11.7 m) above ground in a mixed-species colony. The four or five blue-green eggs usually are laid in April or early May, and incubation takes about 22 days.

Feeding habits: Dashing about with wings spread, the Snowy Egret actively pursues fish and other aquatic animals in shallow water. It also pokes its toes cautiously among submerged plants and debris, apparently to lure small fish out of hiding without frightening them away. The Snowy sometimes hovers above water, descending suddenly upon its prey. The bird may also insert the tip of its bill into the water and vibrate it, apparently in an attempt to attract prey.

Description: This graceful white heron has a black bill, black legs, and

Snowy Egret

bright yellow feet. Immediately before the mating season, the Snowy Egret grows decorative plumes called aigrettes, and at the same time its feet and unfeathered lores turn from bright yellow to golden orange or bright red. By the late 1970s, the Snowy Egret population seemed to have recovered adequately from the ravages of the plume hunters, its recurved aigrettes having been even more highly prized than the straight ones of the Great Egret as ornaments for women's hats in the late nineteenth century. However, in recent years the Snowy Egret population in the Carolinas appears to have begun declining for reasons that have not yet been identified. One possibility is competition for nest sites from the larger and increasingly more abundant White Ibis.

Little Blue Heron (adult)

Little Blue Heron
Egretta caerulea
25–29 in. (63–73 cm)

Range: Little Blue Herons are common permanent residents of our coastal region, though less numerous in winter than during the breeding season. Although the species breeds mostly on the lower coastal plain, small numbers nest locally inland to southeastern Kershaw and central Barnwell Counties, S.C. Birds are seen inland most often during postbreeding dispersal from July through September, but spring visitors are not rare.

Nesting habits: Little Blues nest in colonies with other species of herons, usually occupying the lower branches of the nest trees. Depending on the vegetation, nest heights range from ground level to 10 or 15 feet (3.0 to 4.5 m). The nest may be a rickety platform of sticks 1 to 2 feet

(30 to 60 cm) long or a substantial structure with a well-developed central depression. The four or five pale bluish-green eggs usually are laid in late April, and incubation requires about 23 days.

Feeding habits: Although Little Blue Herons usually feed in shallow water on fish and other small aquatic animals, they can survive in times of drought on insects obtained in grasslands.

Description: Adult Little Blue Herons are handsome, slate-blue birds with maroon head and neck plumage. Immature birds are white with greenish legs and a dark-tipped, bluish bill. "Calico Herons" are birds 1 to 2 years of age that are molting into the dark adult plumage. Adult Little Blue Herons are sometimes confused with dark-phase Reddish Egrets, which are larger birds with dark-tipped, flesh-colored bills.

Tricolored Heron (Louisiana Heron)
Egretta tricolor
24–28 in. (61–71 cm)

Range: A common permanent resident of the coastal region, the species formerly known as the Louisiana Heron is less numerous in winter than during the breeding season. It is rare inland during postbreeding dispersal. In August 1988, interior breeding was documented at Green (Bird) Island on Lake Marion in Berkeley County, S.C.

Nesting habits: Usually nesting about 1 to 15 feet (0.3 to 4.5 m) above ground in mixed-species colonies, the Tricolored Heron uses twigs to build a platform a little more than a foot (30 cm) in diameter. Nests may

Tricolored Heron

Reddish Egret

have a lining of twigs, grasses, or weed stems. In April or early May the female lays four or five bluish eggs that require about 21 days to hatch.

Feeding habits: While feeding, Tricolored Herons often stand or wade in water up to the belly. In shallow water the birds tend to hunt by darting about in the manner of the Reddish and Snowy Egrets.

Description: This is a slate-blue heron with white underparts. Never the target of plume hunters, the Tricolored Heron was the most abundant native heron in the southeastern United States until other species recovered from the years of slaughter.

Reddish Egret
Egretta rufescens
27–32 in. (68–81 cm)

Range: Formerly considered a very rare accidental in the Carolinas, the Reddish Egret became, by the late 1990s, a regular visitor in small numbers along the entire Carolina coast during postbreeding dispersal. The species is most likely to be found in South Carolina at Huntington Beach State Park and in North Carolina at the inlet near Fort Fisher, on Shackleford Banks, and on Portsmouth Island in the Cape Lookout National Seashore from mid-April through September. Individuals linger rarely into winter or, very rarely, into spring. Most birds seen in the Carolinas are immature dark morphs. Immature white morphs and adults of either color phase are rare.

Feeding habits: The Reddish Egret

often shows extremely active feeding behavior in shallow water, dashing about with wings partly open in pursuit of aquatic animals.

Description: Extreme care must be exercised in identifying this species, which is easily confused with the slightly smaller Little Blue Heron. Reddish Egrets, regardless of age or color phase, have dark gray legs and a longer, heavier bill than do Little Blue Herons. Adult Reddish Egrets of both color phases have a flesh-colored bill with a black tip. Little Blue Herons of all ages have pale, greenish legs; white juveniles have dark wing tips. Some juvenile Little Blues may show pink on the lores and base of the bill, but the greenish leg color still separates them from the Reddish Egret. The adult Little Blue Heron's bill is all bluish with a light base and a dark tip.

Cattle Egret

Cattle Egret
Bubulcus ibis
19–21 in. (48–53 cm)

Range: An Old World species that appeared in Venezuela in 1930, the Cattle Egret was breeding from Florida to Battery Island near Southport, N.C., by 1956. Today, the Cattle Egret is a common summer resident of coastal Carolina, occasionally lingering into winter. In South Carolina the species breeds inland to Marlboro, Kershaw, Calhoun, and Barnwell Counties. In 1990 an estimated 300 Cattle Egrets were nesting at the expanding Dunahow Bay heronry in Robeson County, N.C. In April and May as well as after the breeding season, Cattle Egrets wander far from the coast, even into the Appalachian Mountains.

The species can be found at least accidentally throughout the United States and southern Canada. Not surprisingly, breeding now occurs widely in the cattle-raising states west of the Mississippi River.

Nesting habits: Originally feared to be a serious threat to our native herons, the Cattle Egret apparently has had little adverse effect on them because it nests relatively late in the season. It lays clutches of four light blue eggs mostly in May and June when young of other species are well developed. Sometimes Cattle Egrets take over nests vacated by other herons instead of building their own. The incubation period is about 22 to 23 days, and young can fly short distances when about 40 days of age.

Cattle Egret chicks are most easily recognized by the fact that when disturbed they disgorge ticks and insects instead of fish. Considerable evidence exists that some of our native herons prey on Cattle Egret nestlings as a convenient source of food for their own rapidly growing offspring.

Feeding habits: As their name implies, Cattle Egrets feed in pastures, picking ticks from the hides of cattle and capturing insects, amphibians, and mice stirred up by the grazing animals. Cattle Egrets also feed beside highways and airport runways, taking advantage of the fact that moving vehicles act as beaters.

Description: This small, short-necked white heron has yellow legs and bill. Adults in breeding plumage have buffy orange patches on the crest, breast, and back; the bill may then be tinged with orange and the legs with pink.

Green Heron

Green Heron
Butorides striata
16–22 in. (40–56 cm)

Range: Breeding throughout the Carolinas, usually near marshes, ponds, or streams, Green Herons are common summer residents. A few birds remain through the winter along the coast.

Nesting habits: Although they may nest in loose colonies near heronries occupied by other species, Green Herons tend to be more solitary in both breeding and feeding behavior than other members of the family. Breeding usually begins in April. The nest is a loose platform of sticks and twigs placed directly on the ground, in a low bush, or up to 30 feet (9 m) high in a live oak or other large tree. Nests are sometimes found in dry woods, apple orchards, and other sites

well removed from water. The pale greenish-blue eggs number four or five, incubation requires 17 days or slightly longer, and two broods may be raised in a season.

Feeding habits: The Green Heron usually hunts by standing motionless at the edge of water, often leaning forward with its body in a horizontal posture while waiting to strike at passing fish, frogs, crayfish, or other small aquatic animals. Very rarely, a clever Green Heron will grasp a mayfly or some similar insect in its bill and attempt to use it as a lure for fish.

Description: This small, dark, stocky heron has a rather thick neck and a shaggy crest that is raised in alarm. Leg color is a dull greenish yellow except in breeding adults, which may have bright orange legs. Look for the greenish back and dark rufous neck of the adult Green Heron. A sharp *skeow* is the call given in flight. Perched birds often give the knocker call, an irregular and sometimes prolonged series of percussive notes: *kuk kuk kuk kuk kuk*. Immatures are coarsely streaked with brown and easily mistaken for bitterns or immature night-herons.

Black-crowned Night-Heron
Nycticorax nycticorax
23–26 in. (58–66 cm)

Black-crowned Night-Heron (adult)

Range: The Black-crowned Night-Heron is a common permanent resident along the coast, but it is generally rare to uncommon inland to the mountains during migrations and postbreeding dispersal.

Nesting habits: Nests are highly variable, being placed mostly below 10 feet (3 m) high and ranging from frail platforms of twigs to substantial structures used for several seasons. Black-crowneds frequently remove sticks from an old nest for use in constructing a new one. The three to five pale greenish-blue eggs usually are laid in April, and the incubation period is 24 to 26 days.

Feeding habits: Black-crowneds hunt at night, primarily by stalking fish, crayfish, snakes, and amphibians in shallow water.

Description: The adult Black-crowned Night-Heron has a black cap and back, gray wings, white underparts, black bill, and yellow legs. The immature is a streaky brown bird that is easily confused with the immature Yellow-crowned Night-Heron and the immature Green Heron. Gregarious at all seasons, Black-crowneds can be seen at dusk flying in loose flocks from roosts to feeding places. In flight only part

Black-crowned Night-Heron (immature)

of the foot can be seen protruding beyond the tip of the tail.

Yellow-crowned Night-Heron
Nyctanassa violacea
22–28 in. (56–71 cm)

Range: Much less common than the Black-crowned Night-Heron, but more likely to be active by daylight, the Yellow-crowned is a permanent

Yellow-crowned Night-Heron (adult)

resident of the cypress swamps, freshwater ponds, and marshes of the coastal plain. Migration, post-breeding dispersal, and at least occasional breeding bring the species into the piedmont, where it may be of considerably more frequent occurrence than the published records indicate. The species tends to withdraw from most of the Carolinas in winter, but a very few occur in the southern coastal areas during that season.

Nesting habits: Rather solitary birds, Yellow-crowned Night-Herons nest in isolated pairs or in small groups, sometimes occupying the outer fringes of major heronries. The bulky nest usually is saddled on a limb high in a gum or cypress tree. Three or four blue-green eggs are laid in April or May, and incubation requires about 24 days.

Feeding habits: Yellow-crowneds are nocturnal feeders that eat mostly crabs, crayfish, and other crustaceans.

Description: The adult is a mostly gray bird with a black bill and yellow legs. The bold black-and-white face pattern is accented by a touch of yellow just above the bill. Immatures are streaked with brown. Compared with the immature Black-crowned, the immature Yellow-crowned has a lighter-colored crown, a shorter and thicker bill, and longer legs. In flight the entire foot extends beyond the tip of the tail.

Family THRESKIORNITHIDAE: Ibises and Spoonbills

Ibises and spoonbills have faces bare of feathers, lack powder-down, and have poorly developed voice boxes or none at all. Their toes are longer than those of the stork. The hind toe is slightly elevated, and the middle toenail is slightly scalloped. The bills of ibises are long, thin, and decurved, while those of the spoonbills are broad and flat. Ibises and spoonbills fly with the neck extended.

Subfamily Threskiornithinae: Ibises

See comments on family.

White Ibis
Eudocimus albus
22–27 in. (56–68 cm)

Range: First discovered nesting in the Carolinas in 1922 at Fairlawn Plantation near Charleston, S.C., the White Ibis is an abundant breeding bird all along the Carolina coast and now nests northward into Virginia. In South Carolina a substantial

White Ibis (adult in breeding plumage)

White Ibis (immature)

portion of the population nests inland at places like Boykin Mill Pond, east of Columbia in southern Kershaw County. Locally common to abundant in summer and fairly common in winter, the White Ibis is most likely to be found in marshes near heronries. Not surprisingly, inland sightings of White Ibises have increased during the postbreeding dispersal as the coastal populations have proliferated and the species has begun breeding a considerable distance from the immediate coast.

Nesting habits: White Ibis nests are low in trees and bushes or on the ground in stands of grasses or rushes. Laid in late April or early May, the three or four greenish-white eggs are splotched with patches of light or dark brown. Incubation requires 21 days.

Feeding habits: Favorite food items are crayfish, cutworms, grasshoppers, and small snakes. In the coastal plain White Ibises often forage for food on lawns and golf courses.

Description: The adult White Ibis is our only large white bird with pink legs, pink decurved bill, and black wing tips. In some birds, leg, bill, and face color vary from orange to bright red. For a description of the dingy gray young, see Glossy Ibis account.

Hybrids: The Scarlet Ibis (*Eudocimus ruber*) is native to South America, where pairs of the bright red birds breed in colonies with White Ibises. Scarlet Ibises were first found in Dade County, Fla., in November 1954. Those birds probably escaped from a zoo in Lee County. Today a few Scarlet Ibises or pink-and-orange birds, probably crosses between Scarlet and White Ibises, are seen in the wild in southern Florida. Since 1987 several such birds have been reported in South Carolina in association with White Ibises, and one was photographed on a nest. Because of the hybridization problem, the status of the Scarlet Ibis in South Carolina is uncertain.

Glossy Ibis
Plegadis falcinellus
19–26 in. (48–66 cm)

Glossy Ibis

Range: First discovered breeding in the Carolinas in 1940 at Battery Island near Southport, N.C., the Glossy Ibis was nesting in South Carolina by 1947. By 1980 the species was established as a year-round resident of the shallow waters along the Carolina coast. Glossy Ibises are uncommon to common in summer and rare to uncommon in winter from Bodie Island south. A few individuals and small flocks wander inland during postbreeding dispersal, but no nesting colony presently known in the Carolinas is outside the tidewater region.

Nesting habits: Glossy Ibises generally nest in small numbers in mixed-species heronries along the coast. Nesting at a low height in colonies with White Ibises and other herons, the Glossy Ibis builds a substantial cup-shaped nest of sticks and twigs, sometimes with a lining of green vegetation. The three or four un-marked eggs are intense greenish blue. Incubation requires 21 days.

Feeding habits: Favorite food items are crustaceans, grasshoppers, various insects, and small snakes.

Description: The adult Glossy Ibis is our only completely dark bird with a long, dark, decurved bill. Well-feathered preflight young are mostly black with some greenish highlights in the wings, pinkish or whitish patches on the throat and forehead, and a decurved, light-colored bill encircled by dark bands at the tip, middle, and base. Although juvenile White and Glossy Ibises are similar in appearance,

White Ibis young have white on the belly, no light patches on the throat and forehead, no greenish high-lights in the wing, and no bands on the bill. Nestlings of the two species have virtually identical bills until that of the Glossy chick begins to show dark bands.

White-faced Ibis
Plegadis chihi
23 in. (58 cm)

Range: Formerly considered the western race of the Glossy Ibis, the White-faced Ibis ranges west of the Mississippi River and southward into Mexico and parts of South America. The Glossy Ibis ranges east of the Mississippi and south-ward to the islands of the Carib-bean Sea. One White-faced Ibis was photographed as it stood in a ditch at South Nags Head, Dare County, N.C., in early July 2002. It remained in the area for at least a week.

Feeding habits: Similar to those of the Glossy Ibis.

Description: Similar to the Glossy Ibis except for its face, the adult White-faced Ibis in breeding condition generally has a red eye and a red face with a white border extending from above the bill to a point behind the eye and downward to the base of the bill. The Glossy Ibis has a dark face and eye; some individuals may have a narrow, whitish facial border. Intermediate birds cannot be reliably identified to species in the field.

Subfamily Plataleinae: Spoonbills

Only one species occurs in the Carolinas.

Roseate Spoonbill
Platalea ajaja
30–34 in. (76–86 cm)

Range: Very rare visitors in the Carolinas, Roseate Spoonbills are most likely to be seen near the coast during the mid-May to October period of postbreeding dispersal.

Roseate Spoonbill

Feeding habits: Spoonbills feed by wading with half-open bills immersed in shallow water. Swinging their heads from side to side, they grasp small aquatic animals with their bills and occasionally take some vegetable matter.

Description: The Roseate Spoonbill is our only mostly pink bird with a long dark bill that is flattened and becomes wider at the tip. Young birds are faintly pink with yellowish legs and bill. Color gradually intensifies with age.

Family CICONIIDAE: Storks

Only one species is native to the Carolinas.

Wood Stork
Mycteria americana
35–47 in. (89–120 cm)

Range: Our only native stork, the Wood Stork is a locally fairly common summer resident and uncommon winter resident of swamps, marshes, and mudflats in coastal Carolina from Sunset Beach, N.C., southward. At Sunset Beach and Myrtle Beach, the birds show a strong preference for ponds associated with golf courses. Some of the storks seen in the Carolinas have moved north from the nesting colony at Birdville, Ga. However, many are native to South Carolina. First known to nest in the state in 1981, Wood Storks had a breeding population estimated at nearly a thousand pairs by 1996. They breed locally in swamps of the lower coastal plain in Hampton, Colleton, Charleston, and Georgetown Counties, with a fairly large number (100 or more) at each site. Wood Storks

Wood Stork (feeding)

the first week unless the weather is unusually cold or rainy.

Newly hatched chicks are very noisy. Their high-pitched cries become deeper and louder as they mature. For at least 5 weeks one parent is always present to guard the chicks from wandering bands of unmated storks and other predators. Young may remain in the nest for 50 to 55 days before making short flights. They may return to the nest to be fed and to roost at night until they are at least 75 days old. Both parents bring water to preflight young on hot days, "drooling" the liquid from the bill onto the heads of the young birds.

Feeding habits: Wood Storks feed largely on minnows, plus various crustaceans, mollusks, reptiles, tadpoles, frogs, small mammals, insects, and plant materials. Though young rails and grackles have been mentioned, birds do not appear to be a frequent food choice. Wood Storks often ride thermals to a considerable height and then glide to the feeding ground. Sometimes large numbers of these birds may be seen soaring in wide circles and rising to several hundred feet in the air.

wander northward and inland, rarely even into the mountains, during postbreeding dispersal.

Nesting habits: Wood Storks are winter–spring breeders. Built in trees, usually ones standing in water, nests may be placed from a few feet above water to the tops of the tallest cypresses. A single tree may contain several dozen nests. The creamy white eggs have a finely granulated surface and usually number three to four. Laying begins as soon as the nest is complete. Beginning with the laying of the first egg, the pair never leave the nest unattended for the entire 28 to 32 days required for hatching. At the approach of the incoming bird, the one on the nest rises, cocks its tail over the back, opens its bill, and makes a hissing or fizzing sound. Often the returning mate brings a stick, which is added to the nest. Young are not brooded after

Description: The adult is mostly white with black flight feathers, dark legs and bill, and dark unfeathered head. The immature is similar, but it has a yellow bill. Birds of all ages have yellow feet. Wood Storks fly with the neck and legs outstretched, behavior that readily separates them from American White Pelicans.

Family CATHARTIDAE:
American Vultures

Vultures feed almost exclusively on carrion. Their relatively small, un-feathered heads and strong, hooked beaks are useful adaptations to their mode of feeding.

Black Vulture
Coragyps atratus
23–27 in. (58–68 cm)

Range: Common in the lower coastal plain of the Carolinas (except northeastern North Carolina) but uncommon in the piedmont, Black Vultures tend to be rare in the mountains and most numerous in southeastern South Carolina. Locally the species is called "carrion crow" or "South Carolina buzzard."

Nesting habits: Black Vultures have essentially the same nesting habits as the Turkey Vulture. Egg laying usually begins a little earlier, and Black Vulture eggs are greenish white with brown markings.

Feeding habits: More gregarious than Turkey Vultures, Blacks usually gather around large carcasses and ignore small dead animals. Both vultures frequent cattle farms.

Description: The Black Vulture has a bare black head, a short tail, and a conspicuous white patch at the tip of each underwing surface. Smaller than the Turkey Vulture, the Black has a wingspan of 4.5 to 5.0 feet (about 1.5 m). In flight the Black flaps more frequently and more rapidly than does the Turkey Vulture. While soaring, the Black Vulture holds its wings straight out from the body.

Black Vulture

Black Vulture (in flight)

Turkey Vulture
Cathartes aura
26–31 in. (66–81 cm)

Range: Fairly common permanent residents throughout the Carolinas, Turkey Vultures are rare in the mountains in winter. Elsewhere, the local population is increased in winter by the arrival of migrants from the north. Although vultures

Turkey Vulture

Turkey Vulture (in flight)

breed in remote woodlands and swamps, they visit highways and farmlands in search of food. Both Turkey and Black Vultures are considerably less numerous today than they were before the disposal of garbage in sanitary landfills and the burial of dead farm animals became widespread practices.

Nesting habits: Two, rarely three, eggs are laid mostly in early April, though eggs have been found in February and March. Birds nesting in natural cavities in large living or dead trees may pull together some rotten wood from inside the hollow, but no real attempt is made to build a nest. Birds nesting on rocky ledges, in caves, or in abandoned buildings may select a spot with an accumulation of debris, though sometimes eggs are deposited on perfectly bare surfaces. The large eggs are white, splotched with brown and purplish markings. Incubation requires slightly more than a month, and nestlings are ready for flight in about 10 to 11 weeks. If the downy white young are disturbed, they will regurgitate their most recent meal of semidigested carrion.

Feeding habits: Turkey Vultures feed almost exclusively on dead animals, which they locate by sight and by scent. They are frequently seen along highways where animals have been killed by motor vehicles.

Description: These large, brownish-black birds are often seen soaring on rising air currents with wings held motionless, angling upward from the body in a shallow V. Adults have red skin on a head bare of feathers. Immatures have a black head. Look for the two-toned underwing pattern, dark on the leading edge and light on the trailing edge. Wingspan is about 6 feet (2 m).

Order PHOENICOPTERIFORMES: Flamingos

Flamingos are native to Europe, Asia, Africa, and South America. The most striking characteristic of a flamingo is its thick, sharply downturned bill.

Family PHOENICOPTERIDAE: Flamingos

Only the Greater Flamingo occurred naturally as a rare wanderer in the southeastern United States before a captive breeding population was established in 1942 at the Hialeah Race Course in Florida. Given a proper diet, flamingos do well in captivity and maintain their natural color. Therefore, it is not safe to assume that a flamingo seen in the wild in the Carolinas is not an escaped captive just because it appears healthy and is in good color.

Greater Flamingo (American Flamingo)
Phoenicopterus ruber
about 50 in. (127 cm)

Range: Apparently a rare visitor on the Carolina coast from September to January, the Greater Flamingo occurs very rarely in spring. Flamingos visiting the Carolinas tend to linger at one place a week or more. Because this exotic bird sometimes escapes from zoological gardens, all Carolina records are open to question. The natural occurrence of the species in our area is possible, however, particularly in the case of flamingos found in South Carolina prior to 1900. The Greater Flamingo breeds on islands of the Greater and Lesser Antilles and along the northern coast of South America. The birds migrate after breeding and become flightless during the postnuptial molting period.

Feeding habits: A flamingo feeds by immersing its sharply bent bill upside down in shallow water. Muck is pumped through slits in the upper mandible to strain out minute edible plant and animal matter.

Description: The adult Greater Flamingo is our only completely pinkish bird with a stout bill that is sharply bent downward and has a black tip. Juveniles are gray on the wings and bill. Subadults are pale pink. In all plumages the Greater Flamingo has black on the trailing edge of the wing.

The Chilean Flamingo (*P. chilensis*) has been photographed in the Carolinas. The adult has gray legs with a red band at the joint. Although the phenomenon of "reverse migration" has been suggested to explain the presence of the species in eastern North America, the possibility of escape from captivity seems a more likely explanation.

Order FALCONIFORMES: Diurnal Birds of Prey

A large, worldwide order of birds that hunt by daylight, these raptors have keen eyesight, hooked bills, and strong talons.

Family ACCIPITRIDAE: Osprey, Kites, Hawks, and Eagles

In this family the males are generally slightly smaller than the females.

Subfamily Pandioninae: Osprey

The Osprey is one of the most widely distributed birds in the world. It feeds almost exclusively on fish, and its feet are especially adapted for catching and holding its slippery prey. Birds breeding in relatively cold climates move south for the winter.

Osprey

Osprey
Pandion haliaetus
21–25 in. (53–63 cm)

Range: Ospreys breed on or near the Carolina coast in good numbers, but they become rare in winter. Inland, a nest was found in Chowan County, N.C., in 1980. The first nests were reported from the piedmont in 1984 (Jordan Lake and Lake Townsend). Soon thereafter Ospreys were nesting locally throughout piedmont North Carolina. The species occurs as a migrant throughout the Carolinas. Inland nesting has led to an increase in winter stragglers away from the coast.

Nesting habits: "Fish Hawks" build bulky nests of sticks in tall dead trees, on stumps in water, or on man-made platforms such as channel markers. In areas of suitable habitat, breeding populations appear loosely colonial. Returning to the same nest year after year, usually in early March, the birds repair and enlarge the structure each season before the female lays two to four buffy eggs splotched with reddish brown. The eggshells absorb an oily odor from the adults' plumage during the 4 to 5 weeks of incubation. The female does most of the incubating, being relieved by the male only when she is off feeding. Young remain in the nest about 8 weeks.

Feeding habits: Ospreys feed almost entirely on fish obtained by hovering over water and diving headlong upon the prey, impaling it with the claws. In addition to sharply curved nails, their feet have pads with short, stiff spicules that help them hold their slippery prey. When flying to a feeding perch or carrying food to young in the nest, the Osprey holds the head of its catch facing forward, thus reducing wind resistance.

    During the 1960s, Osprey populations in many areas were threatened because some of the fish they consumed had high levels of pesticide residues that caused eggshell thinning or sterility in adult birds. Range extension into piedmont North Carolina, following construction of several major reservoirs, and the consequent population increase are evidence that strict control of the use of persistent pesticides has been beneficial to the species.

Description: A dark bird with white underparts, the Osprey has a white head with a black eye stripe. Watch for the arched position of the wings in flight and for the black spot underneath at the bend of each wing.

Subfamily Accipitrinae:
Kites, Hawks, and Eagles

This subfamily includes all of the diurnal birds of prey found in the Carolinas except the Osprey.

Swallow-tailed Kite
Elanoides forficatus
L 19–26 in., w 50 in.
(L 48–66 cm, w 127 cm)

Range: Today the Francis Marion National Forest in eastern South Carolina hosts the northernmost known breeding population of this strikingly beautiful raptor. The species also nests along the Savannah and Edisto Rivers in southeastern South Carolina. There is some indication that Swallow-tailed Kites may occupy suitable river-bottom habitat farther north in Georgetown and Horry Counties and even along a portion of the lower Cape Fear River

Swallow-tailed Kite

in southeastern North Carolina. In 2003, Swallow-tails were present from May until at least July 19 along the Cape Fear River and over nearby fields from the vicinity of Riegelwood in eastern Columbus County upstream and along NC 87 to the No. 1 Lock on the Cape Fear in southern Bladen County. Only four birds were seen in May, but as many as ten were present in mid-July.

    Swallow-tailed Kites generally arrive on the breeding grounds in mid-March and depart by late August. However, the presence of Swallow-tails in early spring is not evidence of local breeding. The species is famous for overshooting the breeding grounds. Every spring some individuals appear along the Outer Banks of North Carolina or even into New England.

Nesting habits: Swallow-tailed Kites usually form colonies of three to six pairs, with nests in the tops of tall trees that stand within about 300 feet (90 m) of one another in a wetland. Loblolly pines are preferred, but cypress trees are also occupied. When possible, the birds repair and use old nests, which are platforms of twigs and bark mixed with a generous amount of Spanish moss. During the first two weeks in April, adults can be seen carrying nest materials in their talons. Usually placed near the top of the tree, the nest is very inconspicuous. Eggs number two or sometimes three and are white splashed with brown and black markings. The incubation period is 3 to 4 weeks, and young remain in the nest 36 to 41 days.

Feeding habits: Birds nesting in Francis Marion National Forest leave their forest foraging grounds in late morning and fly up to 15 miles to the Santee Delta, a 2-mile-wide open marsh and waterfowl impoundment at US 17 between the North and South Santee Rivers. The birds may spend an hour or two hawking dragonflies and other fairly large flying insects, which are grasped in the talons and passed to the beak while on the wing. Small reptiles and amphibians are also consumed. Some feeding flocks may include Mississippi Kites.

Description: The Swallow-tailed Kite is a black-and-white bird of prey with white on the head, underparts, and wing lining. The black tail is long and deeply forked.

White-tailed Kite
Elanus leucurus
14–17 in. (38–43 cm)

Range: The White-tailed Kite is of accidental occurrence in the Carolinas. It is usually found hunting over marshes, grasslands, and agricultural fields that are likely to harbor mice and other small animals preferred by the species. In recent years it has visited the Carolina coast from Charleston north to the Dare County mainland (Alligator River National Wildlife Refuge, January 14, 2000) and Coinjock in Currituck County (May 16, 2001). Inland, White-tailed Kites have occurred in the Clemson area of South Carolina several times, once from early March to early May; in Davidson County, N.C., in March; and in Haywood County, N.C., in July.

Feeding habits: Kites hunt by hovering and slipping downward feet first to seize their prey. After the capture, they swoop, or kite, upward. The White-tailed Kite's diet consists chiefly of rodents and insects.

Description: Adults have a white head, tail, and underparts; gray back; and gray wings marked with a large black patch at the bend. The long white tail and pointed wings identify the brownish immatures. White-tailed Kites are gull-like in flight.

Mississippi Kite
Ictinia mississippiensis
13–15 in. (33–38 cm)

Range: The Mississippi Kite is a fairly common summer resident of river-bottom forests and adjacent farmlands in the coastal plain of North and South Carolina. Most of the nests have been found in towns at the inner edge of the coastal plain from Silver Bluff Sanctuary near Jackson, S.C., northward to Camden and Cheraw, then in North Carolina to Laurinburg, Goldsboro, Johnston County (Howell Woods), and Roanoke Rapids. A nest with young at Newport, Carteret County, N.C., in June 1996 was uncommonly near the coast. Spring migrants usually

Mississippi Kite

which are captured and consumed while the birds are on the wing.

Description: Adults have a plain gray head and underparts, dark back and wings, and a black tail. When seen from above, adult males have white secondaries, a feature visible on birds perched or in flight. Immatures are brownish with a black tail that is barred with white below. In all plumages, Mississippi Kites have an unusually short outermost primary on each wing.

arrive from late April to early May (earliest known date is March 29, 1982, Dare County mainland [E. F. Potter, unpublished observation]). Postbreeding wanderers, birds displaced inland by tropical storms, and fall migrants occur inland to the mountains mostly from mid-September to late October. Extreme fall dispersal dates are July 6 (Tryon, Polk County, N.C.) to November 21 (west of Creswell, Washington County, N.C.).

Nesting habits: Mississippi Kites usually reach the South Carolina breeding grounds in late April and begin laying about a month later. Made of twigs, leaves, and moss, nests are placed in a fork or crotch of a tree and are usually 100 feet (30 m) above ground. The same nest may be used in successive years. The one, two, or rarely three whitish eggs require about 31 or 32 days for incubation. Young leave the nest when about 5 weeks old and are fed on the wing for several weeks.

Feeding habits: Mississippi Kites often feed in flocks. Their diet is composed almost entirely of insects,

Bald Eagle
Haliaeetus leucocephalus
32–43 in. (81–109 cm)

Range: Bald Eagles have made a remarkable recovery. They are off the list of endangered species and no longer rare in the Carolinas. Most years a significant number of pairs produce offspring, and there are several breeding sites in the piedmont as well as near Lake Mattamuskeet and other traditional nesting places in the coastal plain. Bald Eagles congregate at the major reservoirs in the piedmont, and there are occasional sightings in the mountains.

Nesting habits: The nest, which may be used for many years, is placed in the top of a tall tree and may measure 6 feet (2 m) across and is often just as deep. Boat-tailed Grackles and Great Horned Owls may take apartments in the sides of the massive structure. Breeding begins in December or January, incubation of the two white eggs requires 35 days, and young remain in the nest at least 10 weeks after hatching. Young birds require several years to reach maturity.

Bald Eagle

Feeding habits: Bald Eagles eat mostly fish picked up dead on the shore or robbed from Ospreys. Eagles can capture coots, herons, small mammals, and wounded ducks, but in the Carolinas they almost never take poultry, healthy game species, or fish of commercial value. Bald Eagles and all other birds of prey are fully protected by law in the hope that the end of senseless shooting will enable these magnificent birds to recover from the adverse effects of pesticide pollution. That goal has been at least partly achieved, but there is still need for rigorous protection.

Description: This eagle has a wingspan of more than 6 feet (2 m). Adults are dark brown except for the white head and tail. Immatures are brown and irregularly marked with white until their fourth year. The lower part of the leg is not feathered. Eagles soar with their wings held straight out from the body.

Northern Harrier
Circus cyaneus
17–24 in. (43–61 cm)

Range: A winter resident throughout the Carolinas, the "Marsh Hawk" is uncommon over most of the inland counties, common over coastal marshes and nearby agricultural fields, and most numerous during migrations. The species breeds regularly, but sparingly, south to Carteret County, N.C. Determining the breeding range is complicated by the many migrant birds still present during most of the presumed nesting season (April to June).

Nesting habits: Harriers nest and roost on or near the ground. The species is almost silent except during the spectacular courtship flights. The nuptial flight is a series of nose dives with the bird almost stalling at the peak of each upward swoop before plunging downward again. Such flights have been seen at the Alligator River National Wildlife Refuge on mainland Dare County, N.C., where large numbers of the species winter and a few may be seen in summer. Most of the known Carolina nesting sites are on barrier islands (Ocracoke and Portsmouth) and in marshes around Pamlico and Core Sounds.

Made mostly of sticks and straws, the nest may be well lined with grasses. Susceptibility to flooding seems to determine whether the nest is flimsy or substantial. The four to six dull white or pale bluish-white eggs are generally unmarked. Laying probably begins by mid-

Northern Harrier (female)

Sharp-shinned Hawk

April. However, an adult has been seen carrying long strands of grass as early as February 9. Young are ready to fly when 5 or 6 weeks old. The family group remains together for quite a while, and parents often drop prey for the young hawks to catch in midair.

Feeding habits: Harriers hunt by sailing low over fields, meadows, and marshlands. They eat frogs, insects, and small snakes and birds in addition to mice, rats, and other small mammals.

Description: Both the gray male and the brown female have a long, banded tail and a prominent white rump patch. The breast of the female is more heavily streaked than that of the male. Juveniles are much like the female, brown with an owl-like facial disc, but the underparts are tan and mostly unstreaked. Harriers frequently perch on low posts or directly on the ground.

Sharp-shinned Hawk
Accipiter striatus
10–14 in. (25–35 cm)

Range: The Sharp-shinned Hawk is a fairly common fall migrant, an uncommon winter resident, and a rare to absent breeding species throughout the Carolinas. Although it will hunt in any kind of woods, it prefers conifers for nesting.

Nesting habits: The nest is built of small sticks and twigs in a crotch against the main trunk from 10 to 60 feet (3 to 18 m) above ground. Breeding apparently begins in late April. Eggs usually number three to five, rarely seven, and are nearly spherical, being white splashed with brown. Incubation requires about a month, and young remain in the nest about 23 days.

Feeding habits: The Sharp-shinned Hawk dodges through woodlands in swift pursuit of the small birds that comprise the major portion of its diet. Although the species normally takes birds no larger than thrushes, individuals have been known to capture, or at least pursue, Northern Flickers, Northern Bobwhites, Wood Ducks, and small herons.

Description: Adults are slate blue above and barred with rusty brown below. Immatures are dark brown above and streaked with brown below. Wings are short and rounded. The long, slender tail is squared off when folded, but it may look slightly rounded when fanned. Size overlaps with that of the Cooper's Hawk, which is generally similar in appearance but has a proportionately larger head and a wider tail that is noticeably rounded even when folded. Cooper's Hawks fly with deep, deliberate wing strokes, often with three flaps and a glide. The Sharp-shinned has a comparatively shallow and irregular wing beat.

Cooper's Hawk (in flight)

Cooper's Hawk
Accipiter cooperii
Male 14–18 in. (35–45 cm)
Female 16–20 in. (40–51 cm)

Range: An inhabitant of dense woods and adjacent edges, the Cooper's Hawk is an uncommon winter resident throughout the Carolinas and a rare summer resident found chiefly in the mountains and piedmont.

Nesting habits: The nest is made of sticks and twigs with a lining of bark strips. Usually it is placed 40 to 60 feet (6 to 18 m) above ground in the main fork of a tree. The three to six pale bluish-white eggs usually are laid in April and require 35 to 36 days for incubation. Food for nestlings appears to consist entirely of birds, which are picked bare of feathers before being brought to the young. Although they may leave the nest when about a month old, young are not fully independent until they are about 8 weeks old.

Feeding habits: The Cooper's Hawk is a bold hunter that occasionally visits farmyards to carry away young poultry, thus deserving more than any other of our hawks the name "chicken hawk." This accipiter is sometimes destructive to the Northern Bobwhite. It also eats rats, mice, grasshoppers, and birds that may be considered pests (e.g., Rock Pigeons, blackbirds).

Description: The slate-blue back of adult Cooper's and Sharp-shinned Hawks have given these two species the local name of "blue darter." See

Sharp-shinned Hawk for a comparative description.

Northern Goshawk
Accipiter gentilis
Male about 22 in. (56 cm)
Female about 25 in. (63 cm)

Range: The status of the Northern Goshawk in the Carolinas is uncertain. The species appears to be a rare year-round resident in the North Carolina mountains. Elsewhere in our region, goshawks are very rare transients and winter visitors. The first North Carolina occurrence was reported from Macon County in 1969, and the first South Carolina sighting was at Carolina Sandhills National Wildlife Refuge in 1973. Those and other early Carolina sightings, including one report of probable nesting in Avery County, N.C., coincided with an unprecedented southward movement of the species that apparently resulted in a major range extension. A few goshawks continue to be reported almost every winter somewhere in North Carolina.
Feeding habits: Goshawks eat small birds and mammals, but they are capable of capturing grouse and squirrels.
Description: Larger than a crow, the Northern Goshawk is a robust, barrel-chested hawk with an extremely long rounded tail and longer, more tapered wings than characteristic of our other accipiters. Adults are dark gray above and light gray below. Immatures are brown with a streaked breast. Immature male goshawks can be quite similar to immature female Cooper's Hawks. Caution should be exercised when attempting to identify young birds. Look for the white line above the eye, the robust chest, and the fluffy white undertail coverts.

Red-shouldered Hawk
Buteo lineatus
17–20 in. (43–51 cm)

Range: The Red-shouldered Hawk is a fairly common permanent resident of wet woodlands and nearby farmlands and golf courses in the coastal plain, uncommon in the piedmont, and rare in the mountains, where the scarcity is attributed to the lack of suitable habitat. Formerly more numerous than the Red-tailed Hawk, the Red-shouldered population declined prior to 1980 and remains the less common of the two species. The change appears to be a result of widespread clearing, draining, and flooding of bottomland woods.
Nesting habits: The species has essentially the same nesting habits as the Red-tailed Hawk except that the male Red-shouldered incubates eggs to a much greater extent.
Feeding habits: The Red-shouldered Hawk preys mostly on rats and mice but also takes squirrels, frogs, crayfish, and snakes as well as an occasional bird or amphiuma (popularly known as the "ditch eel"). One Red-shouldered Hawk has been seen snatching young from an Eastern Phoebe nest.
Description: This hawk has reddish-brown underparts and wing coverts, and its tail is boldly banded with black. Overhead, the Red-shouldered has translucent white or light crescents at the base of the

Red-shouldered Hawk

primaries and lacks a belly band. Its cry is a steadily repeated *keeyuur* that is often imitated by Blue Jays.

Broad-winged Hawk
Buteo platypterus
13–19 in. (33–48 cm)

Broad-winged Hawk

Range: Fairly common summer residents in the mountains, becoming uncommon to absent toward the coast, Broad-winged Hawks migrate southward in flocks, often in company with falcons and accipiters. The peak of fall movement usually occurs during the last week of September, when many flocks of 50 or more Broad-winged Hawks pass over the mountains. Although Broad-wingeds may linger in the Carolinas into winter on extremely rare occasions, southern Florida is normally the northern limit of their winter range. Spring migration is protracted, often making it difficult to determine whether certain birds are local nesters or merely late migrants.

Nesting habits: The nest of sticks and twigs is placed 24 to 40 feet (7.5 to 12.0 m) above ground in the crotch of a woodland tree. The two or three eggs, usually laid in April, are whitish with beautiful brown and lilac markings. Incubation, mostly by the female, requires 21 to 25 days, and young may remain in the nest up to 6 weeks.

Feeding habits: This small woodland hawk habitually hunts from a perch for insects and small mammals and reptiles.

Description: Wings have whitish linings and are extremely wide in proportion to their length. The adult Broad-winged has reddish-brown underparts, and its tail is broadly banded with black and white. Dark morphs occur at the western edge of the breeding range and are very rarely seen in the Carolinas as spring or fall migrants.

Swainson's Hawk

Buteo swainsoni
19–22 in. (48–56 cm)

Range: A summer resident of the western United States, this migratory species occurs accidentally on the East Coast. About a dozen records from the Carolinas span the period from early October to late March. Most Swainson's Hawks have been seen only briefly, but a few lingered at one place for several days or even the better part of a month. Records from the coast and lower coastal plain predominate, but at least one was as far inland as Durham, N.C.

Feeding habits: Swainson's Hawk exhibits feeding behavior typical of buteos.

Description: Plumages are highly variable, including adults, juveniles, and second-year birds of dark, light, and intermediate populations. Consult a well-illustrated field guide that treats all North American hawks.

Red-tailed Hawk

Buteo jamaicensis
19–25 in. (48–63 cm)

Range: The Red-tailed Hawk is a fairly common permanent resident throughout the Carolinas. The influx of migrants from the north makes the species more numerous in fall and winter than during the breeding season. These buteos frequently perch on tall poles along busy highways.

Nesting habits: The nest is a bulky structure of sticks lined with finer materials and placed 30 to 60 feet (9 to 18 m) above ground in the crotch of a large tree near the

Red-tailed Hawk

Red-tailed Hawk (in flight)

edge of a patch of heavy timber. Although Red-tailed Hawks prefer to feed in upland habitats, they frequently nest in floodplains. Eggs usually are laid in April, number two to four, and are dull white blotched with varying shades of brown. Incubation takes 28 days with the male feeding the female on the nest and perhaps relieving her from time to time. Both parents feed the young, which remain in the nest about 6 weeks.

Feeding habits: Buteos are soaring hawks that circle overhead and drop (stoop) upon their prey in a steep dive. As a group they are extremely beneficial to people, consuming huge quantities of rats, mice, and other rodents but rarely taking poultry. Other items of diet include rabbits, reptiles, amphibians, and destructive insects such as grasshoppers.

Description: Buteos are large-bodied hawks with rounded wings and broad, fanned tails. Look for the uniformly red tail of the adult Red-tailed Hawk and for the brown belly band that is conspicuous in both adult and immature birds. The species is highly variable, having light phases, dark phases, and many subspecies. A form that winters in the southern Great Plains, the Harlan's Hawk (*B. j. harlani*), occurred once in late January at the Savannah River National Wildlife Refuge in South Carolina. That form has a mostly white tail. The very pale Krider's Hawk (*B. j. kriderii*), native to the western United States and Canada, also has been reported from the Carolinas. Other forms less strikingly different from our breeding population occur from time to time, including the one resident on the Florida peninsula. Variability within a species presents a challenge to every bird student because no bird guide can illustrate every possible variation.

Rough-legged Hawk
Buteo lagopus
19–24 in. (48–61 cm)

Range: This far-northern hawk is a rare and erratic winter visitor in the Carolinas, occurring most frequently in the northern half of North Carolina. Several of these birds may be seen in one winter and none at all the next. Northeastern North Carolina seems to attract Rough-leggeds with some regularity, with the Alligator River National Wildlife Refuge being a good place to look for them and for other rare raptors.

Feeding habits: Rodents comprise the bulk of the diet.

Description: The Rough-legged is our only buteo that has a white tail broadly tipped with black. The legs are feathered nearly to the toes. See field guides for illustrations of dark and light phases.

Golden Eagle
Aquila chrysaetos
31–41 in. (78–104 cm)

Range: The Golden Eagle appears to be a year-round resident of the southern Appalachian Mountains, but no convincing evidence of breeding can be cited. The species is a rare fall transient and winter visitor elsewhere in the Carolinas. Good places to look for Golden Eagles are in the vicinity of Graveyard Fields along the Blue Ridge Parkway, at Mattamuskeet and Alligator River National Wildlife Refuges in northeastern North Carolina, and at the Yawkey Wildlife Center, Georgetown County, S.C.

Feeding habits: Golden Eagles feed mostly on mammals such as

Golden Eagle (immature)

Subfamily Caracarinae: Caracaras

Caracaras are carrion eaters that are more likely to associate with vultures than with the more closely related falcons. Formerly found in almost all parts of Central and South America, this New World subfamily is now represented by only one living species, the Crested Caracara, which is also known as the Common Caracara or the Audubon's Caracara. The Crested Caracara is the national bird of Mexico.

Crested Caracara
Caracara cheriway
20–25 in. (51–63 cm)

Range: Normally not found north of the Kissimmee Prairie region of Florida, the Crested Caracara is a very rare accidental in the Carolinas. Because the species is often kept in captivity, all extralimital records are questionable. The one South Carolina sighting in Charleston on May 1, 1943, is possibly valid. However, the bird photographed in Currituck County, N.C., was remarkably tame and arrived in May 1972, soon after a caracara escaped from captivity in Norfolk, Va.

rabbits, but on occasion they will take game birds up to the size of a turkey. Although in some parts of the country Golden Eagles undoubtedly present a problem for ranchers at calving and lambing time, they probably consume enough rabbits and rodents to be more beneficial than harmful in the long run.

Description: This massive bird has a wingspan of about 6.5 feet (2 m). The adult is dark brown with faint light bands on the tail and golden neck plumes that can be seen only at close range. The immature is similar but has white patches at the base of the tail and near the tip of each wing; it lacks the golden neck plumes. The legs are feathered nearly to the toes.

Family FALCONIDAE: Caracaras and Falcons

Birds in this family are distinguished from other diurnal birds of prey by their long wings that are swept back at the wrist and their tapered tail that, when folded, gently narrows toward the tip.

Subfamily Falconinae: Falcons

Swift flyers with long, narrow, and pointed wings that are swept back at the wrist, the falcons have a notched beak that is used to kill prey by severing the spinal cord at the neck. Females are larger than the males, which falconers call "tercels," a reference to their being a third smaller than the females.

**American Kestrel
(Sparrow Hawk)**
Falco sparverius
9–12 in. (22–30 cm)

American Kestrel (adult male)

Range: The American Kestrel has largely recovered from the effects of pesticide pollution and reclaimed much of its former breeding range in the Carolinas. The "killy hawk" or "kitty hawk" is seen most frequently perched on wires along the roadside, wagging its tail as it watches for prey. The birds are most abundant during migrations and somewhat localized during the breeding season, apparently nesting more often from the mountains to the inner coastal plain than elsewhere in the region.

In the piedmont, breeding kestrels largely depend on the availability of suitable chimneys, church steeples, and crevices in building facades for nesting sites. A pair often nests in downtown Raleigh in the vicinity of the N.C. Department of Agriculture building. In many rural areas, campaigns to remove dilapidated buildings and abandoned chimneys have unintentionally reduced the number of available nesting sites for kestrels and other species that require fairly large cavities, such as Yellow-shafted Flickers, Wood Ducks, and Eastern Screech-Owls. Kestrels probably would respond well to the placement of properly designed and constructed nest boxes in suitable habitat.

Nesting habits: Nesting in natural or man-made cavities, the American Kestrel often appropriates old Pileated Woodpecker nest sites or enlarged Red-cockaded Woodpecker holes. The four or five eggs are nearly spherical in shape with a buffy ground color that is more or less marked with reddish brown. Nesting is somewhat irregular, but most clutches probably are laid in April or May. Incubation requires about a month, with the female assuming most of the responsibility. Both adults feed the preflight young.

Feeding habits: If this bird were named for its most common prey, it would be called "Grasshopper Hawk." Kestrels hunt from a perch and take mice, lizards, small birds, and a variety of insects.

Description: The American Kestrel is the smallest, most colorful, and best known of our falcons. The male has a reddish-brown back and tail, blue wings, and prominent sideburns. The female is similar but has brown wings and a barred tail. Both sexes have the long, pointed wings and tapered tail of falcons. This is our only hawk that regularly perches on roadside wires and wags its tail. The call is frequently a shrill *killy killy killy*.

**Merlin
(Pigeon Hawk)**
Falco columbarius
10–14 in. (25–35 cm)

Range: The Merlin is seen in the Carolinas most frequently as a fall migrant, uncommon inland and fairly common along the coast, where a few spend the winter. Recently there have been numerous reports of Merlins visiting urban and suburban neighborhoods having a good number of bird feeders.

Feeding habits: Merlins capture many birds, including some species larger than themselves, but they rarely molest poultry. They also consume many insects and an occasional small mammal.

Description: The adult male Merlin is blue-gray above and streaked below. He lacks sideburns. The female is brown with a streaked breast. Both sexes have pointed wings and a tapered tail that is boldly barred. Young males resemble the female.

Gyrfalcon
Falco rusticolus
22 in. (56 cm)

Range: A Gyrfalcon in the plumage of a gray morph was seen February 10, 1992, near Bayboro, Pamlico County, N.C., and described convincingly. The largest of the North American falcons, the Gyrfalcon is accidental in the northeastern United States. The North Carolina sighting is the southernmost published report for the species on the Atlantic Coast.

**Peregrine Falcon
(Duck Hawk)**
Falco peregrinus
15–20 in. (38–51 cm)

Range: Completely extirpated from the eastern United States by pesticide pollution, the Peregrine Falcon was reintroduced during the 1980s and once again visits all parts of the Carolinas. Nesting has occurred in recent years on several rocky crags in the southern Appalachian Mountains. Successful nesting has been reported at Chimney Rock Park, Linville Gorge, Whiterock Cliff in Madison County, and Whiteside Mountain near Highlands, all in North Carolina, and at Table Rock State Park in Pickens County, S.C. Peregrines are most likely to be seen along the coast as uncommon to fairly common fall transients in late September and as rare winter residents. Inland, look for them from mid-September to mid-October around major reservoirs and in places where Rock Pigeons

Merlin

Peregrine Falcon (adult)

congregate. Peregrines often perch atop utility poles in open areas.

Nesting habits: The Peregrine does not build a nest. In the mountains of the Carolinas, pairs lay their three or four eggs, which are more or less oval, cream colored, and covered with red-brown blotches, on a high, rocky crag. The site may have a natural depression, which keeps the eggs from rolling off the ledge, or the bird may scrape a hollow in an accumulation of soil, decaying wood, or crumbly rock. Laying may take place from March to June. Incubation requires at least 28 or 29 days for each egg. Females will lay replacement clutches if eggs are destroyed early in incubation, but only one brood is raised each season. Both parents incubate eggs and care for the nestlings. Young fly about 40 days after hatching and do not breed until three years old.

Sometimes Peregrines lay eggs in nests built by other species such as ravens, but that behavior has not been observed in the Carolinas.

Feeding habits: Peregrines feed almost entirely on birds, with waterfowl, shorebirds, and pigeons being among those taken most frequently. Watching a Peregrine put several hundred teal to flight and capture its prey while passing through the flock at a speed possibly in excess of 165 miles (265 km) per hour is one of the supreme thrills of bird-watching. Being near the top of the food chain, the Peregrine Falcon is extremely sensitive to the use of persistent pesticides in any part of its range. Populations that winter where DDT is still used continue to decline even though such use is banned on the breeding grounds.

Description: Adults have blue-gray upperparts, barred underparts, a dark cap, and wide sideburns that sharply contrast with the white throat, plus long pointed wings and a tapered tail that is faintly barred. Immatures are brown with prominent sideburns and a streaked breast.

Prairie Falcon
Falco mexicanus
16–21 in. (40–53 cm)

Range: Although there is no reason to doubt the careful identification of the birds seen in Carteret County, N.C., on May 23, 1968, and at Townville, S.C., in 1977 and 1978, all extralimital records of falcons are subject to question because captive birds frequently escape and are capable of traveling long distances.

Order GRUIFORMES: Rails, Limpkin, and Cranes

Birds in this order have long bills, long necks, long legs, long toes, and short tails. Members of the three families that occur in the Carolinas feed on plants and small animals, but their foraging habits differ greatly.

Family RALLIDAE: Rails, Gallinules, and Coots

Rails are the birds some people are as thin as. Their laterally compressed bodies enable them to slip through densely tangled marsh vegetation, rarely taking flight and rarely being seen by anyone except hunters and bird-watchers. Rails, gallinules, and coots have long legs, long toes, and short, pointed tails. Rails and gallinules normally carry their tails cocked upward, flicking them up and down when agitated.

Yellow Rail

Yellow Rail
Coturnicops noveboracensis
6–8 in. (15–20 cm)

Range: The Yellow Rail is a fall and spring migrant throughout the Carolinas, and it winters along the coast to an undetermined extent. Records place this small, secretive bird in the marsh edges, wet meadows, and grain fields of our region from late September to mid-April. Individuals are sometimes flushed by winter grass fires, indicating that the species may be locally common along the coast. Because the Yellow Rail is seldom flushed by bird-watchers and, unlike our other rail species, is generally silent in winter, its distribution and abundance in the Carolinas may never be fully understood.

Feeding habits: The Yellow Rail's diet appears to be mostly insects and small freshwater snails.

Description: This rail has a short yellow bill and yellowish-brown plumage that is heavily streaked on the back and barred on the sides. In flight the bird flashes a prominent white patch on the trailing edge of each wing near the body.

Instructions for calling Yellow Rails: Locate a safe parking place at an apparently suitable fresh or brackish marsh or wet field during daylight and return in the evening. Try playing a tape recording of the bird's call or clicking rocks together to imitate it. The latter method elicits calls on the breeding grounds, but its effectiveness on the wintering grounds has not been proved.

Black Rail
Laterallus jamaicensis
5–6 in. (12–15 cm)

Range: The Black Rail lives in salt and brackish marshes amid needlerush and cordgrasses. Inland it frequents freshwater marshes, meadows, and grain fields. Nests have been found as far inland as Buncombe County, N.C., but the range of the species is not well known. Most inland nest sites may have been made uninhabitable by changes in farming practices (e.g., drainage and mowing of wet meadows). Records of these extremely secretive birds are mostly for the spring and fall seasons, when they probably are fairly common along the coast. Black Rails appear to be abundant at Cedar Island National Wildlife Refuge in Carteret County, N.C., where at least 80 were heard calling around midnight in late May 1973. The birds arrive in March or early April and remain until October or November, with small numbers apparently spending the winter along the coast.

Nesting habits: The six to ten white or buffy eggs are heavily speckled with brown and lilac. Incubation requires 12 to 14 days. Downy chicks are black and precocial.

Feeding habits: Black Rails apparently eat mostly insects and seeds.

Description: Our smallest rail is mostly black with yellow legs, rusty shoulders, and white barring on the back, wings, and flanks.

Clapper Rail
Rallus longirostris
12–16 in. (30–40 cm)

Range: Clapper Rails are very common permanent residents of salt

Clapper Rail

marshes the entire length of coastal Carolina. Populations increase in autumn with the arrival of migrants from the north. During migrations Clapper Rails occur inland, but sightings are very rare.

Nesting habits: Nests are depressed platforms of marsh grass or sedges usually placed in a clump of grass or attached to a marsh plant over shallow water. In either case the eggs are usually less than 2 feet (61 cm) above water or wet sod. The eight to twelve eggs are creamy buff marked with lilac and brown spots, the incubation period is about 3 weeks, and the black downy young chicks are precocial. Both adults incubate eggs and care for the young. The nesting season may begin as early as March and extend into late summer if eggs are lost repeatedly to predators or high tides. The small, dark race (*R. l. waynei*) breeding from Brunswick County, N.C., southward to Florida, is said to be double-brooded.

Feeding habits: At low tide these secretive birds venture from cover to feed on fiddler crabs and other small aquatic animals found on exposed banks and mudflats.

Description: The "marsh hen" utters a remarkable variety of clacks, grunts, groans, and shrieks. If silence prevails, the birder need only clap his or her hands together smartly to get some idea of how many Clappers are lurking in the marsh. See King Rail for a comparative description.

King Rail
Rallus elegans
15–19 in. (38–48 cm)

Range: The King Rail is found in freshwater marshes throughout the Carolinas in summer. The species winters here, mostly near the coast, where it occurs in fresh and brackish marshes. Listen for the King Rail's grunting *bup-bup-bup* wherever you find good stands of cattails and rushes. If the sun is suddenly covered by clouds on a summer day, birders may be treated to a King Rail chorus arising from every direction throughout the marsh.

Nesting habits: Breeding activity extends from March to July. The nest is a platform of grasses, rushes, and other vegetation placed 6 to 18 inches (15 to 45 cm) above shallow water in buttonwood bushes or tussocks of grass, sedges, or rushes. The eight to twelve eggs are buffy with a few brown specks, and incubation takes about 3 weeks. The precocial young are covered with black down. Both parents incubate eggs and care for the young, as is the case with all our rails.

Feeding habits: King Rails eat small aquatic animals.

Description: This large brown rail has a long, slightly decurved bill. Look for the rusty patch at the bend of

King Rail

the wing and for the prominent barring on the flanks. The Clapper Rail is slightly smaller and grayer than the King Rail, with less distinct barring on the flanks. Clappers prefer salt marshes, but habitat is not reliable for separating the two species because during migration each may visit the habitat preferred by the other.

Virginia Rail
Rallus limicola
8–11 in. (20–28 cm)

Range: The Virginia Rail migrates across inland portions of the Carolinas to winter along the coast, arriving in August and lingering into early May. Though infrequently reported inland, there is some evidence that the species winters and breeds where suitable habitat is available as far inland as Blowing Rock, N.C., and Clemson, S.C. Wintering birds are fairly common in the fresh and brackish coastal marshes. Virginia Rails breed sparingly in Dare County, N.C., along the Savannah River, and at various places in between, such as the extensive brackish marshes on Piney Island in Carteret County, Topsail Island in Onslow County, and Eagle Island in the Cape Fear River near Wilmington.

Nesting habits: Nests are built in clumps of rushes and may contain four to eight pale buff eggs that are lightly spotted with brown, chiefly around the large end. Incubation is shared by both parents and lasts approximately 19 days. The precocial chicks have black down, and the first to hatch often leave the nest while the rest of the eggs are still being incubated. The nesting season is protracted, with territorial pairs found in May and adults still tending downy young in late August.

Feeding habits: Virginia Rails eat seeds, berries, insects, snails, and small crustaceans.

Description: A small, dark reddish-brown rail with heavily barred flanks and large rusty patches in the wings, the Virginia Rail has gray cheeks and a long, slightly decurved bill.

Virginia Rail

Sora

Sora

Porzana carolina
8–10 in. (20–25 cm)

Range: The Sora is a spring and fall transient in most parts of the Carolinas from April through May and from August through October. Common in marshes along the coast, it is generally uncommon inland, where it nevertheless is the rail most frequently seen. Soras are winter residents along the entire Carolina coast. Although some are seen occasionally in summer in coastal North and South Carolina,

no evidence of breeding has been found.

Feeding habits: Soras feed on seeds (especially wild rice), small mollusks (snails), and insects.

Description: This predominantly gray rail has a streaked back and barred sides. The adult has a black throat, a short and thick yellow bill, and yellow legs. Green-legged immature Soras are similar but do not have the black throat.

Purple Gallinule

Purple Gallinule
Porphyrio martinica
12–14 in. (30–35 cm)

Range: Although declining as a breeding species in North Carolina, the Purple Gallinule may still nest locally and erratically as far north as the White Oak River impoundment in Onslow County, N.C. Nonbreeding birds, especially immatures, may appear erratically almost anywhere in the Carolinas at any season.

Nesting habits: Nest building begins in early May, and several incomplete nests usually can be found near the one in which the eggs finally are laid. The nest is a depressed platform of rushes and grass attached to stems of aquatic plants such as pickerelweed or settled into floating islands of dead vegetation. The six to eight creamy eggs are finely dotted with lilac and reddish brown. Clutches usually are completed by late May, and incubation requires about 24 days. The precocial young have black down, yellow feet, and bills mottled with yellow and black.

Feeding habits: Food is primarily the seeds and fruits of aquatic plants, but snails and other animal matter are taken.

Description: The adult Purple Gallinule has an iridescent bluish-purple body, brownish wings, and yellow legs. Its short, stout bill is red with a yellow tip and a white frontal shield. Brown immatures lack the white lateral stripe of the young Common Moorhen. Like moorhens, gallinules nod the head while swimming and, like rails, flick the short pointed tail when agitated.

Common Moorhen
(Common Gallinule)
Gallinula chloropus
12–15 in. (30–38 cm)

Range: More numerous in summer than in winter, the Common Moorhen is a permanent resident on and near the Carolina coast, being locally common in southern South Carolina and becoming uncommon in the coastal plain toward northeastern North Carolina. The farthest inland known nesting site is in North Carolina at Goldsboro in Wayne County. Although the summer range shown in some popular field guides indicates the species is found throughout the Carolinas during the nesting season, the absence of definite breeding records indicates it is only a rare transient in the piedmont and mountains, occurring mid-April to late May in spring and early September to mid-November in fall.

Nesting habits: Beginning in early May, Common Moorhens build their nests in freshwater ponds, rice fields, and backwaters, often

Common Moorhen

American Coot

placing them in clumps of rushes or grass or in willows, buttonwood bushes, or climbing vines. The 10 to 12 buffy eggs are heavily marked with brown and gray. Shared by both sexes, incubation requires about 3 weeks. The precocial young have black down, black feet, and red bills.

Feeding habits: Common Moorhens eat snails, insect matter, and seeds from aquatic plants.

Description: The black body of the adult Common Moorhen has a white stripe along the side, a mark also found on the grayish immature. Adults have long slender toes, long yellow legs with red "garters," and a short stout bill that is red with a yellow tip. Moorhens nod the head while swimming and flick the short pointed tail.

American Coot
Fulica americana
13–16 in. (33–40 cm)

Range: In winter the American Coot is one of the most abundant waterbirds in the Carolinas. Flocks may number a thousand or more along

Wintering flock of American Coots

the coast and on major reservoirs inland. Coots nest locally in the coastal plain of South Carolina and northward at least occasionally to Pamlico and Wayne Counties in North Carolina. Summer stragglers, rarely found inland to the mountains, do not necessarily breed.

Nesting habits: Built by the female, the nest may be placed on a floating platform of vegetation or built like that of a rail, attached to vegetation growing in water. In South Carolina laying may begin in the latter part of April. The eight to twelve buffy eggs are finely dotted with dark brown. Incubation requires 21 to

22 days with both parents in attendance. The precocial chicks have dark down on the body but are reddish orange about the bill and head. Chicks have very large feet for their size and can swim and dive very well from the first day. The pair that nested at the waste treatment plant in Wayne County, N.C., in 1987 produced two broods, with downy young first seen June 12 and August 2. In 1988 five pairs produced 45 young.

Feeding habits: Coots take most of their food, primarily various parts of aquatic vegetation, from the surface of the water, but they will also dive for food.

Description: Like gallinules, coots nod the head while swimming and must patter along the surface of the water for a considerable distance before becoming airborne. Unlike gallinules, coots have lobed toes and waddle awkwardly when they walk. The adult American Coot has a dark gray body and a black head. Its short, stout bill has a frontal shield and is white with a dark band near the tip. A few American Coots have an extensive facial shield and may be mistaken for the Caribbean Coot (*F. caribaea*), which may or may not be a separate species.

Family ARAMIDAE: Limpkin

This large, long-necked wading bird is named for its limping manner of walking.

Limpkin

Limpkin
Aramus guarauna
25–28 in. (63–71 cm)

Range: The Limpkin occurs very rarely in the South Carolina coastal plain inland to Aiken and northward in the lower coastal plain to New Bern, N.C. Limpkins have been seen in the Carolinas from early March to early September. Individuals may linger at one place for several days or even a couple of months.

Feeding habits: The Limpkin's chief item of food is a freshwater snail that is not known to occur north of the Altamaha River in central Georgia. In addition, Limpkins eat other mollusks, small reptiles, amphibians, insects, crayfish, and worms found in swamps and marshlands.

Description: This brown, long-legged wader has white, crescent-shaped spots on the body plumage, a long slender bill that is slightly decurved, and dark legs. Immature night-herons, in spite of their stout bills, are sometimes mistaken for Limpkins.

Family GRUIDAE:
Cranes and Relatives

Although cranes superficially resemble herons, they differ in many respects. Cranes fly with the neck stretched forward, and their tertials form a "bustle" that droops over the tail as the birds forage in marshes and grasslands.

Sandhill Crane

Subfamily Gruinae: Cranes

During courtship, cranes engage in frenzied, leaping dances.

Sandhill Crane
Grus canadensis
33–48 in. (83–122 cm)

Range: Sandhill Cranes are spring and fall transients over the Carolinas, but they usually pass at such a high altitude that they are not seen by people on the ground. However, they are becoming widespread as winter visitors in both states. Astounding was a flock of 100 cranes found in a field near Weaverville, Buncombe County, N.C., on February 16, 2003. Other winter sightings of single birds and small flocks come from Transylvania County, N.C., and many other parts of the Carolinas. A few of the birds have been attracted by captives released at a wildlife management area in South Carolina. Others have escaped from the captive breeding program operated at the Patuxent Wildlife Research Center in Laurel, Md. However, the great majority

appear to be healthy wild birds. It is possible that unusually dry conditions on the wintering grounds in Florida and southern Georgia prompt Sandhill Cranes to move northward in winter.

Feeding habits: Sandhill Cranes wade in marshes and wet fields, where they take small rodents, frogs, and insects.

Description: The uniformly gray adult Sandhill Crane has white cheeks, red crown, dark bill, and dark legs. Immatures are brownish with dark bill and legs. Sometimes gray plumage is stained rusty brown by a ferrous solution in muck where the birds feed.

Whooping Crane
Grus americana
about 45 in. (114 cm)

Range: Although a few Whooping Cranes continue to migrate from the breeding grounds in Canada to the wintering grounds on the Texas Gulf Coast, no member of that extremely rare species had been seen in the Carolinas for more than 150 years when one appeared briefly in Wilkes County, N.C., in mid-April 2003. It was an experimental bird en route from Wisconsin to Florida when its radio signal was lost in that county. Its fate is unknown.

During the northward spring migration, eight young birds from the Florida program appeared near Franklin, N.C., April 1–3, 2004. Birds from the Florida program spent most of the winter of 2004–2005 on the coastal plain of the Carolinas.

Several wintered in South Carolina (Colleton and Beaufort Counties), and three moved into eastern North Carolina. Those three fed on extensive agricultural lands south of Kinston from December 2004 until late March 2005 and apparently roosted in a nearby swamp created by beaver dams. After their departure, all three were tracked in flight as they headed toward Wisconsin, where it is hoped that they will breed. Presence of the experimental Whooping Cranes in the Carolinas was not publicized because their handlers do not want them to become imprinted on human beings.

The last known nineteenth-century record from the Carolinas was a specimen taken on the Waccamaw River in South Carolina. North Carolina has no documented record of a wild Whooping Crane, but the species probably visited the state in colonial times.

Feeding habits: Cranes have feeding habits similar to those of herons and egrets.

Description: The adult Whooping Crane is a very large, white, long-legged wader with black wing tips, black legs, a black facial mask, and a red crown. Immatures have a brownish head, brownish upperparts, and white underparts. Like other cranes, Whoopers fly with the neck extended. Soaring Whoopers may circle higher and higher until they disappear into the clouds.

Order CHARADRIIFORMES:
Shorebirds, Gulls, Terns, and Allies

Shorebirds, including plovers and sandpipers, are predominantly white and gray or brown wading birds with pointed wings and long toes that may be partially webbed. They usually inhabit beaches, mudflats, and other shorelines. Many species, particularly the smaller sandpipers, nest in the Arctic tundra. Shorebirds, including the several species that nest in the Carolinas, lay their protectively colored eggs in depressions in the ground and hatch out precocial chicks with sand-colored down.

Shorebirds generally eat mollusks, crustaceans, and other small aquatic animals, which they usually obtain by probing into mud or wet sand with their long, slender bills. Some species eat insects and an insignificant amount of vegetable matter. Shorebirds may use their feet to stir the water or pat the sand to induce hidden animals to expose themselves. A few species feed primarily by snatching from the surface and rarely probe.

During the middle years of the nineteenth century, great flocks of shorebirds provided easy targets for market hunters who supplied meat for the tables of rapidly growing cities. By 1880 many species had been gunned to the verge of extinction. Following protection from hunting, most shorebirds were able to make a good recovery; however, no species appears to have reached its former level of abundance.

Characteristics of plovers, skuas, gulls and terns, skimmers, and alcids are given under their respective family headings.

Family CHARADRIIDAE:
Lapwings and Plovers

Members of this family are stocky birds with relatively short, sturdy bills used for probing for insects or snatching food from the surface of muddy, sandy, or short-grass substrates.

Subfamily Vanellinae: Lapwing

Lapwings are not native to the Western Hemisphere.

Northern Lapwing
Vanellus vanellus
12 in. (30 cm)

Range: This rare accidental from Europe is most often found in eastern North America on the coast north of the Carolinas. One Northern Lapwing was collected inland at Siler City, N.C., on November 12, 1926, and another appeared near Charleston, S.C., on December 3, 1940. Recently, one was photographed in northeastern North Carolina at the Mackay Island National Wildlife Refuge in Currituck County on December 23, 2004.

Feeding habits: The lapwing feeds in farmlands, grasslands with short turf, and marshy fields, as well as at freshwater margins and coastal mudflats.

Description: Dark above and white below with a long, thin crest, the Northern Lapwing has rusty undertail coverts, a white tail with a black tip, and wings rounded at the tips. This is the only crested shorebird known to have occurred in our region.

Subfamily Charadriinae: Plovers

While feeding, plovers usually run on the ground, stop abruptly, and then run again.

Black-bellied Plover
Pluvialis squatarola
11–12 in. (28–30 cm)

Black-bellied Plover (in breeding plumage)

Range: The Black-bellied Plover can be found along the Carolina coast every month of the year, being common in winter and during migrations but scarce in summer. It does not breed here. As with many other shorebirds, the last northbound birds have just departed from the Carolinas when the earliest nesters leave their precocial young in the Arctic and return to the wintering grounds. The birds of the year follow their parents southward a month or more later. Inland sightings of the Black-bellied Plover are rare in the Carolinas and usually occur in the fall.

Black-bellied Plover (in winter plumage)

wing meets the body. The American Golden-Plover has a relatively thin bill, a dark rump, no wing stripe, and gray axillars.

American Golden-Plover
Pluvialis dominica
10–11 in. (25–28 cm)

Feeding habits: See comments on order.
Description: This gray plover has a thick black bill, a white wing stripe, white rump, barred tail, and black legs. Summer birds have black underparts extending from a facial mask to the belly. Winter birds have a white stripe above the eye and an irregular dark stripe through the eye, giving the appearance of smudged mascara. In flight the Black-bellied Plover flashes black axillars underneath, where the

Range: The American Golden-Plover is an uncommon to rare, but regular, spring and fall migrant inland as well as along the coast. Most spring sightings occur in the mountains between early March and early May. Fall sightings tend to occur toward the coast from mid-August to mid-January. The species is often reported from the Wright Brothers Memorial grounds and the Bodie–

*American Golden-Plover
(in breeding plumage)*

Pea Island area in late summer and early fall when tropical storms drive offshore migrants landward. Although it visits mudflats with other shorebirds, it is more likely to be found in short-grass habitats such as pastures, golf courses, airports, and sod farms.

Feeding habits: This plover takes the usual shorebird fare but apparently favors grasshoppers in spring and crickets in fall.

Description: Similar to the Black-bellied Plover, the American Golden-Plover has a golden hue to the upperparts. Look for the dark rump, gray axillars, and the absence of a wing stripe.

Snowy Plover
Charadrius alexandrinus
about 6 in. (15–16 cm)

Range: A very rare vagrant on the Atlantic Coast north of Florida, the Snowy Plover is known to have visited the Carolina coast several times. One was on North Island in Georgetown County, S.C., from January 9 to February 26, 1992. Another was there in late January 1993. One was also seen at New Drum Inlet, Carteret County, N.C., from April 30 to May 3, 1994. A photograph taken at Deveaux Bank documents the third occurrence of the species in South Carolina. First sighted on November 26, 2003, that Snowy Plover remained in the area until at least February 11, 2004.

Feeding habits: See comments on order.

Description: Similar to the Piping Plover, the Snowy Plover is smaller, with a dark patch on the side of the head between the eye and the neck. Legs are dark gray in all seasons, and the black bill is relatively long and thin.

Wilson's Plover
Charadrius wilsonia
7–9 in. (17–22 cm)

Range: The Wilson's Plover is a fairly common summer resident along most of the Carolina coast from March through October, but it is uncommon along the Outer Banks. Although a few individuals may linger into winter almost anywhere along the coast, the Morehead City, N.C., area appears to be the only place in the Carolinas where the species is a regular winter resident. Inland sightings are very rare and accidental.

Nesting habits: Wilson's Plovers nest on sparsely vegetated beaches or on islands in sounds and bays. The three or four eggs, usually laid in May or June, are buffy splotched with black. They hatch in 24 or 25 days. Both sexes incubate eggs and help care for the precocial young. Sometimes adults stand by the nest

Wilson's Plover

Semipalmated Plover

to shade the eggs and keep them from becoming too hot.

Feeding habits: See comments on order.

Description: The male Wilson's Plover is dark above and white below with one wide black neck band, a white wing stripe, and flesh-colored legs. The female is similar, but her breast band is the same color as her back. Juveniles resemble the female. In both sexes the bill is black and relatively long and thick in comparison with that of the smaller Semipalmated Plover.

Semipalmated Plover
Charadrius semipalmatus
7–8 in. (17–20 cm)

Range: The Semipalmated Plover is an abundant migrant and fairly common winter resident along the Carolina coast. Although present every month of the year, it does not breed here. For this and many other species of shorebirds, the spring and fall migrations cover an extended period of time. Thus, the last northbound birds may be seen here in June, and the earliest south-

bound birds of the same species may arrive in July. Semipalmated Plovers occur rather frequently on inland mudflats, usually in April and May and from August to October.

Feeding habits: See comments on order.

Description: Dark above and white below with one narrow black neck band, the Semipalmated Plover has a white wing stripe, yellowish legs, and a very small, light-colored bill with a dark tip. The species is named for its half-webbed toes. In winter the neck band is dark gray, and the bill may appear to be completely dark.

Piping Plover
Charadrius melodus
6–8 in. (15–20 cm)

Range: The Piping Plover is an uncommon to fairly common winter resident along the Carolina coast from early August to late May. The species is seldom reported inland, where it may occur at sod farms, wastewater treatment plants, and the shores of major reservoirs. Piping Plovers usually remain singly or in small flocks on the relatively dry portions of beaches and mudflats. Recent summer records indicate that Piping Plovers nest sparingly above the high-tide line on beaches from the Cape Hatteras National Seashore southward along the coast to Waites Island, the easternmost barrier island in South Carolina. The Piping Plover is a Federally Threatened Species.

Nesting habits: Eggs are buffy and lightly marked with fine black, blackish-brown, and purplish-gray dots. Sets usually number four, but replacement clutches may be smaller. The shallow scrape may contain bits of shell. Both adults incubate the eggs, which normally hatch in 27 days, and also tend the precocial preflight young. Nesting probably begins in late April, but nests with eggs may be found into July.

Protection of nest sites: Fortunately, most of the known nesting sites in the Carolinas are in remote areas with little human activity. Marking the nesting area, closing it to the public, and designating a few volunteers to watch over the Piping Plovers usually provide adequate protection. However, in the summer of 2005, a pair chose to nest along the route drivers of off-road vehicles use to reach the recreation area at the southern tip of Hatteras Island. In an attempt to balance the safety of the birds with the activities of human visitors, Cape Hatteras National Seashore personnel established an escort service to lead numerous vehicles slowly past the nesting area. Conservationists claimed more could have been done, while the beach drivers resented restrictions on their access to some of the most popular recreation areas within the Seashore.

Feeding habits: See comments on order.

Description: Similar to the Snowy Plover, the Piping Plover is pale gray above and white below with a stubby black bill in winter and orange legs in all seasons. Males in breeding plumage have a yellow bill with a black tip, a narrow black neck band, and a black browline between the white forehead and the gray crown. The breast band is incomplete on the slightly paler females and in some breeding males. The browline and the remnant of the breast band fade to gray in winter.

Killdeer
Charadrius vociferus
10–11 in. (25–28 cm)

Range: The Killdeer is a common permanent resident throughout the Carolinas, but it is considerably less numerous during the breeding season than at other times of the year. Killdeer may visit almost any open ground, such as a pasture, mudflat, golf course, or cultivated field.

Piping Plover (on nest at Cape Hatteras)

Killdeer (adult)

Killdeer (chick)

Nesting habits: Nesting takes place from March through June in open bare to lightly vegetated habitats, including flat rooftops, parking lots, and athletic fields. The four buffy eggs are heavily speckled with blackish brown, and the nest scrape is sometimes lined with a few leaves, grasses, pebbles, or bits of shell. The eggs are large for the size of the bird and conical in shape, lying in the nest with the points toward the center, thus affording maximum efficiency during the 24 to 25 days of incubation. Both sexes incubate eggs and care for the precocial young. Like many other shorebirds, the Killdeer distracts intruders from its eggs or young by fluttering along the ground as if it has a broken wing.

Feeding habits: The Killdeer consumes a great number of grubs and insects, often searching for them in soil freshly turned by the farmer's plow.

Description: Dark above and white below with two black breast bands, the Killdeer has a reddish-orange tail, black bill, and flesh-colored legs. Downy young have only one breast band. The "heartbroken" cry of *kil-dee, kil-dee* is diagnostic.

Family HAEMATOPODIDAE: Oystercatchers

Oystercatchers have long, sturdy, laterally flattened bills that can be inserted into mollusks to pry the shells apart. Only one species is known to occur in the eastern United States.

American Oystercatcher
Haematopus palliatus
17–21 in. (43–53 cm)

Range: The American Oystercatcher is a fairly common permanent resident on the Carolina coast, and apparently more birds of this species winter at Cape Romain than anywhere else on the Atlantic Coast. Inland records are accidental and extremely rare. Numbers appear to be declining as human use of coastal beaches increases.

Nesting habits: The two or three buffy eggs are heavily splotched with dark brown and lavender, making them difficult to see against the sand on open beaches, where oystercatchers usually nest. Clutches normally are laid in April and May.

American Oystercatcher (note the oblong vertical pupil in the eye)

American Oystercatcher (at nest)

Incubation is by both sexes and takes about 27 days. The precocial chicks can swim and dive, as well as run with great agility.

Feeding habits: American Oystercatchers feed on various mollusks, including oysters. They also probe in sand for crabs and worms.

Description: One of our largest shorebirds, the American Oystercatcher is black above and white below with a wide white wing stripe, a white rump, a long orange-red bill, and flesh-colored legs.

Family RECURVIROSTRIDAE: Stilts and Avocets

These graceful waders have long, slender bills and very long legs.

Black-necked Stilt
Himantopus mexicanus
13.0–15.5 in. (33–39 cm)

Range: Generally rare along the Carolina coast, the Black-necked Stilt is locally common from April through August near established nesting sites such as Bodie Island, Pea Island, and Cape Romain. Inland sightings are rare.

Nesting habits: Nesting in loose colonies at shallow impoundments and spoil sites, Black-necked Stilts display in groups with much running about and loud calling. Individuals halt, crouch, and call with extended wings aquiver, or they may stand and call with outstretched wings. Lined with grass, the nest depression is usually made in an elevated mound of mud that is surrounded by shallow water, but dry sites may be used. Both adults incubate the three or four eggs, which hatch in

Black-necked Stilt

American Avocet (in breeding plumage)

21 to 28 days, and both tend the precocial young.

Feeding habits: Stilts feed primarily in shallow fresh water and brackish ponds and impoundments.

Description: Black above and white below with a white tail and rump, the Black-necked Stilt has a long neck, long and thin straight black bill, and very long red or pink legs.

American Avocet
Recurvirostra americana
15–20 in. (38–51 cm)

Range: Small numbers of American Avocets may be found along waterways almost anywhere in the Carolinas, even in the mountains, when spring and fall migrants move across the region. Large flocks (up to several hundred birds) are generally seen only in summer and early fall at impoundments, spoil sites, and other suitable habitat on or near the coast. Most avocets depart from the Carolinas by early October, but a few may linger into spring and even until summer. Although the species normally breeds in western North America,

two day-old chicks were seen at the Pea Island National Wildlife Refuge, N.C., on June 18, 1968. One of the downy chicks was photographed in hand. Three adults were in habitat potentially suitable for nesting near Aurora, N.C., on June 19, 1992. Nests, one of which contained four eggs on May 25, 1996, have been found at the Savannah Spoil Site in Jasper County, S.C., which hosts the largest winter population recorded in the region.

Nesting habits: In the Carolinas, American Avocets tend to nest in impounded marsh and at spoil deposition sites. Nesting in colonies, the birds display in groups, bowing, crouching, and calling with the wings held extended. Scattered nests vary from scantily lined depressions to sizable mounds of debris. They may be placed on a sun-baked mudflat or among plants growing near water. Sites usually are subject to flooding. Laying apparently takes place in late May in the Carolinas. Both parents incubate the four dark-spotted, olive-buff eggs and tend the precocial chicks, which swim readily.

The incubation period is 22 to 24 days, and the young birds become independent in about 6 weeks.

Feeding habits: The avocet feeds by walking through shallow water with its bill submerged. Sweeping its long, recurved bill from side to side, the bird stirs up and consumes a wide variety of aquatic organisms and seeds from marsh plants.

Description: This mostly white bird has a black stripe running the length of the wing and a black bar across the wing where it meets the body. The head and long neck are gray in winter and cinnamon in summer, the long legs are blue-gray, and the long bill is dark and thin, curving upward at the tip. The avocet strikingly exhibits the shorebird habit of resting by standing on one leg and tucking the head beneath a wing.

Family SCOLOPACIDAE:
Sandpipers and Phalaropes

Although phalaropes are mostly pelagic birds except during the nesting season, those that come ashore along the Carolina coast visit the same marshes and shallow impoundments frequented by their close relatives, the sandpipers.

Subfamily Scolopacinae:
Sandpipers

Most sandpipers can be found on mudflats and along the shores of ponds, lakes, and oceans. There are three noteworthy exceptions in the Carolinas. The Common Snipe prefers wet grasslands, the Upland Sandpiper frequents relatively dry grasslands, and the American Woodcock inhabits damp woodlands.

Greater Yellowlegs

Greater Yellowlegs
Tringa melanoleuca
12–15 in. (30–38 cm)

Range: Like many other shorebirds, the Greater Yellowlegs can be found on mudflats along the Carolina coast throughout the year, but it is common only during migrations and does not breed here. The species is fairly common in winter and rare in summer. Inland the Greater Yellowlegs is an uncommon to fairly common spring and fall transient, March to May and August to November, and a rare winter visitor.

Feeding habits: The Greater Yellowlegs feeds on insects and their larvae, snails, crabs, worms, and small fish.

Description: This tall, gray sandpiper has bright yellow legs, a white rump, and a barred tail. The Greater Yellowlegs is distinguished from the Lesser Yellowlegs by the sharp three- to five-note whistle and the relatively long bill that may turn upward very slightly toward the tip. The Lesser has a soft one- to three-note whistle and a bill that is relatively short, slender, and straight.

Lesser Yellowlegs

Lesser Yellowlegs
Tringa flavipes
9–11 in. (22–28 cm)

Range: Generally less widespread than the Greater Yellowlegs, the Lesser Yellowlegs is a fairly common spring and fall migrant and uncommon winter resident along the coast. Migrants occur inland more often in fall than in spring. This species generally avoids saltwater mudflats, and it migrates later in spring and earlier in fall than does the Greater Yellowlegs.
Feeding habits: The Lesser Yellowlegs is similar to the Greater Yellowlegs in feeding habits.
Description: See Greater Yellowlegs for a comparative description.

Spotted Redshank
Tringa erythropus
12.5 in. (32.0 cm)

Range: The Spotted Redshank is a rare accidental on the Atlantic Coast of North America. There are two published reports from northeastern North Carolina. The first bird was seen May 23, 1955, at the Pea Island National Wildlife Refuge. The sec-

ond was present at Cape Hatteras, May 13–17, 1987.
Feeding habits: See comments on order.
Description: Intermediate in size between the Greater and Lesser Yellowlegs, adult Spotted Redshanks can be separated from those two species in flight by the mostly white underwing and a large white area on the rump and lower back. The white flashed by yellowlegs in flight is on the base of the tail. Leg color is not a reliable trait for separating yellowlegs and redshanks because some yellowlegs may have orange legs. In the Spotted Redshank, juveniles (gray with heavily barred underparts) may have yellow or orange legs; nonbreeding adults (gray with some very light barring on flanks) have red legs; and breeding adults (black above and below with white spots on back and wings) may have dark red legs that appear blackish. The major problem is that an intermediate adult with patches of black on the head, neck, and underparts can be dismissed as a yellowlegs partly covered with oil. Both of the birds seen in North Carolina were in intermediate plumage.

Solitary Sandpiper
Tringa solitaria
8–9 in. (20–22 cm)

Range: The Solitary Sandpiper is a fairly common spring and fall migrant from late March to mid-May and from early July to October. It occurs throughout the Carolinas and, like the Spotted Sandpiper, frequents the margins of ponds and streams. Solitary Sandpipers often

Solitary Sandpiper

Willet (in breeding plumage)

visit pig pens and waste treatment plants during migration. Stragglers are very rarely seen into late December.

Feeding habits: Although the Solitary Sandpiper sometimes probes in water or soft mud, it usually feeds by catching insects, their larvae, and various other small invertebrates.

Description: This gray sandpiper has its back and wings dotted with white. Look for the black bill and legs, prominent white eye ring, and barred outer tail feathers. The Solitary Sandpiper often teeters in the manner of a Spotted Sandpiper. The Spotted flies stiffly on bowed wings and has a white wing stripe. The Solitary lacks the wing stripe, and its flight is graceful, almost like that of a swallow.

Willet

Catoptrophorus semipalmatus
14–16 in. (35–40 cm)

Range: The Willet is a year-round resident of coastal Carolina, common in summer and less numerous in winter. It is very rarely found inland, and then mostly during migrations or following the passage of a tropical storm. Boaters rarely see Willets offshore.

Nesting habits: Willets may nest singly or in well-concealed loose colonies. The nest is not easily found unless the adult flushes. Located in sparse to rather dense grasses, often near a marsh or just behind the beach, the cryptic nest is sometimes placed below the high-tide line. The grass-lined hollow in the ground is more or less sheltered by surrounding clumps of waist-high grass. At least once, three of four eggs hatched even though they bobbed in water above the nest twice daily at high tide, encircled by rush stems that kept them from floating away. The falling tide gently returned the eggs to the soggy nest. The conical eggs usually number four, are pale olive splotched with dark brown, and require 21 to 23 days for incubation. Males apparently assist females in incubating eggs and feeding the precocial young. Adults become greatly agitated at the approach of an intruder; they will hover over the curious naturalist and dive at his or her head while giving piercing cries that surely must be avian profanity.

Feeding habits: Willets feed on small aquatic animals obtained by probing or snatching.

Description: This large sandpiper, gray in winter and brown in summer, has black legs and bill. A prominent white stripe runs the length of its wings, which it often holds erect briefly after flight. Its tail is white except for a dark tip. The Willet's loud cry of *pilly-will-willet* is easily learned.

Spotted Sandpiper (in summer plumage)

Spotted Sandpiper
Actitis macularius
7–8 in. (17–20 cm)

Range: The Spotted Sandpiper is present in the Carolinas in all seasons. Common and widespread during migrations, it is scarce in winter but may breed to a greater extent than the few published records indicate. This most characteristic inland sandpiper is a bird of the margins of inland ponds and streams as well as coastal shorelines.

Nesting habits: The breeding season in the Carolinas appears to be from May through July. All of the documented nesting sites are from the mountains or western piedmont of North Carolina, most recently at wastewater treatment facilities in the Winston-Salem area. Spotted Sandpipers may occur along the lower Cape Fear River, at impound-

ments in the Pea Island National Wildlife Refuge, and around ponds in the eastern piedmont of North Carolina during the breeding season; but proof of nesting has not been obtained from those localities. In South Carolina the only known indication of possible breeding is the presence of two birds that were seen together at the Santee Dam on Lake Marion in mid-June 1985.

The female is the dominant partner in courtship displays. Usually located among grasses, the nest is a depression in the ground litter, but it may be lined with grass. Clutches almost invariably consist of four buffy eggs that are irregularly spotted with various shades of brown. Incubation requires about 20 days and is frequently performed by the male, who also assumes responsibility for the precocial young. A female often lays for more than one male, and she may help incubate a late clutch. Even as a newly hatched chick, the Spotted Sandpiper constantly teeters up and down.

Feeding habits: The Spotted Sandpiper forages in mud and shallow water for insects and various other invertebrates.

Description: Mud-colored upperparts contrast with underparts that are white in winter and spotted in summer. Look for the white wing stripe and grayish legs. The Spotted Sandpiper teeters almost constantly while standing or walking. In flight the bird holds its wings stiffly bent downward, alternating a few rapid wing beats with periods of sailing. That behavior makes the species easy to recognize even in its unspotted winter plumage.

Upland Sandpiper
Bartramia longicauda
11–13 in. (28–33 cm)

Range: The Upland Sandpiper is a spring and fall transient from mid-March through early May and from mid-July to October. It is seen most frequently near the coast in early fall. This bird prefers grassy meadows, sod farms, and airports to shorelines. Often only the head

Upland Sandpiper

and neck can be seen above the grass.

Feeding habits: Insects predominate in a diet that also includes some seeds and berries.

Description: Upland Sandpipers have yellow legs and a distinctive silhouette: short bill, small head, long neck, and a longer tail than our other shorebirds. Uplands fly stiffly, much like the Spotted Sandpiper, and hold the wings erect briefly after landing.

Eskimo Curlew
Numenius borealis
12–15 in. (30–38 cm)

Status: Apparently extinct, though possibly sighted in Texas a few years ago, this smallest of our curlews was last positively identified on Barbados in 1963. Historically the Eskimo Curlew nested on Arctic tundra and migrated southward in fall from the Atlantic Maritime Provinces to the Lesser Antilles and South America. Northward migration was mostly over the central part of our continent. The Eskimo Curlew was formerly a very rare transient along the Carolina coast.

Whimbrel
Numenius phaeopus
15–19 in. (38–48 cm)

Range: Although the Whimbrel may be found along the Carolina coast during any month of the year, it is primarily a fairly common to common spring and fall migrant. Parts of the South Carolina coast serve as a staging area for migratory movements. The species winters sparingly at a few sites in both North and South Carolina. Inland sight-

Whimbrel   *Long-billed Curlew*

ings are very rare, but the species may occur even in the mountains.

Feeding habits: In the Carolinas the Whimbrel eats fiddler crabs, crayfish, and other burrowing organisms.

Description: A gray-brown bird with a striped crown, the Whimbrel has long legs and a long, decurved bill. The Long-billed Curlew has cinnamon wing linings and a much longer bill in proportion to its head size. Members of the Eurasian race of the Whimbrel have white on the rump and lower back; aberrant members of the North American race may show white on the upper back and shoulders.

Long-billed Curlew
Numenius americanus
22–26 in. (56–66 cm)

Range: The Carolina coast once swarmed with this largest of our North American shorebirds, but by 1879 the species had been over-hunted almost to the point of extinction. Although still considered a rare species, the Long-billed Curlew now occurs regularly at Cape Ro-

main from late July through March and appears elsewhere along the coast with encouraging frequency. These birds show a preference for extensive mudflats such as those at Portsmouth Island (northeast end of Core Banks), where they may be present from early September to early October, and around New Inlet in southern New Hanover County. Small numbers may winter as far north as the Morehead City area.

Feeding habits: The Long-billed Curlew probes in wet sand or mud, either exposed or covered by shallow water, for various invertebrates. Fiddler crabs are a favored item.

Description: A large brown curlew with long legs, the Long-billed Curlew has an extremely long decurved bill that accounts for about 6 to 8 inches (15 to 20 cm) of its total length. Its bill is approximately four times as long as its head. Look for the unstriped crown and cinnamon wing linings.

Black-tailed Godwit

Limosa limosa
16.5 in. (42.0 cm)

Range: Along the Atlantic Coast
of North America this Eurasian
species is of very rare accidental
occurrence. There are four records
of Black-tailed Godwits from North
Carolina, three of single birds in
fall migration (July, September, and
December) and one of four birds
(two in nonbreeding plumage and
two mostly in breeding plumage)
seen in spring migration at Pea
Island on June 4, 2003. All sightings
were in the Bodie–Pea Island area,
except the bird found in a field near
Goldsboro, Wayne County, N.C., on
September 23, 1999.
Feeding habits: Godwits feed by walking in shallow water and probing
the mud for invertebrates.
Description: Compared with our other
godwits, the Black-tailed tends
to have a straight bill, whereas
the other three tend to have bills
slightly upturned toward the tip.
Unfortunately, some Black-taileds
may have an upturned bill and
some individuals of the Hudsonian
Godwit may have a virtually
straight bill. Both species have a
black tail with white at the base.
The best way to separate standing
birds of these two species, which
are very similar in nonbreeding
plumage, is by the relative length of
the tail and the folded wing. Wing
tips project significantly beyond the
tail of the Hudsonian, but wings
and tail are of approximately the
same length in the Black-tailed. The
Hudsonian may also have a narrow
white terminal band on its tail, but
that is not considered a reliable
field character. In flight the underwing of the Black-tailed is predominantly white; that of the Hudsonian
is dark with a white stripe running
most of its length. Bar-tailed has
no well-defined white stripe in the
wing above or below.

Hudsonian Godwit

Limosa haemastica
15.5 in. (39.0 cm)

Range: One of the least abundant
of North American shorebirds,
the Hudsonian Godwit is very
rare inland and along most of the
Carolina coast, but it appears to be a
regular though uncommon autumn
visitor in the Bodie–Pea Island area
between early August and mid-
November. Some autumn flocks of
this species migrate from Labrador
directly across the Atlantic Ocean to
South America, and the majority of
the birds seen in the Carolinas probably have been forced off course by
storms. Hudsonian Godwits have
been seen in late February at Pea Island and Cape Romain, but the species is very rare in spring because
the northward movement is across
the central United States.
Feeding habits: The Hudsonian Godwit has a long, thin, recurved bill
that is flexible at the tip. The species shows a preference for feeding
in water of a depth about equal to
the length of the bill, which is immersed "to the hilt." Uncharacteris-
tically, a flock of 35 Hudsonians, accompanied by one Marbled Godwit,
visited a sod farm near Orangeburg,
S.C., on August 31, 2002.
Description: Brown with a barred
breast in summer and gray in
winter, the Hudsonian Godwit has

Hudsonian Godwit (in winter plumage)

a white rump and a black tail that may be narrowly tipped with white. The long, thin, recurved bill has a dark tip. Legs are long and dark. In flight, the wing linings are mostly dark and the axillars are black. See Black-tailed Godwit account for a comparative description.

Bar-tailed Godwit
Limosa lapponica
15 in. (38 cm)

Range: This Eurasian godwit is accidental on the coast of North Carolina. All known occurrences of the Bar-tailed Godwit in the Carolinas were in the Pea Island area of Dare County or on Portsmouth Island in Carteret County, just south of Ocracoke Inlet. Fall migration dates are from late July until the middle of October. All spring occurrences (late April to early May) are from Portsmouth Island. Spring birds were identifiable as the European race, *L. l. lapponica*, which has an unbarred white rump patch that extends to a point on the lower back.
Feeding habits: Godwits feed by walk-

ing in shallow water and probing the mud for invertebrates.
Description: Appropriately named, the Bar-tailed Godwit has a heavily barred tail and a barred rump patch that extends to a point on the lower back. In the European race, the rump patch is white and so is the wing lining. The Siberian race has a gray wing lining.

Marbled Godwit
Limosa fedoa
18–20 in. (40–51 cm)

Range: Although recorded on the Carolina coast during every month of the year, the Marbled Godwit does not breed here. Having made a good recovery from overhunting during the nineteenth century, the species is a fairly common fall migrant along the coast. Inland sightings are still rare, being mostly single birds found at major reservoirs. Marbled Godwits winter in

Marbled Godwit (in winter plumage)

good numbers around Charleston, S.C., and in the vicinity of Southport and Ocracoke, N.C.

Feeding habits: Marbled Godwits feed in groups, walking in shallow water and probing the mud for invertebrates.

Description: Predominantly brown, the Marbled Godwit is mottled above and barred below in breeding plumage. Nonbreeding birds have buffy underparts. Its extremely long bill is two-toned, light colored at the base and dark toward the re-curved tip. In flight the bird shows a dark rump, cinnamon wing linings, and a large cinnamon patch on the trailing edge of the upper wing surface.

Ruddy Turnstone

Ruddy Turnstone
Arenaria interpres
8–10 in. (20–25 cm)

Range: A nonbreeding year-round resident of the Carolina coast, the Ruddy Turnstone is fairly common to common except in summer. It rarely occurs inland. Turnstones are often seen on jetties and around rocks as well as on beaches and mudflats.

Feeding habits: The Ruddy Turnstone has a slender bill that is slightly up-turned at the tip and well adapted for flipping over stones, shells, and other debris in search of mollusks, crustaceans, and other inverte-brates. The bill is also used to dig in sand and to crack mollusk shells with woodpecker-like blows.

Description: Winter birds have gray backs and yellow-orange legs; summer birds, brown backs and red-orange legs. In both seasons a wide, curving breast band gives

the impression that the bird wears a dark vest. Watch for the short, upturned bill. In flight, upperparts present a striking black, white, and brown pattern.

Red Knot
Calidris canutus
10–11 in. (25–28 cm)

Range: Found on beaches and flats along the Carolina coast through-out the year, the Red Knot is fairly common to common during migra-tions, mid-April through May and from June to mid-October; it is uncommon in summer and winter. The species does not breed here and rarely occurs inland.

Feeding habits: The Red Knot's diet includes small mollusks, insects, and crustaceans as well as some vegetable matter. Knots forage from the surface or by probing.

Description: This species is sometimes called "robin snipe" because in breeding plumage it has a rusty head and breast. A stocky, medium-sized sandpiper, the winter knot is gray with a white belly, rump, and wing stripe. The white of the rump

Red Knots (on beach during spring migration)

Sanderlings (a winter flock)

Red Knot (in winter plumage)

bird that runs back and forth on the beach like a mechanical toy, following each retreating wave and retreating before each incoming one. Sanderlings probe in wet sand for tiny invertebrates and snatch those exposed by the washing of the waves.

Description: Gray above and white below in winter, the Sanderling has black legs and bill. Breeding adult males are washed with rufous on the foreparts. Breeding females have dull brownish foreparts. In flight Sanderlings display a wide white wing stripe and a black leading edge on each wing. Watch for the feeding behavior described above.

does not extend up the back as it does on the larger, longer-billed dowitchers.

Sanderling
Calidris alba
7.0–8.5 in. (17–22 cm)

Range: Although the Sanderling is a common to abundant resident of our ocean beaches all year, it is least numerous in summer and does not breed here. Spring and fall migrants occasionally occur inland.
Feeding habits: This is the funny little

Semipalmated Sandpiper
Calidris pusilla
about 6 in. (14–16 cm)

Range: The Semipalmated Sandpiper is a common to abundant spring and fall migrant found on mudflats and beaches of coastal Carolina from early April to early June and from early August through October.

The species is an uncommon migrant inland, more frequently seen in fall than in spring.

Feeding habits: Semipalmated Sandpipers feed mostly on aquatic insects or crustaceans obtained by snatching or probing.

Description: Five very small "peep" sandpipers occur in our region. They are the Semipalmated, Western, Least, White-rumped, and Baird's Sandpipers. They are often seen in large mixed flocks. Separation of peep sandpipers in the field requires reference to field guides, and even then accurate identification of some individuals may be impossible.

Semipalmateds have black legs and a relatively short straight black bill. **Westerns** have black legs and a relatively long bill that droops toward the tip. **Leasts** have a dark bill and yellow legs. **White-rumpeds** have a white rump (if the bird will let you see it); nonbreeding adults have a pronounced white line (supercilium) extending from the forehead above the eye to the nape; and folded wings extend beyond tip of tail. Look for the small reddish area on the base of its lower mandible; if visible, it is diagnostic. **Baird's Sandpipers** have black legs, a thin straight bill, and folded wings that extend well beyond the tip of the tail. Baird's are generally slender and less robust birds than the White-rumped.

Bill length, leg color, and wing length are variable characteristics that may be misleading in individual birds. When in doubt, just call them "peeps."

Western Sandpiper

Western Sandpiper
Calidris mauri
5.75–7.0 in. (14.5–17.5 cm)

Range: Despite its name, this bird occurs regularly on the East Coast. Found along the Carolina coast throughout the year, the Western Sandpiper does not breed here. Common to abundant in fall migration, the species is much less common in spring. Western Sandpipers winter in good numbers from Charleston southward, and they are fairly common northward. Inland transients are rare, occurring mainly in the fall. Those birds may visit temporary rainwater puddles along with Least Sandpipers.

Feeding habits: Western and Semipalmated Sandpipers feed together on both freshwater and saltwater mudflats along the coast.

Description: See Semipalmated Sandpiper. Western and Semipalmated Sandpipers are so similar in appearance that even experts often call them "peeps."

Red-necked Stint
Calidris ruficollis
6.25 in. (16.0 cm)

Little Stint
Calidris minuta
6 in. (15 cm)

Range: Both of these Eurasian species are rare postbreeding vagrants to the Atlantic Coast of North America. A Red-necked Stint was reported from the Savannah Spoil Site in Jasper County, S.C., in August 2000 and accepted as a provisional species by the South Carolina Bird Records Committee. An adult Little Stint in worn breeding plumage was seen and photographed while feeding on a mudflat at the margin of the tidal pond at Cape Hatteras, July 22–25, 1989.

Feeding habits: Similar to those of other small sandpipers.

Description: Intermediate in size between Least and Western Sandpipers, both stints have black bills similar to those of our native "peep" sandpipers as well as black legs and feet. The Red-necked Stint in breeding plumage has a rusty cheek and throat, the latter bordered below by a wide necklace of dark spots on its otherwise white underparts. The Little Stint has a rusty cheek, a white throat, and white underparts except for a speckled breast washed with rusty orange.

Least Sandpiper
Calidris minutilla
5.0–6.25 in. (12.5–17.0 cm)

Range: Least Sandpipers occur in the Carolinas every month of the year, but they do not breed here. They are very common in May and from August through October, when large flocks are likely to be seen along the coast in company with flocks of the larger shorebirds. Least Sandpipers are generally uncommon in midwinter. Inland the species is an uncommon to fairly common spring and fall transient. It may be attracted to temporary rainwater puddles.

Feeding habits: When feeding on coastal mudflats with other peep sandpipers, Leasts feed close to the marsh grasses and frequent the muddy channels that wind through the grass.

Description: See Semipalmated Sandpiper.

White-rumped Sandpiper
Calidris fuscicollis
7–8 in. (17.5–20.0 cm)

Range: The White-rumped Sandpiper is an uncommon but regular transient along the coast and a rare one inland. Occurring from late April to mid-October (rarely to mid-November), the species prefers freshwater mudflats, particularly around impoundments.

Least Sandpiper

White-rumped Sandpiper

Feeding habits: The White-rumped Sandpiper may pick animal matter from the surface or probe for it in mud that is exposed or covered by very shallow water. When probing, this species tends to insert the bill very deeply and rapidly several times in one spot, then run forward and repeat the action.

Description: See Semipalmated Sandpiper.

Baird's Sandpiper
Calidris bairdii
7.0–7.5 in. (17.5–19.0 cm)

Range: Formerly considered a very rare spring and rare fall migrant along the Carolina coast and very rarely reported inland in fall, Baird's Sandpiper, though certainly not common, has undergone a change in status. In 1988 numerous reports of one or two birds began coming from all parts of the Carolinas, inland even to the mountains. Whether the change actually reflects an increase in the total population of the species or merely an increase in observer effort cannot be determined. Certainly completion of several new reservoirs in piedmont North Carolina stimulated fieldwork in that area, and there are now numerous reports of birds seen at sod farms, spoil sites, and wastewater treatment plants. Whatever the cause, Baird's Sandpiper now appears to be an uncommon but regular and sometimes fairly common (but never numerous) fall migrant in the inland portions of the Carolinas as well as along the coast between July 10 and November 24 (latest date mid-December). Spring sightings remain very rare in late April and early May (extremes late March and early June).

Feeding habits: Although sometimes found on shores and mudflats, Baird's Sandpipers seem to prefer slightly boggy short-grass habitats. The birds snatch up insects, spiders, and small aquatic invertebrates.

Description: The nondescript Baird's Sandpiper is probably the most difficult peep to identify. It closely resembles the Semipalmated Sandpiper. By comparison, Baird's in the first fall has a much more scaly effect (caused by light feather edgings) in the pattern of the mantle. The buffy or sandy area streaked with dark not only spans the breast but also extends up the sides of the neck and into the cheeks. The bill is slender (not short and stout). The preceding characters plus the dark rump and wings extending well beyond the tip of the tail should help separate most individuals from the rest of the peep sandpipers.

Pectoral Sandpiper

Pectoral Sandpiper
Calidris melanotos
8.0–9.5 in. (20–24 cm)

Range: Along the Carolina coast the Pectoral Sandpiper is a fairly common spring and fall transient, late March to early May and mid-July through October, and a very rare winter visitor. Inland occurrences are uncommon in spring and fairly common in fall. Hunters call this species "grass snipe" because of its fondness for boggy places and the similarity of its flight to that of the Common Snipe. Pectoral Sandpipers are seldom seen near salt water, preferring grassy areas and freshwater impoundments when along the coast.

Feeding habits: Pectorals eat a wide variety of animal matter, but insects predominate.

Description: The Pectoral Sandpiper has a white belly, dark breast and upperparts, dark bill, and greenish legs. A sharp line where the streaking of the breast meets the white of the other underparts is a good field mark. Snipe-like flight and absence of a wing stripe should be noted.

Sharp-tailed Sandpiper
Calidris acuminata
8.5 in. (22.0 cm)

Range: One Sharp-tailed Sandpiper, which nests in Siberia, was seen at a sod farm in Orangeburg County, S.C., July 24–30, 1994. This very rare visitor was an adult just molting out of its breeding plumage. It was in company with Pectoral Sandpipers. Very similar to Pectorals in behavior and appearance, juvenile and breeding adult Sharp-taileds have a rusty cap and a distinct white line above the eye. The breast and sides of the breeding adult are heavily marked with dark spots that become chevrons on the flanks.

Purple Sandpiper
Calidris maritima
8–10 in. (20–25 cm)

Range: From October through April watch for the Purple Sandpiper along the Carolina coast wherever rock jetties are splashed by salt water. First recorded in the Carolinas in 1929, this species is now a regular winter resident, with a few stragglers lingering until the end of May. However, it is seldom numerous and is almost entirely restricted to the jetties scattered along the coastline. The largest winter populations in the Carolinas appear to be at Murrells Inlet and Charleston Harbor in South Carolina and at Masonboro Inlet, Wrightsville Beach, N.C. Birds in the Charleston area apparently roost at high tide on Sullivans Island, where as many as 80 have been counted in late February.

Feeding habits: The Purple Sandpiper

Purple Sandpiper

Dunlin (adult in breeding plumage)

feeds on the various invertebrates that live in the crevices of intertidal rocks or among plants growing on such rocks.

Description: This small, dark gray sandpiper has yellow legs and a thin bill that is yellow at the base and dark at the tip.

Dunlin
Calidris alpina
8–9 in. (20–22 cm)

Range: The Dunlin is an abundant winter resident along the Carolina coast from late August to late May. More than 5,000 have been counted at the Savannah Spoil Site in Jasper County, S.C., in late November, and two stragglers were there as late as June 13, 2002. The Dunlin is a regular migrant inland in fall, with a few lingering around major reservoirs into late December. Small numbers occur inland in spring, those being mostly single birds. On the coast Dunlins frequent tidal mudflats, oyster banks, and beaches, often in flocks of several hundred.

Feeding habits: Food is almost entirely

Dunlin (in nonbreeding plumage)

animal matter obtained by snatching or probing.

Description: Winter birds are mostly gray with black legs and a long black bill that droops near the tip. Summer birds are gray with a reddish-brown back and a black belly patch.

Curlew Sandpiper
Calidris ferruginea
7–9 in. (17.5–22.5 cm)

Range: This Old World species is a rare but regular spring and fall migrant on the Carolina coast, more numerous in fall (mostly early July to October) than in spring (early April to early June). Almost never seen in the United States in winter, a Curlew Sandpiper was found on Portsmouth Island in northeast Carteret County, N.C., on the very late date of January 22, 1993. The banded bird had been there since July.

Feeding habits: General habits are similar to those of the Dunlin, its frequent associate and look-alike in winter plumage.

Description: Birds in breeding plumage are rusty brown above and below with a white eye ring, a white rump, and a dark bill that is long and decurved. Birds in that plumage are most likely to be seen in our area in May and July. Gray birds, juveniles and nonbreeding adults, are noticeable in mixed flocks with Dunlins by their longer wings, longer neck, longer legs, and prominent white rump. Dunlins have white on each side of the tail, but the central tail feathers are dark all the way to the back.

Stilt Sandpiper
Calidris himantopus
7.5–9.25 in. (19–23 cm)

Range: The Stilt Sandpiper is far more numerous in the Carolinas now than it was 25 years ago. Though still generally uncommon as a spring migrant along the coast and inland to the mountains, it is now a fairly common fall migrant

Stilt Sandpiper

that is more numerous on the coast than inland. Most of the spring passage is from early April to late May (extremes February 29 and June 5). Fall dates are mostly from mid-July to mid-November with stragglers through December. The hot spot for Stilt Sandpipers in the Carolinas is the Savannah Spoil Site in Jasper County, S.C. Beginning with the winter of 1995–1996, that place became the northernmost known wintering site for Stilt Sandpipers on the East Coast. At times, several hundred Stilt Sandpipers are present in spring and fall.

Feeding habits: This very deliberate feeder takes a wide variety of small animal matter by snatching and probing. Stilt Sandpipers have been seen swinging the immersed bill from side to side in shallow water, a strategy also used on occasions by yellowlegs.

Description: This is a tall, slender sandpiper with long, greenish legs and a long, slender, dark bill. Summer birds are brown and adorned with a distinctive rusty cheek patch. Winter birds are gray. The clear white rump and the dark upper wing surface are good field marks for birds in flight. The dowitcher is a larger, chunkier bird with white on its back and white on the trailing edge of its wing.

Buff-breasted Sandpiper
Tryngites subruficollis
7–9 in. (17–22 cm)

Range: The Buff-breasted Sandpiper nests in northern Alaska and Canada, near the shore of the Beaufort Sea. The birds migrate through the Great Plains to winter south of the United States. Migrants blown off course may find themselves almost anywhere in the contiguous United States, including all sections of the Carolinas. By 1980 small flocks were being found along the Carolina coast almost annually between July and early November, most frequently in September. Since then, inland reports have become more frequent, but occurrences still fall within the same time period. The only spring record remains a bird taken in South Carolina on May 5, 1844. Many inland reports are from sod farms, spoil sites, and wastewater treatment plants; however, the bird reported from Transylvania County was in a temporary rain pond.
Feeding habits: These remarkably tame birds feed in short grass and other sparse vegetation. A flock feeding amid glasswort (salicornia sp.) on a dry flat on Pea Island remained in the same area for an entire weekend even though they were stalked repeatedly by crowds of curious bird-watchers.
Description: This is our only sandpiper with buffy underparts, pale yellow

Buff-breasted Sandpiper

legs, whitish eye ring, dark bill, and predominantly white wing linings. When flushed, it flies like a snipe, swiftly and erratically.

Ruff
Philomachus pugnax
10.0–12.5 in. (25–31 cm)

Range: This rare visitor from Eurasia was first recorded in the Carolinas when a Reeve, the female of the species, was collected in Wake County, N.C., on May 6, 1892. The second sighting did not occur until 1959. The first known occurrence in South Carolina took place in 1961. In recent years Ruffs have been seen almost annually, mostly along the coast but occasionally inland around major reservoirs, shallow impoundments, and spoil sites. Occurrences are rare in spring (April and May) and very uncommon in fall (mostly mid-July to early September). Fall stragglers linger very rarely into December, once until January 4 at an impoundment in the Mattamuskeet National Wildlife Refuge.
Feeding habits: Ruffs probe for invertebrates in grassy or marshy places.

Description: Similar to a Lesser Yellow-legs, the Ruff has browner plumage and dull yellowish legs. In flight, the Ruff flashes oval white patches on each side at the base of the tail. The species gets its name from the male's enormous nuptial neck plumes that are raised during mock combats on the breeding grounds.

Short-billed Dowitcher
Limnodromus griseus
10–11 in. (25–28 cm)

Range: Although the Short-billed Dowitcher occurs in coastal Carolina throughout the year, it does not breed here. The species is abundant during spring and fall migration but is only fairly common in winter, often being scarce or locally absent in South Carolina. Singles and small flocks of migrants occur regularly inland, even rarely in the mountains. Inland sightings are mostly around major reservoirs and at wastewater treatment plants in May or between mid-July and mid-October.

Feeding habits: The Short-billed Dowitcher eats insects, marine worms, mollusks, and small crustaceans.

Description: Mostly brown in summer and mostly gray in winter, dowitchers have long, greenish-yellow legs and a heavy, long, black bill. The tail is white barred with black, and the white of the rump extends into a triangular white patch that comes to a point about halfway up the bird's back. Short-billed and Long-billed Dowitchers are more easily separated by voice than by appearance. The Short-billed's call is a low and mellow rapid whistle, *too-too* or *too-too-too*. The Long-billed's is

Dowitchers in winter (see Short-billed Dowitcher description)

a single thin *keet* or a series of the same. While feeding, dowitchers often wade belly-deep in water and immerse the long bill full-length with mechanical regularity.

Long-billed Dowitcher
Limnodromus scolopaceus
10.0–12.5 in. (25–31 cm)

Range: The Long-billed Dowitcher is a regular but uncommon fall migrant along the Carolina coast and a rare winter resident and spring migrant. Southbound birds of this species pass our way mostly from mid-September through January, an unusually late time of year for a shorebird. By comparison, the Short-billed Dowitcher's fall migration reaches its peak in July and August. The Long-billed Dowitcher is seldom seen on saltwater mudflats, but it frequents shallow fresh and brackish ponds and mudflats, especially in the Bodie–Pea Island area, where it winters. It also winters around Lake Mattamuskeet, where it sometimes visits flooded fields; in the Wilmington-Southport area; and in South Carolina at the Yawkey Wildlife Management Area in Georgetown County and at the Santee National Wildlife Refuge on Lake Marion. Long-billeds may linger at wintering sites until the end of May or, very rarely, into June. The species is extremely rare as a transient in the piedmont and mountains.

Feeding habits: The Long-billed's feeding habits are similar to those of the Short-billed, but with insects constituting a greater proportion of the diet.

Description: See Short-billed Dowitcher for a comparative description.

Common Snipe

Common Snipe
Gallinago gallinago
10–12 in. (25–30 cm)

Range: The Common Snipe is a winter resident throughout the Carolinas, being uncommon in the mountains and becoming common toward the coast. From late August into May, snipe frequent open areas such as meadows, bogs, grassy fields, and the edges of marshes, ponds, and streams.

Feeding habits: Snipe eat earthworms, cutworms, grasshoppers, and other insects.

Description: Like the American Woodcock, the Common Snipe has a very long bill, is protectively colored, and will remain motionless until it flushes almost under foot. Once flushed, it takes off in a swift, erratic, twisting flight, flashing a russet tail and giving a characteristic explosive *scaipe* note. Although the snipe and woodcock have similar silhouettes, the snipe has comparatively long yellowish legs and mostly white underparts. Its streaked back and russet tail separate the snipe from the dowitchers.

American Woodcock
Scolopax minor
10–12 in. (25–30 cm)

Range: The American Woodcock is a fairly common permanent resident throughout the Carolinas, being more numerous in the coastal plain during the winter months than in summer. It is the only member of the sandpiper group that lives in damp woods as well as the only one that is predominantly crepuscular and nocturnal in habits.

Nesting habits: Following a series of *peent* calls that sound much like a Bronx cheer, the male woodcock makes a spectacular courtship flight. After rising from an opening in the woods to a height of perhaps 300 feet (90 m), twittering all the

American Woodcock

namon-brown plumage is marked above with black, brown, and gray, giving the impression of dead leaves dappled with sunlight.

The woodcock will remain motionless on the woodland floor until the intruder almost steps on it, at the last moment bursting into flight with the wings making a peculiar whistling noise. Dodging behind trees, it soon drops to the ground, once more becoming virtually invisible among the fallen leaves. The American Woodcock is a highly prized game bird both in the field and on the dinner table.

Subfamily Phalaropodinae: Phalaropes

Wintering phalaropes are mostly pelagic birds that rarely visit coastal or inland sites in the Carolinas. An exception is the Wilson's Phalarope, which sometimes visits small ponds. Phalaropes are noted for the way they spin on the surface of the water while feeding.

Wilson's Phalarope
Phalaropus tricolor
8–10 in. (20–25 cm)

Range: Wilson's Phalaropes normally migrate across the western United States, but a few singles and small flocks visit the Carolinas each spring and fall. They are found sparingly and mostly on or near the coast from late March to mid-June (peak in latter half of May) and from early July through September, very rarely in October, November, or early December. The species occurs regularly each fall on ponds in the Bodie–Pea Island area of North

way, he then zigzags downward, uttering a series of descending bell-like notes accompanied by some twittering. Returning to the same small plot of ground, he almost immediately begins calling again. The performance may be repeated many times in a single night, most often in the hour following sunset or the one preceding dawn, but on occasions throughout the night, particularly when the moon is full.

Courtship may begin in January, followed by nesting as early as February. The four buffy eggs are splotched with brown. The nest is an unconcealed, leaf-lined depression in the ground in low, wet woods. The female incubates the eggs 20 to 21 days and cares for the precocial young.

Feeding habits: The American Woodcock's extremely long bill has an upper mandible that is flexible near the tip and remarkably well adapted for probing in soft mud for earthworms and other invertebrates.

Description: This long-billed, stocky bird offers an outstanding example of protective coloration. The cin-

Wilson's Phalarope

Red-necked Phalarope (in winter plumage)

Carolina and at the Savannah Spoil Site in Jasper County, S.C. Inland the species is rare, but it is becoming less so in the vicinity of major reservoirs and wastewater treatment plants. In late May the movement tends to be mostly across the South Carolina coast and inland portions of North Carolina.

Feeding habits: A somewhat terrestrial freshwater species, the Wilson's Phalarope may forage on wet or dry land and wade into water, even submerging the head and neck to feed below the surface. It also spins on the surface like other phalaropes. Its diet includes insects, crustaceans, and seeds of marsh plants.

Description: This phalarope's very thin, straight bill is much longer than its head. Winter birds are gray above and white below. Summer birds are brownish above with a bold stripe running down the side of the neck. In flight, this species can be separated from our other phalaropes by the white rump and the absence of a wing stripe. Breeding females are more colorful than males. Toes are lobed.

**Red-necked Phalarope
(Northern Phalarope)**
Phalaropus lobatus
7–8 in. (17–20 cm)

Range: Although Red-necked Phalaropes are common spring and fall migrants over the ocean well off the Carolina coast, they rarely visit our coastline, probably doing so only as a result of storms. The species is most likely to be seen from early May to early June (rarely mid-April to mid-June) and from mid-August to mid-October (rarely late July to late December). The species is being found with increasing frequency inland to the mountains where major reservoirs, rivers, spoil sites, sod farms, and wastewater treatment plants provide suitable feeding sites.

Feeding habits: In fresh water Red-necked Phalaropes eat insect larvae more than anything else. At sea they feed on tiny invertebrates that eat plankton. Phalaropes spin on the surface of water to stir up food.

Description: The Red-necked Phalarope is dark above and white below with a thin, black bill noticeably shorter than that of Wilson's Phalarope. Summer birds have golden brown streaks on the back, a white throat, and a rusty neck. Toes are lobed.

Red Phalarope
Phalaropus fulicarius
8–9 in. (20–22 cm)

Range: Each spring and fall, large numbers of Red Phalaropes pass the Carolina coast well offshore, usually from mid-March to mid-May and from mid-August to early December. Storm-blown birds are sometimes found on beaches and very rarely as far inland as the Great Smoky Mountains. Reports of large flocks of Red Phalaropes offshore in late December and late January, plus reports of smaller numbers from February and early March, indicate that this species remains off the Carolina coast all winter.
Feeding habits: Feeding habits of the Red Phalarope are similar to those of the Red-necked Phalarope.
Description: The adult breeding Red Phalarope is our only phalarope with a yellow bill; winter adults and all immatures have dark bills. The female breeding adult is more brightly rufous colored than the male. Winter adults are mostly gray above and white below with a heavy black line through the eye.

Family LARIDAE:
Gulls and Allies

In addition to the familiar gulls and terns, the Laridae include two groups of seabirds that visit Carolina offshore waters regularly but are rarely seen from shore: the jaegers and skuas, and the alcids. The best-known alcids are the puffins, which are famous for their large and colorful bills.

Subfamily Stercorariinae:
Skuas and Jaegers

Skuas and jaegers are dark, gull-like birds with elongated central tail feathers, sharply curved claws, and bills hooked at the tip. They are birds of the ocean and rarely come ashore except at their Arctic and Antarctic breeding grounds. They habitually raid nests of other species and rob other birds of their fishy prey.

Great Skua
Stercorarius skua
20–23 in. (51–58 cm)

Range: An uncommon winter visitor to North Carolina offshore waters, the Great Skua is most likely to be seen from early January to early March, but it has been found from early December to early April. A Great Skua banded on the nesting grounds in Iceland was found dead at Cape Lookout in December 1975, its year of hatching.
Feeding habits: See comments on subfamily.
Description: Skuas look like dark, short-tailed, immature Herring Gulls with a dark cap, very slightly elongated central tail feathers, and prominent white patches on each wing at the base of the primaries. Separating the different species by age class and color phase from the deck of a small boat is always difficult and often impossible. Reference to a guide to seabird identification is recommended.

South Polar Skua

Stercorarius maccormicki

21 in. (53 cm)

Range: An uncommon warm-weather
visitor to Carolina offshore waters,
the South Polar Skua nests in Antarctica and visits the northern part
of the western Atlantic Ocean after
the breeding season. The species
is most likely to be found off the
Carolinas from late May to mid-
August, but it has been recorded
from mid-May to late November.
Inland sightings have occurred at
Lake Waccamaw, N.C., and in South
Carolina at Lake Murray on September 23, 1989, following the passage
of Hurricane Hugo.

Feeding habits: See comments on
subfamily.

Description: Similar to the Great Skua,
the South Polar Skua is slightly
smaller and lacks the dark cap.
Reference to a guide to seabird
identification is recommended.

Pomarine Jaeger

Stercorarius pomarinus

20–23 in. (51–58 cm)

Range: The Pomarine Jaeger occurs off
the Carolina coast throughout the
year, becoming scarce at midwinter
and midsummer. Although it is
generally uncommon, the species
is seen regularly in fall and early
winter from shore along the Outer
Banks and occasionally elsewhere
along the coast. Tropical storms
often drive Pomarine Jaegers onshore and well inland, and there are
a few inland sightings not directly
associated with storms.

Feeding habits: See comments on
subfamily.

Description: Jaegers are easy to recog-

Pomarine Jaeger (adult in flight)

Pomarine Jaeger
(immature on beach in fall)

nize (see comments on subfamily)
but hard to identify by species.
The Pomarine is the largest of our
jaegers and the one most often
seen in our region. The scarcity of
published records can be attributed
to the great difficulty of identifying
immature birds and molting adults.
Consult guides to identification of
seabirds for details on plumages of
the various species of jaegers, their
color phases, and age classes.

Parasitic Jaeger
Stercorarius parasiticus
15–21 in. (38–51 cm)

Range: The Parasitic Jaeger is found off the Carolina coast every month of the year, but sightings are most frequent from mid-May to mid-June and from mid-September to early December. The spring peak is in late May, and the fall peak is in October. The species occurs inland very rarely during migration. Because Parasitic Jaegers frequent inshore waters, they are the jaeger species most likely to be seen from shore, over sounds and inlets, and actually standing on the beach. They are also most likely to be swept inland by tropical storms.
Feeding habits: See comments on subfamily.
Description: See Pomarine Jaeger.

Long-tailed Jaeger
Stercorarius longicaudus
20–23 in. (51–58 cm)

Range: Found in Carolina waters from mid-April to mid-December, the Long-tailed Jaeger is most frequently seen in the region from mid-May to mid-June and from mid-September to mid-October. Onshore sightings occur mostly in May. However, one adult appeared at Stumpy Point on the Dare County mainland August 31, 1995, and remained until September 2, flying over marsh, pocosin, and highway. Boaters on Lake Norman, north of Charlotte, N.C., watched as a Long-tailed Jaeger spiraled upward and disappeared toward the south on September 9, 1998. Neither inland occurrence was related to an unusual weather event.

Long-tailed Jaeger

Feeding habits: See comments on subfamily.
Description: Adults wearing the extremely long central tail feathers are unmistakable. Those two plumes may account for 6 to 10 inches (15 to 25 cm) of the total length of the bird. Immatures and molting adults are easily confused with other jaeger species. See Pomarine Jaeger.

Subfamily Larinae: Gulls

Gulls are heavy-bodied birds with webbed toes, long pointed wings, and a stout bill that is hooked at the tip. They eat small fish, assorted mollusks and crustaceans, and other animal matter. Large gulls tend to be scavengers, and at times thousands may be seen at garbage dumps, landfills, or docks for fishing boats. Adults generally have white bodies and predominantly gray or black mantles (back and upper wing surfaces). Immature gulls are brownish, and in some large species they do not acquire adult plumage until several years old. Gulls build substantial nests, usually on the ground, and their downy chicks are precocial. At feeding time the adults regurgitate partly digested food on the ground, and the young help themselves.

Laughing Gull
Larus atricilla
15–17 in. (38–43 cm)

Range: The Laughing Gull is the only common black-headed gull in the Carolinas. It is a permanent resident in coastal and tidewater Carolina, abundant in summer and uncommon to locally absent in midwinter. Inland sightings (other than those related to hurricanes and tropical storms) occur at lakes and are rare, but they are increasing in frequency and in the number of birds involved.

Nesting habits: Laughing Gulls nest in colonies, and several hundred nests may be found on a single small, grassy, coastal island. Partly or completely concealed, the substantial nests of seaweeds, grasses, and sedges are raised a little off the sand or mud on grassy islands or high marshes that may be partially covered with shallow water at high tide. Eggs usually number three and are dark olive, splotched and scrawled with black. Laid in May or early June, they require about 20 days for incubation. Both sexes incubate eggs and care for the precocial downy chicks, which remain in the nest only a few days.

Feeding habits: See comments on subfamily. Laughing Gulls regularly follow our coastal ferries, competing for handouts of food tossed into the air by passengers. These gulls also eat various animal foods plucked from the surface of ground or water.

Laughing Gull (in flight, summer plumage)

Laughing Gull (winter plumage)

Description: The adult Laughing Gull has a white body and tail, a dark mantle with a white border on the trailing edge of the wing, and dark feet and bill; its black head molts to become mostly white in winter. See a field guide for illustrations of the immature plumages. The name of the species is derived from its call, which sounds like high-pitched, cackling laughter.

Franklin's Gull
Larus pipixcan
13.5–15.5 in. (34–39 cm)

Range: A bird of the prairies, Franklin's Gull rarely occurs east of the Appalachian Mountains. A specimen was collected on the Catawba River in North Carolina, just above the state line, in October 1952. On May 8, 1975, one was found following a tractor in a field near Townville, Anderson County, S.C. Single birds were seen at Huntington Beach State Park on September 26, 1976, and at Lake Greenwood on April 2, 1978. In November 1988 there was an unprecedented eastward movement of Franklin's Gulls that brought singles to Figure Eight Island and Henderson County, N.C., and to the Savannah Spoil Site in Jasper County, S.C., plus a flock of 10 birds to Lake Robinson in Darlington County, S.C. Since the 1988 invasion, Franklin's Gulls have appeared somewhere in North Carolina almost annually. The species is still rare in the Carolinas, but it may be more numerous than the published reports indicate. Similarity of Franklin's Gull to the Laughing Gull may cause the Franklin's to be overlooked by bird students who are not aware that the species sometimes occurs in the Carolinas.

Feeding habits: This gull eats insects more than anything else. It often follows the plow and is adept at catching insects in flight.

Description: Although similar to the adult Laughing Gull, the adult Franklin's in flight has a white band separating the gray wing from the black wing tip. In first-winter birds, the Franklin's black band at the tip of the tail does not extend all the way to the edge of the tail, leaving small white outer corners. Differences in head patterns are subtle and require use of a well-illustrated field guide.

Little Gull
Larus minutus
11 in. (28 cm)

Range: A Eurasian species that breeds erratically in Canada from the Great Lakes to Hudson Bay, the Little Gull was first confirmed as occurring in North Carolina waters in December 1971. Since then, the species has become a regular winter visitor along the coast, where it is locally fairly common inshore along the Outer Banks among the huge flocks of Bonaparte's Gulls that are present mostly in February and March. Inland sightings are rare. In South Carolina small numbers have been reported from December to April, including several sightings of single birds at the Savannah Spoil Site in Jasper County. The species has been seen three times inland at Jordan Lake, twice in February and once in March.

Feeding habits: Less a scavenger than the larger gulls, the Little Gull takes insects, small fish, and other small aquatic animals.

Description: Watch for the small size, rounded wings, and ternlike flight of the Little Gull. The adult has a gray mantle and a black underwing. Its head is black in summer but mostly white in winter. Consult a field guide for the immature and winter plumages.

*Black-headed Gull
(in nonbreeding plumage)*

*Bonaparte's Gull (on water in
adult nonbreeding plumage)*

Black-headed Gull
Larus ridibundus
14–15 in. (35–38 cm)

Range: A rare transient and winter
visitor, this Eurasian gull has been
found on or near the Carolina coast
between early August and late
April. Inland sites include Jordan
Lake, Lake Mattamuskeet, the ferry
landing at Aurora, N.C., and the Savannah Spoil Site in Jasper County,
S.C. The bird seems to favor spoil
sites, shallow impoundments, tidal
pools, and wastewater treatment
plants near the coast. Winter birds
in the Carolinas may associate with
Bonaparte's Gulls.
Feeding habits: See comments on
subfamily.
Description: Similar in general appearance to the Bonaparte's Gull,
the adult Black-headed is a slightly
larger bird with a larger, dark red
bill and with primaries that are
dark underneath. In breeding plumage the head is very dark brown.
Birds seen in the Carolinas in April
usually are in breeding plumage.
Consult field guides for further
information.

*Bonaparte's Gull (immature,
nonbreeding plumage)*

Bonaparte's Gull
Larus philadelphia
12–14 in. (30–35 cm)

Range: Basically a somewhat erratic
winter resident along the Carolina
coast from late August to mid-May,
the Bonaparte's Gull is generally
fairly common to common but
occasionally abundant for short
periods. This species visits large
inland lakes mostly from November
through early May but becomes
scarce in midwinter.
Feeding habits: Although the Bona-

parte's Gull eats much insect matter, it also takes small fish, crustaceans, and other small aquatic animals. It often plucks food from the surface of the water while on the wing.

Description: Similar to the Laughing Gull, Bonaparte's has a large, white, triangular patch extending from the bend of the wing toward the tip. The white of the primaries is visible underneath as well as from above. See a field guide for illustrations of the differences between Bonaparte's and the rarely seen Black-headed Gull.

Black-tailed Gull
Larus crassirostris
18.5 in. (47.0 cm)

Range: An adult in winter plumage was seen at Pea Island, N.C., on December 28, 2001, providing the first and so far only record of this East Asian/Pacific species in the Carolinas. Only recently has the Black-tailed Gull been found elsewhere on the East Coast, notably at the Chesapeake Bay Bridge-Tunnel.
Feeding habits: See comments on subfamily.
Description: Approximately the size of a Ring-billed Gull, the Black-tailed is not easily separated from that common species in the field. A black tail, white rump, dark mantle, and all-black wing tips suggest a Black-tailed Gull, but all gulls with black tips on the tail are not Black-tailed Gulls. Reference to a well-illustrated field guide is necessary for proper identification of a suspected Black-tailed Gull.

Mew Gull
(Common Gull)
Larus canus
16 in. (41 cm)

Range: Two populations of the Mew Gull occur on the East Coast of North America as far south as Cape Hatteras, N.C. *Larus c. brachyrhynchus*, which breeds in Alaska and western Canada, appears to be the form very rarely found on the East Coast. A first-winter bird was seen on the Ocracoke side of Hatteras Inlet on December 27, 1983. The form more likely to be seen on the East Coast is *L. c. canus*, the Common Gull of Europe and Asia. There are several reports of the Common Gull from Cape Hatteras and vicinity between December 27 and February 19.
Feeding habits: See comments on subfamily.
Description: Intermediate in size between the Laughing Gull and the Ring-billed Gull, *Larus c. canus* is often described as a "Ring-billed Gull without the ring." This form is extraordinarily variable in plumage characteristics. Reference to a well-illustrated field guide is necessary for proper identification of the two subspecies.

Ring-billed Gull
Larus delawarensis
18–20 in. (45–51 cm)

Range: An extremely abundant winter resident of coastal and tidewater Carolina, the Ring-billed Gull is found inland more frequently and in larger numbers than are our other gulls. A few can be found occasionally even in the mountains. Sometimes they visit large parking

Ring-billed Gull (adult in winter)

California Gull
Larus californicus
21 in. (53 cm)

Range: A bird of western North America, the California Gull is accidental in the eastern United States. First recorded in North Carolina at a landfill near Newport in Carteret County on January 29, 1983, the species has become a regular winter visitor at Cape Hatteras. Several different individuals may be identified in the vicinity of Oregon Inlet and Cape Hatteras Point during a winter season. One was reported at a landfill near Raleigh, N.C., in January 2005. California Gulls usually arrive in November or December and depart before the end of March. A complete surprise was an adult in the vicinity of Lockwood Folly Inlet at Holden Beach on August 4, 2002. The early date suggests the bird had spent the summer in the Carolinas.

Feeding habits: See comments on subfamily.

Description: The nonbreeding adult California Gull looks like a small Herring Gull with a dark tip on its bill and yellow or greenish-yellow legs. The species is highly variable. Reference to a well-illustrated field guide is necessary for proper identification.

Slaty-backed Gull
Larus shistisagus
25 in. (64 cm)

Range: The first, and so far only, report of the Slaty-backed Gull in the Carolinas is of one seen at Cape Hatteras, N.C., on February 15, 2003. About the size of a Herring Gull, this very rare wanderer from Siberia closely resembles the Western

lots, where they may perch on light fixtures, causing sensors to turn on lights in daytime. The species is present along the coast all year, but it is not known to breed in the Carolinas.

Feeding habits: In the coastal plain Ring-billed Gulls often feed on waste grain and hunt insects behind farm tractors. They visit large reservoirs in the piedmont, and flocks of several thousand may gather at a landfill. Otherwise their feeding habits are like those of the other gulls.

Description: The adult Ring-billed is a white gull with a gray mantle and black wing tips; it has yellow legs and a yellow bill with a dark band encircling it near the tip. The immature is mottled with gray and has pinkish legs and a dark-tipped, flesh-colored bill; its tail is white with a black band bordered by a narrow white tip.

Gull and some members of the Vega (Siberian) population of the Herring Gull.

Herring Gull
Larus argentatus
22–26 in. (56–66 cm)

Range: A permanent resident of coastal and tidewater Carolina, the Herring Gull is abundant except during summer. It was first discovered nesting in North Carolina's Pamlico Sound in 1962. The species now breeds, often in close association with Laughing Gulls, at several sites from Oregon Inlet to Cape Lookout. Two nests with eggs on Portsmouth Island in late June 1983 and large flightless young there in late July represent the first known nesting on a barrier island in North Carolina. In winter, Herring Gulls are generally uncommon to rare inland in the Carolinas unless there is a major fish kill at a lake.

Herring Gull (adult)

Herring Gull (immature)

Nesting habits: Although in other parts of the country Herring Gulls sometimes build nests in trees, the North Carolina nests have been well-cupped mounds of grass and other vegetation placed directly on the ground. Eggs number two or three and are highly variable with ground colors ranging from blue to gray to light brown and with specks, blotches, and streaks of brown, black, and lilac. Incubation varies from 24 to 28 days, chicks are precocial, and both adults incubate eggs and care for young. The species is single-brooded.
Feeding habits: See comments on subfamily.
Description: The adult Herring Gull is white with a gray mantle and black

wing tips; it has pink legs and a yellow bill with a red spot on the lower mandible. Immatures are brownish and have no white band on the tip of the tail.

Yellow-legged Gull
Larus cachinnans
24–25 in. (61–64 cm)

Range: Formerly considered a race of the Herring Gull, the Yellow-legged Gull breeds around the Mediterranean Sea and east into Turkey and the Caucuses. The species is a very rare visitor to the East Coast of North America. One was present at

Cape Hatteras Point from December 30, 1994, through March 13, 1995, at which time photographs were obtained.

Feeding habits: See comments on subfamily.

Description: Almost impossible to distinguish reliably from the Herring Gull in the field, the nonbreeding adult Yellow-legged Gull strongly resembles the nonbreeding adult Herring Gull except for the yellow legs and the larger, "squarer"-looking head with a heavy, blunt-tipped, bright yellow bill. Breeding adults have a red orbital ring and a red gape. Excellent optical equipment, well-illustrated field guides, and lots of experience watching gulls are essential for anyone hoping to identify a Yellow-legged Gull that might stray into the Carolinas.

Thayer's Gull
Larus thayeri
23 in. (55 cm)

Range: First reported in Dare County, N.C., on October 26, 1971, Thayer's Gulls normally winter in waters along the Pacific Coast of North America. A few are reported from the East Coast every winter, including two or three from the Cape Hatteras area. Very rarely one appears inland at a landfill. Thayer's Gulls generally arrive in early December and linger until mid-March.

Feeding habits: See comments on subfamily.

Description: Formerly considered a race of the Herring Gull, Thayer's Gull has a brown iris, a medium gray mantle, and flesh-pink legs and feet. The Herring Gull has a yellow iris, but it also has pinkish legs. Anyone hoping to identify a Thayer's Gull needs to have excellent optical equipment, the best-illustrated field guides that are available, and an abundance of patience.

Iceland Gull
Larus glaucoides
23–25 in. (58–63 cm)

Range: As its name implies, the Iceland Gull breeds in the far north, but in winter it may wander all the way to southern Florida. It is a rare but regular visitor along the Carolina coast, particularly in the vicinity of landfills, sometimes arriving as early as mid-October and lingering into early May. Most sightings are from December through February. Iceland Gulls are very rarely found inland.

Feeding habits: See comments on subfamily.

Description: Most of the Iceland Gulls found in the Carolinas are immatures, which are difficult to distinguish from the immatures of the similar but slightly larger Glaucous Gull. Only reference to well-illustrated field guides can clarify the differences between the two species.

Lesser Black-backed Gull
Larus fuscus
21–22 in. (53–56 cm)

Range: This Eurasian species is a regular but uncommon winter visitor on the Carolina coast south to Huntington Beach State Park in Georgetown County, S.C., and rarely as far south as Otter Island in Colleton County. Landfills in Craven, Carteret, and Horry Counties seem

*Lesser Black-backed Gull
(in winter plumage)*

Glaucous Gull (first-winter bird)

to be popular feeding sites. A few birds visit some large reservoirs and landfills in piedmont North Carolina annually. Lesser Black-backed Gulls may be expected from late August to April. Summer stragglers have been found occasionally since 1993, but there is no suggestion of breeding in the Carolinas.

Feeding habits: See comments on subfamily.

Description: Slightly smaller than a Herring Gull, the Lesser Black-backed is almost identical to the Great Black-backed except for size, grayer mantle, mottled head, and leg color, which is yellow instead of pink.

Glaucous Gull
Larus hyperboreus
26–32 in. (66–81 cm)

Range: The Glaucous Gull is a rare winter visitor along the entire Carolina coast, but individuals are most likely to be seen along the Outer Banks. A few Glaucous Gulls occur occasionally at landfills and major reservoirs in the piedmont. Birds are present somewhat erratically from early September to late May, but mostly from October through March.

Feeding habits: See comments on subfamily.

Description: The adult Glaucous Gull is larger than a Herring Gull and nearly all white. Its feet are pinkish, and its bill is yellow with a red spot on the lower mandible. Second-winter Glaucous is similar, but the bill is flesh-colored with a dark tip. First-winter Glaucous is mottled with gray and has a dark-tipped, flesh-colored bill. Iceland Gulls are similar but are generally smaller than a Herring Gull and have a relatively small head and bill. First-winter Iceland has a completely dark bill. The relative length of the tail and the folded wings is not a reliable field mark. Some individuals apparently cannot be identified accurately in the field.

Great Black-backed Gull
Larus marinus
28–31 in. (71–78 cm)

Range: The Great Black-backed Gull is an abundant winter resident in the vicinity of Oregon Inlet. Southward along the Carolina coast it becomes a fairly common to uncommon winter visitor. It also occurs regularly in tidewater North Carolina in winter and is increasing as a winter visitor around landfills, wastewater treatment plants, and major reservoirs in the upper coastal plain and piedmont. In summer the Great Black-backed Gull is found mostly in the Pamlico Sound area, where it nests among Herring Gulls on islands of dredged material. The southernmost documented nesting site in eastern North America is near Cape Lookout.

Nesting habits: Great Black-backed Gulls build bulky, well-cupped nests of dry grasses placed directly on the sand. The two or three pale olive-buff eggs are blotched with dark brown and black. Incubation takes about 26 days. Although the precocial downy gull chicks may stay in or near the nest for a day or two, they are soon able to run about. Both parents incubate eggs and care for the young, sheltering chicks from the hot sun until they are well feathered and feeding them until they are old enough to fly.

Feeding habits: See comments on subfamily.

Description: Adults are white with a black mantle, a yellow bill, and pale pink legs. Immature Great Black-backed Gulls are separated from young Herring and Ring-billed

Great Black-backed Gull (adult)

Gulls by their large size, whitish head, and completely black bill.

Sabine's Gull
Xema sabini
13.5 in. (34.0 cm)

Range: First sighted in the Carolinas from the beach north of Oregon Inlet, N.C., on May 27, 1972, Sabine's Gull has been found south along the coast to Charleston harbor and the Savannah Spoil Site in Jasper County, S.C. It has occurred inland in North Carolina to Lake Norman and Salem Lake in Forsyth County. Most sightings, however, have been offshore. Sabine's Gull is a rare transient along the East Coast in late spring and early fall when it normally migrates along the Pacific Coast between the Arctic breeding grounds and a wintering territory south of the equator. Known spring occurrences in the Carolinas are between March 10 and May 31 (peak in May). Fall reports are from mid-July to early November (peak in September).

Feeding habits: Sabine's Gull eats

Sabine's Gull

Black-legged Kittiwake (adult; note the sharply defined, solid black wing tip)

small fish and other suitable animal matter.

Description: The adult Sabine's Gull has a black bill tipped with yellow, a dark head in summer, a white body, a white tail that is slightly forked, and a mantle boldly marked with triangular patches of black, white, and gray. The immature is similar; but its forked tail has a black band at the tip, and its bill is completely dark.

Black-legged Kittiwake
Rissa tridactyla
16–18 in. (40–45 cm)

Range: A bird of the open seas, the Black-legged Kittiwake occurs mostly out of sight of land, but occasionally it visits beaches, inlets, and harbors in the Carolinas. First recorded off Cape Hatteras in February 1940, the species is now known as a regular, though never abundant, winter visitor along the Carolina coast from October through March. The species has been found rarely as early as August 29 (Hunting Island State Park, S.C.) and as late as May 30 (Oregon Inlet).

Black-legged Kittiwake (immature in flight)

Feeding habits: Less a scavenger than the larger gulls, the kittiwake snatches small fish, crustaceans, and other animal matter from the surface of the sea.

Description: The adult Black-legged Kittiwake has a white body; a gray mantle with sharply defined, solid black wing tips; a yellow bill; and black feet and legs. Immatures have a somewhat mottled mantle that creates a bold M pattern in flight, a black bill, a black band across the back of the neck, and a black tip on the very slightly forked tail.

Subfamily Sterninae: Terns

More slender and graceful in flight than gulls, terns have webbed toes, a pointed bill, long narrow wings, and a forked tail. They feed by diving from the air upon insects and small fishes. Migrants and storm-driven terns occur far inland, but sightings of terns in the piedmont of the Carolinas in winter are much less common.

Tern nests are usually simple depressions in the sand, but sometimes they are lined with shells or grasses. Both parents incubate eggs and care for the precocial young. They also shelter eggs and chicks from the hot sun. Adult terns feed the offspring by poking fish into their gullets. Terns, like gulls, are colonial nesters.

Gull-billed Tern (at nest)

Gull-billed Tern
Sterna nilotica
13–15 in. (33–38 cm)

Range: An uncommon to fairly common summer resident along the Carolina coast, the Gull-billed Tern is usually present from mid-April to September. One seen at Huntington Beach State Park on February 13, 1999, set a record early date for the Carolinas. Inland occurrences are accidental. First found breeding in South Carolina on Cape Island in May 1929 and in North Carolina on Ocracoke Island in June 1933, the species is approaching the northern limit of its breeding range on the East Coast when it nests in northeastern North Carolina. Gull-billed Terns have never been abundant in the Carolinas. There has been a noticeable decline in the Carolinas since 1990. However, a count of 110 at an impoundment in Carteret County, N.C., on July 28, 2002, and juveniles seen in August 2004 are encouraging signs.

Nesting habits: Laying begins in May, and the two or three brown-spotted, greenish-buff eggs hatch in 22 or 23 days. One brood is raised each season. Small colonies of Gull-billed Terns are usually associated with those of Common Terns or Black Skimmers. The Gull-billed colony at Cape Romain is unusually large, numbering about 700 pairs in some seasons.

Feeding habits: Gull-billed Terns feed extensively over marshes and consume numerous insects as well as vertebrates such as small lizards. Occasionally Gull-billeds are seen feeding over soybean or corn fields near the edge of Pamlico Sound or following a tractor near the Pamlico River in Beaufort County, N.C.

Description: This predominantly white tern has a slightly forked tail and a very thick black bill. Unlike most of our other terns, the Gull-billed molts scattered feathers throughout its crown, giving it a salt-and-pepper gray look in winter. Most other tern species found in the Carolinas molt gradually from bill to nape, creating a "receding hairline" effect. The adult Caspian Tern is also salt-and-pepper gray-headed in winter, but not at all likely to be confused with the much smaller Gull-billed.

Caspian Tern
Sterna caspia
19–23 in. (48–58 cm)

Range: Fairly common along the Carolina coast from mid-April to late May and from August to early November, the Caspian Tern winters regularly in South Carolina and southeastern North Carolina. Stragglers may be found farther north along the North Carolina coast until early January. Inland to the mountains, the species occurs as a spring and fall transient, usually around large lakes in late April or early May and from August through September. Apparently, inland migrants are going to and from major breeding sites around the Great Lakes and in central Canada. Small numbers of Caspian Terns occur in Carolina coastal waters in summer, and a few nests can be found almost every summer at Oregon Inlet, Hatteras inlet, and Cape Romain. The small, disjunct breeding population in the Carolinas does not even rate a dot on the range maps in popular field guides, but a few nests have been found here almost annually for more than 30 years.

Nesting habits: The 1970 Cape Island, S.C., nest contained two eggs and was situated in a colony with Black Skimmers and Gull-billed Terns. The nest was an unlined depression in the sand, and the incubation

Caspian Tern (adult beginning to lose black cap)

period was apparently no less than 28 days. (In some regions the Caspian Tern builds a fairly elaborate nest, and the incubation period is reported as being only 20 days.) In North Carolina, Caspian Terns nest on bare or nearly bare sandy domes of islands created by dredging operations. Scrapes lined with small shell fragments, the nests contain one or two eggs or chicks. Breeding pairs in North Carolina may associate with colonies of Black Skimmers, Common Terns, or Royal Terns.

Feeding habits: See comments on subfamily.

Description: See Royal Tern.

Royal Tern
Sterna maxima
18–21 in. (45–53 cm)

Range: The Royal Tern is a permanent resident of coastal and tidewater Carolina, abundant most of the year but only fairly common from late December to late March. Inland sightings are rare and often associated with passage of a hurricane.

Nesting habits: The nesting season starts in May, but if eggs are destroyed by high tides, the birds will lay a second, third, or rarely a fourth time. Sometimes several thousand pairs of Royal Terns breed in a single colony on a small sandy island. Nests may be placed so close together that the distance between centers is only 12 to 14 inches (30 to 35 cm). Each scrape usually contains a single egg, although clutches of two or three eggs do occur. Incubation requires 3 to 4 weeks, which means that any Royal Terns nesting on low sandflats must lay eggs within a week after lunar high tide in order to hatch successfully before the passing of a lunar month. Soon after hatching, the precocial young flock together near the nesting site but a safe distance from the bills of adults still incubating eggs. The number of nests in South Carolina has declined since 1990, apparently because of erosion at traditional nesting sites. In North Carolina the species appears to be holding its own.

Feeding habits: See comments on subfamily.

Colony of Royal Terns with downy young

Description: The Royal Tern has a shaggy black crest. Note the orange bill, white forehead, and well-forked tail. The similar Caspian Tern is a larger bird with a blood-red bill, darker wings, and a slightly forked tail. Royals have a black cap extending all the way to the bill only for a short time during the nesting season, but Caspians have some dark feathers on the forehead even in winter.

Sandwich Tern
Sterna sandvicensis
14–16 in. (35–40 cm)

Range: A fairly common but very local summer resident of coastal Carolina, the Sandwich Tern is usually present from April to October. Stragglers occur until late December, and on very rare occasions a few linger throughout the winter. Oregon Inlet appears to be the northernmost area along the Atlantic Coast where this mostly subtropical species breeds in appreciable numbers.

Nesting habits: Sandwich Terns nest in colonies with Royal Terns. In early June they lay one to three

Royal Tern (adult in flight, beginning to lose black cap)

Sandwich Terns (at nesting site)

slightly smaller eggs in scrapes that tend to be clustered among those of the larger and more abundant Royals. Incubation requires about 21 days, and the species is single-brooded. Young Sandwich Terns normally have a dull, slightly orange bill that quickly becomes black with a pale yellow tip upon fledging. However, rare juveniles may have a completely yellow bill; one at Cape Hatteras had a bright yellow bill and yellow legs as well. Such birds should not be confused with the "Cayenne Tern," a South American counterpart of our Sandwich Tern, which may have a yellow bill as well as yellow legs and feet. That South American Sandwich Terns might visit North Carolina is entirely possible. A Sandwich Tern banded at Cape Lookout on June 23, 1978, was found dead six months later in the Netherlands.

Feeding habits: See comments on subfamily. Sandwich Terns tend to feed offshore.

Description: Similar to the Royal Tern but smaller, the Sandwich is our only tern with black legs and feet and a yellow-tipped black bill.

Roseate Tern
Sterna dougallii
13–17 in. (33–43 cm)

Range: Mostly a rare coastal transient from late March to mid-May and from late July to October, the Roseate Tern is accidental in June and July. It became known as a breeding species in North Carolina in the summer of 1973 when one pair nested near Core Banks in Carteret County. The presence of Roseate Terns in summer and observations of courtship behavior indicate additional local nesting can be anticipated. The species nests both north (New York to Nova Scotia) and south (Florida) of the Carolinas.

Nesting habits: See comments on subfamily.

Feeding habits: See comments on subfamily.

Description: The summer adult has a thin black bill, a black cap on a rounded head, a light gray mantle, and a very long and very deeply forked tail that is completely white and extends well beyond the tip of the folded wings. Underparts of breeding birds are lightly washed with pink. Legs are short compared with those of our other terns of similar size.

Common Tern
Sterna hirundo
13–16 in. (33–40 cm)

Range: Common Terns can be found somewhere along the Carolina coast during all seasons of the year. They are common to abundant during migrations, but they tend to be uncommon or locally absent during the breeding season and in winter. In fact, winter occurrences can be

Common Tern (in flight)

Common Tern (adult at nesting site)

open or sparsely vegetated sand or sand/shell beaches. Common Terns usually nest in association with other species, such as Black Skimmers and Gull-billed Terns. The two or three blotched eggs are laid in a depression in the sand that may have a lining of shell fragments or dry grass. Incubation requires about 23 to 26 days. Common Terns are single-brooded.

Feeding habits: See comments on subfamily.

Description: In summer the adult Common Tern has a black cap, a bright red-orange bill that is more or less dusky at the tip, a deeply forked tail that is mostly white, and a gray mantle that becomes noticeably darker toward the outer primaries. The tail is usually shorter than the tips of the folded wings. Consult a field guide for identification of immatures and winter adults, all of which have black bills.

Arctic Tern
Sterna paradisaea
14–17 in. (35–43 cm)

Range: The Arctic Tern breeds, as its name implies, in the Arctic region and winters as far south as Antarctica. The southward fall migration of the Arctic Tern is primarily far offshore over the waters of the eastern North Atlantic, and the northward movement is mostly far offshore over the western North Atlantic. Therefore, sightings along the coast and over the offshore waters of the Carolinas are more numerous in spring than in fall; but they are still unusual because the species generally remains far offshore, mostly beyond the range of

expected only in extreme southeastern South Carolina. Common Terns occasionally visit large inland lakes all the way to the mountains, usually in April and May and from July to October. They breed in colonies on small sandy islands in Pamlico Sound and southward along the coast to Charleston, S.C. The central coast of South Carolina appears to be the present southern limit of breeding along the Atlantic Coast of the United States. The future of the Carolina nesting population is uncertain as it is presently undergoing a period of decline.

Nesting habits: Nesting sites are on

one-day boating trips. Nonetheless, following the passage of Hurricane Hugo, an Arctic Tern in breeding plumage came to rest in a parking lot at Shelby, N.C. Spring occurrences are from mid-April through June, with the peak in the latter half of May. Fall sightings are from mid-August to late October, with the single October 24 report being a month later than all other available reports of southbound Arctic Terns found in the region.

Feeding habits: See comments on subfamily. Arctic Terns are capable of hovering and plunging in the manner of a Least Tern.

Description: The Arctic is a small-headed, long-tailed, long-winged tern with a light gray mantle, white underwing, black cap, and white body except in the breeding adult, which has a gray body. The outer web of the outermost tail feather is dark gray. The bill is short, thin, and sharply pointed; it is black except in the breeding adult, which has a blood-red bill. Because virtually all Arctic Terns seen along the Atlantic Coast of the United States are in transitional plumage (e.g., red bill, white body, white forehead), the most important field marks are on the wing. In all plumages, the primaries are narrowly tipped with black on the trailing edge of the wing. The translucence of the primaries may or may not be apparent, depending on light conditions. In flight the bird may appear to have a black V narrowly edging the tip of each wing. A standing Arctic Tern has reddish-orange feet and very short legs.

Forster's Tern (in winter plumage)

Forster's Tern
Sterna forsteri
14–15 in. (35–38 cm)

Range: Forster's Tern is a common winter resident along the Carolina coast. Inland, the species visits large lakes all the way to the mountains in spring and fall, and a few occur in winter on some large lakes in South Carolina. The species breeds fairly commonly in Pamlico and Core Sounds in northeastern North Carolina, and since 1987 Forster's Terns have been nesting in the Bulls Bay area of South Carolina, apparently the southernmost breeding site in the southeastern United States.

Nesting habits: In the Carolinas, the birds lay their two to four well-speckled eggs on drifts of vegetation in salt marshes or on isolated low sandy islands. The incubation period is 23 days, and the young remain in the nest a few days. The species is single-brooded.

Feeding habits: See comments on subfamily.

Description: Although similar to the Common Tern, Forster's has more white in the primaries, and its deeply forked tail is mostly pale gray, lacking the dark outer webs found on that of the Common. Calls are much like those of the Common Tern, but lower-pitched and with a more wooden or rasping quality.

Least Tern
Sterna antillarum
8.50–9.25 in. (21–24 cm)

Least Tern (adult on nest)

Range: Once nearly extirpated by plume hunters, the Least Tern is now a fairly common summer resident along the Carolina coast from April to October and rarely into early November. Least Terns winter from Central America southward.

In the eastern United States, the species traditionally nested near the oceanfront. Forced from much of that habitat by development and recreational activities, the birds have adapted by also nesting around inland lakes in the coastal plain and lower piedmont of South Carolina, on bare islands of dredged material, and on flat rooftops covered with pea-gravel at New Bern and Wilmington, N.C., and in South Carolina at Myrtle Beach, Charleston, and Shaw Air Force Base in Sumter County. The base is about 85 miles (136 km) from the coast. Rooftop nesting and protection of coastal nesting sites may enable the Least Tern to maintain its breeding population in the Carolinas in spite of heavy development in the coastal region. However, there is concern that changes in design and construction practices may eliminate the use of gravel on flat roofs.

Nesting habits: Least Terns usually begin nesting in May. Two or three eggs are laid in a scrape on a beach, a shell bank, a sand bank formed by channel dredging, or with increasing frequency the flat, gravel-topped roofs of large buildings. The eggshells are so mottled and splotched that they are almost invisible among the pebbles, debris, or fragments of seashells around the nesting site. Incubation requires about 3 weeks, and the young can fly when about 24 days old. Second broods may be attempted in the southern part of the species' range, but one is the usual number in the Carolinas. Least Tern nests are often destroyed by adverse weather conditions, sometimes resulting in several nesting attempts in a single season.

Feeding habits: See comments on subfamily. Least Terns can hover on wings that flutter much like those of a butterfly and plunge-dive on prey in shallow water.

Description: Noticeably smaller than our other terns, the Least has a mostly yellow bill during the nesting season and a white forehead.

Bridled Tern
Sterna anaethetus
14–15 in. (35–38 cm)

Range: The Bridled Tern has been recorded in the Carolinas from mid-April to mid-October, plus once on January 18. The species is a fairly common summer visitor offshore from late June to late September. Commonly associated with a well-developed drift line, Bridled Terns, like other pelagic terns, often rest on floating wooden crates and boards.

Feeding habits: See comments on subfamily.

Description: Similar to the Sooty Tern, the Bridled has a dark gray mantle and tail. Note the light collar across the back of the neck.

Sooty Tern
Sterna fuscata
15–17 in. (38–43 cm)

Range: Storm-blown Sooty Terns may appear anywhere in the Carolinas at any season, but most of the records are coastal and concentrated in the period from early May through September, when this pantropical species is an apparently uncommon but regular summer visitor offshore. Almost every summer a few Sooty Terns can be found at one or more of the various Common Tern and Black Skimmer colonies from Charleston County, S.C., north to Cape Hatteras, N.C. A few of those birds attempt to nest, and one was seen brooding a Black Skimmer chick.

Nesting habits: Adults may arrive at the colony site as early as late April. The nest is a depression in the sand, and a single egg is laid, perhaps as

Sooty Tern (in flight)

early as May 30. Hatchling chicks were seen at Cape Hatteras in July 1993, the first record of young Sooty Terns in North Carolina. A day-old chick had previously been found dead on July 15, 1988, at Cape Romain, S.C. There is no evidence that a chick has been reared successfully anywhere in the Carolinas.

Feeding habits: The Sooty Tern snatches fish from the surface of the water without diving.

Description: Black above and white below, the Sooty Tern has a black bill, a white forehead above the black eye line, and a deeply forked black tail that is narrowly edged with white on each side. The immature is mottled dark brown and has a moderately deep fork in the tail.

White-winged Tern
Chlidonias leucopterus
9.5 in. (24.0 cm)

Range: A casual visitor to the Great Lakes region and a rare vagrant on the Atlantic Coast of the United States, the White-winged Tern is a Eurasian species. It has been reported from the pond at Bodie Island Lighthouse, Dare County,

N.C., on August 13, 1994, and from the Savannah Spoil Site in Jasper County, S.C., on November 15, 2000.

Feeding habits: See comments on subfamily. Instead of plunge-diving, White-winged Terns prefer to pluck their food from the surface of the water.

Description: The White-winged Tern is so similar to the Black Tern that reference to a well-illustrated field guide is necessary for identification.

Black Tern (during fall migration)

Black Tern
Chlidonias niger
9–10 in. (22–25 cm)

Range: Black Terns nest in the inland portions of the northern United States and southern Canada. The birds migrate in spring and fall over the eastern United States and near-shore waters of the western Atlantic Ocean. Spring migrants pass through the Carolinas mostly along the coast in May and early June. Inland migrants are fairly common in fall, mostly from late July through August, occasionally to early September. Fall migrants pass through the Carolinas mostly as single birds or in small flocks and may visit large inland lakes. It is very easy not to notice them.

Feeding habits: Instead of plunge-diving, Black Terns prefer to hawk insects on the wing or pluck food from the surface of the water.

Description: The breeding adult is a handsome bird. Almost completely dark above and below, it has a slightly forked gray tail and a light gray underwing surface. Immatures and winter adults are mostly gray with variable amounts of black and white. The nonbreeding adult re-

tains black on the crown and a spot behind the eye; the immature has a mostly gray crown and a black spot behind the eye.

Brown Noddy
Anous stolidus
12–16 in. (33–40 cm)

Range: A very rare accidental, the pantropical Brown Noddy is seldom seen in Carolina offshore waters except during or immediately after hurricanes. Occurring from late May to mid-October, the species has been recorded along the Carolina coast from Hilton Head Island north to an area off Oregon Inlet. Tropical storms and hurricanes may drive noddies onshore and even inland as far as Lake Norman, north of Charlotte, N.C.

Feeding habits: This highly pelagic tern feeds without diving.

Description: The Brown Noddy has dark wings and body, a white forehead below a pale gray cap that blends into a darker gray hind neck, and a dark, wedge-shaped tail. Immature birds have little or no white on the head.

Subfamily Rynchopinae:
Skimmers

Skimmers have bills that are laterally compressed into knife-like blades. The upper mandible, being short and having a single cutting edge, fits snugly into a groove in the double-edged lower mandible. Their habit of feeding on a rising tide, whether by night or by day, has given skimmers the nickname "flood gull."

Black Skimmer
Rynchops niger
16–20 in. (40–51 cm)

Black Skimmer (at nest)

Black Skimmer (feeding in flight)

Range: Permanent residents of coastal Carolina, Black Skimmers are common to locally abundant in summer, and they remain fairly common in winter north to Cape Lookout. Although the species normally occurs only along the coast, storm-blown birds are occasionally found inland. Rarely, skimmers feed over freshwater impoundments and flooded fields in the coastal plain during winter.

Nesting habits: Skimmers nest on remote coastal islands or beaches, laying clutches of three to five eggs in bare scrapes in the sand during June or July. The creamy eggs are blotched and scrawled with dark brown. Although single-brooded, the females will lay again if clutches are destroyed by high tides, storms, or predators. Renesting sometimes leads to an erratic and prolonged nesting season. Incubation requires 21 to 23 days. Adults will feign injury if the nest is disturbed. Precocial chicks are covered with buffy down and have mandibles of equal length. When newly hatched, they will scratch a hole in the sand and freeze at the approach of danger, remaining motionless even if picked up; but very soon they can outrun the curious naturalist. There is no apparent explanation for the fact that the number of skimmers nesting in the Carolinas has declined in recent years.

Feeding habits: Skimmers feed by flying along just above the water with the tip of the lower mandible shearing the surface. When a shrimp or small fish strikes the bill, the upper mandible snaps shut. Then the bird can carry its prey to the nestlings or simply flip it out of the water and swallow it while still skimming the shallows. Black Skimmers feed mostly when the water is calm in early evening and at night. Their nocturnal habits often startle people taking moonlight strolls along the beach.

Description: Strikingly black above and white below, the Black Skimmer has a long orange bill that is tipped with black, and its lower mandible is longer than the upper (see comments on subfamily).

Dovekie

Family ALCIDAE:
Auks, Murres, and Puffins

Alcids are the northern counterpart of the Antarctic penguins. Web-footed, heavy-bodied, short-winged, and awkward on land, alcids nevertheless are strong fliers as well as excellent swimmers and divers. They use their wings for "flying" underwater in active pursuit of small fish and crustaceans. Alcids have increased dramatically in the Carolinas during the past 20 years, both in the number of individuals seen and in the diversity of species found.

The extinct Great Auk (*Pinguinus impennis*), last positively recorded alive in 1844, reportedly wintered in the Atlantic Ocean as far south as South Carolina. Although it was flightless, the Great Auk, unlike penguins, had well-developed flight feathers.

Dovekie
Alle alle
7–9 in. (17–22 cm)

Range: Offshore winter visitors along the Carolina coast from late October through February, Dovekies may be fairly common some years and

go unreported in others. If a storm coincides with a major southward movement, Dovekies may be found surprisingly far inland, as was the case in December 1950 when they occurred inland to Raleigh, N.C. Following a good winter influx, as in January–February 1996, there may be onshore sightings and stragglers into spring. That year a Dovekie in breeding plumage was at Cape Hatteras Point on the extraordinary date of May 27.

Feeding habits: See comments on family. Dovekies feed on shrimp, crabs, and other small crustaceans, which they pursue and catch below the surface of the water.

Description: This small alcid is mostly black above and white below. It has a stubby bill and several short white streaks on its black back.

Common Murre
Uria aalge
17.5 in. (44.5 cm)

Range: There are only two reports of the Common Murre from the Carolinas. One in nonbreeding plumage was seen at Huntington Beach State Park, S.C., on January 17,

1995. Another in the same plumage was photographed in the surf at Cape Hatteras Point February 2 and 3, 2001. One was seen at Huntington Beach State Park by several different observers between December 30, 2004, and January 29, 2005.

Feeding habits: See comments on family.

Description: Distinguishing this species from the very similar Thick-billed Murre requires reference to field guides illustrating both species.

Thick-billed Murre
Uria lomvia
18 in. (46 cm)

Range: A rare winter visitor, the Thick-billed Murre is most likely to be found offshore from December to February or, very rarely, until late March. Most sightings are of single birds, but small flocks have been seen.

Feeding habits: See comments on family.

Description: Distinguishing this species from the very similar Common Murre requires reference to field guides illustrating both species.

Thick-billed Murre

Razorbill
Alca torda
15–18 in. (38–45 cm)

Range: Prior to 1994, the Razorbill was known only as a rare to very rare winter visitor on the Carolina coast. In early February 1994 local fishermen reported 2,000 to 3,000 Razorbills offshore, and a record onshore count of 1,184 was made on February 14. Smaller numbers were reported south of the Outer Banks, and two were at Cape Lookout as late as March 27. A new maximum count of more than 9,000 was made at Cape Hatteras Point February 15, 2004. The Razorbill is now considered a winter resident off the Outer Banks from early November to mid-March. Numbers diminish southward, but a few can be expected in the Huntington Beach–Murrells Inlet area almost annually.

Feeding habits: See comments on family.

Description: Our only alcid with an extremely thick, black bill, the adult Razorbill in breeding plumage has a white line extending from the eye forward to the bill and curving downward across it. Winter adults may show just a white vertical line near the tip of the bill. In flight the Razorbill shows a sharply pointed black tail and narrow white feather tips on the trailing edge of the wing near the body.

Black Guillemot
Cepphus grylle
12–14 in. (30–35 cm)

Range: Black Guillemots normally winter in the northwestern Atlantic

Ocean, but they occur casually south to New Jersey. They rarely visit the Carolinas. A sickly bird of this species was seen at the mouth of Charleston Harbor on September 21, 1958. An apparently healthy Black Guillemot was about 500 feet (150 m) offshore from Huntington Beach State Park, S.C., on April 17, 1975. A juvenile appeared at the park on November 27, 1992, and was photographed there on December 4. It remained in the Murrells Inlet area for most of the winter, feeding along the rock jetty in company with a Thick-billed Murre. A guillemot changing from first-winter to breeding plumage visited a jetty at Wrightsville Beach, N.C., April 24 to 30, 1993. On January 29, 1994, a guillemot was again seen with murres in the ocean off Litchfield Beach, S.C. After nearly 10 years with no additional reports of guillemots in the Carolinas, one was found at Kill Devil Hills, N.C., on February 15, 2003.

Feeding habits: See comments on family.

Description: The adult Black Guillemot is the only Atlantic alcid with a large white wing patch. Juveniles of the Atlantic population are heavily barred with black and white on the back and inner portion of the upper wing surface.

Long-billed Murrelet
Brachyramphus perdix
10 in. (25 cm)

Range: A rare visitor from Siberia, the Long-billed Murrelet has been found in the Carolinas three times. One was photographed November 19, 1994, near the jetties at Huntington Beach State Park, S.C. Another was found at Jordan Lake, Chatham County, N.C., on December 9, 1994. The third sighting for the Carolinas was made at Fort Macon, N.C., on December 15, 2002.

Feeding habits: See comments on family.

Description: Separating the Long-billed Murrelet from the very similar Marbled Murrelet, formerly considered a separate race of the same species, requires use of a well-illustrated field guide.

Atlantic Puffin
Fratercula arctica
12.5 in. (32.0 cm)

Range: The Atlantic Puffin reaches its southwestern limit of breeding in northeastern Canada. It is regular in winter offshore to southeastern Virginia, and it is rarely found offshore as far south as the Outer Banks of North Carolina in February and March. The largest number recorded on a single date was 31 on February 19, 2005. A major surprise was one in breeding plumage seen in the Gulf Stream off Oregon Inlet on August 14, 1993. An injured bird found at Topsail Island, N.C., on March 28, 2005, died during surgery to repair a broken humerus and became the first specimen for the state.

Feeding habits: See comments on family. Unlike most other alcids, which seldom fly more than 5 feet (1.5 m) above water, puffins may fly up to a height of 30 feet (9 m).

Description: Adult puffins are distinctive because of the large face patch (white in breeding plumage and gray in nonbreeding) and the large, laterally compressed, triangular bill. In the Atlantic Puffin, the base of the bill is dark slaty blue, and the tip is orange.

Order COLUMBIFORMES: Pigeons and Allies

All members of this order are land birds with thick, heavy plumage consisting of feathers that are loosely attached in the skin. All eat vegetable matter and feed their young by regurgitating cells sloughed from tissue lining the large crop. Sandgrouse and pigeons are said to be the only birds in the world that can immerse the bill in water and drink without having to raise the head to swallow.

Family COLUMBIDAE:
Pigeons and Doves

Doves and pigeons are small-headed, swift-flying birds that bob their heads while walking. During incubation the lining of the adult's crop thickens. The tissue sloughs off into a cheesy curd that is regurgitated to provide the first food for the nestlings. Pigeons' milk has about the same food value as mammals' milk. Later the young poke their beaks into the throats of the parents to obtain regurgitated semidigested grain.

Rock Pigeon
Columba livia
about 11 in. (28 cm)

Range: Formerly known as the "Rock Dove" or "Domestic Pigeon," this introduced species has become thoroughly naturalized in all but the most remote regions of the Carolinas. Pigeons avoid woodlands and are most numerous in urban habitats. Much to their surprise, some bird-watchers saw a Rock Pigeon offshore from Hatteras on August 23, 1997.

Young pigeons (squab) are a table delicacy, and historically pigeons have served as message carriers and ornamental birds for parks.

Nesting habits: Rock Pigeon nests are crude platforms of twigs and straws placed in the eaves and crannies of large buildings wherever caves and cliffs are not available. Pigeons in urban habitats may nest throughout the year in the Carolinas, and two or more broods are raised annually. Reproduction is generally limited by the food supply. The two white eggs hatch in about 17 days. Both sexes incubate, the male usually by day and the female by night. Altricial young pigeons and doves are brooded and fed by both parents until ready to leave the nest when 2 or 3 weeks old. See comments on family for further information on feeding of young.

Feeding habits: See comments on order.

Description: Rock Pigeons may be gray, brown, or pure white, often mottled or touched with iridescence. The white rump readily separates Rock Pigeons from all other doves and pigeons found in the Carolinas.

Band-tailed Pigeon
Patagioenas fasciata
14.5 in. (37.0 cm)

Range: A bird of the western United States and Mexico east to the Rio Grand River valley in western Texas, the Band-tailed Pigeon is accidental in the Carolinas. One was seen near Devil's Courthouse on the Blue

Ridge Parkway on June 10, 1980, and two were heard in the same vicinity June 16, 2001. In addition, one was reported near Sumter, S.C., in 1980, and one frequented a chinaberry thicket in Georgetown, S.C., in August 1991. One seen in a Charlotte neighborhood in February 1994 stayed until spring.

Feeding habits: See comments on family.

Description: Our largest pigeon, this lanky, long-tailed bird might easily be mistaken for a small hawk. In all plumages, the species has a broad gray band across the tip of the tail. Its voice is a deep, owl-like hooting.

Eurasian Collared-Dove
Streptopelia decaocto
13 in. (33 cm)

Range: Two species in the genus *Streptopelia* have been introduced in eastern North America, and the Eurasian Collared-Dove has spread rapidly north along the coast from Florida into the Carolinas. By the summer of 2000 there were signs of colonies inland to Goldsboro, Wayne County, N.C., and the Conover area of Catawba County, N.C. Copulation by a pair was observed in a parking lot in Brevard, N.C., in the spring of 2004. The similar Ringed Turtle-Dove (*S. risoria*), an escaped cage bird, is not yet known to have established a breeding population in the southeastern United States.

Nesting habits: Believed to be similar to those of the Rock Pigeon.

Feeding habits: See comments on family.

Description: The very pale gray Eurasian Collared-Dove has a black

Eurasian Collared-Dove

band across the back of its neck. It can be distinguished from its even paler look-alike, the Ringed Turtle-Dove by the color of the undertail coverts, gray in the Eurasian and white in the Ringed.

White-winged Dove
Zenaida asiatica
11.0–12.5 in. (28–31 cm)

Range: Mostly a rare winter visitor from Mexico and the southwestern United States, the White-winged Dove is more likely to occur along the Carolina coast than inland, but transients may be found inland to the mountains. A few of these doves may linger into spring or summer as far inland as the vicinity of Columbia, S.C., where a flock of six was seen on June 6, 1998. The first documented nesting in the Carolinas occurred at Beaufort, Carteret County, N.C., in the spring of 1999. There is no proof of an established wild population in the Carolinas, although at least one White-winged Dove remained in Beaufort in the spring of 2002.

Nesting habits: At Beaufort, N.C., a

White-winged Dove

Mourning Dove

fully feathered, preflight young bird was found on June 12, 1998. Two adults were seen at a nest containing one nestling on July 5. Copulation occurred as late as July 21, suggesting the possibility of as many as three broods in a single nesting season.

Feeding habits: See comments on family.

Description: About the size of a Mourning Dove, the White-winged has a tail that is not pointed but is tipped with white except on the central rectrices. In flight, each upper surface of the wing is broadly marked with a curved band of white coverts sharply contrasting with very dark flight feathers. When the bird is perched, the white of the wing shows as a crescent along the side of the bird extending from the bend of the wing toward the rump.

Mourning Dove

Zenaida macroura

11–13 in. (28–33 cm)

Range: An abundant permanent resident throughout the Carolinas,

the Mourning Dove is valuable not only as a game bird but also as a consumer of weed seeds. It occurs in open country habitats such as fields, woodland margins, and suburban neighborhoods, but it is scarce in dense woods.

Nesting habits: Although limited nesting occurs every month of the year in the warmer portions of our region, Mourning Doves normally lay the first of their two or three annual clutches in March. The male gathers nesting materials, and the female does the building. The nest usually is a frail platform of twigs and pine needles built on the ground, in vines or bushes, or on a horizontal limb of a tree 15 to 30 feet (4.5 to 9.0 m) above ground. Sometimes doves take over old robins' nests. Mourning Doves lay two pure white eggs that hatch in 12 to 14 days. Care of young is essentially the same as for Rock Pigeons.

Formation of large autumn and winter flocks makes the Mourning Dove subject to great hunting pressure, but the species seems to have no trouble maintaining its numbers.

Feeding habits: See comments on order.

Description: A buffy gray-brown bird with a small head and a long, pointed tail that is edged in white, the Mourning Dove often perches on roadside wires, where its distinctive silhouette is easily seen.

Common Ground-Dove

Passenger Pigeon
Ectopistes migratorius

Extinct: Once an extremely abundant transient in the mountain and piedmont regions of North Carolina and a winter resident in South Carolina, the Passenger Pigeon was last reliably reported in the two states in 1894 and 1895, respectively. Excessive hunting and habitat destruction are thought to have caused the extinction of the species.

Common Ground-Dove
Columbina passerina
6–7 in. (15–17 cm)

Range: Although the Common Ground-Dove formerly bred along the coast northward to Carteret County, N.C., the species is now only a rare accidental in the piedmont and coastal plain. After extirpation of the small breeding population in southeastern North Carolina, Horry County, S.C., became the northernmost site of nesting by the Common Ground-Dove on the Atlantic Coast. The species may still occur very locally inland to Anderson, Kershaw, and Chesterfield Counties in South Carolina, but most of the breeding birds are found in the eastern part of the state.

The population of the species appears to be declining throughout its range. The cause of the decline is often stated as development, and certainly loss of scrub/shrub habitat is a significant factor. However, ground-doves will nest close to houses and visit bird feeders. Predation by feral cats, yard cats, and fire ants along with changes in farming practices, mortality during hurricanes, and incidental shooting by Mourning Dove hunters may be more detrimental to the species than residential and commercial development in the coastal region. The Common Ground-Dove and other ground-nesting species such as the Bobwhite are certainly in need of assistance from wildlife managers.

Nesting habits: Nesting usually begins about mid-April and lasts until fall, with as many as four broods sometimes being raised. The flimsy nests of twigs, grasses, and pine needles may be placed on the ground, on a stump, on a cross-rail of a grape arbor, or in a bush, waxmyrtle being a popular choice. The two white eggs hatch in 12 to 14 days, and care of the young is essentially the same as for other doves.

Feeding habits: See comments on order.

Description: The Common Ground-Dove looks like a House Sparrow–sized Mourning Dove with a short rounded tail and rufous wing patches.

Order PSITTACIFORMES: Parrots and Allies

This distinctive group of colorful and essentially arboreal birds includes many species that are popular as caged birds. Parrots and their allies have large heads and short necks; large, strongly down-curved, hooked bills; and strong, grasping feet with two toes turned forward and two behind. Some species have patches of bare skin around the eyes, and all have sparse plumage with powder-down scattered through it.

The only member of the order native to the Carolinas is the Carolina Parakeet (*Conuropsis carolinensis*), which was last positively found in the region during the mid-1800s. Carolina Parakeets were persecuted by fruit growers and shot for the millinery trade as well as for the collectors of bird skins. Egg collectors also helped push the species into extinction.

In modern times, several species have escaped from captivity and survived for a short time in the wild. Two, the Budgerigar (*Melopsittacus undulatus*) and the Monk Parakeet (*Myiopsitta monachus*), bred successfully in the wild but have not established enduring populations.

Order CUCULIFORMES: Cuckoos and Allies

Cuckoos and their allies are long-tailed birds that have slightly hooked beaks and feet with two toes in front and two behind.

Family CUCULIDAE: Cuckoos, Roadrunners, and Anis

This large family is widespread in the Old World, but only a few species occur in North America. Members characteristically have a long tail that may appear to be loosely attached to the body.

Black-billed Cuckoo

Subfamily Coccyzinae: Cuckoos

Although North American cuckoos are not obligate brood parasites, they are known to engage in that practice from time to time, laying eggs in the nests of other cuckoos or those of birds belonging to other families.

Black-billed Cuckoo
Coccyzus erythropthalmus
11–12 in. (28–30 cm)

Range: The Black-billed Cuckoo is a rare to uncommon summer resident of extensive deciduous woodlands in the North Carolina mountains, mostly in the upper hardwood and transition zones (3,550–4,575 ft. [1,065–1,366 m]). Although the species has bred at least sparingly and erratically in the piedmont and coastal plain of North Carolina, it is primarily a transient in those regions and throughout South Carolina. During the 1990s bird students detected a definite migratory movement

of Black-billed Cuckoos along the Outer Banks in late May.

Nesting habits: The Black-billed Cuckoo is not known to differ significantly from the Yellow-billed in nesting habits. The incubation period is 10 to 11 days.

Feeding habits: The Black-billed Cuckoo is a useful species that consumes numerous insects. On the mainland of Dare County, N.C., the species feeds in stands of loblolly bay (*Gordonia lasianthus*), an evergreen shrub or small tree having leaves that generally show considerable insect damage.

Description: Similar to the Yellow-billed Cuckoo, the Black-billed has a completely black bill and much smaller tail spots. The adult Black-billed has a red eye ring; the imma-ture has a white one. First-spring Yellow-billed Cuckoos hatched from a late clutch may still have an all-dark bill and a dark orbital ring (juvenile traits) well into summer of the next year. Birds still in juvenile plumage have been known to mate and rear young successfully, undergoing the change in bill color and molting into adult plumage during the process. Observers should check the tail pattern before deciding that a dark-billed cuckoo is really a Black-billed Cuckoo.

Yellow-billed Cuckoo
Coccyzus americanus
11–13 in. (28–33 cm)

Range: A fairly common to common summer resident of deciduous woodlands throughout the Carolinas, the Yellow-billed Cuckoo arrives about mid-April and departs about mid-October, with a few stragglers remaining into November or early December.

Nesting habits: During the May to August or September breeding season, cuckoos can be heard calling to each other by day and by night; but after the young are on the wing, the birds are mostly silent. The cuckoo's resonant call is thought by many to foretell the coming of rain, hence the local name "rain crow." There may be some scientific basis for this bit of folklore, because cuckoos apparently adjust the timing of their nesting effort to the temporary abundance of suitable prey, which in many cases coincides with periods of rainfall.

Occasionally, North American cuckoos lay eggs in nests built by members of their own or other species. Such behavior is similar to that of their European relatives, which are notorious brood parasites. Normally, the Yellow-billed Cuckoo builds a shallow nest of twigs that is lined with a few skeletonized

Yellow-billed Cuckoo

dry leaves and adorned with pine needles on the rim. Placed 4 to 20 feet (1.2 to 6.0 m) above ground in a bush or low tree, the nest is built by both adults and may still be under construction when the female lays the first of her two to four greenish-blue eggs. Incubation begins with the laying of the first egg. During the first day or two of incubation, the male may continue to bring twigs and pine needles for the female to add to the nest, and he may rearrange the nest materials while he is incubating.

In one North Carolina nest, single eggs were laid on four successive days, and each egg hatched on the ninth day after laying. The normal incubation period appears to be 9 to 11 days, which is a very short time for a bird the size of a Yellow-billed Cuckoo. Apparently both parents share more or less equally in the care of eggs and young. However, the bird on the nest at the beginning of rainfall normally remains there until the rain ceases.

At hatching, the black-skinned chick is blind and nearly naked. Pinfeathers begin to appear on the second day, and by the fifth day the nestling is covered with long, sheathed quills. On the palate and tongue nestlings have several soft whitish spots (papillae) that enable them to grasp the bill of the adult during feeding. At first they receive semidigested food regurgitated by the adults, but within 24 hours after hatching, they are fed whole caterpillars, butterflies, and katydids; some of the caterpillars are so large that the parent must give them a couple of pokes before the chick can close its beak.

Young cuckoos develop rapidly and are able to stand on the rim of the nest by the third or fourth day. Parents swallow or carry away fecal sacs until the chicks begin expelling feces over the side of the nest when about 6 days old. On the sixth day after hatching, the sheaths burst, within several hours transforming the nestling into a dark-billed, bob-tailed version of the adult Yellow-billed Cuckoo. Young may leave the nest at 7 days of age or remain up to several days longer. The period of 16 or 17 days between onset of incubation and freedom from the nest is one of the shortest known for any bird, precocial or altricial.

Although records of adults incubating eggs as late as September 22 in the Carolinas suggest the possibility of second clutches, there is no positive evidence that Yellow-billed Cuckoos are double-brooded.

Feeding habits: The Yellow-billed Cuckoo is a useful species, being among the few birds that will eat tent caterpillars.

Description: Brown above and white below, the Yellow-billed Cuckoo has a decurved bill that is mostly yellow near the base. The wings are marked with rufous patches near the tips, and the long tail has large white spots underneath.

Subfamily Crotophaginae: Anis

Anis are tropical American birds that occur accidentally in the Carolinas. They are gregarious, and females deposit their eggs in communal nests that may contain more than two dozen eggs.

Smooth-billed Ani
Crotophaga ani
14.5 in. (37.0 cm)

Range: An ani, originally believed to be a Smooth-billed Ani but now considered unidentified as to species, was found dead at Huntington Beach State Park, S.C., on November 29, 1978. On December 5, 1981, two identified as Smooth-billed Anis were seen perched in low Chinese tallow trees (*Sapium sebiferum*) at Hope Plantation near Jacksonboro in Colleton County, S.C. A single specimen record for North Carolina is generally considered to be that of an escaped captive bird. It was taken at Edenton, Chowan County, on August 23, 1866. The specimen was donated to the Philadelphia Academy of Natural Sciences.

Feeding habits: Insects, sometimes plucked from the hides of cattle, are the chief source of food for anis, but fruits and berries are also consumed.

Description: Black and about the size of a female Boat-tailed Grackle, anis often appear to be disheveled. Both species have large, triangular black bills. The grooves on the bill are not a very good field mark because the

Smooth-billed Ani may have weak grooves, and those of the Groove-billed Ani may be difficult to see. The lower mandible of the Groove-billed is relatively thin and has a very slight gonydeal angle (a bend in the lowermost ridge of the lower mandible); that of the Smooth-billed is relatively stout with a pronounced gonydeal angle.

Groove-billed Ani
Crotophaga sulcirostris
13.5 in. (34.0 cm)

Range: A Groove-billed Ani remained at the Savannah River National Wildlife Refuge, near Hardeeville, Jasper County, S.C., from October 27 until at least December 9, 1979. A bird believed to be a Groove-billed Ani had previously been found dead on the beach at Waite's Island, near Cherry Grove Beach, Horry County, S.C., on January 23, 1976. Unfortunately, the specimen was lost before it could be positively identified to species. The only North Carolina record is a sight report from Atlantic Beach dated October 14, 1996.

Feeding habits: See Smooth-billed Ani.
Description: See Smooth-billed Ani.

Order STRIGIFORMES: Owls

Owls have soft, fluffy plumage that enables them to fly silently in pursuit of rodents and other small animals, which they catch with their hooked beaks and strong feet. The indigestible portions of their prey are coughed up in elongated pellets that can be found scattered about the roost and examined to determine the diet of each species.

Although owls appear to be short necked, their necks actually are rather long, allowing them to twist the head a full 180 degrees to right or left. Owls have large, forward-looking eyes set in a pronounced facial disk. Contrary to folklore, they are not blind in the daytime. Their nictitating membrane, or third eyelid, is well developed to protect the sensitive retina from bright light. Owls also have highly developed ears concealed by the feathered facial disk, which functions to absorb sound waves and direct them to the ears. Many species, including the Barn Owl, hunt primarily by sound rather than by sight. The ear opening is an unadorned hole on each side of the bird's head. The "ears" of the Long- and Short-eared Owls, like the "horns" of the Great Horned Owl, actually are tufts of feathers.

Most owls build little or no nest, preferring to lay their eggs in a natural cavity or in the vacant nest of another species. Owl eggs are pure white and almost spherical. Blind and helpless, newly hatched owlets are covered with white down. Both parents care for the young until they are ready to fly, which in some large species may be 8 to 10 weeks.

Family TYTONIDAE: Barn Owls

Barn Owl
Tyto alba
15–21 in. (38–53 cm)

Range: Rare to uncommon at most localities, the Barn Owl is a permanent resident everywhere in the Carolinas except on the highest mountains. The population is increased slightly in winter by the arrival of migrants from the north. The species is seen most frequently over coastal marshes at dusk during the winter months.

Nesting habits: Barn Owls appear to mate for life, nesting year after year in the same hollow tree, barn loft, silo, church steeple, duck blind, or abandoned building. No nest is built by the Barn Owl, and eggs

Barn Owl

may be laid at any time of year.
The four to nine eggs are deposited
at irregular intervals. Because
incubation begins with the laying
of the first egg, it is possible to find
unhatched eggs and young from
the same clutch at several stages of
development. The female incubates
each egg for 21 to 24 days. She is fed
regularly by her mate.

Feeding habits: See comments on
order. Birds living in cities make
long flights to hunt in rural
fields and marshes, but rarely in
woodlands.

Description: Golden brown above and
very light below, the Barn Owl has
a heart-shaped face resembling
that of a monkey. The unbirdlike
screams, chuckles, and snores of
Barn Owls undoubtedly have given
many an old building the reputation for being haunted.

Family STRIGIDAE: Typical Owls

Eastern Screech-Owl
Megascops asio
8–10 in. (20–24 cm)

Range: The Eastern Screech-Owl
is a fairly common to common
permanent resident of woodlands,
preferably conifers, throughout the
Carolinas.

Nesting habits: Screech-owls nest in
natural cavities, old woodpecker
holes, unused chimneys, and large
nest boxes from 3 to 50 feet (1 to
15 m) above ground. The two to six
eggs usually are laid in April and require about 26 days for incubation.
The species is single-brooded.

Feeding habits: See comments on
order.

Description: The Eastern Screech-Owl

Eastern Screech-Owl (gray phase)

is our only small owl with ear tufts.
Despite its name, the bird calls in a
plaintive, tremulous whistle that is
musical and not at all unpleasing.
This owl, like others, will snap its
bill menacingly when disturbed.
Both nestlings and adults exhibit
two color phases, one red and the
other gray, which bear no relation-
ship to age, sex, or season. The
red phase, however, seems to be
dominant in the race that breeds
in the western counties, while the
gray phase appears to be the more
common form for the race breeding
in the eastern counties.

Great Horned Owl
Bubo virginianus
18–25 in. (45–63 cm)

Range: Uncommon to fairly common,
the Great Horned Owl is primarily
a permanent resident of upland
forests throughout the Carolinas.
Nonetheless, on February 23, 1992,

Great Horned Owl

eyes and with ear tufts set wide apart. This is the "hoot owl" whose deep, resonant call is a series of four to seven hoots, perhaps *hoo-hoo, hoo-hoo-o-o,* with a final rising inflection, or more commonly *hoo-hoo, hoo-hoo-hoo, hoo, hoo.*

Snowy Owl
Bubo scandiacus
20–27 in. (51–68 cm)

Range: This bird of the Arctic tundra is a rare and irregular winter visitor in the Carolinas, having been found from the mountains to the coast between late October and early February. Occurrences probably are related to a shortage of rodents in the far north and the simultaneous arrival of unusually cold weather in our region. In the Carolinas, Snowy Owls usually stay on the move and are hard to find on consecutive days.

Feeding habits: See comments on order.

Description: The Snowy is our only predominantly white owl. Adults are almost pure white, but the immatures have dark spots on most of the feathers.

the species was found nesting on an Osprey platform far from woodlands at North Pond in the Pea Island National Wildlife Refuge, Dare County, N.C.

Nesting habits: Although capable of building a skimpy nest, the Great Horned Owl almost always takes over one built by a hawk or crow, uses and vacates an Osprey nest before the return of the owner, or may even take an apartment in a Bald Eagle nest, with both species incubating at the same time only a few feet apart. The two, or sometimes three, eggs are laid very early, from late December to March, and require about a month for incubation.

Feeding habits: See comments on order. Although Great Horned Owls occasionally consume poultry and game birds, they are fully protected along with all other birds of prey.

Description: The Great Horned Owl is a large brown owl with large yellow

Snowy Owl

Burrowing Owl

Burrowing Owl
Athene cunicularia
9–11 in. (22–28 cm)

Range: The Burrowing Owl is a very rare accidental along the Carolina coast. Single birds were found at Beaufort, S.C., in December 1943; on Hatteras Island, N.C., in February 1967; near Morehead City, N.C., from June to early September 1972; at Charleston, S.C., on December 30, 1975; and at Huntington Beach State Park, S.C., on June 24, 1976. Two of the birds were roosting beneath unused boats on the shore, and another was using an old dredge pipe. One bird apparently had enlarged a sand crab tunnel some distance from its boat and divided its time between the two sites. The Hatteras bird proved to be of the Florida race, *A. c. floridana.*

Feeding habits: Burrowing Owls hunt by day, hovering on the wing in pursuit of small mammals and insects, especially locusts, crickets, and grasshoppers.

Description: The Burrowing Owl is a small, long-legged, sandy-colored owl that frequently bobs up and down while standing still.

Barred Owl

Barred Owl
Strix varia
18–24 in. (45–61 cm)

Range: Barred Owls are fairly common permanent residents of swamps, river bottoms, and moist woodlands throughout the Carolinas.

Nesting habits: Nesting begins early, often in January or February, with the two or three eggs usually being laid in a natural tree cavity, but occasionally in the abandoned nest of a hawk or crow. Incubation requires about 28 days.

Feeding habits: Barred Owls eat rodents, insects, small birds, frogs, and sometimes fish. They rarely molest poultry.

Description: The Barred Owl is a large, gray-brown bird with dark eyes and no ear tufts. Its clearly accented raspy hoots are typically given in two consecutive groups of four or five syllables each, the second ending with a distinctive, descending aww. The phrases are sometimes rendered as "Who cooks for you? Who cooks for you a-l-l?"

Long-eared Owl
Asio otus
13–16 in. (33–40 cm)

Range: A very uncommon winter visitor from late September through March, the Long-eared Owl frequents dense growths of cedars, pines, and other evergreen trees. It probably is more numerous than the few published records indicate. As many as three birds were present for two consecutive winters in pines near a Voice of America transmitter site in Beaufort County, N.C., and single birds have been reported from various sites in the coastal plain south to Charleston, S.C.

In western North Carolina, one was present on Grandfather Mountain at The Glades (4,600 ft. [1,380 m]) on the Shanty Spring Trail in June and July 1984. Frequency of calling indicated a probability of nesting well south of the previously reported southern limit at Mount Rogers in southwestern Virginia.

Nesting habits: Long-eared Owls show a preference for pines in selecting a nesting site and are likely to take over an old hawk or crow nest, repairing it by building up the sides and adding a lining of dry grasses, dead leaves, and their own down feathers. Sometimes they adapt an old squirrel nest or occupy a hollow tree. Also, there are recorded instances of nests on the ground. Eggs number three to eight. They are oval and pure white with a smooth, rather glossy texture. The incubation period appears to be about 21 days, beginning with the laying of the first egg. Young begin to leave the nest when about 4 or 5 weeks old. The role of the male in incubation is uncertain, but he remains close to the nest and helps feed the young.

Feeding habits: See comments on order. Up to 90% of the food items taken by this species are rodents.

Description: The Long-eared Owl is similar to the larger Great Horned Owl, but the slender ear tufts stick up directly above the relatively small yellow eyes.

Short-eared Owl
Asio flammeus
13–17 in. (33–43 cm)

Range: The Short-eared Owl is a bird of open prairies, meadows, and salt marshes. On barrier islands, it frequents dunes and shrubbery adjacent to marshes, hunting at twilight and on overcast days. The species is an uncommon visitor along the Carolina coast from late October to late April. Inland sightings occur mostly during migration and throughout the winter where land has been recently cleared, as in preparation for creating a major reservoir.

Nesting habits: The Short-eared Owl does not normally nest in the Carolinas, and no active nest has been found in our region. However, six birds were at the Alligator River National Wildlife Refuge, on mainland Dare County, N.C., on May 16, 2001. Four were still present the first of June and remained throughout the summer. Two adults and a juvenile

Short-eared Owl

Northern Saw-whet Owl

were seen there on August 15, 2001, indicating the probability of local breeding.

Feeding habits: Much like our other owls in feeding behavior, the Short-eared is somewhat diurnal and therefore more likely than other owls to be active during daylight hours.

Description: The Short-eared Owl frequently perches on the ground in open, grassy habitats. When flushed, it strongly resembles a completely brown Northern Harrier with dark spots near the bend of each wing. The ear tufts are so small that they can be seen only at very close range.

Northern Saw-whet Owl
Aegolius acadicus
7.5–8.0 in. (19–20 cm)

Range: Breeding in the Canadian zone forests of the North Carolina mountains and wintering in dense pines and cedars at least to a limited extent throughout the Carolinas, the Northern Saw-whet Owl is one of the rarest owls found in our region. The species occurs most frequently in the transition habitat where spruce-fir stands meet hardwoods above 4,360 feet (1,300 m). Evidence of breeding in the southern Appalachians rests primarily on the sighting of immature birds at Richland Balsam and Mount Mitchell State Park in 1965. The first active nest in North Carolina was not found until the summer of 1989. It was built in a nest box erected for flying squirrels at a site along Brush Fence Ridge on the Yancey-Buncombe county line. On a calm night from late March to mid-June, saw-whets can be heard from numerous places along the Blue Ridge Parkway where it passes through the owl's preferred habitat. Stops in the vicinity of Devil's Courthouse are popular with hopeful listeners.

Nesting habits: According to reports from other states, Northern Saw-whet Owls lay their four to seven eggs in April, nesting 14 to 60 feet (4.3 to 18.4 m) above ground in old woodpecker cavities, preferably those of the Northern Flicker. Rapping on the tree trunk may cause the incubating bird to poke its head out the entrance hole, behavior that is in keeping with the species' general reputation for tameness. Once an adult spent an entire day roosting in a bush near a door to an elementary school at Kernersville, N.C.

Feeding habits: See comments on order.

Description: The Northern Saw-whet Owl is smaller than the Eastern Screech-Owl and has no ear tufts. Fledglings are plain brown with a white forehead. The call sounds remarkably like someone sharpening a saw. Fledgling screech-owls lack ear tufts and are easily mistaken for saw-whets.

Order CAPRIMULGIFORMES:
Nighthawks, Nightjars, and Allies

These nocturnal birds are very widely distributed in temperate and tropical zones, with the exception of New Zealand and most of the oceanic islands. They are referred to collectively by the misnomer "goatsuckers." The myth of the goatmilkers survives in the Latin names for the order, family, one subfamily, and one genus.

Family CAPRIMULGIDAE:
Nighthawks and Nightjars

Nighthawks and nightjars, like other nocturnal birds, wear somber plumage. They can shuffle a few steps on their small feet, but they seldom do so, preferring to fly even short distances. When they perch in a tree, they sit lengthwise on the limb. Nighthawks and nightjars feed on the wing, capturing night-flying insects with an extremely wide mouth. The underside of the middle toenail bears serrated notches similar to those found on herons. Although the function is unknown, the comb is assumed to be used in grooming.

Subfamily Chordeilinae:
Nighthawks

Mostly gray and black with white spots, nighthawks feed and nest in open areas. In cities they may nest on flat roofs covered with gravel; in rural areas they nest on the ground in fields or along beaches. Where large cables are strung fairly low beside a highway, a nighthawk can sometimes be spotted perched lengthwise, apparently napping in broad daylight. As their name implies, nighthawks feed on the wing, capturing night-flying insects with their extremely wide mouths.

Lesser Nighthawk
Chordeiles acutipennis
9 in. (23 cm)

Range: Native to Mexico and adjacent portions of the southern United States, the Lesser Nighthawk is known to have occurred in the Carolinas only once. The bird found dead in Carteret County, N.C., in December 1998 is preserved in the collections of the N.C. State Museum of Natural Sciences in Raleigh.
Feeding habits: Similar to Common Nighthawk.
Description: Because three very similar species occur in the United States, reference to a well-illustrated field guide is necessary.

Common Nighthawk
Chordeiles minor
9–10 in. (23–25 cm)

Range: A common transient in the western counties along the edge of the Blue Ridge Mountains and an uncommon to fairly common summer resident across the Carolinas, the Common Nighthawk is usually present from mid-April to October, but earlier and later sightings frequently occur. During migration, particularly in fall, nighthawks are sometimes found in dense flocks numbering into the thousands.
Nesting habits: The male nighthawk

Common Nighthawk (on nest)

performs an elaborate courtship ritual, beginning by inflating the membrane that lies beneath his white throat patch and making gutteral croaking sounds. Better known and easier to observe is the male's spectacular courtship dive. Descending from a great height, he pulls up at the last second with a great rush of wind through the primaries, ending with a loud booming sound. The performances continue during much of the nesting period, until his energy is needed to feed the young.

Usually laid in May or early June, the two grayish-white eggs are thickly spotted with various drab colors. Nesting in open situations, the female lays her eggs directly upon a sand dune, the ground between rows of field crops, or the flat, gravel-topped roof of a building. In the inland portions of the Carolinas, urban rooftops now appear to be the preferred nesting sites. Incubation requires about 19 days, and the adult will distract an intruder by feigning injury. Almost always returning to the eggs from the same direction, incubating nighthawks

sometimes gradually and unintentionally move the clutch as much as 50 feet (15 m) before the downy young emerge from the shells. The young require some degree of parental care for about 4 weeks.

Feeding habits: Nighthawks constantly give buzzing nasal calls while on the wing. More diurnal than nightjars, Common Nighthawks can be seen wheeling and diving high above marshes, pastures, and business districts by day in pursuit of insects. After dark, "bullbats" often feed around street lights and illuminated signs.

Description: This gray bird has long, slender, pointed wings and a slightly forked tail. Its throat is white, and there is a white bar across each wing as well as across the tail near the tip.

Antillean Nighthawk
Chordeiles gundlachii
8.5 in. (22.0 cm)

Range: Native to the Florida Keys, the Antillean Nighthawk normally winters south of the United States, but one was in the vicinity of the campground at Cape Hatteras, August 6–14, 1994.

Feeding habits: Essentially the same as those of the Common Nighthawk.

Description: Similar to the Common Nighthawk but slightly smaller, this species usually can be identified in the field only by its voice. Listen for calls of three or four notes: *kiddy-kiddic, kitty-dik,* or *pitty-pi-tik, pitty-pit-pit.*

Subfamily Caprimulginae: Nightjars

Mostly brown and black with spots of white, the North American nightjars look like sun-dappled dead leaves by day as they rest motionless on the ground or perch lengthwise on a tree limb with lids covering their large eyes. Nightjars feed on the wing, capturing night-flying insects with their extremely wide mouths, gaping up to 2 inches (5 cm) in the Chuck-will's-widow, which occasionally swallows small birds such as wrens, warblers, and sparrows.

Nightjars have long, forward-pointing facial bristles thought by some ornithologists to increase the effective span of the mouth and by others to protect the eyes and nostrils during feeding flights. Although nighthawks, swifts, and swallows have similar feeding habits, those species have rictal bristles that are poorly developed, or none at all. That fact only compounds the mystery.

Chuck-will's-widow
Caprimulgus carolinensis
11–12 in. (28–30 cm)

Range: The Chuck-will's-widow is a fairly common but local summer resident of pine woods (both loblolly and longleaf, some stands being as young as 15 years old) and oak-pine woodlands adjacent to fields throughout most of South Carolina and in the eastern and central counties of North Carolina. The species becomes uncommon toward the mountains, where it is known mostly as a transient. However, the species was recently discovered nesting regularly in northern hardwood forests above

Chuck-will's-widow (on nest)

3,000 feet (900 m). Here, the birds prefer very mature, open hardwood forests, but not necessarily a site in or near an opening.

Males return to the breeding grounds throughout the region from late March to mid-April, soon to be followed by the females. Chuck-will's-widows generally depart for the tropics by late September, but a few birds of undetermined origin apparently winter near the Carolina coast.

Nesting habits: Nests can be found year after year in virtually the same location. Birds return in early April, and nest excavation begins in late April. Most clutches are completed by mid-May. Eggs are laid in a shallow scrape in the leaf-carpeted ground. The two deep cream eggs are variously marbled and spotted with colors ranging from pale blue to dark brown. Incubation requires about 20 days, and calling ceases when the young emerge from their shells.

Chicks are covered with silky, protectively colored down. Most young fledge during the last week of June. Young remain in or near the nest and require parental care until they can fly well enough to capture their own food. If eggs are taken, the female will lay again and again. The sitting bird will feign injury and lead intruders from the nest. Reports of nightjars removing eggs or chicks from a disturbed nest apparently have a basis in fact.

Feeding habits: See comments on subfamily. Chuck-will's-widows have a taste for serviceberry (*Amelanchier* spp., also known as Juneberry and shadbush), and many berries are fed to nestlings.

Description: The Chuck-will's-widow is larger and more reddish brown than the Whip-poor-will. The throat patch is reddish-brown in the male Chuck, buffy in the female Chuck, and generally brownish or gray in Whips. Both species wear a light-colored necklace separating the throat from the breast. It is whitest and widest in the adult male Whip, dingy white in the male Chuck, and buffy in the females. Chucks and Whips flash variable patches of white or buffy plumage on each side of the tail at the tip.

Nightjars are best identified by their loud and persistent calls, often given hundreds of times in succession. The Chuck may seem to have three, four, or five syllables, according to the distance the bird is from the listener. The soft initial *cluck* is not heard at a great distance. Some people hear only four syllables as in the common name, but others hear the bird saying "Kiss William's widow." The Whip-poor-will normally says its name, with the emphasis on the first syllable, but sometimes "whip" seems to be the last syllable.

After nesting is under way, the birds become quiet and are hard to find without playing a tape-recording of their vocalizations. That practice should be used briefly and infrequently.

Whip-poor-will
Caprimulgus vociferus
9–10 in. (22–25 cm)

Range: A fairly common to common summer resident of woodlands in the mountains, piedmont, and inner coastal plain, the Whip-poor-will becomes less common toward the coast during the breeding season and may be locally absent, but winter stragglers are not particularly rare.

Nesting habits: See Chuck-will's-widow account.

Feeding habits: See comments on subfamily.

Description: See Chuck-will's-widow for a comparative description.

Order APODIFORMES: Swifts and Hummingbirds

Although superficially quite different in appearance, swifts and hummingbirds share the characteristic of having very short bones in the section of the wing before the final bend. Birds in this order also have weak legs and feet.

Family APODIDAE: Swifts

Eight species occur in North America, but only four are found regularly in the contiguous United States. Of those, only one is known from the Carolinas.

Subfamily Chaeturinae: Chimney Swift and Allies

Chimney Swifts are named for their habit of nesting and roosting in chimneys.

Chimney Swift
Chaetura pelagica
4.25–5.5 in. (12–14 cm)

Range: Chimney Swifts begin arriving in the Carolinas in March and are generally abundant through October. Some may linger into early November. They migrate by day and roost overnight in large chimneys such as those found at schools, churches, and industrial sites.

Nesting habits: Although a few Chimney Swifts still nest in large hollow trees, the great majority nest and roost in chimneys. Both sexes help build the nest. Late in May they can be seen hovering at the tips of limbs while breaking off dead twigs.

With saliva they fasten the twigs to the inside of the chimney and to each other, fashioning an unlined, semicircular basket that may be attached almost anywhere between the top and the bottom of the flue. Our species is related to the Asian swift whose entirely glutinous nest is the basis for bird's-nest soup. The three to six pure white eggs usually are laid before mid-June, and incubation requires about 18 days.

Both adults incubate eggs and care for the altricial young, which stay in the nest for a relatively long time, 24 days or longer. The nestlings' eyes do not open fully until the fourteenth day. Using their short, stiff tails to brace themselves against the vertical walls, they exercise their wings while preparing to emerge from the chimney fully capable of extended flight. After the nesting season, swifts flock together, and a thousand or more may roost in a single large chimney.

Feeding habits: Chimney Swifts wheel about the sky in pursuit of insects. They usually fly high above the trees, but on cloudy days they sometimes swoop almost to the ground. While feeding over still water, they sometimes do "belly-busts," apparently their way of wetting the feathers prior to preening. Chimney Swifts are also known to fly behind waterfalls, which may be another way of wetting the feathers while on the wing.

Description: The Chimney Swift is a dark gray bird with a short wide

few fine black or brown spots about the large end. First clutches usually are laid in late April, and incubation apparently requires about 14 days. Almost nothing is known about the care of the young or their development, but the male parent is thought to share in all the nesting chores. Two broods are raised each season, and a third nesting may be attempted under favorable conditions.

Feeding habits: See comments on family.

Description: This is our only vireo that has two white wing bars, yellow spectacles, and yellow sides. The white iris of the adult is distinctive, but immature birds have dark eyes and may be mistaken for Bell's Vireos. The song, often imitated by the Yellow-breasted Chat, can be rendered as *chick-per-a-wheeo-chick*, with the first and last syllables accented and the middle ones slurred together. Rarely, the first and last syllables are omitted, leaving a short song that is strikingly like that of an Eastern Wood-Pewee. Another short version is *chick-peeear*.

Bell's Vireo
Vireo bellii
4.25–5.0 in. (10.8–12.5 cm)

Range: Bell's Vireo is a western species that breeds eastward to the Mississippi River, throughout Illinois, in most of Indiana, and into northwestern Ohio. The species occurs east of the Appalachian Mountains as a very rare transient and apparently winters, at least sparingly, in Florida. A fall migrant was seen in open mixed woods at the edge of a golf course in Wake County, N.C., on August 10, 1974, and at the same site again on October 7, 2002. On the latter date, the bird was leaf-bathing in shrubbery being sprayed with a garden hose. An immature female Bell's Vireo was caught in a mist net at Hog Island near Mount Pleasant, Charleston County, S.C., on October 14, 1985. Single birds of this species were reported from the Broad River Wildlife Management Area in the fall of 1991 and from the Caw Caw Interpretive Center near Charleston in April 2000. The last South Carolina report is the only published spring sighting for the Carolinas.

Feeding habits: See comments on family.

Description: This very small vireo is easily confused with the immature White-eyed Vireo, which lacks the white iris and yellow spectacles of the adult. First-summer White-eyed Vireos have dark eyes and faint white spectacles that usually are replaced with yellow ones before the end of summer or during early fall.

In a suspected Bell's Vireo, look for its small size (about the same as the Northern Parula), black eye, thin white spectacles with a thin dark line through the eye, pale yellow sides and undertail coverts (eastern population), and two white wing bars (upper one short and faint, the lower long and faint or perhaps fairly prominent).

The bill of a Bell's Vireo is relatively thin compared with that of a White-eyed Vireo, but still thicker than that of a Northern Parula. Both of the Bell's Vireos seen in Wake County were from the eastern population, which has brighter yellow on the underparts and a slightly shorter tail than that found on birds from the western population.

Yellow-throated Vireo
Vireo flavifrons
5–6 in. (12.5–15.0 cm)

Range: The Yellow-throated Vireo is a fairly common summer resident of mature woodlands in all sections of the Carolinas from early April to early October. A few may arrive in mid-March or linger into December. The species normally breeds in the mountains only at elevations below about 3,000 feet (900 m).

Nesting habits: Suspended from a fork of a limb 20 to 60 feet (6 to 18 m) above ground, the cupped nest is woven of plant fibers and is camouflaged on the outside with lichens. The three or four eggs are much like those of the White-eyed Vireo and require 12 to 14 days for incubation. Offspring are thought to remain in the nest about 2 weeks. The species is double-brooded, and the male shares in nest construction, incubation, and care of the young.

Feeding habits: See comments on family.

Yellow-throated Vireo

Description: The Yellow-throated Vireo has two white wing bars, yellow spectacles, yellow throat and breast, and a blue-gray rump. The heavy, hooked bill and yellow spectacles separate it from the Pine Warbler. The song is similar to that of a Red-eyed Vireo, but somewhat slurred and delivered with a husky, burry accent.

Blue-headed Vireo (Solitary Vireo)
Vireo solitarius
5.5–6.0 in. (14–15 cm)

Range: Blue-headed Vireos are fairly common spring and fall transients in woodlands throughout the Carolinas. Fairly common winter residents in southeastern South Carolina, they winter sparingly northward along the coast and inland, very rarely even in the mountains. Blue-headed Vireos breed commonly at all elevations throughout the mountains of the Carolinas in both coniferous and deciduous forests. The species also breeds to an undetermined extent in mature pine woods of the foothills, eastward in North Carolina to Granville and Wake Counties, and throughout the sandhills. There are strong indications that the Blue-headed Vireo is increasing its population east of the mountains, as evidenced by nesting activity not only in piedmont South Carolina at Sumter National Forest, in Newberry County, but also as far south and east as Jasper and Williamsburg Counties.

Nesting habits: Blue-headed Vireos arrive on their breeding grounds about mid-March, ahead of the

Blue-headed Vireo

main passage of spring migrants. Nest building begins in late April, and eggs usually are laid in early May for the first clutch and in June for the second. The nest, eggs, and family life are essentially the same as for our other vireos. The nest usually is placed rather low, and the incubation period probably is 11 days or longer. Nest materials may include the soft, white inner layer of oak galls in an early stage of development. The species has a reputation for abandoning a nest under construction if an intruder approaches the site too closely or too frequently.

Feeding habits: See comments on family.

Description: The adult Blue-headed Vireo has a dark blue-gray head that contrasts noticeably with the greenish back. Other field marks include prominent white spectacles, white wing bars, and yellowish sides. The blue-gray head and relatively large size separate this species from Bell's Vireo, which has faint white spectacles rather than the prominent ones of the Blue-headed. The song of the

Blue-headed is similar to that of the Red-eyed but about an octave higher in pitch and more sweetly musical. The most common scold is an emphatic, descending *shu-shu-shu-shu*. A common call is a sharp, descending, cat-like mewing that may be heard as *vee-u*. Fledglings sometimes attempt to imitate the song of a neighboring White-eyed Vireo.

Warbling Vireo
Vireo gilvus
5.0–5.5 in. (12.5–14.0 cm)

Range: In most parts of the Carolinas, the Warbling Vireo is a transient, rare in spring and very rare in fall, occurring from early April to mid-May and from late August to mid-October. In the mountains of north-western North Carolina, however, the species breeds in open groves of deciduous trees adjacent to rivers in the broad valleys and plateaus below 3,000 feet (900 m). Scattered late spring and summer records suggest that Warbling Vireos may breed eastward across the northern edge of North Carolina to eastern Halifax County. The extralimital population found in June 1991 in Clarendon County, S.C., at the Bluff Unit of the Santee National Wildlife Refuge plus documented breeding in Orange County, N.C., in 1999 and subsequent years strongly indicate that significant range extension is in progress in the Carolinas.

Nesting habits: The nest of the Warbling Vireo is a neatly woven basket of plant fibers that is lined with grasses, horsehair, and other soft materials. It is usually suspended 20 to 50 feet (6 to 15 m) above ground among leafy twigs close to the topmost branch of a tree.

Active nests have been found in North Carolina in May and June, and the species apparently is single-brooded. The three to five white eggs have a few scattered spots of reddish brown, dark brown, or blackish brown, with the darker spots predominating. Incubation requires 12 days, and the young do not leave the nest until 16 days after hatching.

Newly fledged Warbling Vireos are oddly pale, almost white, in general appearance. Both adults share in nest building, incubation, and care of young. The nest is so well hidden that the male often sings with impunity while sitting on the eggs.

Feeding habits: See comments on family. Sometimes Warbling Vireos consume many ladybugs, much to the displeasure of gardeners who like the beneficial little beetles.

Description: This drab, gray vireo has only one distinguishing feature: a broad, white eye line that is not bordered by black. Its call is a harsh, nasal mewing. Its song is a husky, rapid warble given without pause until the final emphatic *VEET.* Some people interpret it as "When I *see* you, I will *seize* you and I'll *squeeze* you till it *squirts!"*

Philadelphia Vireo
Vireo philadelphicus
4.5–5.0 in. (11.5–12.5 cm)

Range: An uncommon and rarely seen migrant, the Philadelphia Vireo moves northward primarily west of the Carolinas, but a fairly good number come across our moun-

tains, mostly in late April and early May. During fall migration Philadelphias may be found in all sections, even on the Outer Banks, from early September through the first week in October (extreme dates: August 25 to October 28).

Philadelphia Vireos usually frequent woodland edges and deciduous scrub, but autumn migrants often travel with other species and visit a wide variety of habitats. Look for them in mixed flocks of warblers, woodpeckers, titmice, chickadees, kinglets, and nuthatches. The Philadelphia Vireo seems to be a frequent companion of Bay-breasted, Cape May, and Blackburnian Warblers.

Feeding habits: See comments on family.

Description: Easily mistaken for a warbler, the Philadelphia is our only vireo with plain wings and a yellow breast.

Red-eyed Vireo
Vireo olivaceus
5.5–6.5 in. (14.0–16.5 cm)

Range: The Red-eyed Vireo is a common summer resident in all sections of the Carolinas from early April through mid-October. During the breeding season this species occurs in the mountains up to 5,000 feet (1,500 m) and occasionally a bit higher, but it is found mostly at elevations below 4,500 feet (1,400 m). A few postbreeding wanderers and fall transients occur at the highest elevations from late June through early October.

Nesting habits: This persistent singer nests in both wet and dry deciduous woodlands, and in the latter

Red-eyed Vireo

rous diet with a number of berries, the bright red seeds of magnolias being among their favorite foods in autumn.

Description: The Red-eyed Vireo is distinguished by the absence of wing bars and the presence of a gray crown, black-bordered white eye line, and red iris. Two other vireos that occur regularly in our region do not have spectacles or wing bars. The Philadelphia has predominantly yellow underparts, and the Warbling has a white eye line that is not bordered with black. The song of the Red-eyed Vireo is two three-note phrases often rendered as "Here I am. Where are you?" given in robin-like phrases with the first part slurred downward and the second slurred upward. The song may be repeated over and over for long periods of time almost without a pause. The call is a generally soft, descending cat-like mew.

habitat it is usually the most abundant breeding species. The nest is a deep cup woven of bark, grass, and other plant fibers and lined with pine needles or other soft materials. It may be decorated on the outside with bits of lichen. Caterpillar silk is used to bind the nest together and to suspend it by the rim from a slender fork near the tip of a drooping limb. Nests are placed from 2 to 60 feet (0.6 to 18.0 m) above ground in a deciduous shrub or tree.

The three or four eggs are white, lightly sprinkled with reddish-brown dots that are concentrated near the large end. First clutches generally are laid in May and second ones in June. Incubation requires 12 to 14 days. The male shares in nest construction, incubation, and care of the young, which stay in the nest about 12 days.

Feeding habits: Red-eyed Vireos supplement their highly insectivo-

Black-whiskered Vireo
Vireo altiloquus
5.5 in. (14.0 cm)

Range: The Black-whiskered Vireo breeds in mangroves and hammocks of southern Florida and the Florida Keys. On April 1, 1960, about the time this bird normally migrates from South America to Florida, one was found dead but still warm beneath a telephone wire on the causeway to Wrightsville Beach, N.C. During the preceding two days there had been a good flow of tropical air on the Atlantic Coast, with strong winds from the southwest. The second North Carolina record occurred May 8, 1983, also in New Hanover County. A Black-whiskered

Vireo exhibited territorial behavior at Cape Lookout on May 23, 1994, and remained there until July 2. On May 20, 2000, a Black-whiskered Vireo was found not far from the place occupied in 1994. One on Baldhead Island, Brunswick County, N.C., was present June 6 to 22, 2001. It appeared to have been joined by a second bird that was heard but never confirmed by sight. Obviously some of those birds must have passed over South Carolina, but there is not yet a published sighting of the species in that state.

Feeding habits: See comments on family.

Description: This species has the general appearance of a Red-eyed Vireo, but it has a prominent black line extending from the base of the bill down both sides of the throat.

Blue Jay

Family CORVIDAE:
Jays and Crows

Bold, noisy, and aggressive birds, the corvids figure prominently in folklore, literature, and everyday speech: "sassy as a jaybird" or "as the crow flies." Jays and crows are medium to large in size with long strong legs, large strong feet, and strong straight bills. The nostrils usually are covered with short, stiff, forward-directed bristles. Most corvids will eat anything they can swallow and are thus able to survive changing conditions in a wide variety of habitats.

Blue Jay
Cyanocitta cristata
10–12 in. (25–30 cm)

Range: The Blue Jay is a very common permanent resident throughout the Carolinas, with the population in-creased in winter by flocks of birds that migrate from the northern part of the species' range. Blue Jays are at home in any kind of woodlands, but they prefer fairly open pine-oak woods. They are rather quiet about their nests, but they will engage in noisy pursuit of hawks, owls, and snakes, giving alarm cries that are recognized by almost all woodland birds and mammals.

Nesting habits: The nest is a bulky and rather untidy affair made of sticks, twigs, leaves, roots, pine needles, rags, waste paper, and mud. It may be placed in a small tree, but high horizontal limbs of large oaks and pines seem to be preferred. Often 20 to 50 feet (6 to 15 m) or more above ground, the nest is usually not far from the main trunk of the tree.

The three to five olive-buff eggs are thickly spotted with brown. First clutches of the season are laid in April and usually contain a larger number of eggs than second ones. The incubation period is about 17 days, and bobtailed young leave the nest 17 to 21 days after hatching, though they are still dependent on the parents for another week or more. First broods often leave the nest the latter part of May, and second broods do so about mid-July.

Because the sexes are indistinguishable in the field, no one seems to know exactly the role of the male in nesting activities. Blue Jays do engage in courtship feeding, and males apparently participate in nest construction, feed the incubating female, and help tend the young. Some reports indicate that males relieve the female on the nest, but apparently just to cover the eggs or nestlings during the absence of the female rather than providing true incubation or brooding.

Feeding habits: The Blue Jay is omnivorous, but vegetable matter apparently comprises a major portion of its diet. Although the jay has a bad reputation for robbing nests of other birds, it is only one of many such predators including crows, rat snakes, and feral cats. The nest that is not well hidden or well defended will be raided, if not by the jay then by some other animal.

Tool use: Captivity often forces birds to show their ingenuity. One captive Blue Jay learned to tear a strip from the paper lining its cage and use that strip to rake sunflower seeds spilled on the counter close enough to be reached with its bill. Jays, like nuthatches, wedge acorns and other large seeds into crevices in the bark of trees to hold them still for cracking with blows from the bill.

Description: This is our only blue bird with a crest and a dark neck band. The Blue Jay has an imposing vocal repertoire that includes hawk imitations and raucous cries. One of its most delightful renditions is the rather musical pump-handle call, which is accompanied by an appropriate bobbing motion.

American Crow
(Common Crow)
Corvus brachyrhynchos
16–21 in. (40–53 cm)

Range: The American Crow is common and conspicuous throughout the Carolinas at all seasons, but it does not breed at the higher elevations in our mountains, where it is mostly an infrequent summer visitor. Though seen in a wide variety of fields and open country habitats, crows nest and roost in rather dense woods.

Our winter crow roosts are thought to be composed chiefly of flocks that have migrated from the north. When crows flock for the winter, they post lookouts to warn the feeding or roosting birds of impending danger.

Nesting habits: Crows mate early in February and begin nest building later that month. During the nesting season the birds are quiet and secretive, remaining in solitary pairs. Usually placed 25 to 70 feet (7.5 to 21.5 m) above ground and near the trunk on a large horizontal limb of a conifer, the nest is a rather large structure made of sticks and twigs and lined with leaves and grass.

American Crow

Eggs for first clutches are laid during the first half of March. Numbering four to six, they vary in color from pale blue to olive green and are spotted and blotched with dark brown. Incubation requires about 18 days, and young remain in the nest about a month. Both adults share in nest construction, incubation, and care of the young. In the Carolinas a second brood may be raised.

Feeding habits: The American Crow's diet is mostly vegetable matter, notably corn, wheat, oats, and wild berries. Animal matter includes many insects as well as crayfish, snakes, lizards, mice, rats, young rabbits, and the eggs and young of other birds. Thus, from an economic standpoint, the crow is both beneficial and detrimental. Because of its fondness for corn and young poultry, it has been shot, trapped, bombed, and poisoned; but this wary species continues to thrive.

Description: This big black bird is best recognized by its voice, the familiar *caw*. The slightly smaller Fish Crow calls in a less strident, somewhat nasal *ca* or *ca-ha*. Crows fly with a steady, rowing wingbeat.

Fish Crow
Corvus ossifragus
15–17 in. (38–43 cm)

Range: The Fish Crow is another passerine that is in the process of extending its range in the Carolinas. Prior to 1960 the species was regarded as a common permanent resident along the entire Carolina coast and inland along the Savannah River and its tributaries to Greenwood, S.C., where a nest was found on April 1, 1925. In March 1962, four Fish Crows were seen in Raleigh, Wake County, N.C., and in April 1972 a nest was found in a medium-height pine grove in residential Raleigh. By 1982 the species was a year-round resident in rural Wake County. By the mid-1990s, reports indicated the presence of Fish Crows during the breeding season and in winter as far inland as Clemson and Rock Hill, S.C., as well as at Tryon and Winston-Salem, N.C. Huge roosts have been found in winter near Manteo, N.C., and at several sites in southeastern South Carolina. Although the species is becoming more and more numerous in the piedmont and inner coastal plain, at present there is no indication that Fish Crows are common in the foothills or that they have invaded the southern Appalachian Mountains.

Fish Crows first appeared in central North Carolina soon after Common Grackles began breeding locally, and they have been observed in the act of raiding nests in a grackle colony. Because grackles are generally restricted to open habitats below 3,000 feet (900 m), there is a chance that if and when

Fish Crows invade the mountains, they also will not nest in the middle and high elevations.

Nesting habits: On the Carolina coast, nesting begins in late April, and some Fish Crow nests still contain eggs in early June. The nest and four or five eggs are like those of the American Crow but smaller. Incubation takes 16 to 18 days, and young remain in the nest about 3 weeks. Both parents appear to share fully in building the nest, incubating eggs, and caring for the offspring. Only one brood is raised, but if the first set of eggs is lost, another will be laid, sometimes in the same nest. Although nests are usually built 30 to 100 feet (9 to 30 m) high in pines and other tall trees, they may be situated in waxmyrtle bushes only 5 or 6 feet (1.5 to 2.0 m) above ground.

Little is known about the nesting habits of the inland Fish Crow population. These birds appear to begin nesting in late March or early April, and they place their nests in pine groves, the same habitat preferred by the Common Grackle at inland localities.

Fish Crows may nest well removed from others of their kind or in small colonies with several pairs breeding within a radius of a few hundred yards. In autumn, Fish Crows flock in preparation for migration, and winter roosts may number several thousand birds. Nonetheless, substantial numbers of the Fish Crows breeding inland in the Carolinas appear to remain in the vicinity of their nesting sites throughout the winter.

Feeding habits: Fish Crows breeding on the coast habitually raid heron, gull, tern, and shorebird colonies. In addition to the eggs and young of other birds, Fish Crows consume a variety of aquatic life, including eggs of turtles, and many wild fruits and berries from plants such as the mulberry, grape, palmetto, holly, and magnolia. Inland, Fish Crows apparently do not feed around lakes to any appreciable extent. They frequent city dumps, shopping centers, and the nesting sites of Rock Doves and Common Grackles.

Description: The Fish Crow is a slightly smaller, shorter-legged version of the American Crow. Its call is a nasal *ca* or *ca-ha* that can be confused with the calls of young American Crows.

Common Raven
Corvus corax
22.0–26.5 in. (56–67 cm)

Range: The Common Raven is an uncommon but conspicuous permanent resident in our higher mountains at elevations above 3,500 feet (1,090 m). In South Carolina, breeding birds returned to Caesar's Head State Park in 1986 after a long absence and hatched three young in 1987. Nesting as low as 2,400 feet (720 m) at Pilot Mountain State Park in Surry County, N.C., was considered unusual until recently. About the same time the ravens returned to Caesar's Head, they also invaded the foothills and upper piedmont of North Carolina. They are nesting successfully at a quarry in Forsyth County and on tall buildings in downtown Winston-Salem. Nesting activity has been seen at other quarries at Stokesdale in

Common Raven

young birds even after departure, and the family group leaves the nesting area together. The following nesting season, only the adults return to the nest site.

Ravens do not always conduct their nesting activities by the book. At Winston-Salem, a nest with young was found as early as February 15. During May, in downtown Winston-Salem, a pair fed a chick in one nest while simultaneously incubating eggs in a second nest nearby.

Feeding habits: Ravens are omnivorous, having a taste for carrion, birds, snakes, and small mammals; but they readily accept anything edible at the garbage dump. In some parts of the country they have learned to rip open plastic garbage bags in search of food.

Description: Larger and heavier than a crow, the Common Raven has a shaggy throat and a wedge-shaped tail. Its voice is a hoarse croak.

Family ALAUDIDAE: Larks

Larks have slender bills, sing in flight, usually walk on the ground, and seldom perch in trees or shrubs.

Horned Lark
Eremophila alpestris
6.75–8.0 in. (16–20 cm)

Range: Horned Larks are birds of barren ground, stubble fields, airports, golf courses, sod farms, and other extensive areas of short vegetation and bare earth. Once confined to naturally open country such as prairies and tundra, the species moved eastward in the nineteenth century as removal of forests and cultivation of land modified the

Guilford County and near Reidsville in Rockingham County. Nesting has also been reported from the vicinity of South Mountains State Park in south central Burke County, and single birds have been seen as far east as Raleigh, Wake County, N.C.

Nesting habits: In February or early March, in a tall conifer or on some small rock shelf protruding from a cliff or a skyscraper, ravens build a nest of sticks and twigs lined with matted moss or wool. The four to six greenish, brown-splotched eggs usually are laid in March, and incubation takes about 3 weeks. The male feeds the female on the nest, but he normally does not sit on the eggs except when she must leave them in cold or wet weather.

Young remain in the nest about a month, or until early May in our area. When young are reluctant to leave the nest, the parents may begin destroying it to force departure. The adults continue to feed

Horned Lark

earth. Taking place mostly at noon and sundown, singing reaches a peak during nest building, egg laying, and incubation. The territory, probably 300 feet square (10,000 sq. yd. [8,200 sq m]) or larger, is usually defended by the male. Both adults feed almost entirely within its boundaries.

Nesting reportedly begins when the mean temperature rises above 40°F (4.4°C) for two consecutive days, which sometimes happens in our area in early March. The mating ritual is much like that of the House Sparrow. The male Horned Lark struts before the female, who crouches and flutters her wings.

The nest is constructed by the female. Using her beak and feet, she excavates a shallow depression on the sheltered side of a clump of grass. Here she builds a nest of coarse leaves and stems lined with grasses. The rim is level with the ground, and the area near the rim may be paved with pebbles and lumps of dirt. Construction requires from 2 to 4 days.

The female lays two to five greenish-gray eggs that are finely speckled with cinnamon brown, often in a dense ring at the large end. Early clutches tend to be smaller than late ones. Performed by the female, incubation takes about 11 days and usually does not begin until the clutch is complete. The male may help care for the young during their 10 days in the nest. Newly hatched Horned Larks have brown skin and long, buffy down. Young just out of the nest hop instead of walking like the adults, and 5 days after departure they can fly.

habitat to suit its needs. Traveling in flocks, Horned Larks are rather localized winter residents south to eastern North Carolina and central South Carolina, being most numerous in the piedmont from December through March. Horned Larks may be fairly common or even common at one place and absent from nearby habitat that appears equally suitable.

The species breeds from the North Carolina mountains, mostly on balds in the northern counties (e.g., Watauga and Ashe), eastward to Martin and Washington Counties, N.C., and Sumter, S.C. First discovered nesting in the piedmont of North Carolina in 1937 and in the piedmont of South Carolina in 1950, Horned Larks generally can be found year-round in the vicinity of established colonies.

Nesting habits: Male Horned Larks may begin singing in January and delineate their territories in early February. They sing, mostly for the benefit of other males, either from the ground or in flight at altitudes of several hundred feet. The flight song ends with a spectacular dive to

Nests have been found in the Carolinas from early March to mid-July, the species having two or three broods per year in our region. Pairs will continue to renest on the same territory throughout the breeding season unless growth of vegetation makes the habitat unsuitable. Singing ceases after the nesting season, and the birds gather for the winter in flocks sometimes numbering into the hundreds.

Feeding habits: Horned Larks consume mostly grass and weed seeds plus some grasshoppers, weevils, spiders, and other animal matter.

Description: The Horned Lark's tiny "horns" are seen only at close range. The species is best recognized by its high-pitched sibilant flight notes, bold black breast band, and unnotched dark tail with white outer feathers. The Prairie Horned Lark (*E. a. praticola*) is the race breeding in the Carolinas. The winter population comprises that race plus some Northern Horned Larks (*E. a. alpestris*). The line above the eye is yellow in the northern race and white in the prairie race.

Family HIRUNDINIDAE:
Swallows and Allies

Slender bodied with long, pointed wings, swallows have a tail that may be slightly notched or deeply forked. To separate swallows from swifts, note the distance between the bend of the wing and the side of the body. If it is very short, the bird is a swift. Swifts are more closely related to hummingbirds than to swallows.

Subfamily Hirundininae:
Swallows

Flying low over waterways, meadows, grain fields, and other open places in pursuit of moths, flies, mosquitoes, and various other insects, swallows emit typically harsh but rather cheerful twitters. A large flock of mixed species may number several hundred birds, or rarely into the thousands, and can be quite noisy while feeding on the wing or resting on wires over open terrain.

Purple Martin
Progne subis
7.25–8.50 in. (18.5–21.5 cm)

Range: A summer resident throughout the Carolinas, the Purple Martin is fairly common to common in the coastal plain and thrives locally inland to the mountains. Among our earliest spring migrants, martins arrive in coastal South Carolina and extreme southeastern North Carolina in February or early March, rarely in late January, and reach inland localities by mid-March or early April. Fall migration is quite leisurely, beginning in late July, when local birds gather into large flocks of perhaps one to several thousand birds, and continuing into October.

Nesting habits: In primitive times Purple Martins nested in old woodpecker holes and other natural cavities in trees and cliffs. Native Americans erected gourd houses to attract martins to their villages, and early European settlers adopted the practice. Nesting boxes for martins should be placed in open terrain from 15 to 25 feet (4.5 to 7.5 m) above ground.

Purple Martins (male at center and female on left)

Martins will return to the same site year after year, with the adult males arriving before the females and young males hatched the previous season. If the birds come while their apartment house is down for cleaning and repairs, or to prevent its use by House Sparrows, martins will circle the exact spot where it should be and even perch on it as it is being set in place.

Both sexes build the nest of grass, leaves, and other convenient materials such as twigs, feathers, mud, rags, paper, and string. Nests may be started several weeks before eggs are laid. The four or five slightly glossy white eggs may be laid from mid-April through May. The incubation period varies from 12 to 20 days with 15 apparently the average duration.

The female normally assumes all responsibility for incubation, but the male sometimes sits on the eggs. The male assists in feeding the young, often bringing as many food items during a period of observation as does his mate. Young stay in the nest 24 to 28 days, at which time the adults cease feeding them. One or both of the parents remain nearby, waiting for the offspring once they have flown from the nest. The family party stays together until the young are fully independent, a period of about 3 weeks. Then the group may join other martins to form a huge flock for the southward migration.

Purple Martins usually are single-brooded and will not renest if even one nestling survives from the first clutch; however, second clutches may be laid when the first nesting is a total failure, and some third clutches have been reported.

Feeding habits: Purple Martins feed mostly on day-flying insects, showing a distinct preference for beetles, dragonflies, wasps, and other fairly large prey. Although they do on occasions take a good number of mosquitoes, their consumption of those predominantly night-flying pests has been greatly exaggerated by some writers.

Description: The adult male Purple Martin is completely dark above and below. Females and immature males have dusky throats and whitish bellies. To distinguish them from swallows, watch for the martins' larger size and broader wings and tail, and the adult male's iridescent purple head and body.

Tree Swallow
Tachycineta bicolor
5.0–6.25 in. (12.5–16.0 cm)

Range: During the late 1900s, Tree Swallows rapidly extended their breeding range in the southeastern United States. The first evidence of that activity in the Carolinas was a

Tree Swallow

pair feeding young in an old woodpecker cavity beside the New River
in northeastern Ashe County, N.C.,
in June 1979. By the turn of the century, nesting was occurring south
to Oconee County, S.C.; around large
lakes in the piedmont; and sparingly in the coastal plain, though
apparently not yet as far south as
Charleston.

Near the Carolina coast the Tree
Swallow remains a common spring
and abundant fall migrant. It also
winters there erratically, often
being uncommon at a locality for
a few weeks and then suddenly
becoming common, especially during cold and windy weather. The
species is a common spring migrant
from early March through May and
an uncommon fall migrant from
July to early November over most
of our inland counties, becoming
scarce toward the mountains.

Nesting habits: Tree Swallows normally nest in isolated pairs, placing
grass, straw, and white feathers
in a natural cavity, martin gourd,
or wooden nest box. They do not
linger about the nesting site once
the young are well on the wing,

but soon gather in flocks and begin
moving southward.

At Table Rock State Park, Pickens
County, S.C., a pair inspected a nest
box on April 13, 2001, and had a nest
completed by May 2. Three eggs
were in the nest by May 4. In spite
of disturbance by a predator, there
were at least nine eggs by May 29
and five nestlings on June 14. The
young fledged on June 27. In 2002,
nest building began after bluebirds
had fledged from the box on May 14.

Feeding habits: See comments on
subfamily. Although 80% of their
annual diet is animal matter, Tree
Swallows consume many berries
from waxmyrtle and bayberry
bushes, especially in winter, when
flying insects may be scarce.

Description: The adult male Tree
Swallow is the only swallow with a
blue-green back that occurs in our
region. Brownish young birds may
be confused with Bank and Rough-
winged Swallows, but the white
throat and absence of a breast band
separate the Tree Swallow from
those two species.

Northern Rough-winged Swallow
Stelgidopteryx serripennis
5.0–5.75 in. (12.5–14.5 cm)

Range: The Northern Rough-winged
Swallow is a fairly common summer resident throughout the Carolinas, with local abundance varying
considerably according to the availability of suitable nesting sites. At
many sites, tree growth or roadside
beautification projects have destroyed bare, red clay embankments
formerly used for nesting.

In the mountains the species
does not breed above the middle

Northern Rough-winged Swallow

cm) to a maximum of about 6 feet (2 m) into the bank, terminating in a shallow depression that is lined with dry grasses and rootlets. The bulk of the nest varies considerably according to the size of the cavity, and the material rarely includes feathers.

Six or seven pure white eggs are laid between early May and early June. Incubation requires about 16 days, with the female sometimes assisted by the male. Young remain in the nest up to 3 weeks, and only one brood is raised each year.

Feeding habits: See comments on subfamily.

Description: Named for the series of small barbs on the outer web of the outermost primary feather, the Northern Rough-winged Swallow is a mostly brown bird. Its dusky throat and absence of a well-defined breast band separate it from our other brown-backed swallows.

elevations, but birds forage over the highest peaks. On the Outer Banks the Rough-winged Swallow is only a rare transient. Breeding birds apparently arrive in the Carolinas about mid-March and depart soon after the young are strong on the wing, normally between early July and early September. Winter stragglers are very rare in North Carolina, but a few individuals may linger in coastal South Carolina until late January.

Nesting habits: Rough-winged swallows nest in cracks and crevices in rock cliffs or brick and stone structures such as dams, bridges, and tunnels; take over kingfisher burrows or protruding drainpipes; or excavate their own burrows in road cuts or natural embankments. Normally only one to several pairs will use a single site, but sometimes rather large colonies form at particularly favorable places such as Cliffs of the Neuse State Park near Goldsboro, N.C.

Excavation most often begins about the first of April. Usually dug near water, the burrow extends from a minimum of 9 inches (22.5

Bank Swallow
Riparia riparia
4.75–5.50 in. (12–14 cm)

Range: The Bank Swallow is an uncommon to locally fairly common spring and fall transient from late March through May and from early July through September. It is a very rare winter straggler. The main thrust of the migratory movement for this species seems to be across the piedmont in both seasons, but amazing numbers of fall transients, up to an estimated 2,000 birds, have been noted at a sod farm in Orangeburg County, S.C. The species nests locally in the mountains and western piedmont of North

Carolina. The presence of breeding Bank Swallows may go undetected in the eastern counties because of the birds' close resemblance to the Northern Rough-winged Swallow or an assumption that the individuals were only late migrants.

Nesting habits: Both parents participate in excavation of the burrow near the top of a nearly vertical embankment. At the end of the burrow, which usually is 2 to 3 feet (0.5 to 1.0 m) deep, they build a nest of grass stalks interwoven with finer plant materials and lined with feathers. The four to five pure white eggs hatch in about 14 to 16 days. Both adults incubate eggs and care for the young, which remain in the nest about 18 to 22 days. Shortly before departure they gather at the mouth of the cavity and may take short flights.

Feeding habits: See comments on subfamily.

Description: The Bank Swallow is brown above and white below with a narrow brown breast band contrasting sharply with the white throat.

Cliff Swallows (pair at nest)

Cliff Swallow
Petrochelidon pyrrhonota
5–6 in. (12.5–15.0 cm)

Range: An uncommon transient throughout the Carolinas from early April to late May and from late July to mid-September, the Cliff Swallow breeds locally in all sections of the Carolinas, showing a preference for nesting sites on tall dams and beneath high bridges crossing large man-made lakes. First reported nesting in South Carolina at Hartwell Dam on the upper Savannah River in the spring of 1965, the species soon was discovered breeding in North Carolina at Kerr Lake on the Roanoke River, at Tuckertown Lake on the Yadkin River, and at other sites in piedmont North and South Carolina. In 1977 and 1978, one nest was found at Moore's Landing in coastal South Carolina. By the turn of the century, nesting was occurring throughout the Carolinas at sites near water but not necessarily associated with tall dams and high bridges; however, reports of confirmed nesting from the mountains and the immediate coast remain rare.

Nesting habits: Cliff Swallows return to their colonies about mid-April. Some nests may be completed by the end of the month, while construction of others does not begin until early June. Building requires 5 days or longer. Scooping up balls of mud in their mouths, both adults help build the flask-shaped nest, which often has a neck protruding near the top and curving downward 5 to 6 inches (12 to 15 cm). Although the walls may be slightly reinforced with straw and horsehair, these mud structures must be placed in sheltered sites to keep them from being washed away by rainfall. Some pairs renovate nests built the previous year.

The nest chamber is scantily lined with feathers and dried grass stems. The four or five eggs are white, perhaps tinged with a creamy or pinkish shade, and almost always spotted with various shades of brown, sometimes in a ring around the egg. Incubation usually lasts about 14 days, and sometimes two broods are raised, the second ones fledging about mid-July.

Young are tended by both parents and leave the nest at 16 to 24 days of age. In late July or early August the adults and offspring of a colony may be seen perched on wires along the highway, which is enough to attract the attention of even a casual observer. Later they will flock with swallows of their own and other species prior to fall migration. Noted for their gregariousness, Cliff Swallows sometimes nest in mixed colonies with Barn Swallows.

Feeding habits: See comments on subfamily.

Description: The Cliff Swallow is identified in flight by its buffy rump and unforked tail. At close range the pale forehead, rusty throat, and streaked back can be seen.

Cave Swallow
Petrochelidon fulva
5.5 in. (14.0 cm)

Range: In the fall of 1999 and again in the late fall of 2002, major flights of Cave Swallows invaded the East Coast, including the Carolinas. Prior to 1999, only a few members of that species had been seen in North Carolina: one in Carteret County on December 17, 1987; two at New Bern on December 16, 1991; one at Sneads Ferry, Onslow County, on February 5, 1995; and one adult at Bodie Island, Dare County, on May 19, 1995. A Cave Swallow was found dead at Fort Macon, Carteret County, on December 2, 1999, and preserved as a museum study skin. The only previous specimen record from the Carolinas was one found near death on October 31, 1993, at Folly Beach, Charleston County, S.C. Both specimens are of the race *P. f. pallida*, and the South Carolina bird was the first member of the population from the western United States and Mexico documented as occurring in eastern North America.

The 1999 invasion brought the first known Cave Swallow to piedmont North Carolina. One was found in Iredell County on December 20, 1999. Reports were also received from the Savannah Spoil Site in Jasper County, S.C., and from several places along the immediate coast. The 2002 invasion started in late fall and continued into winter, bringing individuals north to Carteret County, N.C., and as many as forty birds to Sunset Beach, N.C.

Feeding habits: See comments on subfamily.

Description: Any "Cliff Swallow" seen in the Carolinas in late fall or winter should be examined very closely. Cliff and Cave Swallows are essentially the same size, shape, and color; but the Cave Swallow has a buffy throat patch that extends around the neck. Most Cliff Swallows are dark chestnut and blackish on the throat and around the neck. The cinnamon forehead of the Cave Swallow is not a reliable field character because a primarily southwestern race of the Cliff Swallow also has a cinnamon forehead, and juvenile Cave Swallows have a pale forehead and rump much like those of a Cliff Swallow. The Caribbean race of the Cave Swallow is rufous on the rump, sides, and throat. To clarify the confusing differences, consult a well-illustrated field guide.

Barn Swallow (adult at nest)

Barn Swallow
Hirundo rustica
6.0–7.5 in. (15–19 cm)

Range: The Barn Swallow nests throughout the Carolinas, being common in most areas but least numerous in southeastern South Carolina. The earliest birds may arrive in mid-March, and a few may linger along the coast into early winter. Abundant during migrations, Barn Swallows pass northward through the Carolinas mostly from early April to early June, and the return flight is mostly from late July through September.

Nesting habits: The bowl-shaped nests of mud pellets mixed with grass and straw are placed atop a rafter or sheltered ledge in a seldom-used building or beneath a bridge or pier. A small projection such as a nail or a mud dauber nest may offer a suitable starting point for a nest flattened against a wall. Having very weak feet, as do all swallows, the birds of both sexes scoop up and carry the mud pellets with their beaks. The nest usually is lined with white feathers.

The four to six white eggs may be spotted with reddish brown all over or mostly in a ring at the large end. Incubation is by the female and requires about 15 days. The male Barn Swallow sleeps beside the nest and may sit on the eggs when the female is absent, but he apparently does not have a functional brood patch. Both adults care for the young, which remain in the nest 18 days or longer.

Active nests have been found in the Carolinas from April to early August, the species being double-brooded in our region. The same nest may be used again, not only for the second brood but also in the succeeding year.

Feeding habits: See comments on subfamily.

Description: The Barn Swallow has a dark blue back, rusty underparts, and a deeply forked tail. Details such as the rusty forehead and white tail spots can be seen at close range. Immature birds have lighter underparts than the adults and may be confused with the Cliff Swallow.

Family PARIDAE:
Chickadees and Titmice

The Paridae are small, very active, and highly insectivorous birds with nostrils partly covered by short bristles. They have such strong feet and legs that they can perform amazing acrobatics while extracting seeds from cones, plucking berries from the tips of branches, or searching crevices in bark for insects and larvae. They are among the first birds encountered by the novice bird-watcher because they usually are the first birds in the neighborhood to discover a new bird feeder.

Carolina Chickadee

Carolina Chickadee
Poecile carolinensis
4.25–4.75 in. (10.8–12.0 cm)

Range: The Carolina Chickadee is a common permanent resident of woodlands throughout the Carolinas. The species is scarce in the mountains at elevations above 4,500 feet (1,380 m), but it may occur as high as 6,000 feet (1,800 m) in habitats not occupied by the slightly larger Black-capped Chickadee. Along the immediate coast, Carolina Chickadees may be locally scarce or absent wherever trees are few and far between.

Nesting habits: Carolina Chickadees sometimes take over nest boxes put up for bluebirds or wrens, but they usually prefer to excavate their own nest cavities even where old woodpecker holes are available. Both adults work about 2 weeks at digging the hole in the soft wood of a fence post, decaying stump, or dead stub on a living tree. Height above ground ranges from 2 to 12 feet (0.6 to 3.7 m), with an average around 5 or 6 feet (1.5 to 2.0 m).

At the bottom of the burrow, which may be 6 to 12 inches (15 to 30 cm) below the entrance hole, is the nest proper. This is made of plant down and other soft plant fibers, moss, hair, fur, and feathers matted together rather than woven. One side of the nest is built higher than the other to form a blanket that is drawn over the eggs when the bird leaves the nest. April is the usual month for nesting, but egg laying often begins in March and in some seasons does not occur until early May.

The four to eight white eggs are speckled with reddish brown, the spots often forming a wreath at the large end of the egg. Incubation requires about 12 to 13 days. The male feeds the incubating female and helps care for the young during their 17 days in the nest. The species is generally considered to be single-brooded, but some pairs apparently rear second broods. After the nesting season, Carolina Chickadees flock with titmice, nuthatches, kinglets, and other small birds.

Feeding habits: See comments on family.

Description: This tiny gray bird has a black cap and a black bib framing a white cheek patch. Its hurried *chick-a-dee-dee-dee* and whistled *fee-bee, fee-bay* are among the first songs learned by beginning bird students in the Carolinas. Separating the Carolina Chickadee from the Black-capped is a tricky field problem. Outside the known range of the Black-capped in the mountains of North Carolina, chickadees found in our region should be assumed to be Carolinas until proved otherwise.

Black-capped Chickadee
Poecile atricapillus
4.75–5.75 in. (12.0–14.5 cm)

Range: The race of the Black-capped Chickadee that reaches the southern limit of its range in the Great Smoky, Great Balsam, and Plott Balsam Mountains of North Carolina is *P. a. practicus.* That form appears to have been extirpated from all our other lofty peaks, including Mount Mitchell. Black-capped Chickadees breed mostly in the high-altitude spruce-fir forests above 4,000 feet (1,200 m). In winter Black-cappeds tend to withdraw to lower elevations and mingle with Carolina Chickadees. Where Black-capped and Carolina Chickadee breeding populations come together, hybridization may occur. In the Great Smokies and adjacent northern Great Balsams, the Black-capped is regarded as a fairly common permanent resident with no problem of hybridization with Carolina Chickadees. The Plott Balsam population appears to be

sound above 5,000 feet (1,500 m), but there is some evidence of little breeding between the two species below that elevation. The status of the Black-capped population in the southern Great Balsams has not been determined.

Because of the potential for hybridization and because Carolina Chickadees breed in some high-elevation habitats where Black-cappeds are not present, one cannot safely assume that any chickadee is a Black-capped simply because it is seen in spruce-fir forest above 4,000 feet (1,200 m). Nonetheless, there are published sight records for three family groups of Black-cappeds in spruce-fir above 5,000 feet (1,500 m) on Grandfather Mountain in 1984. Also, a singing Black-capped and a silent one were found at Mount Mitchell on June 23, 1989. Because the genetic identity of those birds was not established and reports of subsequent sightings are lacking, any claim for resident breeding populations of Black-capped Chickadees on those peaks would be premature.

Nesting habits: In late April and early May, pairs of Black-capped Chickadees dig their nest cavities from 5 to 60 feet (1.5 to 18.0 m) above ground in the trunks of dead trees. At the bottom of the cavity they build a nest of soft plant fibers, hair, wool, feathers, and insect cocoons. Eggs are like those of the Carolina Chickadee but usually larger. Incubation takes 12 to 14 days, and young remain in the nest about 16 days. The male feeds the female during incubation and helps her care for the young. Nesting activities for Black-cappeds begin 2 or 3 weeks later than for Carolinas.

Feeding habits: See comments on family.

Description: Separating Black-capped and Carolina Chickadees in the field is very difficult and indeed impossible for some individual birds, especially where hybrids occur in parts of the range. Compared with the Carolina, the Black-capped is slightly larger, has whiter cheeks and rustier sides, and has broader white edgings to the wing feathers. Observers should keep in mind that members of a northern population of the Carolina Chickadee, sometimes found in the mountains and northern piedmont of North Carolina, also have uncommonly rusty sides; but bill length is shorter than that of the Black-capped.

Black-cappeds tend to be tamer than Carolinas, or at least more curious about human activities. Vocalizations are not entirely reliable field characters because some individuals of both species occasionally deliver incomplete or incorrect songs that can be misleading. If identification is based on song, repetition of the song is essential. The Black-capped sings a clearly whistled *fee-bee*, and its *chick-a-dee-dee-dee* call is slow, deliberate, and about an octave lower in pitch than the hurried call of the Carolina.

Tufted Titmouse
Baeolophus bicolor
6.0–6.5 in. (15.0–16.5 cm)

Range: A common permanent resident throughout the Carolinas, the Tufted Titmouse is a bird of

Tufted Titmouse

deciduous and mixed woodlands, but it normally does not occur at the highest elevations in the mountains.

Nesting habits: Because Tufted Titmice do not excavate their own cavities, they readily accept nest boxes and old woodpecker holes. The chosen natural or man-made site may be 4 to 50 feet (1.2 to 15.0 m) above ground. Both sexes help build the nest. If the cavity is too deep, the birds will put in a filling of dead leaves, grass, and seed stems. The nest proper is made of green moss and leaves and is lined with cotton, hair, fur, feathers, and other soft fibers. In coastal South Carolina, a piece of cast snakeskin is almost always present.

The four to eight white or creamy eggs are profusely spotted with reddish brown. Laying may begin in mid-March in parts of South Carolina or be delayed until early June in the mountains. Requiring 12 to 14 days, incubation is performed entirely by the female, who is fed by the male. When she must leave her eggs, she covers them with soft nest materials. Young remain in the nest 15 or 16 days, being fed by both adults and brooded chiefly, if not wholly, by the female. The species is single-brooded, and after the nesting season titmice flock with chickadees, nuthatches, and other small birds.

Feeding habits: See comments on family.

Description: This small gray bird has rusty sides, a crest, and a shiny black eye. Its calls are much like those of the chickadee, but its whistled *peter-peter-peter* is distinctive.

Family SITTIDAE: Nuthatches

Members of this family are small, tree-dwelling birds that live in forests in the Northern Hemisphere. Only four species occur in North America.

Subfamily Sittinae: Typical Nuthatches

Nuthatches are small woodland birds that feed mostly by picking insects from crevices in bark while hitching nimbly headfirst up or, more often, down the trunks of trees. Not having stiffened tails to serve as props while they forage on tree trunks, they must depend entirely on their stout legs, long toes, and sharp claws. Nuthatches also eat seeds and nuts, which they wedge in crevices and pound open with their long, heavy bills. That behavior is a form of tool use, comparable to a person's using a vise to hold something in place while working on it. The crevice and the vise constitute a "third hand," so to speak. The nuthatches' habit of shelling nuts probably is the origin of the family name.

Red-breasted Nuthatch
Sitta canadensis
4.5 in. (11.5 cm)

Range: An erratic winter visitor in piedmont and coastal Carolina, the Red-breasted Nuthatch is fairly common to common some years from mid-September to early May and rare or absent others. Winter visitors frequent pine forests, often in association with other small birds. The species is a permanent resident in the spruce-fir and hemlock forests of the North Carolina mountains, being common from April through November. Depending on the local abundance of food, weather conditions, and the influx of migrants from the north, the Red-breasted Nuthatch may be common or absent at high elevations during the winter.

Sightings below 3,000 feet (900 m) are rare in the breeding season, but when the spruce-fir seed crop is poor, Red-breasted Nuthatches move down the mountains to feed on the seeds of other conifers. Extralimital breeding was noted in Rockingham County, N.C., in 1975. Although Red-breasted Nuthatches have been found in the mountains of South Carolina during the nesting season since the 1980s, that activity was not documented until April 28, 2003, when a nest was found in the picnic area of the Chattooga Recreation Area in Oconee County, adjacent to the Walhalla Fish Hatchery (elevation 2,574 feet [780 m]). The picnic area contains a stand of old-growth white pines and Canada hemlocks. The nest was in a dead stub of a living birch tree.

Red-breasted Nuthatch

Nesting habits: Red-breasted Nuthatches mate in March and remain together all year, rarely associating with the flocks of unmated birds. Although a pair may take over an old woodpecker hole, they are more likely to hollow out their own cavity in a rotten stub or dead limb. Height above ground or water may vary from 2 to 120 feet (0.6 to 37.0 m), but 10 to 15 feet (3.0 to 4.5 m) is average.

Both adults share in nest construction, lining the burrow with a pad of soft plant and animal fibers and plastering the surface around the entrance hole with pitch. Applications are made from the beginning of construction and continue as long as eggs or young remain in the nest. The pitch may prevent insects or predators from entering the nest cavity. The four to seven eggs are white with reddish-brown spots. Fresh clutches have been found as early as May 10 and as late as June 14. Incubation, apparently performed chiefly by the female, requires 12 days, and young leave the nest 14 to 21 days after hatching. Both adults care for the offspring, and the species is single-brooded.

Feeding habits: See comments on subfamily.
Description: See White-breasted Nuthatch.

White-breasted Nuthatch
Sitta carolinensis
5–6 in. (12.5–15.0 cm)

Range: The White-breasted Nuthatch is a permanent resident of mature deciduous forests in all sections of the Carolinas. It is fairly common in the mountains except in the spruce-fir forests, where it is scarce or absent; uncommon in most of the piedmont; and fairly common in swamps and floodplains throughout the coastal plain except near the immediate coast. Usually seen as single birds or isolated pairs, White-breasted Nuthatches remain mated all year and nest much earlier than do most other small birds.
Nesting habits: White-breasted Nuthatches rarely hollow out their own nest holes. They almost always take over deserted woodpecker holes or other natural cavities from 20 inches to 40 feet (0.5 to 12.0 m) above ground. Both adults help line the burrow with bark strips, feathers, fur, caterpillar silk, and other soft fibers. Egg laying begins by early March in coastal South Carolina and by early April in the mountains. The four to six white eggs sometimes have a rosy tinge and always are profusely speckled with reddish brown and lavender. Incubation requires 12 days, and the male brings food to the incubating female. Both parents feed the young in the nest and during their 2 weeks of dependency following departure. The species is single-brooded.

White-breasted Nuthatch

Feeding habits: See comments on subfamily.

Description: This small, upside-down bird has a blue-gray back and white breast. The male White-breasted Nuthatch has a solid black cap; the female, a gray one. The Red-breasted Nuthatch is similar, but it has rusty underparts and a dark line through the eye. The male has a black crown; the female, a slate-blue one. The Brown-headed Nuthatch has a brown cap and a light spot on the back of its neck; the sexes are alike.

Brown-headed Nuthatch
Sitta pusilla
4 in. (10 cm)

Range: The Brown-headed Nuthatch is a common permanent resident of open pine woods throughout the coastal plain and in most of the piedmont, but in the mountains the species is very local in winter and at low elevations during the nesting season. Successful nesting has been documented in Buncombe County several times, and there is

Brown-headed Nuthatch (at nest hole)

one report suggestive of breeding in Clay County, N.C.

Nesting habits: Brown-headed Nuthatches hollow out their own cavities in a partly decayed fence post, tall stump, or dead limb. Several holes may be started before one is selected for use and dug to a depth of about 6 inches (15 cm) below the entrance. Elevations above ground vary from a few inches to about 90 feet (28 m), the usual height being less than 15 feet (4.5 m). The nest chamber is lined with soft plant materials, prominent among them being the thin, transparent sheaths from pine seeds.

The four to six white or creamy eggs are heavily and rather evenly speckled with reddish brown and lavender. Eggs may be found from early March in coastal South Carolina to mid-May elsewhere in the Carolinas. Incubation requires about 14 days, with the male bringing food to the female. Both parents feed the young, and the family party remains together long after the nesting season is over. The species is single-brooded in southeastern South Carolina. Where their ranges overlap, Brown-headed Nuthatches associate with Red-cockaded Woodpeckers. Other frequent companions are kinglets, titmice, chickadees, Pine Warblers, Downy Woodpeckers, Chipping Sparrows, and Eastern Bluebirds.

Feeding habits: Brown-headed Nut-hatches feed largely on pine seeds and a wide variety of insects.

Description: See White-breasted Nuthatch.

Family CERTHIIDAE: Creepers

Creepers are an Old World family of small birds with long, slender, decurved bills and stiffened tail feathers. The tail is used as a prop as the creeper climbs about the trunks and limbs of trees searching crevices in the bark for hidden insects and larvae. There are only six species worldwide, and all are confined to the Northern Hemisphere.

Subfamily Certhiinae: Typical Creepers

Five of the six species in the Certhiidae are members of this subfamily, only one of which occurs in North America.

Brown Creeper
Certhia americana
5.0–5.75 in. (12.5–14.5 cm)

Range: The Brown Creeper is a fairly common winter resident from mid-October to mid-April in the

Brown Creeper

coastal plain and piedmont sections of the Carolinas. In the mountains of North Carolina it is a permanent resident, breeding mostly in the high-elevation spruce-fir forests, though territorial pairs have been reported as low as 2,600 to 3,000 feet (700 to 900 m). Brown Creepers winter at all elevations, but most commonly at the lower ones. Sometimes the species is rare or absent in winter on certain high peaks such as Mount Mitchell.

Nesting habits: Brown Creepers place their nests in knotholes and natural cavities, behind a slab of loose bark on a tall tree stub, or beneath a loose shingle on a building. Lined with feathers, the nest is a loosely formed mass of lichens, moss, grasses, rootlets, spider cocoons, and shredded bark. Nests built behind bark scales may be fastened in place with spider webs and built upward on the sides a little above the nest cup, giving the whole a crescent shape. Although the male brings materials to the nest site, construction apparently is the work of the female. Completion of the nest may require several weeks.

Singing may begin in mid-February, but from late March through June is the usual nesting period. In the southern Appalachians, nest construction has been noted from late April to mid-June. The five or six eggs may be sparingly or profusely dotted with reddish brown. Incubation takes about 14 days. The male brings food to the female both during nest building and while she is sitting on the eggs. The male also helps feed the young, which leave the nest about 14 days after hatching. Newly fledged birds have been seen in North Carolina from late June to early August. After the breeding season, Brown Creepers are often found with chickadees, Golden-crowned Kinglets, and Red-breasted Nuthatches in woodlands of various types.

Feeding habits: The Brown Creeper typically feeds by spiraling up the trunk of one tree to search for insects and then flying to the base of the next tree in preparation for another climb. When bright sunlight strikes the trunks of trees, creepers respond by climbing up the shady side of the tree, often approaching the edge of the shade but never moving onto the sunny side of the trunk. Under the same conditions, creepers searching the side of a house move straight up one shadow and fly to the base of the next one. In very cold weather the process may be reversed, with the creeper foraging in the warmth of

the sunlight and only occasionally moving into the edge of the shady side of the tree trunk.

In winter, Brown Creepers may feed heavily on pine seeds. They also collect insects from cobwebs beneath overhanging roofs or from crevices in the siding of wooden buildings, and they may roost on window ledges and porches. Such close association with human habitations seems surprising in a woodland species that rarely visits bird feeders.

Description: This small brown bird is more easily recognized by its feeding behavior than by its markings. Look for the long slender decurved bill, white eye line, rusty rump, and long stiff tail feathers.

Family TROGLODYTIDAE: Wrens

Wrens are small brown or brownish-gray birds with short strong legs, short rounded wings, sharp and usually decurved bills, and tails frequently cocked. They are highly insectivorous birds that live chiefly in hedges, brushy places, woodland tangles, and grassy marshes, foraging mostly on or near the ground. These pugnacious birds greet the intruder with harsh, scolding calls. The sexes look alike, and both sing throughout most of the year. Indeed, wrens are among the most gifted and persistent singers in the bird world.

The family name means "cave dweller" and derives from the shape of the large and typically domed nest with an entrance on the side. The male may build several nests as part of the mating ritual. The female selects one, usually the best constructed or best hidden, finishes the inside to suit herself, and lays and incubates the eggs. Males often roost in a cock nest, and cowbirds sometimes are fooled into laying there rather than in the real nest. Male wrens rarely incubate, but they may feed the female on the nest and regularly help care for the young. Wrens usually are multibrooded, and some are polygamous.

Carolina Wren
Thryothorus ludovicianus
5–6 in. (12.5–13.0 cm)

Carolina Wren

Range: South Carolina's official state bird, the Carolina Wren, is a common permanent resident in all sections of the Carolinas. However, in such specialized habitats as salt marshes and high-elevation spruce-fir forests, this species is known only as a postbreeding wanderer. Although Carolina Wrens are found in remote swamps and woodlands, they also frequent farmyards and the residential sections of cities. Their bubbling songs and scolding notes are heard all year long. A mated pair will remain together from one breeding season to the next, perhaps nesting in the same place for several successive years.

Nesting habits: Carolina Wrens build their bulky and often partly domed nests of dead leaves, twigs, rootlets, moss, pine needles, and other convenient materials in natural cavities, woodpiles, birdhouses, mailboxes, flower pots, or almost any other sheltered nook, including clothespin bags, caps, and the pockets of coats left hanging on porches or in garages.

Eggs number four to six per clutch and are whitish, well spotted with brown and lilac. Incubation,

performed wholly by the female, takes 12 to 14 days. Remaining in the nest about 2 weeks, the young are fed by both adults. Two broods are raised ordinarily, but three are common in coastal South Carolina, where first clutches are laid in late March or early April, with the second and third ones appearing in early June and mid-July. Northward and inland, first clutches are laid a little later, and third clutches are not common. This extraordinarily high rate of reproduction is possible because the female lays the next clutch in a nest the male has already prepared for her, and she may begin incubation while he is still feeding the offspring of the previous nesting.

Feeding habits: See comments on family.

Description: The largest of our wrens, the Carolina has a plain brown back, a prominent white eye stripe, and buffy underparts. One of its songs can be rendered as *cheerily, cheerily, cheerily* and another as *T-shirt, T-shirt.*

Bewick's Wren
Thryomanes bewickii
5.0–5.5 in. (12.5–14.0 cm)

Range: Formerly a common summer resident in the mountains of North Carolina, where it was one of the several most numerous birds found in the cities and towns prior to 1900, the Bewick's Wren (pronounced like the name of the Buick automobile) frequented farmyards and ranged to the highest peaks. Outside the mountains, breeding occurred occasionally eastward to Forsyth County, N.C., and to Chester and Aiken Counties, S.C. By the 1930s, the population had declined sharply. Although conclusive data are not available, the almost complete disappearance of the Bewick's Wren from the urban areas of western North Carolina appears to have taken place about the time the House Sparrow and European Starling invaded the region. Arrival of the Brown-headed Cowbird in Buncombe County by the early 1930s may have been the final blow. Bewick's Wren is among the parasitized species known to have raised young cowbirds.

Today the endemic Appalachian race of Bewick's Wren is believed to be extinct. The last known nesting in the Carolinas was near Mount Pisgah on the Blue Ridge Parkway in 1971. All subsequent reports from the region appear to have been transients from the migratory population that breeds outside the Appalachian Mountains in Kentucky and Tennessee. Most likely to be found in brushy places and woodpiles or around abandoned cars and buildings, the Bewick's Wren is easily attracted into view by squeaks, scolds, and Screech Owl imitations.

Feeding habits: See comments on family.

Description: Bewick's Wren has white underparts, a prominent white eye line, and mostly white outer tail feathers. The tail is long and rounded at the tip. The bird habitually jerks its tail sideways. The Carolina Wren also has a plain brown back, but its buffy underparts readily separate it from the Bewick's Wren.

House Wren
Troglodytes aedon
4.25–5.25 in. (11–13 cm)

Range: The House Wren is a common winter resident of brushy areas, thickets, and woodland margins in eastern South Carolina and coastal North Carolina from mid-September to early May, but the species becomes uncommon or rare westward throughout the two states. The House Wren nests in the lower and middle elevations of the North Carolina mountains and southward throughout the South Carolina mountains. In the mountains it is mostly a summer resident. The species also breeds at least locally throughout the piedmont of both states and adjacent portions of the inner coastal plain of North Carolina (e.g., Rocky Mount, Selma, Fayetteville, and Laurinburg). In the remainder of the North Carolina coastal plain, House Wrens nest locally and sporadically, mostly in recently burned clear-cuts and pocosins. The species, which was first known to nest in the

House Wren

North Carolina piedmont in 1922 and in western South Carolina in 1950, has extended its breeding range significantly in the past 50 years and may continue to do so in the decades ahead.

Nesting habits: Breeding birds arrive in early April and usually depart by mid-October. In many places, House Wrens nest only in towns, preferring open residential developments with lots of shrubbery. They seldom nest in exposed sites and readily accept a gourd or birdhouse, which the male sometimes fills to overflowing with twigs. The five to eight eggs are white and thickly speckled with reddish brown at the rounded end of the shell. The incubation period is 13 days, and young remain in the nest about 2 weeks.

Two broods are raised annually, and some males are polygamous. The female may begin finishing a nest for her second clutch before the first brood is fully independent. She may mate the second time with the same male or move into the territory of another male. If she deserts her first family, the young may perish because the male cannot

brood nestlings. If the young are old enough to regulate their own body temperature, they may survive, for the male will continue feeding them in the absence of his mate.

Feeding habits: See comments on family.

Description: The House Wren is a small, grayish-brown bird with no conspicuous markings. It has a faint eye line and a moderately long tail. The Winter Wren has heavily barred underparts and a very short tail. Bewick's and Carolina Wrens have prominent white eye stripes. The Marsh and Sedge Wrens have white streaking on their backs.

Winter Wren
Troglodytes troglodytes
3.5–4.25 in. (9.0–10.8 cm)

Range: The Winter Wren is a fairly common permanent resident of the high-elevation spruce-fir community where it breeds and associates with species such as the Golden-crowned Kinglet, Brown Creeper, and Red-breasted Nuthatch. The Winter Wren may withdraw from the highest peaks about mid-November and return in late March or early April. Regardless of elevation, the species shows a preference for moist, cool habitat. Winter Wrens sing throughout the year, but their concert reaches a peak from late April until mid-July. These birds sometimes perform antiphonally, with the refrain carried by two or more musicians.

Outside the mountains, the Winter Wren is a fairly common winter resident, occurring from mid-October to mid-April. This woodland species is usually found about stream banks, fallen trees, and dense tangles.

Nesting habits: Little is known about the breeding habits of the Winter Wren in the southern Appalachians. The small amount of data available indicates that nests are concealed in upturned roots of fallen trees. The four or five eggs are white, finely dotted with reddish brown. Laying probably begins about mid-May, and the incubation period is thought to be 14 to 16 days. Young apparently stay in the nest nearly 3 weeks, departing before the end of June. No published records suggest a second brood in the North Carolina population.

Feeding habits: See comments on family.

Description: This very dark brown wren has a stubby tail, indistinct eye line, and heavy barring on the underparts. Along the path from the parking lot to the tower atop Mount Mitchell, a Winter Wren often sings persistently from the bare top of a standing dead conifer, ignoring the hundreds of tourists who may pass on a busy spring weekend.

Sedge Wren
(Short-billed Marsh Wren)
Cistothorus platensis
4 in. (10 cm)

Range: The Sedge Wren is a fairly common to common winter resident of freshwater and brackish marshes on and near the Carolina coast. Inland the species becomes rare or absent in winter. Fall migrants have been seen inland from early August to early October, and spring migrants occur from late April to mid-May. Although Marsh and Sedge Wrens often winter in the same habitat, the latter usually prefer marshes with scattered shrubs.

Nesting habits: There is no firm evidence that the Sedge Wren breeds in the Carolinas, but its globular nests should be sought in northeastern North Carolina amid the sedges, grasses, and other low herbage at a height of not more than 1 or 2 feet (30 to 60 cm) above ground, mud, or very shallow water. Usually the nest is very well hidden, with blades of the growing green grass woven into the ball and arching over it. The eggs are pure white, and the shells are very thin and fragile. The peak of the Sedge Wren's nesting season is from early June to early July.

Marsh Wrens also lay clutches of white eggs occasionally, but their nests tend to be more conspicuous, slightly ovate, attached to taller plants, and over slightly deeper water.

Feeding habits: See comments on family.

Description: The very tame little Sedge Wren has a short bill, a stubby tail, an indistinct eye line, and a brown back with narrow white streaks that extend into the crown. Its song is a series of very sharp, staccato chips followed by a more rapid series of notes somewhat like a less staccato version of the rattle given by a Common Yellowthroat. The call note is a rich *chip* or *chip-chip*.

**Marsh Wren
(Long-billed Marsh Wren)**
Cistothorus palustris
4–5 in. (10.0–12.5 cm)

Marsh Wren

Range: The Marsh Wren is a common permanent resident of the great coastal marshes. It is found not only in salt marshes but also amid the tall reeds and cattails of freshwater marshes. Some of the breeding birds may withdraw southward in winter, but they are more than replaced by the influx of birds from the north. During migrations, Marsh Wrens occur inland to our mountains, and an occasional straggler may spend the winter in some marsh far from the coast.

Marsh Wrens sing energetically, often several at a time, at any hour of day or night. Suddenly a bird will fly upward for several yards, singing on the wing, and then drop silently into the marsh again.

Nesting habits: Although they may nest singly, birds of this species tend to be fairly gregarious and often nest in loose colonies. Attached to the stem of a marsh plant growing in shallow water, and woven of wet, pliable marsh grass, the nest is a hollow ball about the size of a grapefruit and has an entrance on the side. Four or five dummy nests may be constructed in addition to the one selected by the female.

The five to eight eggs are light brown, heavily marked with darker shades of brown. Incubation takes about 13 days. The species is often triple-brooded, and eggs have been found from late April through early August. The chief cause of nesting failure is high water; thus, the Marsh Wren may be comparatively scarce along our coast the year following the passing of a major storm during the nesting season.

Feeding habits: In addition to insects common in the diet of all wrens, this species consumes many snails and small crustaceans.

Description: The Marsh Wren has a prominent white eye stripe and a dark brown back narrowly streaked with white at the shoulders. The song is a musical, liquid gurgling sound followed by brief rattling. The series may be introduced by a brief nasal gran note. The alarm call is a sharp *tsuk* or *tsuk-tsuk*.

Family REGULIDAE: Kinglets

These small, very active birds have thin bills and weak feet and legs. Most species are Eurasian in distribution or circumpolar in the Northern Hemisphere. The latter is the case with the two species that occur in the Carolinas.

Golden-crowned Kinglet

Golden-crowned Kinglet
Regulus satrapa
4.0–4.25 in. (10.0–10.8 cm)

Range: The Golden-crowned Kinglet is a common permanent resident in the hemlock and spruce-fir forests of the North Carolina mountains and at least locally as far south as the Walhalla Fish Hatchery and the Chattooga Recreation Area in Oconee County, S.C., where nesting activity was first observed in June 1986 and an active nest was found in April 2003. The previously known southern limit of breeding in the eastern United States was near Highlands, N.C.

Outside the mountains, the Golden-crowned Kinglet is a common winter resident of the Carolinas from early October to mid-April, frequenting stands of evergreens and rarely visiting bird feeders.

Nesting habits: Built 4 to 60 feet (1.1 to 18.0 m) above ground among the slender twigs of spruces or other evergreens, the nest of the Golden-crowned Kinglet is a ball of green mosses mixed with lichens or bits of dead leaves and lined with strips of soft inner bark, fur, rootlets, or feathers. The opening is at the top with the rim contracted above the hollow holding the five to ten creamy eggs that are variably dotted or splotched with brown. The nest is so small that large clutches are deposited in two layers. Late May or early June appears to be the peak of egg laying in the Appalachian Mountains. The South Carolina nest, however, was discovered on April 28, 2003, and the pair were feeding young in the nest on June 2. The incubation period and length of time offspring remain in the nest apparently are unknown. Young birds have been found in nests in North Carolina in late June.

A Maine observer reported that newly hatched kinglets are about the size of bumblebees and are fed by both parents, at first by regurgitation and later with whole insects and caterpillars. After the nesting season, Golden-crowned Kinglets associate in loose flocks with chickadees, Red-breasted Nuthatches, Brown Creepers, and other small birds.

Feeding habits: Golden-crowned Kinglets pick insects, spiders, and other minute animal life from twigs and leaves of trees.

Description: The Golden-crowned Kinglet is a tiny, olive-green bird with two white wing bars. It has a dark line through the eye, a white line above it, and a black edge to the golden crown. The female has a yellow crown patch, but the male has a central orange streak dividing the yellow of the crown. Kinglets are very active birds that constantly flick their wings while on the move.

Ruby-crowned Kinglet

Ruby-crowned Kinglet
Regulus calendula
3.75–4.50 in. (9.5–11.5 cm)

Range: The Ruby-crowned Kinglet is
a common winter resident east of
the mountains from late September
to early May. In the mountains the
species is mostly a spring and fall
transient at the higher elevations,
preferring the coves and valleys
as a winter home. Ruby-crowneds
occur in a wide variety of habitats
including residential shrubbery,
woodland margins, and forests,
often showing a preference for conifers. Even in the mountains, summer kinglets are best considered
vagrants unless there is definite
evidence of nesting activity.
Feeding habits: Constantly flicking
its wings and often hovering at
the tips of branches, the restless
Ruby-crowned Kinglet feeds almost
entirely on animal matter, only occasionally consuming a few berries
and weed seeds.
Description: The Ruby-crowned
Kinglet is a tiny, olive-green bird
with two white wing bars and a
white eye ring that is broken at the

top. The male's red crown is seldom
seen except when the bird erects
those feathers. Ruby-crowneds
begin singing in April while still on
the wintering grounds. The song is
remarkably loud and rich in tone
for so small a creature.

Family SYLVIIDAE:
Old World Warblers

There are nearly 400 species of these
small, active, insect-eating warblers
that are not related to the wood
warblers of the Western Hemisphere.
Two Old World warblers are known
to have reached the North American
Arctic, where they occur mostly in
willows.

Subfamily Polioptilinae:
Gnatcatchers

The gnatcatchers are a distinctly
New World subfamily of birds that
have thin bills and weak feet and
legs. Eight species live from South
and Central America northward, with
only one reaching the eastern United
States.

Blue-gray Gnatcatcher
Polioptila caerulea
4.0–5.5 in. (10–14 cm)

Range: The Blue-gray Gnatcatcher is
a common summer resident of bottomland hardwoods in all sections
of the Carolinas, but it usually is
not found in the mountains above
2,500 to 3,400 feet (750 to 1,000
m). Gnatcatchers begin arriving in
the Carolinas about mid-March,
and most of them depart in early
October, although a few spend the
winter in the lower coastal plain,
mostly from Wilmington south.

Blue-gray Gnatcatcher

Occasionally gnatcatchers winter as far north and inland as Lake Mattamuskeet and Goldsboro. Sightings of stragglers in the piedmont and coastal plain during December or early January suggest but do not prove overwintering.

Nesting habits: Both adults aid in construction of the nest, which is a lichen-covered cup of grasses, plant down, and feathers saddled on a lateral limb of a tree from 4 to 35 feet (1.2 to 11.0 m) above ground, rarely as high as 80 feet (24.5 m). Placed in both deciduous and evergreen trees, gnatcatcher nests closely resemble the somewhat smaller ones built by Ruby-throated Hummingbirds. The four to six eggs are white, tinged with green or blue, and speckled with chestnut.

Laying takes place from mid-April to early May. Both sexes incubate eggs, which hatch in about 13 days. Young remain in the nest 10 to 12 days and are fed by both parents. Although the species is single-brooded over most of its range, a second brood may be raised in parts of the Carolinas, mostly in southeastern South Carolina. After

the breeding season, gnatcatchers roam through upland woods with chickadees and titmice.

Feeding habits: Gnatcatchers are almost wholly insectivorous, taking cotton leafworms, woodborers, and flies in addition to gnats.

Description: This tiny blue-gray bird has a prominent white eye ring and white outer tail feathers. Its body may be slightly smaller than that of a kinglet, but the longer tail gives it a greater overall length. Some individuals are very tame, even gleaning insects beneath a wooden table occupied by a couple of picnickers.

Family TURDIDAE: Thrushes

Thrushes are migratory woodland birds that are noted for their sweet, flute-like songs. They are highly insectivorous, although in season they eat a wide variety of both wild and cultivated fruits and berries, those of flowering dogwood, American holly, and pokeweed being among their favorites in the Carolinas.

Northern Wheatear
Oenanthe oenanthe
5.5–6.0 in. (14–15 cm)

Range: A bird having the appropriate field marks and behavior of this species was seen on a Charleston, S.C., golf course on October 1, 1960. Subsequently, five sightings have been made of single birds in North Carolina: at Franklin, Macon County, October 11, 1981; near Avon, Dare County, October 2, 1987; at Hatteras Campground, September 22 to October 29, 1994; at Ocracoke, October 6–7, 1995; and an adult female of the Greenland race at the dam on Lake Tiaroga, Connestee Falls community, Transylvania County, October 14, 2003. The wheatear seen at Franklin was associating with a flock of Eastern Bluebirds.

Wheatears are a group of Eastern Hemisphere thrushes that have moved out of the woodlands to frequent open country. Breeding in tundra from northern Alaska to Greenland, the Northern Wheatear winters in the Old World and is a rare accidental southward in the Western Hemisphere to Louisiana, Cuba, and Bermuda.

Description: The only distinctive feature on this predominantly gray species is its tail. The bird is white on the rump and at the base of the tail, which is broadly banded with black at the tip. The black of the central tail feathers is noticeably wider than on the others. A field guide should be consulted for identification of this and all other rare or uncommon species.

Eastern Bluebird (male)

Eastern Bluebird
Sialia sialis
6–7 in. (15.0–17.5 cm)

Range: Eastern Bluebirds are fairly common permanent residents of our open woodlands, orchards, farmyards, and roadsides. They are locally scarce or absent on and near the coast and at high elevations in the mountains.

Nesting habits: Bluebirds build a simple nest of grass or pine needles in the bottom of a natural cavity in a tree or wooden fence post. They readily accept properly constructed birdhouses and often appropriate rural and suburban mailboxes. Most of the nesting materials are gathered by the female. Four or

Eastern Bluebird (female)

five pale blue eggs usually are laid, but clutches of white eggs are also found. Rarely, there may be four blue eggs and one very pale blue egg speckled with reddish brown.

The female normally does all the incubating, and eggs hatch in 12 or 13 days.

The male helps feed the young, which remain in the nest 15 to 18 days. Nesting activity begins early (March or even February in some parts of South Carolina), and three broods may be raised in a season. Eggs have been found from early March to the first of August in the Carolinas. Birds of the year remain with the parents and may help feed the young of subsequent broods. Family bands of Eastern Bluebirds are joined after the nesting season by birds of several other species such as the Pine Warbler, Carolina Chickadee, Tufted Titmouse, Brown-headed Nuthatch, and Chipping Sparrow.

Many bluebirds are killed by ice storms, but by far the greatest threat to the species is the shortage of suitable nesting sites. Farmers and suburban homeowners who remove dead trees and branches or erect metal fences must provide nest boxes if they want to keep their bluebird neighbors.

Feeding habits: See comments on family. In winter, bluebirds may be attracted to a feeder by offerings of suet, raisins, mealworms, or suet cake containing peanut butter.

Description: The adult male Eastern Bluebird has a blue back, red breast, and white belly. The female is similar but grayish about the head. Dingy young birds have speckled breasts and prominent white eye rings. The red breast is acquired during a molt that usually occurs prior to the first winter. Very rarely a female with a speckled breast, probably hatched from a late brood

the previous year, may nest successfully during her first spring.

An all-blue bird believed to have been a male Mountain Bluebird (*S. currucoides*) was seen perched on a nest box in Buncombe County, N.C., on June 15, 1985; but there was no evidence that a mate was present. A second report of that species came from Celo, Yancey County, N.C., where a male was present for several days in January 2004. The Mountain Bluebird is a very rare straggler east of the Mississippi River.

Townsend's Solitaire
Myadestes townsendi
8.5 in. (22.0 cm)

Range: The Townsend's Solitaire is a highly migratory western species that occurs casually in eastern North America in fall and winter. A single bird was seen near the top of Table Rock Mountain, Pickens County, S.C., on December 3, 1994.

Feeding habits: Wild fruits and berries predominate in the diet of the Townsend's Solitaire, which also takes a good number of insects, especially caterpillars.

Description: A long-tailed gray bird with white eye rings and white outer rectrices, the Townsend's Solitaire has an erect posture, a small bill, and a buffy wing stripe. Juveniles look much like juvenile Eastern Bluebirds, but with a longer tail.

Veery
Catharus fuscescens
6.5–7.5 in. (16.5–19.0 cm)

Range: In southwestern North Carolina and adjacent Georgia, the Veery

Veery

reaches its southern limit of breeding in the mountains of eastern North America. The species can be found not only in the spruce-fir zone above 5,000 feet (1,500 m) but also in deciduous woods from 3,500 to 5,000 feet (1,070 to 1,500 m), where it overlaps the upper range of breeding for the Wood Thrush.

From late May to late July the parking lot at Clingman's Dome in the Great Smoky Mountains National Park is a good place to listen for the Veery's loud, descending series of rapid, flute-like notes. The evening chorus of the Veery continues until dark. Outside the mountains the species is a fairly common transient that is found mostly in April and May and in September and October. It is uncommon near the coast.

Nesting habits: Typically, nests are placed on or near the ground in woods, and those nests closest to the ground often rest on a bed of leaves. The peak of laying is from late May to early June. The three or four greenish-blue eggs are slightly smaller than those of the Wood Thrush. The female incubates the eggs for 10 to 12 days. The male guards the nest and helps care for the young, which remain in the nest at least 10 days. There is no evidence that the species has a second brood.

Feeding habits: See comments on family.

Description: See Wood Thrush.

Gray-cheeked Thrush
Catharus minimus
7–8 in. (17.5–20.0 cm)

Range: An uncommon spring and fall migrant, the Gray-cheeked Thrush, like the Swainson's Thrush, has been reported along the coast in winter, but such sightings lack convincing documentation. The Gray-cheeked is seen most often in the upland hardwood forests during May and early October (extremes April 25 to June 19 and September 9 to November 17).

Feeding habits: See comments on family.

Description: See Wood Thrush for a comparative description. See Bicknell's Thrush for song comparison. Very rarely a Gray-cheeked Thrush may have black feet and a

Gray-cheeked Thrush

great deal of black in feathers that normally are brown, but the gray cheek patch generally remains recognizable at very close range.

Bicknell's Thrush
Catharus bicknelli
6.25 in. (16.0 cm)

Range: Bicknell's Thrush is a very rarely seen species that migrates through the Carolinas en route from breeding grounds in eastern Canada and New England to wintering grounds south of the United States.

Feeding habits: See comments on family.

Description: Formerly considered a subspecies of the Gray-cheeked Thrush, Bicknell's Thrush is not easily identified in the field. It is a brown-backed thrush with a reddish-brown tail, which makes it look very much like the Hermit Thrush. If the apparent Hermit Thrush does not cock and droop its tail, the bird in question may be a Bicknell's Thrush. The three-phrase, Veery-like songs of the Gray-cheeked and Bicknell's Thrushes are distinctive. The Gray-cheeked song drops during the first and last phrases but rises in the middle. Bicknell's song rises during the first and last phrases but drops in the middle.

Swainson's Thrush
Catharus ustulatus
6.5–7.5 in. (16.5–19.0 cm)

Range: Fairly common spring and fall transients in upland hardwood forests, Swainson's Thrushes move northward in April and May, and they pass through the Carolinas on

Swainson's Thrush

their return trip to the tropics in September and October. Occasional birds may linger into winter along the coast, but the species is very unusual as a winter visitor in the Carolinas.

Feeding habits: See comments on family.

Description: See Wood Thrush for a comparative description.

Hermit Thrush
Catharus guttatus
6.5–7.5 in. (16.5–19.0 cm)

Range: A fairly common winter resident of woodlands throughout the Carolinas from mid-October to early May (extremes September 15 to May 12), the Hermit Thrush is less abundant in the mountains than toward the coast. As early as 1979 there was a singing male apparently on territory at Roan Mountain, N.C. Summer birds were heard singing in spruce-fir forests on Grandfather Mountain, Mount Mitchell, and Unaka Mountain in Mitchell County, N.C., in 1984, 1989, and 1992, respectively. Although numbers heard on Roan Mountain

Hermit Thrush (feathers fluffed for warmth)

and Mount Mitchell continued to increase, the first proof of breeding in North Carolina was not obtained until 2001, when three fledglings were seen in Buncombe County at an elevation of 5,470 feet (1,658 m) on June 21. During July 2002 there were three singing birds along Heintooga Road in the Great Smoky Mountains National Park, the southernmost locality reported in the Appalachian Mountains during the nesting season. A male was singing at Devil's Courthouse through May 2004, but nesting was not confirmed.

Nesting habits: A Hermit Thrush typically builds its nest on the ground in coniferous or mixed conifer-hardwood forests. The nest is often sheltered by a low limb of a conifer. Occasionally the nest may be placed low in a tree, 2 to 4 feet (0.6 to 1.2 m) above ground. A ground-level nest may be in a slight depression and usually is well hidden beneath a small tree, bush, or fern. The bulky but compact structure of twigs, bark, and various plant fibers is lined with conifer needles, plant fibers, and rootlets. The female alone builds the nest and incubates the eggs, but the male feeds her during incubation. The smooth, oval, pale blue and slightly glossy eggs number three or four and hatch after about 12 days. Both parents tend the altricial young, which leave the nest when about 10 to 12 days old.

Feeding habits: Hermit Thrushes normally eat worms, insects, fruits, and berries. They are not at all shy when visiting bird feeders at homes located in or near woodlands. Apple cores and a paste made of peanut butter, corn meal, and melted suet are favorite feeder foods. Hermit Thrushes will also pluck berries from an arrangement of bittersweet in a container beside an exterior doorway.

Description: This small brown bird with an indistinctly spotted breast and a conspicuous eye ring is easily recognized by its reddish-brown tail, which it raises and lowers several times a minute. The Hermit Thrush rarely sings its beautiful, liquid song while wintering in the Carolinas. Apparently it sings only briefly just before sunrise and occasionally at dusk, doing so most frequently soon after arrival in fall and shortly before departure in spring. Throughout the daylight hours it gives only a low but distinctive call note, a whiny *wee* that is slurred upward, and sometimes a lower-pitched *chuck*. See Wood Thrush and Bicknell's Thrush for comparative descriptions.

Brown-backed thrushes in winter: The only brown-backed thrush that is supposed to winter in the Carolinas is the Hermit Thrush. Failure of a single bird to cock its tail during a brief period of observation does not automatically make it a Veery, a Gray-cheeked Thrush, a Bicknell's, or a Swainson's. Any brown-backed thrush found dead in winter (unless obviously a Hermit Thrush) may be a bird of special interest and therefore should be deposited in the scientific collections of a university zoology department or a museum with an ornithologist on staff.

Wood Thrushes (pair at nest with young)

Wood Thrush
Hylocichla mustelina
7.5–8.5 in. (19.0–21.5 cm)

Range: The Wood Thrush is a common summer resident from coastal Carolina to the lower and middle elevations of the mountains, but in the spruce-fir zone it is replaced by another thrush, the Veery. Wood Thrushes return to their breeding territory in April and depart for their tropical wintering grounds in October. Although there are a few winter records for the Carolinas, mostly in late December, no known report documents overwintering in the region.

Nesting habits: Wood Thrushes almost always nest amid mature trees of swamps, woods, and dooryards, but the nest is usually placed in a shrub or in the main fork of a sapling about 8 to 15 feet (2.5 to 4.5 m) above ground. Occasionally a nest may be saddled on a large horizontal limb of an oak overhanging an opening in the woods. Loss of mature trees to storm damage or logging often causes a noticeable decline in the local Wood Thrush population.

The nest is essentially like that of the American Robin; but the outer wall usually has more leaves and bits of paper or plastic, and the mud cup usually has a lining of rootlets. Eggs normally number three or four and are greenish blue, decidedly lighter in color than those of the Gray Catbird. First clutches generally are laid in late April or early May. Incubation requires 13 or 14 days and is performed by the female. She broods the young during their 12 or 13 days in the nest. Males guard the nest and help care for the young. The species is double-brooded in the Carolinas, and the second nest may be under construction only a couple of days after young leave the first one.

Feeding habits: See comments on family.

Description: This species and the five spotted-breasted thrushes listed above are separated from the Brown Thrasher by their smaller size, shorter tails, and generally olive-brown upperparts. The Wood Thrush is reddish brown about the head and has rounded breast spots that contrast sharply with the white underparts. It is also readily identified by its ringing song, often three liquid, flute-like notes followed by a trill given emphatically at a higher pitch. The song may sound like *pur-co-lo-reee.*

The other five species have comparatively indistinct breast spots. The Hermit Thrush has a conspicuous eye ring and a reddish tail, which it constantly raises and lowers. Bicknell's Thrush also has a reddish tail, but it is not constantly raised and lowered. Swainson's Thrush has a buffy eye ring, a buffy cheek patch, and a buffy wash on the upper breast. Gray-cheeked Thrush has a gray cheek patch, whitish breast and throat, and an eye ring that, if present at all, is whitish and indistinct. The Veery has completely reddish-brown upperparts. Neither Swainson's nor Gray-cheeked Thrushes have red in the upperparts, and many fall birds of those two species are so similar that they cannot be readily separated in the field. Consult a well-illustrated field guide for help in identifying this difficult and confusing group of birds.

American Robin
Turdus migratorius
9–11 in. (22–28 cm)

Range: The American Robin is the best known and most widely distributed of the North American thrushes. This abundant species winters throughout the Carolinas and breeds in all sections of the two states, but in summer it tends to be scarce or absent along the coast

American Robin (at pyracantha bush)

and at elevations above 4,000 feet (1,200 m). During the 1970s, robins became well established in the vicinity of McClellanville, S.C., the southernmost point on the Carolina coast where nesting was then known to occur regularly. Since that time, the breeding range has expanded into the Charleston area.

Robins nest mostly near residences where lawns, shrubs, and scattered trees are found. After the breeding season, robins flock and roost in dense cover such as wooded swamps, where they are often found in company with European Starlings and blackbirds. When our dooryard birds move south for the winter, they are replaced by flocks of migrants from the north. In spring, northbound flocks of robins visit pastures and large lawns.

Nesting habits: The robin usually builds her nest in a crotch if the tree has small limbs or atop a large horizontal limb, but exposed beams of a porch or storage shed will suffice. Sometimes one or more nests may be started and abandoned before one is completed and occupied. Height above ground is variable, 15 to 50 feet (4.5 to 15.0 m) being commonplace; but ones as low as about 3 feet (1 m) are very rare.

The male usually brings nesting materials, but the female is primarily responsible for construction. The nest of grasses, twigs, rootlets, leaves, or perhaps yellowed daffodil foliage is given rigidity with mud, which the bird forms into a cup by pressing her breast against the inner wall while turning her body. The mud is often collected from earthworm castings. The mud cup is lined with dry grasses. Three or four clear blue-green eggs are laid, usually about mid-April for first clutches. However, a series of warm days in January may result in nest construction and clutches of eggs laid by early February. Such nests are almost never successful.

Eggs are generally found from early April to late July in the Carolinas. Incubation requires 12 to 14 days, young remain in the nest about 2 weeks, and two or even three broods may be raised each season. The male does not incubate or brood, but he does help guard the nest. He helps feed the young in the nest and assumes full responsibility after their departure. That frees the female to begin making preparations for the laying of the next clutch.

Robins are among the few birds known to feed the young of other species. Very unusual was a robin feeding young Eastern Bluebirds still in the nest box.

Feeding habits: Robins eat worms, insects, fruits, and berries.

Description: The American Robin is dark above and rusty below. The head of the male is darker than that of the female. Young robins have heavily spotted breasts until the first molt, which for birds of the first brood usually begins in early July in the Carolinas. During their first winter, young birds have red breasts like the adults.

Varied Thrush
Ixoreus naevius
9.5 in. (24.0 cm)

Range: Varied Thrushes breed on the West Coast from northern Alaska and western Canada southward along the coast to northern California. The species winters south to southern California. Nonetheless, Varied Thrushes occur accidentally throughout the contiguous United States. An adult male was photographed in a yard at Edisto Beach, S.C., on October 6 and 10, 1993. A second report was for a winter straggler found at Spartanburg, S.C., by participants in a Christmas Bird Count. The third sighting for South Carolina occurred at James Island on November 30, 2002.

Feeding habits: See comments on family.

Description: Only slightly smaller than an American Robin, the Varied Thrush in all plumages has an orange stripe above the eye, orange throat, and orange wing bars. The juvenile has a breast band that is wide and mottled gray and orange. It is narrow and gray in the adult female, and narrow and black in the adult male. Both adults have mostly orange underparts below the breast band. The male has a black crown, a wide black eye stripe, and a blue-gray back. The adult female is dark or medium gray in those same areas. Undertail coverts are white, contrasting sharply with the dark tail.

Family MIMIDAE: Catbirds, Mockingbirds, and Thrashers

Probably descended from some thrush-like ancestor, all members of this New World family are excellent singers, and most are skillful mimics. The three species found regularly in our region can be separated by voice according to the number of times in succession identical phrases are given. The Northern Mockingbird will sing the same phrase three or more times in a row, the Brown Thrasher but twice, and the Gray Catbird only once. A catbird may give several consecutive mewing sounds, but each will have a different inflection. The voice of the catbird, which conveys a sense of sadness to some hearers, is more liquid and normally less strident than that of our other mimics. A Chippewa Indian naturalist bestowed upon the catbird a name meaning "the bird that cries with grief."

Gray Catbird
Dumetella carolinensis
8–9 in. (20–22 cm)

Range: The Gray Catbird is found in all sections of the Carolinas at all seasons, but only along the coast is it a true year-round resident. In the mountains, catbirds are common from mid-April to mid-October, even on some of the highest peaks, but in winter they become rare or absent, lingering only at the lower elevations. In the piedmont, catbirds are common in summer and rare or absent in winter. In the coastal plain, catbirds are fairly

Gray Catbird

common during the breeding season, uncommon in winter, and abundant only during migrations. Although they breed but sparingly along most of the immediate coast, catbirds are fairly common there in winter and may be locally abundant in both summer and winter at certain coastal sites, such as the Bodie–Pea Island area. Catbirds frequent residential neighborhoods having dense shrubbery as well as all sorts of thickets, especially damp ones.

Nesting habits: The male catbird uses song to establish a territory and attract a mate. He woos her by chasing after her, by strutting before her with wings drooped and tail cocked, and by courtship feeding. The nest is a deep cup of twigs, dead leaves, and grasses; it is lined with rootlets and secluded in briers, bushes, and trees with thick foliage. Height above ground generally ranges from 3 to 15 feet (1.0 to 4.5 m), but some nests have been discovered as high as 60 feet (18 m).

Both the male and the female work on the nest. If a bird of either sex happens to be present when the other arrives with additional materials, the latecomer will turn the load over to the first bird and begin to search for another suitable item. Construction normally takes 5 or 6 days, but sometimes pairs that have lost a first clutch to a predator will build a new nest very quickly by using almost all the pieces of the first one.

The four or five deep greenish-blue eggs are laid about mid-May for the first clutch and in June for the second. Once incubation is well under way, the female rarely leaves her eggs. She is fed on the nest by her mate. Incubation requires 12 or 13 days, and young remain in the nest for 10 days. Although males neither incubate nor brood, they do help feed the nestlings and clean the nest. Banding studies indicate that a pair may remain mated to each other through the entire season, or the male may retain a certain territory over a period of years and have a different mate for each of several successive nestings.

Feeding habits: Catbirds eat both animal and vegetable matter, the latter primarily fruits and berries.

Description: The Gray Catbird is uniformly dark gray except for its black cap and rusty undertail coverts. See comments on the family for a description of catbird vocalizations.

Northern Mockingbird
Mimus polyglottos
9–11 in. (22–28 cm)

Range: Mockingbirds are our most versatile singers, giving remarkable concerts by day and night throughout most of the year. Some individuals have been reported as being

Northern Mockingbird

able to imitate the songs of thirty other species. Singing males face the sun when it is low in the sky. Nocturnal singers orient toward any light source that may be available. Such orientation is believed to enhance the conspicuousness of the singer. Perched atop some tall snag, chimney, or television antenna, the mocker sometimes becomes so rapturous that it will fly straight up for several feet and drop to its perch again without missing a note. The bird may move from one perch to another, singing all the way.

This magnificent songster is a common to abundant permanent resident in all sections of the Carolinas, but in the mountains it is confined to the lower elevations, rarely going as high as 3,400 feet (1,020 m).

Nesting habits: A bird of the roadsides, woodland edges and thickets, and dooryards, the Northern Mockingbird builds its nest 3 to 12 feet (1.0 to 3.5 m) above ground in bushes, vines, and trees. The bulky cup of small sticks, twigs, and leaves is normally built by the male and lined with grasses and rootlets by

the female. Construction usually requires 3 or 4 days. The three to five
greenish-blue eggs are spotted and
splashed with reddish brown. The
female incubates the eggs for 12 to
14 days. Her mate usually assists in
caring for the young, which remain
in the nest about 2 weeks.

The nesting season begins early
in April with eggs for the first brood
being laid about the middle of the
month, the second clutch in June,
and the third in late July or early
August. Mockingbirds are quite
bold in defense of their nests, at-
tacking humans, cats, snakes, and
other birds with a ferocity that does
not encourage a second visit.

During courtship, the pair face
each other and raise their wings
repeatedly in a highly stereotyped
dance. Pairs may stay mated from
2 to 4 years, and some remain
together up to 8 years. Wing flashing is seen in single birds at other
seasons, possibly a recrudescence
of the courtship performance, possibly to startle insects into movement—or just as likely for some
reason not yet considered by ornithologists. The white wing patch
is larger in males than in females.
Within the male population, the
size of wing patches is greater in
mated birds than in unmated ones.
Therefore, patch size is deemed
useful in communication and mate
selection.

Feeding habits: Mockingbirds
consume nearly equal amounts
of animal matter and vegetable
matter. However, insects are taken
mostly in spring; fruits and berries,
mostly in fall and winter. Mockers
have a habit of driving other species
from bird feeders during winter.

Blue Jays may gang up on the bully
mocker, taking turns harassing it
until it becomes exhausted or at
least decides the goodies in the
feeder are not worth the effort of
defending them.

Description: The gray Northern Mockingbird has white outer feathers on
its long tail and large white patches
in its wings. See comments on the
family for descriptions of vocalizations by this species and our other
mimic thrushes.

Sage Thrasher
Oreoscoptes montanus
8–9 in. (20–22 cm)

Range: A Sage Thrasher was seen
near Nags Head, N.C., on October 5,
1965. A second bird of this western
species was collected near Southern
Pines, N.C., on September 19, 1973.
There are several other records from
the East Coast, but the species is
generally rare east of the Mississippi River.

Feeding habits: The Sage Thrasher
is highly insectivorous, but it also
takes some vegetable matter.

Description: Much smaller and grayer
than the Brown Thrasher, the Sage
Thrasher has white tips on its outer
tail feathers and streaking on the
back as well as the breast. Prominence of streaks varies with age
and time of year.

Brown Thrasher
Toxostoma rufum
10.5–12.0 in. (26–30 cm)

Range: Found in all sections of the
Carolinas at all seasons, the Brown
Thrasher is most common in the
piedmont during the breeding season, and it tends to be absent at the

Brown Thrasher

higher elevations in the mountains. In winter most Brown Thrashers withdraw from the inland counties, but a few hardy birds remain all winter even in the mountains, though only at the lower elevations. In eastern South Carolina and southeastern North Carolina, the Brown Thrasher is common in winter because of the influx of birds from regions with colder climates. The thrasher is a bird of overgrown fields, woodland margins, and residential neighborhoods, favoring drier habitats than those that appeal to the Gray Catbird.

Nesting habits: The bulky, deeply cupped nest of small sticks and twigs is often well lined with a layer of leaves, grasses, paper, and other soft materials followed by a layer of small twigs and grass stems with an inner lining of well-cleaned fine rootlets. Late-season nests may be less carefully constructed.

In the Carolinas, nests are placed anywhere from less than 1 foot (0.3 m) above ground to 5 or 6 feet (1.5 to 2.0 m) high in briers, vines, and bushy trees. First clutches normally are laid by mid-May, and two or three broods may be raised in a season. Eggs have been found in the Carolinas from early April to early July.

The three to six eggs are tinged with green or blue and thickly dotted with reddish brown. The incubation period is said to be from 11 to 14 days. The nestling period varies from 9 to 12 days, with the average young probably leaving the nest at 11 days of age. Both parents share fully in all nesting chores.

Feeding habits: Acorns, wild fruits, and berries are major items in a diet that also includes a large number of beetles and caterpillars. Unusual items such as crayfish, fiddler crabs, lizards, salamanders, and tree frogs are taken opportunistically.

Tool use: Acorns are a major food item even though the Brown Thrasher's bill is not well adapted to shelling them, and they are too large to be swallowed whole. Thrashers often drive acorns into soft ground to hold them in an upright position for the shelling process. Occasionally the birds may excavate a hole especially for that purpose. Such behavior is a form of tool use, comparable to a woodworker's placing a piece of wood in a vise to hold it in place for shaping.

Description: The Brown Thrasher, often mistakenly called "brown thrush," is reddish brown above and coarsely streaked with brown below. The long tail and long, decurved bill separate it from several species of brown-backed thrushes with spotted breasts. The adult Brown Thrasher has a yellow eye. See comments on family for a comparative description of vocalizations by thrashers, mockingbirds, and catbirds. Sometimes a Brown Thrasher will run through its repertoire in a lovely, soft whisper song, which is given from a secluded perch and heard only by a fortunate few of its human neighbors.

Family STURNIDAE: Starlings

Several species of this Old World family have been introduced in North America, but only one, the European Starling, is widespread and found in the Carolinas. Others are relatively small populations of mynas.

European Starling
Sturnus vulgaris
7.5–8.5 in. (19.0–21.5 cm)

Range: Sixty European Starlings were released in New York City's Central Park in March 1890. They began to breed at once, and by the early 1920s this introduced species was nesting in the Carolinas. Today starlings are found on the Atlantic Coast from Labrador and Newfoundland south to the Florida Keys, westward to the Pacific Coast, as far north as Alaska, and south to Baja California. The species has also invaded portions of northern Mexico bordering the United States eastward to the Gulf of Mexico.

Nesting habits: Starlings breed in the Carolinas throughout the year, though more frequently and in greater numbers during spring and summer than in fall and winter. Pairs place their bulky pad of dried vegetable matter in any convenient crevice around buildings and do not hesitate to evict bluebirds, flickers, martins, and other native cavity-nesting species from their

European Starling (breeding adult)

homes, often destroying their eggs and young in the process. The starling's four to six eggs are pale bluish and unspotted. Incubation requires about 14 days, and both parents sit on the eggs. Both adults feed the young, which remain in the nest until fully fledged, a period of 2 to 3 weeks. Each season two or three broods are raised in the same nest. Most passerines swallow or carry away the fecal sacs until the offspring are able to defecate over the side of the nest. Starlings, however, do not practice nest sanitation, so the site becomes caked with droppings.

In autumn, starlings form huge flocks, often traveling and roosting with native blackbirds. Starlings frequently roost in noisy hordes on ledges of downtown buildings, where their droppings are unsightly and a hazard to pedestrians. People who must live or work in the vicinity of a major roost are not impressed by the fact that starlings consume many harmful insects. Ornithologists say that the first great population explosion has ended along the Atlantic Seaboard and that the wintering flocks are gradually diminishing.

Feeding habits: Insects, caterpillars, and other animal matter compose about half the food taken by the starling. Vegetable matter includes various fruits and berries, notably mulberries and cherries.

Description: The winter European Starling is a heavily speckled, brownish bird with a short tail and a pointed dark bill. In spring the bill turns bright yellow and the plumage becomes iridescent. Although its own song is squeaky and unimpressive, the starling possesses an outstanding ability to imitate other birds and a variety of sounds.

Family MOTACILLIDAE:
Wagtails and Pipits

Wagtails and pipits are sparrow-sized birds with slender, warbler-like bills. While searching for insects, they walk slowly, pumping their tails up and down.

Wagtails are highly variable, with several breeding populations distributed circumpolarly in the Northern Hemisphere. Populations range from Greenland to northern Scandinavia and Siberia and even to northwest Alaska. In winter, wagtails range from the Azores to the Philippines. In North America, they visit from Baja California to Newfoundland and, recently, the southeastern United States. They may occur singly on expanses of open ground, most likely near water. The birds shown in some field guides as "Black-backed Wagtails" are now considered part of the White Wagtail species.

Pipits often visit grassy areas, and they tend to forage in flocks.

White Wagtail
Motacilla alba
7.25 in. (18.5 cm)

Range: A White Wagtail photographed at Huntington Beach State Park, S.C., on April 16, 1998, constitutes the first documented report of the species from the eastern United States. It is attributed to the *M. alba alba* population that breeds in Siberia. A White Wagtail photographed October 22, 2002, at Falls Lake, N.C., is attributed to the *M. alba lugens* (Black-backed Wagtail) population that breeds in western Europe.

Feeding habits: See comments on family.

Description: White Wagtails are highly variable black, white, and gray birds that change in appearance by breeding population, age, and season. Refer to a well-illustrated field guide for noteworthy field marks. Adult males in breeding plumage can be separated by the color of the back, which is black in *M. a. lugens.* "Black-backed" adult males are usually separable from the predominantly white population. Females, subadults, and birds in transitional plumage are nearly impossible to identify accurately in the field or in photographs.

M. a. alba and *M. a. lugens* are now considered one species, the White Wagtail (*M. alba*). The Yellow Wagtail (*M. flava*), which has not been seen in the Carolinas, is considered a separate species.

American Pipit (Water Pipit)
Anthus rubescens
6–7 in. (15.0–17.5 cm)

Range: The American Pipit is an uncommon and erratic transient

American Pipit

(October–November and March–May) and a rare winter visitor in our mountains. A few visit high mountain balds, but flocks of 200–300 may occur in fields and grassy areas below 3,000 feet (900 m). In the piedmont and upper coastal plain, the species is a transient and uncommon winter resident. In the low country, however, American Pipits abound from late October to early May in large open fields that have been freshly plowed or burned. Huge flocks are almost invisible against the dark, damp soil as the birds search for food in the furrows and occasionally perch on a dirt clod or bit of stubble. Pipits also visit sandy shores, mudflats, golf courses, and airports. In broad, grassy areas they seem to favor the bare spots. An estimated 12,000 flew by Fort Moultrie, S.C., in a single hour during a snowstorm on January 23, 2003.

Feeding habits: See comments on family.

Description: The American Pipit looks like a thin-billed sparrow with a light eye line, white outer tail feathers, and black legs. The very similar Sprague's Pipit has yellowish legs.

Sprague's Pipit
Anthus spragueii
6–7 in. (15.0–17.5 cm)

Range: Sprague's Pipit is a western species that probably visits the Carolinas far more frequently than the few published records indicate. These pipits occur as fall migrants in the mountains and on the Carolina coast from late October through November. Winter residents have been found on dunes and jetties at Huntington Beach State Park, at Santee National Wildlife Refuge, and at sod farms in Orangeburg County, S.C. The only suggestion of wintering in North Carolina comes from Rocky Mount, where the species was once present from January 5 through March 9. Spring migration may begin in March and last until early May. In the Carolinas, Sprague's Pipits seem more likely to be found in fields and pastures near Savannah Sparrows than among American Pipits.

Feeding habits: See comments on family.

Description: Sprague's Pipit has yellowish legs, a pale face, and a streaked back but is otherwise similar to the American Pipit. This is a somewhat solitary species that tends to stay hidden in tall grass or weeds, often flies rather high when flushed before dropping into another clump of vegetation, and does not wag its tail as frequently as does the American Pipit.

Family BOMBYCILLIDAE:
Waxwings

Waxwings are named for the colorful wax-like appendages found on some of their wing feathers. The purpose of those waxy droplets, if any, has not been discovered.

Cedar Waxwing
Bombycilla cedrorum
6.5–8.0 in. (16.5–20.0 cm)

Cedar Waxwing

Range: Formerly believed to nest in the mountains of North Carolina and to be only a winter visitor elsewhere in the Carolinas, the Cedar Waxwing now is known to have been nesting locally and erratically as far south and east as Lane, Williamsburg County, S.C., as early as June 1968. Today, anyone who sees a Cedar Waxwing anywhere in the Carolinas from late May through early September should look for signs of local nesting. As yet there is no proof of nesting along the immediate coast, but several waxwings were present on the Dare County mainland all summer in 1996. Huge, restless flocks roam the Carolinas in winter, stripping berries from bushes in one neighborhood and then moving on in search of a fresh supply of food.

Nesting habits: Billing and courtship feeding are part of the mating ritual for waxwings. The nesting period begins about mid-May and extends throughout the summer with eggs still in some nests in late August. Waxwings are very erratic in their nesting habits, moving from place to place to take advantage of the local abundance of fruits and berries instead of returning year after year to a chosen site. Although solitary nesting seems to be the usual in our region, small or loose colonies have been reported from the Oconee Nuclear Station in South Carolina and from Forsyth

and Franklin Counties in North Carolina. Breeding birds seem to feed on ripe fruits found within a mile (1.6 km) of their nesting site.

Nests have been found from 4 to 50 feet (1.2 to 15.0 m) above ground, but the average appears to be about 20 feet (6 m). Nests may be placed in forks or on horizontal limbs of shrubs, deciduous hardwoods, pines, or firs. Built by both adults, nests are bulky baskets of *Usnea* lichens, twigs, weed stems, grasses, pine needles, plant down, moss, wool, feathers, twine, and almost any other convenient item, with the softer materials being used for the lining. The three to five eggs are ashy gray, sparingly and irregularly dotted with black, blackish brown, or purple. Incubation is primarily, if not entirely, by the female.

Hatching takes place in 10 to 16 days, with 12 to 14 probably being average. The female broods the nestlings almost constantly for the first few days, until they have sprouted some feathers. Both parents feed insects to the young during the remainder of their 14 to

18 days in the nest. Two broods may be raised in a season.

Feeding habits: Cedar Waxwings eat a variety of wild and cultivated fruits and berries. Privet and pyracantha berries constitute a major source of food in winter. Waxwings also eat some insects and caterpillars, and in spring they eat the buds of fruit trees. While they usually do not visit bird feeders, they do like to drink and bathe where water is available.

Description: This crested, brownish bird has yellowish underparts, a black mask about the eyes, and a yellow-tipped tail. Adults usually have wax-like red appendages on a few of the wing feathers. Young birds are streaky brown and lack the "sealing wax" on the wings. The Bohemian Waxwing (*B. garrulus*) of the western United States and Canada has not been recorded in the Carolinas. This larger and grayer species has cinnamon undertail coverts. Cedar Waxwings have white undertail coverts.

Family PARULIDAE:
Wood Warblers

Wood warblers are a New World family of small and highly insectivorous woodland birds with thin, straight bills. Most of the warblers that breed in the eastern United States and Canada migrate to Central and South America, or at least to the southeastern United States, for the winter. These migratory flights are made at night, often leading to great mortality in rainy or foggy weather. Some birds crash against television towers, high bridges, and tall buildings. Others become attracted to lighthouses and airport ceilometers, flying in circles about the bright light until they drop from exhaustion or from collisions with one another. In spite of those hazards, warbler migration provides one of the greatest thrills in bird study.

Budding spring woodlands that were deserted the day before are alive with flitting, singing warblers the morning after the arrival of a big wave of migrants. Upland groves of open, mature hardwoods often teem with warblers in April and May. Another good place to look for warblers in spring is in moist woodlands having good stands of ironwood (*Carpinus caroliniana*), so named because of the sinewy appearance of its gray bark, but also known as "blue beech." A small defoliating insect attacks the leaves of *C. caroliniana* at the peak of warbler migration, thus providing an abundant food supply.

The fall passage is prolonged and quiet, but no less a challenge to the field student. Young birds of the year and postbreeding adults may look quite different from the spring adults, and the few sounds they make are of little help in identifying them. In the fall, migrating warblers occur in a great variety of habitats, and they are frequently seen near the ground along woodland edges and in mixed flocks with the resident Eastern Bluebirds, Pine Warblers, Chipping Sparrows, Carolina Chickadees, and other small birds. If you see one bird chasing another during spring or fall migration, look quickly to see who is being chased. Quite often it will be a new species for the neighborhood.

Many fall migrants that will not visit a feeding station will come to water. Some come to bathe on the wing in the spray of a lawn sprinkler or on the ground in puddles around it. Such birds can be studied at leisure while they shake and preen on a low perch. Aphid infestations and ripe pokeberries also attract fall migrants.

Bachman's Warbler
Vermivora bachmanii
4.25–4.50 in. (10.8–11.5 cm)

The rarest of American wood warblers and an endangered species, the Bachman's Warbler may be extinct. There has been no published sighting from the Carolinas for more than 25 years. The species was discovered by the Reverend John Bachman (1790–1874), who was pastor of Saint John's Lutheran Church in Charleston, S.C., for 60 years. A truly remarkable naturalist, Bachman not only discovered two avian species new to science (Swainson's Warbler and Bachman's Warbler) but also befriended John James Audubon while he labored to complete *The Birds of America*. Bachman wrote the entire text for the pioneer book on American mammals, The *Viviparous Quadrupeds of North America*. For more information about the remarkable clergyman-naturalist, read *Had I the Wings: The Friendship of Bachman and Audubon* (University of Georgia Press, 1995), which was written by the late South Carolina naturalist Jay Shuler, a past president of Carolina Bird Club.

Blue-winged Warbler
Vermivora pinus
5.0 in. (12.5 cm)

Range: The Blue-winged Warbler occurs sparingly during the breeding season in the extreme southwestern tip of North Carolina

Blue-winged Warbler

at elevations between 1,500 and 2,000 feet (450 to 600 m). Territorial males have been found mostly in Graham and Cherokee Counties, N.C., but also as far north as Buncombe and Ashe Counties, N.C., and as far south as Pickens and Oconee Counties, S.C. However, there is no proof of nesting anywhere in the Carolinas. Outside the mountains, Blue-winged Warblers are spring transients from mid- to late April and fall transients from mid-July to mid-October.

Nesting habits: The Blue-winged Warbler has essentially the same nesting habits as the Golden-winged Warbler, but the nest is often very deep and narrow, like an inverted cone.

Feeding habits: See comments on family.

Description: The Blue-winged Warbler resembles a Prothonotary, but it has a black line through the eye and two white wing bars. Its buzzy song (*bee-buzz*) is quite different from the ringing tones of the Prothonotary.

Hybrids: Where their ranges overlap, Golden-winged and Blue-winged

Warblers hybridize. The well-marked offspring of such matings once were thought to be separate species, the Brewster's Warbler and the Lawrence's Warbler. Both hybrid forms have been found in the Carolinas, mostly as spring migrants. Consult a field guide for information on identification of hybrid warblers.

Golden-winged Warbler
Vermivora chrysoptera
5.0 in. (12.5 cm)

Range: In the mountains of southwestern North Carolina, including Sassafras Mountain on the North Carolina–South Carolina state line, the Golden-winged Warbler is a locally fairly common summer resident at the low to middle elevations, mostly from 1,800 to 4,000 feet (540 to 1,200 m) and occasionally up to 5,000 feet (1,500 m) or very rarely 6,000 feet (1,830 m) where old fields and forest clearings are growing up in bushes and young trees. The right-of-way for high-voltage transmission lines is also a good place to look for Golden-wingeds. Males sometimes sing from perches on the huge towers. The species was formerly fairly common in Ashe County, N.C., but in recent years tidy rows of Christmas trees have replaced many of the old apple orchards and overgrown pastures that formerly hosted breeding pairs. The warblers arrive on the breeding grounds about mid-April and depart by late September.

Golden-winged Warblers are rare transients in the piedmont, very rare in the coastal plain, and

Golden-winged Warbler

apparently absent on the immediate coast except as a very rare fall migrant. Spring migrants occur mostly in late April or early May. Fall migrants are found from mid-August to early October, rarely as late as October 21 in southeastern South Carolina.

Nesting habits: The coarse, bulky nest of bark strippings, grass, and other plant fibers may be placed on bare ground, on a mat of dead leaves, or very near the ground in clumps of weeds, ferns, or briers. The birds tend to tilt the nest opening so the plant materials on the ragged upper rim can partly conceal the cup below. The four or five eggs are white, variably spotted or wreathed with gray and reddish brown. Laying apparently begins in the Carolinas in late May; incubation is by the female and requires 10 to 11 days, and young stay in the nest about 10 days. The species appears to be single-brooded.

Feeding habits: See comments on family. Despite their habit of nesting on the ground, Golden-winged Warblers frequently feed very high in tall trees, foraging at the tips of branches even before the buds open in spring.

Description: The male is a mostly gray bird with a black bib, black eye patch, yellow crown, and large yellow wing patch. Females and immatures have the same general pattern, but they are less boldly marked.

Tennessee Warbler
Vermivora peregrina
4.5–5.0 in. (11.5–12.5 cm)

Range: During spring migration the Tennessee Warbler is uncommon in the mountains and appears to be confined to the lower and middle elevations. It becomes rare toward the eastern piedmont and is almost completely absent from the coastal plain in spring. The peak of northward migration comes in late April and early May. Southbound Tennessee Warblers are more numerous, being common in the mountains and occurring from the highest peaks to the barrier beaches from mid-August through October (extremes August 11 to November 27). Huge numbers—hundreds, perhaps thousands—have been found along a road high in the Great Smoky Mountains in early September, and 74 were counted on the campus of Clemson University in South Carolina on October 24, 1984.

Feeding habits: See comments on family. Look for Tennessee Warblers in deciduous woods, usually in the treetops. Many fall-migrant warblers, including this species, have been noticed visiting trees heavily infested with aphids.

Description: Spring males resemble a Red-eyed Vireo with a dark eye and a bill that is thin even for a warbler. This is our only warbler that has completely white underparts in spring. Fall birds can be confused with the Philadelphia Vireo. Consult a field guide for tips on identifying spring females and fall birds of both sexes.

Orange-crowned Warbler
Vermivora celata
5.0 in. (12.5 cm)

Range: Usually found in the Carolinas from early October through early May, the Orange-crowned Warbler is a fairly common winter resident in southeastern South Carolina, becoming uncommon northward along the coast and rare to very rare inland, where it is known only as a transient and unexpected winter visitor.

Feeding habits: See comments on family. The Orange-crowned Warbler often forages on or near the ground.

Description: This dull greenish bird is

Orange-crowned Warbler (in winter)

best recognized by the absence of tail spots, wing bars, and prominent head markings. The orange crown is rarely seen, the dark stripe through the eye may be indistinct, and there is faint streaking on the underparts. Immature Tennessee Warblers have white undertail coverts, but those on the Orange-crowned Warbler are yellow.

Nashville Warbler
Vermivora ruficapilla
4.5–5.0 in. (11.5–12.5 cm)

Range: The Nashville Warbler is a rare spring and fall migrant that is more likely to be seen in the central and western counties than in the coastal plain. Migrants pass through the Carolinas mostly from late April to mid-May and from mid-August to mid-October. While still far from common, this species appears to be more plentiful east of the Appalachians now than it was in the 1950s. It is now a rare, but not unexpected, winter visitor or winter resident in the lower coastal plain of the Carolinas from mid-November to mid-March, with more reports from Lake Mattamuskeet, N.C., than any other site.

Feeding habits: In spring the Nashville Warbler usually is a treetop bird, but in fall it often forages near the ground in thickets and woodland edges. It sometimes feeds by hovering at the tip of a tree limb.

Description: The mostly greenish Nashville is our only warbler that has a gray head, prominent white eye ring, unstreaked yellow throat and breast, no wing bars, and no tail spots.

Northern Parula (male carrying food)

Northern Parula
Parula americana
4.5 in. (11.5 cm)

Range: A fairly common to common summer resident of swamps and damp woodlands throughout the Carolinas, the Northern Parula is most numerous near the coast, scarce in the western piedmont, and generally absent from the mountains above 5,200 feet (1,600 m). Spring migrant parulas begin arriving in southeastern South Carolina—where a few individuals may spend the winter—in early March, but they do not reach most of our region until late March or early April. The species is rarely seen in the Carolinas after October, but winter stragglers are not unexpected, for the species winters regularly in southern Florida. From mid-April to early May, when the majority of spring migrants pass through the Carolinas, parulas frequently sing from large shade trees well removed from water.

Nesting habits: Nest building begins soon after Northern Parulas return to their breeding grounds. The nest is usually suspended about 23 feet (7.5 m) high from a lateral branch of a tree standing in or near water. Where Spanish moss (*Tillandsia usneoides*) is available, the nests invariably are concealed in its streamers, the nest proper being woven of fine grasses and strands of moss. Elsewhere the birds weave together strands of a beard-like gray lichen (*Usnea* sp.). The entrance to the nest is always on the side of the cluster.

The three to five eggs are white, speckled around the large end with reddish brown and lilac. Laying for first clutches usually takes place in late April or early May. Incubation apparently is the duty of the female, and it probably requires 12 to 14 days. Both parents care for the young, but the duration of the nestling period has not been determined. Two broods are often raised near the coast; one probably is the usual number per season in the mountains. Singing decreases rapidly in July, and the ascending buzzy trill is rarely heard in late summer and autumn.

Feeding habits: See comments on family.

Description: The Northern Parula is our only blue-backed warbler with a yellow throat. The adult male has an irregular rusty band separating the yellow of the throat from the yellow upper breast; that mark is absent in females and immatures. Both adults have a greenish patch on the back.

Hybrids: Parulas occasionally interbreed with Yellow-throated Warblers, producing the extremely rare hybrid known as Sutton's Warbler.

Yellow Warbler
Dendroica petechia
4.5–5.25 in. (11.5–13.0 cm)

Range: The Yellow Warbler breeds from the lower elevations—up to about 5,000 feet (1,500 m)—in the mountains of North and South Carolina eastward across the piedmont to Chester County, S.C., and Wake County, N.C., and very sparingly in the northern coastal plain of North Carolina. The species is fairly common in northwestern South Carolina and in the mountains and western piedmont of North Carolina. It becomes uncommon to rare or locally absent toward the eastern edge of its range in the Carolinas. Yellow Warblers have been seen in June along the North Carolina coast from Corolla south to Buxton; however, no proof of breeding has been obtained.

Nesting birds arrive from early April to the middle of the month in wet thickets and streamside shrubbery, especially willows. In the mountains they also nest in farmyards. Migrants passing northward through the breeding territory frequent both lowland and upland groves, arriving from 2 to 4 weeks after the summer residents. Yellow Warblers seldom are seen around their nesting places after July, and during that month they reappear in coastal South Carolina, where they do not breed.

Outside its breeding range, the Yellow Warbler is a transient from early April through May and from July through October. Winter stragglers are rare, but they have been found in the coastal plain, especially in the vicinity of Lake

Yellow Warbler (male)

Mattamuskeet, N.C., a known migrant-holding location.

Nesting habits: The male may help the female build the nest, which usually is situated about 7 to 12 feet (2.0 to 3.5 m) above ground in a crotch of a small tree, shrub, or climbing rose bush. The compact, symmetrical cup of cotton, plant down, or other soft plant fibers is often lined with hair. In May or June the Yellow Warbler lays four or five white eggs that are generously speckled and splashed with shades of brown and lilac.

If the nest is parasitized by a cowbird, the Yellow Warbler almost always builds another nest atop the one containing the alien egg. Sometimes a nest may have five or six stories.

The incubation period is about 11 days. The male does not sit on the eggs or brood young, but he stands guard and feeds the female on the nest. Young remain in the nest about 9 to 12 days, being fed by both parents. The birds begin moving southward as soon as the offspring are fully independent.

Feeding habits: See comments on family.

Description: This is our only warbler with a yellow breast and yellow tail spots. The male has conspicuous reddish streaks on the breast; the female has faint streaks.

Chestnut-sided Warbler
Dendroica pensylvanica
5.0 in. (12.5 cm)

Range: The Chestnut-sided Warbler is a fairly common spring transient in the mountains and western piedmont between mid-April and mid-May, rarely into early June. It becomes uncommon to very rare toward the coast. As a fall migrant from mid-August to late October, the species is fairly common in the eastern counties, but it remains rare along the immediate coast.

Chestnut-sideds are common summer residents in our mountains, generally breeding at elevations of 2,000 to 6,300 feet (600 to 1,900 m) southward to Caesar's Head State Park, Greenville County, S.C. They can be found at overlooks along the Blue Ridge Parkway and almost everywhere else people and nature have created suitable openings in the forest. This species thrives in the brushy habitat that springs up following forest fires and lumbering operations. No doubt the Chestnut-sided is more plentiful now than it was before the arrival of white settlers, when it was largely confined to mountain balds.

Nesting habits: Built by the female, the nest of weeds, grasses, and leaves is lined with fine grasses, rootlets, and hair. It is placed in

Chestnut-sided Warbler (male)

a fork or crotch about 3 feet (1 m) above ground in bushes, vines, or small saplings. The three or four eggs are white, variously speckled and splotched with brown and gray.

The peak of laying in our region appears to be from late May through early June. Incubation requires about 12 days and is performed by the female, but both adults feed the young, which remain in the nest about 10 to 12 days. The species appears to be single-brooded.

Feeding habits: See comments on family.

Description: Both sexes have a greenish-yellow crown, a narrow black patch about the eye, and white underparts marked only by a chestnut streak down each side. Consult a field guide for tips on identifying the immature, which has a plain yellowish-green back, two yellow wing bars, and solid white underparts.

Magnolia Warbler
Dendroica magnolia
4.5–5.0 in. (11.5–12.5 cm)

Range: In the mountains and piedmont, the Magnolia Warbler is a fairly common spring transient and a common one in fall, becoming uncommon eastward. The species is more likely to be seen along the coast in fall than in spring. The spring passage takes place from late April through mid-May, and the fall passage occurs mostly from late August through October.

In the late 1800s the Magnolia Warbler was reported as breeding in Buncombe County, N.C., and there are several modern reports of singing males apparently on territory in spruce-fir forests at Roan Mountain (June 2 to July 14, 2003), Grandfather Mountain, Mount Mitchell, Potato Knob in the Black Mountains (June 25, 2003), and Black Balsam Mountain (late June 2002) in Haywood County, N.C. The last site is considerably south of the other peaks that have hosted territorial males in North Carolina. Despite the recurrent sightings of territorial males, there is no documentation from the Carolinas for a breeding pair, an active nest, or preflight young in more than a hundred years.

Feeding habits: See comments on family.

Description: The Magnolia Warbler is our only warbler that has a rectangular white patch on each side of the tail about midway along its length. The tail spots are noticeable only when the tail is fanned. The spring male looks much like a Yellow-rumped Warbler with a

Magnolia Warbler (male)

Magnolia Warbler (female)

yellow throat, a yellow breast, and a broad white wing patch instead of two white wing bars. Magnolias have yellow on the rump but not on the crown.

Cape May Warbler
Dendroica tigrina
5.0–5.5 in. (12.5–14.0 cm)

Range: The Cape May Warbler is primarily known in the Carolinas as a spring and fall transient. In late April and early May the species is fairly common in the mountains and most of the piedmont, becoming uncommon to very rare in the

eastern piedmont and throughout the coastal plain. During fall migration the species occurs throughout the Carolinas from late August to early November, with the peak of fall passage probably being from late September through mid-October. Like most transient warblers, this species is usually seen in hardwoods in spring and in various types of woods and thickets in fall.

Although there is as yet no proof of nesting in the North Carolina mountains, there are several reports of males singing during June and early July in suitable habitat at places like Grandfather Mountain and Roan Mountain.

Nesting habits: Cape May Warblers typically nest in open stands of coniferous trees. They invariably place the nest either as near as possible to the tip of the uppermost spire in the crown of a spruce or fir or near the top of the main trunk. Resting in twigs and foliage, such nests cannot be seen from the ground even with the aid of field glasses or a spotting scope. Height above ground usually ranges from 30 to 60 feet (about 9 to 18 m). The female builds the bulky structure, using green moss (sphagnum) interwoven with twigs and fine grass stems bound together with plant down. The nest is lined with a soft mat of hair, rootlets, fur, and feathers. Eggs usually number six or seven. The creamy white shell has little or no gloss and is well spotted with reddish brown at the large end and occasionally marked with black scrawls. The incubation period is unknown. Following the female to the nest is reportedly very difficult because she usually lands at the base of the tree and works her way upward through the dense evergreen boughs.

Feeding habits: Although Cape May Warblers are highly insectivorous, they have a taste for ripening grapes and may inflict considerable damage on vineyards during fall migration.

Description: The adult male Cape May Warbler is unmistakable with his heavily streaked yellow underparts, rusty cheek patch, large white wing patch, and yellow rump. Females and immatures are very difficult to identify, and use of a field guide is recommended.

Black-throated Blue Warbler
Dendroica caerulescens
5.0 in. (12.5 cm)

Range: The Black-throated Blue Warbler is a common summer resident in the mountains of North and South Carolina from mid-April through mid-October. Breeding has been confirmed as far south as Caesar's Head, Greenville County, S.C. As a spring and fall transient, the species is found throughout the Carolinas, more commonly in the western counties than toward the coast, from mid-April to mid-May and from early September through October. Very unusual was one that lingered in Transylvania County, N.C., into early winter, visiting a suet feeder from late November 1995 until early January 1996.

Nesting habits: Black-throated Blue Warblers are gregarious, and it is not unusual to find several pairs close together in suitable habitat during the nesting season. Generally nesting near a brook, spring, or

Black-throated Blue Warbler (male)

seepage in hardwood forests above 2,800 feet (850 m) in elevation, this warbler places its nest from 10 inches to 3 feet (25 to 90 cm) above ground in the fork of a shrub (rhododendron or mountain laurel) or in rank weeds (often rattleweed) and ferns growing between rocks and fallen trees in heavily timbered ravines.

Accompanied by the male, the female gathers all the nesting materials and does all the construction. The nest exterior is composed chiefly of bark strippings (rhododendron and grapevine) bound together with spider webs and interwoven with other kinds of bark, rotten wood, and moss. The interior of the cup is neatly lined with moss, fern rootlets, hair, or fine grasses.

The four eggs are laid in late May or early June. They are whitish and marked with brown and lilac either all over or in a wreath at the large end. The female incubates the eggs for about 12 days and broods the young, which stay in the nest about 10 days. The male helps feed the offspring and clean the nest. Well-feathered young are out of the nest by early July. It is not unusual to hear Black-throated Blue Warblers singing in August and September, after the nesting season.

Feeding habits: See comments on family.

Description: Both the handsome male, with his blue back, black throat and sides, and white belly, and the dingy female can be distinguished by the small white patch near the base of the primaries. Young males look almost exactly like the adult males.

Cairns's Warbler (*D. c. cairnsi*) is the race of the Black-throated Blue Warbler that breeds in our mountains. It is named for John S. Cairns, a resident of Weaverville, N.C., who did a great deal of important ornithological work in the North Carolina mountains during the 1890s.

Yellow-rumped Warbler (Myrtle Warbler, Audubon's Warbler)
Dendroica coronata
5–6 in. (12.5–15.0 cm)

Range: The Yellow-rumped (Myrtle) Warbler is a common winter resident of the Carolinas from late September or early October to mid-May (extreme dates August 29 to June 19). In midwinter Myrtle Warblers may become scarce or absent in our mountain counties and locally absent in the piedmont, but they are abundant throughout the winter along the coast. Summer birds seen at Mount Mitchell, Roan Mountain, and Linville Falls suggest that the southward extension of breeding range by the Myrtle Warbler population in the East may have reached

Yellow-rumped Warbler (in winter plumage)

beyond West Virginia, where the species has become a regular breeder in the spruce-fir zone.

Feeding habits: In winter Myrtle Warblers eat the fruits of various plants, especially those of the waxmyrtle and bayberry. They also eat many small insects, which they may pick from the bark and leaves of trees and shrubs or pursue on the wing like tiny flycatchers. Myrtle Warblers frequently visit bird feeders and bird baths, thus usually becoming one of the first warbler species met by the beginning bird student.

Description: The Yellow-rumped Warbler is our only bird that has a yellow cap, yellow rump, and a yellow patch on each side of the breast. In many brownish fall Myrtles the yellow patches are dull and difficult to see.

Among the vast numbers of Yellow-rumped Warblers wintering in the Carolinas, a very rare individual may be of the western subspecies known as the Audubon's Warbler (*D. c. auduboni*). One such bird was collected at Rocky Mount, N.C., on February 28, 1970. Others have been found at several different places in eastern North Carolina and in Horry, Clarendon, and Charleston Counties in South Carolina.

Black-throated Gray Warbler
Dendroica nigrescens
4.5–5.0 in. (11.5–12.5 cm)

Range: This species breeds in the western United States and occurs accidentally on the East Coast. One was seen on Bulls Island, S.C., on December 13, 1941, and another was collected on Wadmalaw Island, Charleston County, S.C., on March 29, 1972. The first known North Carolina occurrence was a bird found at Orton Plantation near Wilmington on December 30, 1965. There are now additional reports of single birds from coastal and piedmont North Carolina between late September and mid-February: at Wilmington, January 5–22, 1986; at Greensboro, February 24, 1992; at Wilmington, January 31–February 16, 1995; on Roanoke Island, October 7, 2000; at Fort Fisher, September 30, 2001; and a female at Lake Norman, January 5, 2003.
Feeding habits: See comments on family.
Description: The pattern of black, white, and gray in the plumage bears striking similarity to that of a chickadee. In all plumages there is a black cap, a white line above the eye, a black line through it, and a

white line extending from the base of the bill below the eye to the nape. The underparts are white with streaks on the sides (black in adults, grayish in immatures). The adult male has a black throat. The adult female has a black band across the upper breast and a mostly white throat. The breast band is incomplete in the immature female. In all plumages, the species has two white wing bars and a diagnostic yellow spot in front of each eye.

Black-throated Green Warbler
Dendroica virens
4.50–5.25 in. (11.5–13.0 cm)

Range: During spring migration the Black-throated Green Warbler is fairly common in our western counties from mid-April to mid-May, becoming uncommon to very rare eastward across the piedmont. Fall migrants pass throughout the Carolinas, mostly from mid-September to early November.

As breeding birds in the southern Appalachians, Black-throated Green Warblers may be locally common in high-elevation glades and around suitable clearings in spruce-fir forests, but they are seldom encountered elsewhere in the mountains. Although the species breeds very locally and in small numbers on portions of the inner coastal plain, it is widely distributed in the cypress swamps and river bottoms of the lower coastal plain, often being found where Atlantic white cedar is present. The relatively large population on the Dare County mainland appears to be very important in maintaining the breeding population that extends southward

Black-throated Green Warbler
(male in spring)

Black-throated Green Warbler
(in fall plumage)

near the coast approximately to the Charleston area.

Birds arrive on the breeding grounds in late March or early April. During the nesting season the mountain birds sing continuously from dawn to dusk and may still be in full song in late July. Those nesting on the coastal plain tend to be silent after early June, which probably results from the earlier onset of nesting there than in the mountains. After the nesting season, Black-throated Green Warblers slip away with the influx of southbound birds passing through the Carolinas. One at Brevard on November 14, 2002, was exceptionally late. Extreme dates for the Carolinas are March 23 (mainland Dare County, N.C.) and January 31 (Lake Mattamuskeet, Hyde County, N.C.).

Nesting habits: Nests are placed 3 to 75 feet (1 to 23 m) or higher on horizontal limbs of large trees, in crotches of tall saplings, or in tangles of vines. The nest is a neat cup of bark strips, grass, leaves, rootlets, and conifer needles. The female appears to be chiefly responsible for nest construction, incubation, and brooding, but a male Black-throated Green Warbler has been seen making repeated trips to gather soft, fuzzy fibers from newly emerged fiddleheads of cinnamon fern. Egg laying occurs on the coast between mid-April and mid-May and in the mountains between mid-May and mid-June. The three or four eggs are white, speckled and wreathed with brown and lilac at the large end. Incubation is thought to require about 12 days, and the young probably stay in the nest about 10 days. Both adults feed the young and clean the nest.

Feeding habits: See comments on family.

Description: This is our only warbler with wing bars and a large yellow face patch that encircles the eye. Several western species are confusingly similar, but only one of them, the Townsend's Warbler, has been reported in our region. Reference to field guides is recommended.

Townsend's Warbler
Dendroica townsendi
4.5–5.0 in. (11.5–12.5 cm)

Range: This western species is a very rare accidental in the eastern United States. A male and a possible female were reported from Nantahala in the North Carolina mountains on April 24, 1975. Since that time, a color photograph was obtained of a bird seen on November 7, 1992, at the Pea Island National Wildlife Refuge, and a specimen was salvaged from a boat off the North Carolina coast on September 20, 1999. In addition, a male was present for one day, April 27, 2000, in the Elizabethan Gardens on Roanoke Island.

Feeding habits: See comments on family. The bird seen at Pea Island was flycatching with a flock of Myrtle Warblers.

Description: Townsend's Warbler is confusingly similar to the Black-throated Green Warbler, but it has darker auriculars (feathers covering the ear openings) and more yellow in the underparts. Reference to a well-illustrated field guide is essential for accurate identification.

Blackburnian Warbler
Dendroica fusca
4.25–5.50 in. (10.8–14.0 cm)

Range: The Blackburnian Warbler is a fairly common spring and fall transient in the North Carolina mountains and in northwestern South Carolina, becoming uncommon to very rare toward the coast. The peaks of migration are from late April through mid-May and from late August to mid-October. Although Blackburnian Warblers

Blackburnian Warbler (male)

have been found in the mountains of South Carolina in June, no evidence of breeding has been obtained.

Blackburnian Warblers are fairly common summer residents in the mountains of North Carolina, mostly at elevations above 3,000 feet (900 m). They arrive on the breeding grounds in our spruce-fir, hemlock, and northern hardwood forests about mid-April and depart by mid-October. In May, the Pink Beds area of Transylvania County is a very good place to find Blackburnian Warblers on territory. The site is adjacent to the Cradle of Forestry Interpretive Center on Route 276.

Nesting habits: The nest usually is placed from 5 to 80 feet (1.5 to 24.5 m) above ground in a coniferous tree, often a hemlock. At times it is near the tip of a drooping branch, but more often it is saddled on a horizontal limb 6 to 10 feet (1.8 to 3.0 m) from the main trunk. The nest is rather bulky, usually a densely woven mass of small twigs, plant down, lichens, and rootlets lined with horsehair, fine grasses, and feathers.

Egg laying begins in late May in our region, but some females may still be building nests in mid-June. The four or five white eggs are dotted and splashed with brown and gray, often in a wreath around the large end. The incubation period is unknown, and little is known about the family life of this species except that both parents feed the young.

Feeding habits: See comments on family.

Description: The male Blackburnian is our only warbler with an orange cap and a bright orange throat patch. The adult female can be confused with the Yellow-throated Warbler; look for her tiny yellow crown patch and the white streaks on her back.

Yellow-throated Warbler
Dendroica dominica
4.75–5.75 in. (12.0–14.5 cm)

Range: The Yellow-throated Warbler is a common breeding species throughout the coastal plain and a fairly common one elsewhere in the Carolinas. In the mountains, however, it is confined to the lower elevations, favoring pines below 2,500 feet (750 m) but sometimes ranging up to 3,000 feet (900 m).

The birds arrive on the breeding grounds from early March to early April and depart by late September or early October. The species is an uncommon but regular winter resident in southeastern South Carolina and a rare winter straggler northward along the coast.

Nesting habits: Nest construction is entirely by the female. In the swamps and bottomlands of the coastal plain, Yellow-throated

Yellow-throated Warbler (male in spring)

Warblers prefer to build their nests, composed of bits of bark, rotten wood, fine grasses, weeds, and feathers, in a clump of Spanish moss with the entrance hole on one side of the garland. Elsewhere, the birds build in pine woods, placing the nest near the tip of a horizontal branch in a cluster of needles and burrs. Nests are usually 15 to 60 feet (4.5 to 18.0 m) above ground, but they have been found from 3 to 100 feet (1 to 30 m) or higher. The four greenish-white eggs are spotted near the large end with brown and lavender gray.

Very little is known about the family life of the Yellow-throated Warbler. The incubation period is thought to be about 12 days. In coastal South Carolina the species is double-brooded, first broods often being fully fledged by late April. No one has determined how far northward and inland the Yellow-throated Warbler is able to raise two broods per season, but apparently the species is single-brooded in the mountains, where young leave the nest about mid-June.

Feeding habits: See comments on family.

Description: The Yellow-throated Warbler is a gray-backed bird with a white eye line, black sideburns, yellow throat, white belly, heavily streaked sides, two white wing bars, and white tail spots. The hybrid Sutton's Warbler (see Northern Parula) is similar to the Yellow-throated except for the unstreaked sides and a greenish patch on the back. This very rare form has been found in South Carolina several times, but there is no published record from North Carolina.

Pine Warbler

Pine Warbler
Dendroica pinus
5.0–5.75 in. (12.5–14.5 cm)

Range: The Pine Warbler is a common permanent resident of pine forests throughout South Carolina and in all but the upper piedmont and mountain counties of North Carolina. In the mountains the species is found only at low elevations. Here and in the upper piedmont of North Carolina, it is a fairly common transient, an uncommon summer resident, and a rare winter straggler. An influx of migrants causes the Pine Warbler to become locally very common in the eastern counties in fall and winter.

Nesting habits: The breeding season for the Pine Warbler extends from March to June, and during that time the birds may raise as many as three broods. Nests are usually 30 to 50 feet (9 to 15 m) above ground, but they range from 10 to 135 feet (3 to 41 m). Invariably located in pine trees, they may be saddled on a large horizontal limb, concealed in needles at the tip of a branch, or hidden in a cluster of cones. The nest is a compact cup of bark strips, weed stems, twigs, and grasses and is lined with pine needles, hair, or feathers. Nests lined with Eastern Bluebird or Northern Cardinal contour feathers are particularly colorful. The outside may be decorated with cobwebs.

The four or five grayish-white eggs are speckled with brown and lilac, often with a wreath at the large end. The incubation period is thought to be about 12 days, and the male assists the female. Both adults feed the young, but the duration of the nestling period has not been determined.

During the nesting season Pine Warblers tend to stay high in the trees, but in August they flock with Eastern Bluebirds, Chipping Sparrows, Brown-headed Nuthatches, Carolina Chickadees, and Tufted Titmice. Throughout the autumn the mixed flocks spend much time feeding and bathing on or near the ground, often attracting rarely seen migrants as temporary companions.

Feeding habits: See comments on family. This species spends more time foraging in and beneath pines than do our other warblers.

Description: The coloration of Pine Warblers is highly variable, ranging from spring males with brilliant yellow breasts to fall females with only a hint of yellow. Learn the Pine Warbler's trill, which is slower and more musical than that of the Chipping Sparrow, and watch for this combination of field marks: two prominent white wing bars, white tail spots, white belly, unstreaked back, and indistinct eye stripe. The bill of the Pine Warbler is longer and thicker than average for warblers.

Kirtland's Warbler
Dendroica kirtlandii
5.5–6.0 in. (13–15 cm)

Range: Once believed to have numbered fewer than a thousand individuals, the Kirtland's Warbler made a good comeback after biologists and volunteers began removing Brown-headed Cowbird adults and their eggs from the nesting area of the rare and endangered species. Kirtland's Warblers nest primarily among jack pines growing in a small section of the Lower Peninsula of Michigan. Careful management of the species' specialized breeding habitat was also undertaken, and that apparently was an important factor in rebuilding population numbers.

Trips to and from their winter range in the Bahama Islands carry Kirtland's Warblers over some portions of the Carolinas. The straight-line route takes southbound birds from Michigan through Ohio and southward to northeastern Tennessee, western North Carolina (Alexander, Wilkes, and Iredell Counties), and central South Carolina (Sumter and Richland Counties) to the Charleston area before beginning the overwater journey to the Bahama Islands. Other Kirtland's Warblers travel from Michigan to southern Pennsylvania, eastern Virginia (Kerr Lake), and eastern North Carolina (Rocky Mount and Ocracoke Island) before heading toward the Bahamas.

The fall migration begins in late August, and nearly all Kirtland's Warblers have left the breeding grounds by mid-September. There are fall records for the Carolinas from August 25 to October 29, all October sightings being from South Carolina. Apparently the hatching-year birds depart first from mid-August to early September. The young birds are followed by the adults, with perhaps a few of them lingering among the jack pines until late September.

There are only six reports of spring migrants from the Carolinas. Ones from Beaufort, Cherokee, and Kershaw Counties, S.C., and Jackson and Haywood Counties, N.C., indicate a return by the straight-line route. However, two spring birds from the edge of a beaver pond on Moccasin Creek near Zebulon, Wake County, N.C., suggest a northward route east of the mountains to southern Pennsylvania and then westward over the Appalachians at a relatively low elevation.

In our region, migrating Kirtland's Warblers tend to frequent thickets and woodland edges on high ground just beyond the wet margins of lakes, ponds, and swamps. Two other facts about their behavior during fall migration are of interest. First, they tend to associate with members of other warbler species, particularly Pine, Palm, and Myrtle Warblers. Second, the males sometimes sing after leaving the breeding grounds, as did one at Mayesville, Sumter County, S.C., on August 25, 2001.

Feeding habits: See comments on family.

Description: Kirtland's Warbler is gray above and predominantly yellow below with black streaks on the back and sides, two white wing bars, white tail spots, white belly, and a white eye ring that is interrupted on each side where the upper and lower eyelids meet. This very tame, relatively large species is the only gray-backed warbler that occurs in our region and wags its tail. However, the movement is more like that of a Hermit Thrush (cock and droop) than a Palm Warbler (bobbing up and down).

Prairie Warbler (male)

Prairie Warbler

Dendroica discolor

4.25–5.0 in. (10.8–12.5 cm)

Range: From late March or early April to mid-October, the Prairie Warbler is a very common summer resident along the North Carolina coast. The species becomes less numerous inland toward the mountains, where it is locally uncommon or fairly common in brushy places on open hillsides at low elevations. It also becomes scarce as a breeding bird in southern South Carolina. A few Prairie Warblers may be found in December and January as far north as Hatteras Island and Lake Mattamuskeet, N.C., but the species apparently does not normally occur throughout the winter in our region. It does winter regularly in most of Florida.

Nesting habits: The nest is usually 2 to 10 feet (0.6 to 3.0 m) above ground in a sapling standing in an overgrown field, thicket, or second-growth clearing. The well-made cup of weeds, plant down, grasses, and leaves is lined with hair, fine grasses, or pine needles. First clutches may be laid in April, but early May probably is the rule over most of our region. The four or five white eggs are speckled and wreathed with spots of brown and lavender. Incubation requires 12 to 13 days, and young remain in the nest 8 to 10 days. The female apparently does all the nest building, incubating, and brooding, but both adults feed the young. It is not clear whether late egg dates represent second broods or result only from renesting after loss of the first clutch.

Feeding habits: See comments on family.

Description: Both the Prairie Warbler and the Palm Warbler are tail waggers. Olive green above and mostly yellow below, the Prairie Warbler has two white wing bars, black streaks on its sides, white tail spots, and white undertail coverts. The adult male may have rusty streaks on his back, and his song rapidly ascends the chromatic scale. Prairie Warblers habitually wag their tails and closely resemble another tail wagger, the Palm Warbler, which has a yellow rump and yellow undertail coverts. Palm Warblers have rusty caps in spring.

Palm Warbler
Dendroica palmarum
4.5–5.5 in. (11.5–14.0 cm)

Range: Over most of our region the Palm Warbler is a fairly common transient found in spring from early April to mid-May and in fall from mid-September through November. It is very common along the Carolina coast in fall. As a winter resident, it is common in southeastern South Carolina but irregular elsewhere in the two states. This tail-wagging warbler frequents hedgerows, edges of fields, yards, gardens, roadsides, and the sandy barrier islands.

Feeding habits: Palm Warblers feed on or near the ground. Fall migrants apparently eat a variety of berries as well as insects, some of which may be captured on the wing by flycatching from perches near the ground.

Description: See Prairie Warbler for a comparative description of the two species. Two forms of the Palm Warbler occur in the Carolinas,

Palm Warbler

both of which are commonly seen during fall migration. Both have white tail spots, a yellow rump, and yellow undertail coverts. In fall the Western Palm Warbler has a dingy grayish breast with faint lateral streaks. The Yellow Palm Warbler has mostly yellow underparts with grayish streaks on the sides in fall. In breeding plumage, both forms have a bright rufous crown, and the Western has matching bright rufous streaks on its breast and sides.

Bay-breasted Warbler
Dendroica castanea
5–6 in. (12.5–15.0 cm)

Range: Known only as a transient in the Carolinas, the Bay-breasted Warbler is an uncommon spring migrant in the western counties but a common one in the fall. The species is very rare toward the coast in spring but more likely to occur in the eastern counties in fall. Spring migrants pass through our region from late April to mid-May, rarely as late as May 30. The considerably more plentiful fall migrants can be expected from early September through October. Twenty or more have been sighted on a good day in late September at Jackson Park in Henderson County, N.C. Fall and winter stragglers have been reported in South Carolina on November 2 (Simpsonville), November 9 (Clemson), and January 5 (near Anderson).

Feeding habits: See comments on family.

Description: The spring male has a streaky back and two white wing bars that, along with the chestnut crown, throat, and sides, clearly distinguish him from all our other warblers. Spring females and fall birds are easily confused with other species. Identification of some individuals may be impossible even with the aid of a well-illustrated field guide.

Blackpoll Warbler

Blackpoll Warbler

Dendroica striata

3.0–5.75 in. (7.6–14.6 cm)

Range: In both spring and fall, the Blackpoll Warbler is among the last of the migrating warblers to arrive. A majority of the northbound birds pass through the Carolinas between late April and early June (very rarely as late as June 15). The peak of passage is usually about mid-May. Fall migrants may be found mostly from mid-September to mid-November, but the peak period is in the latter half of October, when the species may be surprisingly numerous along the coast.

In spring the Blackpoll is a common migrant in the central portion of our region, being only fairly common in the mountains and near the coast. In fall it is rare in the moun-

tains and generally uncommon to fairly common elsewhere.

Feeding habits: See comments on family.

Description: In spring the male Blackpoll has a distinctive solid black cap, a white cheek patch, and yellow feet and legs; otherwise, he resembles the Black-and-white Warbler. Spring females and fall birds are finely streaked and difficult to identify, but their yellowish feet and legs help separate them from similar species. A field guide should be consulted.

Cerulean Warbler

Dendroica cerulea

4–5 in. (10.0–12.5 cm)

Range: During spring and fall migration, the Cerulean Warbler is uncommon in the mountains, becoming rare or absent toward the coast. The spring passage occurs from early April to early May, and the fall passage occurs from late July until mid-September, but chiefly during August in the mountains and extreme western piedmont. Cerulean Warblers breeding in the eastern

United States appear to be sustaining a trend of population increase that was noted prior to 1980.

In summer the species is a rare to locally common resident in open, mature deciduous forests, often where large tulip trees dominate in cove hardwoods from 1,200 to 4,000 feet (360 to 1,200 m). Individuals rarely range above 5,000 feet (1,500 m). Birds singing and apparently on territory or carrying food have been found locally from southeastern Ashe County and adjacent Wilkes County south to Graham and Polk Counties, N.C., and in Caesar's Head State Park, Greenville County, S.C. In eastern North Carolina there is a substantial breeding population along the Roanoke River from the Occoneechee Neck section of Northampton County downstream into Bertie and Martin Counties. The species formerly nested at Morganton, Statesville, and Greensboro, N.C.

Nesting habits: Cerulean Warblers tend to be gregarious during the breeding season, favoring the canopy of mature hardwood forests with an open understory then as well as during migration. As many as twenty males may be heard singing at a particularly favorable locality, but the nests apparently are rather widely dispersed throughout the general vicinity.

The shallow, compact cup of bark fiber, weed stalks, lichens, moss, and grass is bound on the outside with spider silk and resembles a Blue-gray Gnatcatcher nest. Placed high in a deciduous tree, well away from the main trunk amid a cluster of twigs, the nest usually is impossible to see from the clearing below

Cerulean Warbler (male)

even when an adult is making regular trips to it to feed the begging nestlings. The three to five eggs are white, variably dotted or blotched with brown.

Incubation apparently is performed entirely by the female, and the incubation period is estimated to be 12 to 13 days. The male may assist in the feeding of offspring. In North Carolina, adults have been seen feeding young out of the nest as early as May 28 and others still in the nest as late as June 16.

Feeding habits: See comments on family.

Description: The Cerulean is our only warbler with a blue back and white throat. The female is paler than the male and lacks the narrow dark band that separates his white throat from the white breast and streaked sides.

Black-and-white Warbler
Mniotilta varia
5.0–5.5 in. (12.5–14.0 cm)

Range: Although the Black-and-white Warbler is most abundant during spring and fall migrations, it can

Black-and-white Warbler (male)

be found somewhere in our region during every season of the year. A common summer resident in the mountains, it breeds mostly below 5,000 feet (1,500 m) and wanders into higher elevations after the nesting season. The species also nests in the piedmont and upper coastal plain, becoming uncommon in summer at the eastern edge of its breeding range in the lower coastal plain. Breeding birds arrive between mid-March and early April, and most depart by mid-October, although a few linger throughout the winter in the coastal plain, particularly around Lake Mattamuskeet and in southeastern South Carolina.

Nesting habits: The Black-and-white Warbler usually breeds in mature hardwood forests, but in parts of the piedmont and coastal plain, it nests in swamp hardwoods and pine plantations. The nest is placed on the ground, often under an exposed root at the base of a tree or under a mat of pine straw beside a fallen log. It blends so well with its surroundings that it is practically invisible from above. Composed of bark strippings, grasses, and leaves, the nest is lined with hair or rootlets.

The four or five white eggs are dotted with reddish brown and lavender gray, sometimes in a wreath pattern. Incubation apparently is primarily, if not entirely, by the female and requires about 12 days. Both adults care for the young, and the species is single-brooded. When disturbed by an intruder, the sitting bird may perform a broken-wing act. The period of nestling life is 8 to 12 days, and very shortly after emerging from the nest, the young can climb trunks and branches of trees.

Feeding habits: Black-and-white Warblers are insectivorous, and they so closely resemble nuthatches and Brown Creepers in their feeding behavior that the species formerly was called "Black-and-white Creeper."

Description: Heavily streaked with black and white, this species has a black crown divided by a white central stripe. The male has a black cheek patch and a black throat patch with white lines separating the cheek from the crown and the throat. Females and immatures lack the dark cheek and throat patches. Black-and-white Warblers can be confused with male Blackpolls, which have a solid black cap. The song of the Black-and-white is a high-pitched "squeaky wheel" sound.

American Redstart
Setophaga ruticilla
5.0–5.5 in. (12.5–14.0 cm)

Range: The American Redstart is found throughout the Carolinas as a spring and fall migrant, and it breeds extensively in the inland portions of the two states. Redstarts nest in the mountains up to about 4,600 feet (1,380 m), throughout the North Carolina piedmont, and at least sparingly in the North Carolina coastal plain. In South Carolina, evidence of breeding outside the mountains and foothills comes from Laurens, York, Chesterfield, Richland, Sumter, Georgetown, and Berkeley Counties. That list of sites suggests breeding statewide except for the southern tip.

American Redstart (male)

Spring migrants begin arriving in early April and are most numerous in the piedmont. Fall migration occurs from mid-August through October, with redstarts often very common during that season. Stragglers are rare in winter, but one was at a feeder in Seneca, Oconee County, S.C., January 1 and February 3, 2002, and one was seen on February 6, 2001, in Charleston County, S.C. At Morganton, N.C., a female redstart was present from January 14 to February 24, 1993.

Nesting habits: Breeding birds frequent wooded streams, especially extensive bottomland forests, placing nests 5 to 20 feet (1.5 to 6.0 m) above ground in a fork of a bush or small tree, often a birch. Built by the female, the nest is a deep, compact cup of shredded plant fibers bound together with spider webs and lined with grass, fine plant fibers, and hair.

The four white eggs are speckled with gray and brown, chiefly around the large end, and usually laid about mid-May. Incubation requires about 12 days and is performed by the female. She also does all the brooding, but the male helps feed the young and clean the nest. Offspring remain in the nest about 9 days. The species normally is single-brooded.

In piedmont North Carolina many breeding males are first-year birds and therefore have little or no black in the plumage. Their resemblance to females may cause some bird students to overlook mated pairs.

Feeding habits: See comments on family. Redstarts feed by flycatching more often than do most of our other warblers.

Description: The fully adult male American Redstart is our only predominantly black warbler. The sides, bases of the flight feathers, and bases of the outer tail feathers are touched with orange. The female is gray above and white below with white spectacles and yellow spots on the sides, wings, and tail. First-year males resemble females, but the yellow spots may be tinged with orange, and the throat and upper breast may be irregularly dotted with gray and black. Young males wear the female-like plumage through the first nesting season.

Prothonotary Warbler
Protonotaria citrea
5.0–5.5 in. (12.5–14.0 cm)

Prothonotary Warbler (male)

Range: The Prothonotary Warbler is a common summer resident from early April to mid-September along the coast and throughout the coastal plain. It also breeds sparingly throughout piedmont South Carolina and inland to Gaston, Forsyth, Iredell, and Cleveland Counties in North Carolina. The species is a rare spring migrant in the mountains from late April to early May. Winter stragglers are extremely rare. Although probably most abundant in cypress swamps, the species nests in other types of swamps and in heavily wooded borders of lakes and streams.

Nesting habits: Both adults work on the nest of small twigs, leaves, and moss placed in a natural cavity in a tree, stump, or wooden structure. A discarded crate or a conveniently located birdhouse may be occupied. The nest usually is low, only 3 to 15 feet (1.0 to 4.5 m) high, and usually over water. The four to seven almost spherical eggs are white and generously splashed with bright reddish brown. Incubation requires about 13 days and seems to be performed by the female alone, with the male feeding her on the nest

to some extent. Both adults tend the young, which leave the nest at 10 to 11 days of age. The species is double-brooded in our region, eggs usually being laid in early May for first broods and in late June for second ones.

In 1984 and 1985, one pair built nests in an atypical site, an overturned boat on the shore of the Cape Fear River at Elwell's Ferry, which is near Kelly in Bladen County, N.C. The first year, when it became necessary to repair the boat, workers removed the nest, which contained young, and placed it at the base of a nearby cypress. Later, a grass-cutting crew moved the nest to a box placed aboard the ferry. Throughout those changes, the parents continued to care for the young, carrying food from the original feeding territory to the nest regardless of its current position as the ferry moved back and forth across the river. The young eventually fledged.

Feeding habits: See comments on family.

Description: The Prothonotary Warbler is predominantly yellow with a shiny black eye and blue-gray wings and tail. Males are more golden yellow than the females. Named for the papal chief notary, who wears a yellow robe, the Prothonotary Warbler probably should be called the "Golden Swamp Warbler." Then, at least, bird-watchers would not have to wonder whether to accent the second syllable, as is heard quite frequently, or the third, as logically should be preferred. Both pronunciations are acceptable.

Worm-eating Warbler (male)

Worm-eating Warbler
Helmitheros vermivorum
5.0–5.5 in. (12.5–14.5 cm)

Range: The Worm-eating Warbler migrates throughout the Carolinas, being an uncommon transient from mid-April to mid-May and from mid-August to early October. In late September it may be locally numerous in brushy mountain lowlands. The species is uncommon to fairly common as a breeding bird in the mountains, preferring hilly deciduous forests from 1,800 to 3,000 feet (550 to 900 m) in elevation. It is locally uncommon to rare or absent in the piedmont and locally uncommon in the coastal plain during the breeding season. In the coastal plain, breeding birds are often found around Carolina bays and in swamps and pocosins. This is a terrestrial bird, feeding for the most part on the ground and nesting there.

Nesting habits: Well hidden under a drift of dead leaves, the nest of decayed or partly skeletonized leaves usually is lined with hair, fine grasses, or the reddish-brown fruiting stems of hair moss. The three to six slightly glossy white eggs are variably spotted with brown, the markings usually being somewhat concentrated at the large end. The female incubates the eggs about 13 days, with the male sometimes feeding her on the nest. Young leave the nest about 10 days after hatching and remain with the parents for some time after departure. Apparently, only one brood is raised each season.

Incubating females are close sitters. When flushed from her nest, one walked away silently with tail fanned and wings fluttering. Another flew directly to the ground in front of the observer. With lowered head and body, she crept away, flicking the feathers of her raised tail and making an excited *chit* note.

Feeding habits: The species' name appears to be a misnomer. Although the Worm-eating Warbler consumes a wide variety of animal matter, including bees, spiders, insects, and insect larvae, worms apparently are not a significant source of nourishment. The species forages by walking on the ground and along limbs.

Description: See Swainson's Warbler for a comparative description. The song of the Worm-eating Warbler is a very high-pitched, rapid buzz, similar to that of the Chipping Sparrow but normally faster and more like an insect.

Swainson's Warbler
Limnothlypis swainsonii
5.5–6.5 in. (14.0–16.5 cm)

Range: The Reverend John Bachman of Charleston, S.C., discovered this elusive warbler on the Edisto River in 1833, and J. J. Audubon (a frequent guest in the Bachman household) named it for the English artist-naturalist William Swainson.

Swainson's Warbler

Present from early April to late September, the Swainson's Warbler breeds in suitable habitat throughout South Carolina and in both the coastal plain and the mountains of North Carolina. Birds of the mountain population apparently do not occupy their territories in western North Carolina until late April. The species is absent from piedmont North Carolina except as a rare transient and a very local nester.

In the eastern counties, Swainson's Warblers usually nest where there are impenetrable swampy thickets, often those with extensive stands of cane. In the mountains, they nest below 3,000 feet (900 m) in the steep, rugged, densely vegetated river gorges draining the southeastern Blue Ridge escarpment, possibly as far northeast as Chimney Rock Park, Rutherford County, N.C. Here the species is usually found in thickets of rhododendron, laurel, and doghobble. In both situations the habitat effectively discourages all but the most dedicated ornithologists.

Nesting habits: Nests are bulky masses of leaves lined with fine rootlets. Built by the female, they are placed 1 to 10 feet (0.3 to 3.0 m) above ground in palmettos, cane, bushes, or tangled vines. The general appearance is that of a cluster of dead leaves lodged in a crotch by high water.

The three or sometimes four eggs are globular and creamy white, occasionally lightly spotted with reddish brown or tinged with blue or green. Eggs have been found in the Carolinas from early May to early July. Incubation is by the female and requires 14 or 15 days. The female is a very close sitter, at least once having accepted insects from the fingers of an intruder. If forced from the nest, she will feign a broken wing.

Both parents share in the feeding of the young, which remain in the nest 10 to 12 days or slightly longer and beg food from their parents an additional 2 or 3 weeks. Males may continue singing into August, but there is no firm evidence of a second brood.

Feeding habits: See comments on family.

Description: This very plain brown warbler has a solid rusty cap, a white line above the eye, and a dark line through it. Swainson's Warbler resembles the brownish Worm-eating Warbler, which has a dark crown that is divided and bordered by conspicuous buffy streaks. The song of the Swainson's Warbler is easily confused with that of the Louisiana Waterthrush, but Swainson's typically has fewer syllables, often three low notes that are slurred downward and followed by an ending much like the last two notes of the Hooded Warbler's song.

Ovenbird (adult at nest)

Ovenbird
Seiurus aurocapilla
5.5–6.5 in. (14.0–16.5 cm)

Range: The Ovenbird is a common summer resident from early April through October in the mountains of North and South Carolina up to about 5,000 feet (1,500 m) and across the piedmont of both states. The species also breeds to some extent in the Carolina coastal plain, but not along the immediate coast. During the breeding season Ovenbirds are fairly common in suitable habitat in northeastern North Carolina, becoming less numerous southward to Brunswick County, near Leland, N.C., and to Horry, Georgetown, Berkeley, Orangeburg, Bamburg, and Barnwell Counties, S.C. Range extension into the South Carolina coastal plain was first recorded in Horry County in June 1984. A decade later the species had become widespread, though still spotty, in the South Carolina coastal plain, where there is evidence of ongoing range expansion.

Ovenbirds occur as transients throughout the Carolinas. They are more abundant inland than along the coast, but one landed on a boat 50 miles (31.1 km) off Murrells Inlet on May 16, 2003. Winter stragglers are found occasionally, particularly in southeastern South Carolina, and a few winter annually in the vicinity of Buxton, N.C. Very rare and unexpected was one in Transylvania County, N.C., throughout December 1995.

Nesting habits: During the nesting season, the Ovenbird favors rather dry hilly forests with a moderate understory. The canopy may be either pines or hardwoods. Built entirely by the female, the ground-level nest is made of grass, leaves, pine needles, and other plant materials. It has a domed roof and a side entrance. Beneath the dome is a lining of hair and fine rootlets or grass upon which the bird deposits four or five eggs, spotted mostly at the large end with brown and gray or lilac. The oven-like nest is usually placed in a slight depression near a path or other opening in the forest and is often sheltered by a shrub, fallen branch, or leaf litter.

The female incubates the eggs about 12 days, and she occasionally may be fed on the nest by the male. Both adults feed the young, which stay in the nest 8 to 10 days. The family party remains together until the offspring are about 5 weeks old. Although single-brooded, Ovenbirds will lay again if the first nesting attempt should fail.

Feeding habits: While foraging on the ground for insects and small mollusks, Ovenbirds and waterthrushes walk with a teetering motion in the manner of the Spotted Sandpiper. The genus name *Seiurus* means "tail waving."

Description: The Ovenbird has a plain olive back and a heavily streaked breast. Its head pattern separates it from the waterthrushes, which also feed on the ground and wag their tails. Look for the Ovenbird's prominent white eye ring and black stripe above the eye. Adults have a rusty crown. See Northern Waterthrush account for a comparative description. More easily heard than seen, Ovenbirds migrating through the Carolinas sing *Teach-er, Teach-er, Teach-er* (just like the many recordings that are available). However, our southern breeding birds, in the mountains as well as the eastern counties, usually sing a shorter version, perhaps *tea-er, tea-er, tea-er* or just *teach, teach, teach.*

Northern Waterthrush

Northern Waterthrush
Seiurus noveboracensis
5–6 in. (12.5–15.0 cm)

Range: A fairly common spring and fall transient across the central part of the Carolinas, the Northern Waterthrush is uncommon toward the mountains and the coast. The main passages occur from mid-April through May and from mid-August through October. Winter stragglers are found almost annually, sometimes as late as mid-February, which is not particularly surprising in a species that winters regularly in southern Florida.

Feeding habits: Waterthrushes are likely to be found feeding in the margins of sluggish water in swamps, wet thickets, woodland streams, and even along the edges of marshes. They often forage on floating debris.

Description: Olive brown above and heavily streaked below, the two waterthrushes are separated by their head patterns. The Northern Waterthrush has a creamy stripe above the eye, its throat is finely streaked between the heavy lateral throat stripes, and its comparatively short bill is almost conical. The Louisiana has a prominent white stripe above the eye, its throat is white between the heavy lateral stripes, and its long bill is rather heavy for a warbler. Ovenbirds have a complete eye ring and a dark stripe above the eye. All three species walk with a teetering motion in the manner of a Spotted Sandpiper.

Louisiana Waterthrush
Seiurus motacilla
6 in. (15 cm)

Louisiana Waterthrush

Range: In the Carolinas, the Louisiana Waterthrush is a fairly common spring and fall migrant and summer resident from mountains below 3,500 feet (1,070 m) eastward to the fall line. During the breeding season the species is fairly common in the Great Dismal Swamp and at Merchants Millpond State Park in Gates County, N.C., and nests at least sparingly in the inner coastal plain southward to Georgetown, Bamburg, and Barnwell Counties, S.C. It is limited as a nesting bird in the coastal plain because of its habitat requirements. Sites along streams with steep banks and a noticeable current are scarce east of the fall line. Throughout the coastal plain the species is an uncommon to rare migrant. Breeding birds arrive in the Carolinas by late March and begin moving southward about mid-July, nearly all having left the Carolinas by early September. Winter stragglers are exceedingly rare.

Nesting habits: Louisiana Waterthrushes inhabit the borders of woodland streams, especially rocky, fast-flowing ones. The nest is placed in a sheltered nook in the steep bank of a stream, often in the outer curve of a bend, perhaps under some exposed roots or overhanging ferns. On a substantial platform of wet leaves stuck together by the mud on them, the waterthrush builds a neat cup of twigs, mosses, and weed stems and lines it with dry grasses and hair. The four or five eggs are white or pinkish white, speckled all over with brown and gray. Incubation requires 12 to 14 days; apparently the female does all the incubating and brooding, but the male participates in nest construction and assists in feeding the young, which probably remain in the nest about 10 days.

Feeding habits: Although the Louisiana Waterthrush consumes mostly insects and spiders, it sometimes eats snails, other small mollusks, and tiny fish. It often forages on floating debris.

Description: See Northern Waterthrush for a comparative description.

Kentucky Warbler

Kentucky Warbler
Oporornis formosus
5.5 in. (14.0 cm)

Range: The Kentucky Warbler is a fairly common summer resident in the mountains below 3,500 feet (1,070 m) and eastward to the fall line. It breeds locally wherever there is suitable habitat in the coastal plain. The birds arrive in the bottomland hardwoods of the breeding grounds from early to late April and depart mostly from August to mid-September, but a few stragglers may be found in October.

Nesting habits: Usually built on or very near the ground at the base of a bush and often beside a trail, the nest is a bulky mass of dead leaves lined with grass, bark strips, rootlets, and dried pine needles. Laid in May or June, the four or five white eggs are sprinkled with reddish brown and lilac gray. Incubation requires 12 or 13 days. If an unsuspecting hiker pauses too near her home, the female will rush off the nest to defend her offspring.

Apparently the female is solely responsible for nest construction, incubation, and brooding; but the male helps feed the young, particularly after they leave the nest. The period of dependency may last nearly a month, 10 days in the nest and up to 17 days after departure. The brief sojourn on the breeding grounds and the male's minor role in the care of the young indicate that the species is single-brooded.

Feeding habits: See comments on family.

Description: Olive green above and completely yellow below, the Kentucky Warbler has yellow spectacles and black sideburns.

Connecticut Warbler
Oporornis agilis
5.75–6.0 in. (13–15 cm)

Range: Migrating Connecticut Warblers frequent thickets, both wet and dry, but they probably prefer the wet ones. These rare transients are found throughout the Carolinas in spring and fall. Spring migration tends to be mostly, but not exclusively, in the mountains and western piedmont. In the eastern counties Connecticut Warblers are seen more often in fall than in spring, with most of the birds occurring along the coast. Spring migrants usually pass through the Carolinas in early May (extremes April 26 to May 30), with mountain occurrences being most frequent about May 14 to 23. Fall migrants occur mostly from mid-September to mid-October (extremes September 2 to December 31).

Feeding habits: This species forages on the ground, walking in the manner of the Ovenbird, but without teetering.

Description: Two gray-hooded warblers occur in the Carolinas, the Connecticut and the Mourning. Both have olive backs and yellow underparts extending from the base of the hood to the tip of the undertail coverts. The Connecticut is the larger of the two. It has relatively pale yellow coloration and a prominent complete eye ring, white in the adult and buffy in the immature. The Mourning Warbler has a dark line through its eye, breaking its narrow white eye ring and giving the adult an unusually dark face. Immature Mournings also have a dark smudge across the breast where the adult will have a black area at the base of its gray hood.

Mourning Warbler
Oporornis philadelphia
5.0–5.75 in. (12.5–14.5 cm)

Range: The Mourning Warbler is a regular, but still rare, spring and fall migrant found in all regions of the Carolinas. Spring migrants occur mostly in the latter half of May (extremes very late April to May 30) and tend to be more numerous in the mountains and piedmont than in the coastal plain. Fall migrants occur from mid-August to mid-October (extremes July 15 to October 30). The species is regular in the coastal plain, though never numerous. One was seen off Cape Hatteras in late May 2000, and another was banded at Charleston, S.C., August 24, 1994.

Singing males were seen and heard during four consecutive breeding seasons (1983–1986) at Jenkins Ridge Overlook on the Blue Ridge Parkway (Mile Post 460.8). In July 1984 a pair were on territory, and the adult male was seen carrying a caterpillar. However, no conclusive proof of nesting was obtained. Behavior suggestive of local breeding has also been observed at Mount Mitchell and at Roan Mountain from late May into early July.

Feeding habits: This slow-moving and secretive bird usually forages close to the ground in woodland clearings and thickets.

Description: See Connecticut Warbler for a comparative description.

MacGillivray's Warbler
Oporornis tolmiei
5.25 in. (13.0 cm)

Range: MacGillivray's Warbler nests in western Canada and the western United States. It winters as far north as the southern tip of Baja California and adjacent portions of western Mexico. Vagrants are very rare east of the Mississippi River and north of Florida. An immature male was found freshly killed on a road near Lake Mattamuskeet, Hyde County, N.C., on November 6, 1998. The specimen was donated to the North Carolina State Museum of Natural Sciences.

Feeding habits: The species generally forages for insects while skulking on or near the ground in dense vegetation. It hops instead of walking, as do many other warblers that feed on the ground. Its rather quick and furtive movements include switching the tail sideways.

Description: Similar to the Mourning and Connecticut Warblers, MacGillivray's Warbler is best separated from them by the bold white arcs above and below each eye, a trait shared by the immatures as well as both adults. The Connecticut Warbler has a complete eye ring in all plumages, and the Mourning has a narrow complete eye ring (adult female and immatures), a narrow partial eye ring (some adult males), or none at all (most adult males).

Common Yellowthroat
Geothlypis trichas
4.5–5.5 in. (11.5–14.0 cm)

Common Yellowthroat (male)

Range: From late March or early April to mid-October, the Common Yellowthroat is found throughout the Carolinas, being a very common species over most of the region, even in the mountains below 5,000 feet (1,500 m). Above that elevation, the species is only fairly common. Yellowthroats winter from the eastern piedmont throughout the coastal plain of the Carolinas, becoming more numerous along the coast than inland. They prefer habitats such as brushy fields, hedgerows, wet thickets, and marshes.

Nesting habits: The nest usually is well hidden in low bushes, cane, cattails, or clumps of grass, often only a few inches above ground or water. Made of coarse grass, leaves, and strips of bark, the rather bulky structure is lined with fine grasses. The male apparently does not regularly assist the female with construction.

The three to five eggs are white, variably spotted with black and brown. In coastal Carolina, first clutches are laid in late April or early May; second ones, in June. Incubation requires about 12 days and is performed by the female.

Common Yellowthroat (female)

The male sometimes brings food to the nest for the female to eat while she is incubating or for her to feed to the newly hatched nestlings. On the fourth day he begins delivering food directly to the young, which remain in the nest 9 or 10 days.

Feeding habits: See comments on family.

Description: Olive above and mostly yellow below, the male Common Yellowthroat has a broad black mask and sings *witichity-witichity-witichity*. The wrenlike female is brownish with a pale yellow throat. Look for the white belly that in all plumages separates the yellow throat and breast from the yellow undertail coverts.

Hooded Warbler
Wilsonia citrina
5.5 in. (14.0 cm)

Range: The Hooded Warbler is a common summer resident of moist deciduous woodlands throughout the Carolinas, arriving on the coast in late March and at inland localities in early to mid-April. Fall migration begins in early August, and most of the birds have moved southward by early October, though stragglers are found very rarely from early November until late January.

Nesting habits: Usually the nest is built 2 to 4 feet (0.6 to 1.2 m) above ground in a low bush or in the top of a clump of cane. Tangles of briers are favorite sites. Normally the compact nest is made of cane leaves, bark strips, weed stems, and pine needles. It may be lined with fine grasses, hair, rootlets, or the black inner fiber of Spanish moss.
Early May appears to be the peak of egg laying. The three to five creamy eggs are variably marked with brown and lilac. The incubation period is 12 days. Apparently the female builds the nest and does all the incubating and brooding, but the male assists in feeding the young. When they leave the nest at 8 days of age, the offspring are unable to fly, but they have well-developed legs and are remarkably self-sufficient. Although most pairs probably raise only one brood per season, second and third sets of eggs have been reported.

Feeding habits: See comments on family.

Hooded Warbler (male)

Hooded Warbler (female on nest)

Description: The yellow forehead and cheeks of the male Hooded Warbler are surrounded by a black cap, neck band, and bib that are joined together to form the hood. Plain olive back, plain yellow underparts, and white tail spots are like those of the female, which usually has a dark cap and a yellow throat. Female Hoodeds are easily confused with Wilson's and Bachman's Warblers, both of which lack white in the tail. Listen for the male Hooded's loudly whistled *weet-a-wee tee-o* rendered with a rising inflection on the next to the last syllable.

Wilson's Warbler (male)

Wilson's Warbler
Wilsonia pusilla
4.5–5.0 in. (11.5–12.5 cm)

Range: An uncommon to rare spring and fall transient, Wilson's Warbler is more likely to be found in the piedmont and mountains than in the coastal plain. That is because the species migrates northward across the Gulf of Mexico west of the Florida peninsula, where it occurs only accidentally. The spring passage takes place mostly from late April through mid-May. The fall movement extends from mid-August through September, with stragglers sometimes found later. Since the 1980s there has been increasing evidence that a few Wilson's Warblers winter occasionally in the piedmont and coastal plain of the Carolinas, at least as far northwest as Winston-Salem, N.C. This species likes thickets, especially willows.

Feeding habits: See comments on family.

Description: Plain light olive above and plain bright yellow below, the male Wilson's Warbler has a small black cap that sharply contrasts with the bright yellow forehead. Females and immatures are similar, but with an olive crown. In all plumages the Wilson's Warbler lacks white in the tail.

Canada Warbler
Wilsonia canadensis
5.0–5.75 in. (12.5–14.5 cm)

Range: Although the Canada Warbler is a fairly common to common summer resident in the North Carolina mountains from 3,400 feet (1,040 m) to the tops of the highest peaks, the species is an uncommon migrant in the piedmont counties and is generally rare to absent toward the coast. Spring migrants are found mostly in May (extreme dates April 23 to May 29), and fall migrants occur outside the mountains mostly from late August through late September (extreme dates August 6 to November 6).

After mid-August the breeding birds begin wandering into the lower elevations of the mountains; but fall migration does not begin until late August, and it continues into early October. Canada Warblers frequent dense growths of rhododendrons and other shrubs, especially those near small mountain streams.

Nesting habits: The bulky nest of dry weeds is lined with fine plant fibers and hair. It is placed on or near the ground, often on a moss-covered log or stump. Beneath the projecting bank of a stream is another favored site. The four to five white or slightly buffy eggs are speckled with brown or gray, primarily around the large end. Egg laying

Canada Warbler (male)

apparently takes place in late May
or early June, but the incubation
period (probably about 12 days) and
number of days the young stay in
the nest are unknown. The female
is believed to do all the incubating
and brooding, with the male helping feed the young and clean the
nest.

Feeding habits: See comments on
family.

Description: Plain gray above and
bright yellow below, the male Canada Warbler has yellow spectacles
and a black necklace across his
upper breast. The necklace may be
faint or even lacking in females and
immatures, but the yellow spectacles (very pale around the eyes)
and somewhat greenish, unspotted
tail make identification of poorly
marked birds possible.

Yellow-breasted Chat
Icteria virens
6.75–7.25 in. (17–19 cm)

Range: The Yellow-breasted Chat is a
fairly common summer resident in
deciduous thickets at the low and
middle elevations in the mountains

*Yellow-breasted Chats (male, at left,
bringing food to nest with young)*

and throughout the Carolina piedmont. Its numbers decrease across
the coastal plain and along the
immediate coast. The birds generally begin arriving on the breeding
grounds in mid-April, but some
may be on territory near the coast
in mid-March. Most chats have
departed by the end of September;
however, banding recoveries indicate that this very secretive species
winters sparingly in the lower
coastal plain of the Carolinas. Winter stragglers have been reported
inland to the foothills.

Nesting habits: Placed 1 to 5 feet (0.3 to
1.5 m) above ground in briers (often
blackberry) or a sapling, the bulky
nest is made of weed stems, grass,
and leaves. It is lined with fine
grasses and rootlets. Both adults
apparently participate in nest
construction.

The three to five white eggs are

variably marked with brown spots. The incubation period has not been determined definitely, but 11 days is thought to be normal for the species. Although the female does all the incubating and brooding, the male at least assists in the feeding of the offspring, which remain in the nest 8 days or perhaps slightly longer.

From time to time during the breeding season, the chat may be seen singing lustily while making a clownish, floppy-winged flight, either rising into the air and returning to the same perch or moving from one perch to another. Flight songs have also been reported in other warbler species, including the Common Yellowthroat, Louisiana Waterthrush, Ovenbird, Blue-winged Warbler, and Prothonotary Warbler.

Feeding habits: Although the Yellow-breasted Chat is predominantly insectivorous, it consumes many wild fruits and berries in season.

Description: More easily heard than seen, the chat is a ventriloquist that makes its presence known with a noisy repertoire of squawks, chuckles, whistles, and imitations of other species, notably the White-eyed Vireo. Chats usually stay well hidden in dense tangles of saplings, bushes, and briers.

This large, heavy-billed warbler has a plain olive back, white spectacles, bright yellow throat and breast, and white belly and undertail coverts. The white under-tail coverts and large size clearly separate the chat from the Common Yellowthroat, which has the same general color pattern except for its yellow undertail coverts.

Family THRAUPIDAE: Tanagers

Tanagers comprise a large New World family of colorful, mostly fruit-eating birds. Only five of the more than 200 species occur regularly in the United States. Two species nest in the Carolinas, and a third is a casual winter visitor.

Summer Tanager
Piranga rubra
7–8 in. (17.5–20.0 cm)

Range: The Summer Tanager is a common summer resident throughout the Carolinas, but in the mountains it breeds only at the lower elevations, mostly below 2,000 feet (600 m). Pairs and family parties are present in wooded residential districts and open woodlands from mid-April to mid-October. Winter stragglers are very rare.

Nesting habits: The male is not known to participate in nest construction. Nests are shallow cups of grass placed well out from the main trunk on a horizontal limb of a pine or a deciduous tree, often an oak. The site is usually 10 to 40 feet (3 to 12 m) above a roadway or a clearing in the woods.

The three or four greenish-blue eggs are dotted with brown and lavender. Eggs usually are laid in late May or June, and the species is single-brooded. Incubation lasts about 12 days and is performed by the female. The male feeds his mate during incubation, helps defend the nest, and helps feed the young and clean the nest. Under normal conditions, offspring probably remain in the nest about 12 days.

Feeding habits: Summer Tanagers eat a variety of fruits and berries, but

Summer Tanager (male)

Summer Tanager (female)

red ones are found from time to time. Compared with the female Scarlet Tanager, the female Summer has less darkness in the wings, more orange-yellow in the underparts, and a larger, lighter-colored bill. Nestlings and fledglings are brownish above and white streaked with brown below. After their postjuvenal molt, young of both sexes are yellow and resemble the adult female; young males begin acquiring the red plumage during their first spring after hatching.

Scarlet Tanager
Piranga olivacea
6.5–7.5 in. (16.5–19.0 cm)

Range: The Scarlet Tanager is a common summer resident in the southern Appalachian Mountains, breeding mostly at elevations between 1,500 and 5,000 feet (450 to 1,500 m). The species also breeds throughout the piedmont of North Carolina and northwestern South Carolina, where it may locally outnumber the formerly more abundant Summer Tanager.

The Scarlet Tanager population also appears to be increasing in the inner coastal plain of North and South Carolina. Nesting has been documented in Sumter County, S.C., and it appears to be occurring as far east as Gates County in northeastern North Carolina and along the Martin-Washington County line, as well as eastward to Bladen and Brunswick Counties in the southeastern part of the state. That dramatic change is particularly surprising because Scarlet Tanagers are generally rare migrants below the fall belt.

insects apparently constitute the bulk of their diet in most seasons. They consume many wasps and bees, and they may hover beneath the eaves of a house while foraging for spiders and insects. They also hunt from a perch like a flycatcher.
Description: The adult male Summer Tanager is our only all-red bird without a prominent crest, though he can raise the feathers on his crown when agitated. The bill is pale yellow. Unlike the Scarlet Tanager, he retains his bright plumage throughout the year. Although the females normally are dull greenish-yellow birds, partly and completely

Scarlet Tanager

Partial to deciduous forests, the Scarlet Tanager arrives on its breeding grounds by late April or early May, and most individuals have left for the tropics by mid-October. It is a very rare winter straggler.

Nesting habits: The nest, probably built by the female, is a shallow cup of grasses placed on a horizontal tree limb, often that of an oak, well out from the main trunk and usually about 20 to 40 feet (6 to 12 m) above ground. The three to five eggs are greenish blue, speckled with reddish brown. Performed by the female, incubation requires 13 to 14 days. Young remain in the nest about 2 weeks. Males may help feed their offspring until the young are fully fledged, or the female may become almost fully responsible for the rapidly maturing juveniles. The species is single-brooded.

Feeding habits: Although Scarlet Tanagers occasionally eat fruit, they are mostly insectivorous with a strong taste for caterpillars.

Description: The breeding male Scarlet Tanager is our only bird with a bright red head and body and jet-black wings and tail. In the fall, males molt and temporarily resemble females. The female is greenish yellow with dark wings and tail; her bill is smaller and darker than that of the female Summer Tanager.

Western Tanager
Piranga ludoviciana
6.5–7.5 in. (16.5–19.0 cm)

Range: Since about 1990, the Western Tanager has become an annual winter vagrant in the Carolinas, occurring mostly as a visitor at feeding stations from December through March, but occasionally seen as early as September 8 (Lugoff, S.C.) and as late as May 31 (Bat Cave, N.C.). The species normally winters south of the United States.

Feeding habits: Insects provide most of the food, but a significant amount of fruit is taken.

Description: The male is mostly yellow with black tail and wings, one wing bar yellow and the other white, and a variable amount of red on the head. The female is similar, but she has no red about the head. Her bill is variably tinted with orange.

Western Tanager

Family EMBERIZIDAE:
Towhees, Sparrows, and Allies

All members of this widespread family have conical bills, and most are secretive and well adapted for feeding on the ground. Most consume both seeds and insects in proportions that vary from season to season. The family includes towhees, sparrows, longspurs, and *Emberiza* buntings. Towhees and many of their relatives are noted for their ability to scratch in dirt, leaf litter, and snow to reach buried food.

Green-tailed Towhee
Pipilo chlorurus
7.0–7.75 in. (17.5–19.5 cm)

Range: A very rare accidental from the western United States, the Green-tailed Towhee has been documented only twice in the Carolinas. One was collected in Charleston County, S.C., on January 18, 1921. Another was photographed near Southport, N.C., where it was present from January 5 until April 15, 2002.

Feeding habits: See comments on family and Eastern Towhee account.

Description: Smaller and less colorful than our other towhees, Green-tailed adults and first-winter birds can be recognized by their greenish wings and tail, rufous crown, and white throat.

Spotted Towhee
Pipilo maculatus
7.5 in. (19.0 cm)

Range: Native to the western United States, the Spotted Towhee is accidental east of the Mississippi River. One was trapped and collected as a scientific specimen at Fayetteville, N.C., on February 14, 1957. Another was trapped and collected on February 19, 1967, at Spartanburg, S.C. There are no published sight records for the Spotted Towhee from the Carolinas. This species was until recently considered to be a subspecies of the Eastern (Rufous-sided) Towhee.

Feeding habits: See comments on family and Eastern Towhee account.

Description: The western counterpart of our familiar Eastern (Rufous-sided) Towhee, the Spotted Towhee has numerous spots of white on its back and wings.

Eastern Towhee
(Rufous-sided Towhee)
Pipilo erythrophthalmus
7.5–8.25 in. (10–22 cm)

Range: The Eastern Towhee is a common permanent resident throughout the Carolinas, but the species tends to withdraw from the higher mountains during the winter. Towhees are birds of thickets, overgrown fields, woodland margins, and residential shrubbery.

Nesting habits: On or very near the ground, the female builds the cup of bark strips, grasses, and other plant fibers. The two to five white eggs are generously marked with reddish-brown spots that tend to be heaviest at the large end, where they may form an almost solid cap. Incubation lasts 12 to 13 days and is performed by the female, but occasionally the male may bring food to her. Although brooding is left entirely to the female, the male regularly helps feed the young, which develop very rapidly and remain in

Eastern Towhee (male)

Eastern Towhee (female)

the nest only 7 days. Normally two broods are raised, and third ones are not uncommon under favorable conditions. First clutches may be laid in April, but early May is the usual time.

Feeding habits: While feeding, towhees often make a great deal of noise by scratching with both feet to expose seeds and insects hidden beneath leaf litter.

Description: The black-backed male and the brown-backed female Eastern Towhees are easy to recognize, but the streaky-brown fledglings do not favor either parent. The careful observer may notice that some adult males have red eyes, while others have white or yellowish eyes. Some birds have more white in their tail feathers than others, and the voices are distinctly different. Those variations occur among three different races that breed in the Carolinas and a fourth that is a very rare winter visitor. Often called "joree" or "chewink" in imitation of its call notes, the Eastern Towhee sings *drink-your-tea,* ending with a highly variable trill.

Bachman's Sparrow
Aimophila aestivalis
5.5–6.25 in. (14–16 cm)

Range: During the breeding season Bachman's Sparrows are most likely to be found in the same habitat preferred by Red-cockaded Woodpeckers: open stands of longleaf pine with an undergrowth of scattered bushes and wiregrass. Elsewhere in the coastal plain Bachman's Sparrows breed in open pine woods, especially in tracts recently thinned by fire. They are hard to find because they move from one tract to another as the undergrowth becomes too tall or thick for their needs, and they appear to be decreasing even where apparently suitable habitat is available. In the piedmont, Bachman's Sparrows have been known to nest in abandoned fields with scattered saplings and tall grasses; however, that population appears to have been generally displaced by changes in habitat. In winter Bachman's Sparrows tend to withdraw southward, but some remain all year at least as far north as southeastern North Carolina.

Nesting habits: The grass nest is

Bachman's Sparrow

American Tree Sparrow

usually domed or arched over and very difficult to find. Built on the ground at the base of a bush or clump of grass, it often has a hidden passageway extending outward from it. The female builds the nest and incubates the four or five eggs, which, unlike those of most sparrows, are pure white. The nesting season is highly variable, but first clutches usually are laid by late April or early May.

The incubation period apparently is about 12 to 14 days, and most observers agree that the male helps feed the young. Two or three broods may be raised in a season. This sparrow, except for singing males, is so secretive that very little is known about its breeding habits.

Feeding habits: More insectivorous than many other sparrows, this species also eats grass, sedge, and pine seeds.

Description: At a glance, which usually is all you get, Bachman's looks like a dingy Field Sparrow. The bill, however, is not pink; the upper mandible is dark, and the lower one is light, perhaps a bit yellowish. Reference to field guides is recommended.

American Tree Sparrow
Spizella arborea
6.0–6.5 in. (15.0–16.5 cm)

Range: A rare winter resident of the mountains and northwestern piedmont counties of North Carolina, the American Tree Sparrow occurs irregularly eastward to the coast and southward to Hilton Head Island, S.C., from late October to early May. Apparently the species avoids high elevations in the mountains.

Feeding habits: American Tree Sparrows are usually found in small flocks, often along with other species of sparrows, feeding on weed seeds in old fields or perching in the sun on nearby trees and bushes.

Description: The American Tree Sparrow resembles a Field Sparrow with a dark central breast spot. Look for its two-toned bill (dark above and yellow below), dark jaw stripe (often faint in winter birds), and dark legs.

Chipping Sparrow
Spizella passerina
5.0–5.75 in. (12.5–14.5 cm)

Range: Although at least a few can be found in all sections of the Caroli-

Chipping Sparrow

nas throughout the year, Chipping Sparrows are most numerous in the western counties during the breeding season. In winter they occur over much of the piedmont but are much more numerous toward the coast, where they are uncommon in summer. Chippies frequent open pine woods, woodland edges, roadsides, residential lawns, golf courses, and brushy fields.

Nesting habits: The female builds a nest of fine weed stems, rootlets, dry grasses, and leaves, lining it with hair or fine grasses. Nests may be placed on the ground, in vines or bushes, in the top of a young pine, or on horizontal limbs of trees as high as 30 or 40 feet (9 to 12 m) above ground. The three to five pale greenish-blue eggs are wreathed at the large end with dots of black and purple. Fed by her mate, the female incubates the eggs for 11 to 14 days,

depending on air temperature. She eats the shells after the chicks emerge, and both adults begin feeding the nestlings less than half an hour after hatching.

The female does almost all of the brooding, but she may be relieved by the male in cool weather. Young can leave the nest when 10 days old and are capable of sustained flight in another 4 days. First clutches usually are laid in May, and two or even three broods may be raised in a season. When nesting is over, Chipping Sparrows form flocks, often in company with Eastern Bluebirds, Pine Warblers, and Field Sparrows. Resident flocks of Chipping Sparrows and their companions are often joined for a day or two at a time by one or more migrant warblers.

Feeding habits: See comments on family.

Description: This small, clear-breasted sparrow has a black bill, a rusty crown, a white stripe over the eye, a black stripe through it, and a gray cheek patch. The gray rump and cheek are apparent even in young birds with streaky crowns.

Clay-colored Sparrow
Spizella pallida
5.0–5.75 in. (12.5–14.5 cm)

Range: A rare transient, the Clay-colored Sparrow is seen along the Carolina coast in fall from mid-September to mid-November, but most often in October. This western species occurs on very rare occasions in the piedmont in fall and spring. In North Carolina it has been seen during October in

Clay-colored Sparrow

Field Sparrow

Orange and Franklin Counties. As a spring transient, it has been found between April 20 and May 9 as far east as Raleigh, N.C., and as far west as Clemson, S.C. The Clay-colored Sparrow has visited Charleston, S.C., in December and early January, but it is not considered a regular winter resident there. Several have also been found to winter at some sites in eastern North Carolina.

Feeding habits: See comments on family.

Description: Similar to the immature Chipping Sparrow, the Clay-colored has a striped crown, brown cheek patch, dark chin stripe, and buffy rump. Young Chipping Sparrows have a gray rump, and the streaky crown lacks a clearly defined central stripe. Reference to a field guide is recommended.

Field Sparrow
Spizella pusilla
5.5–6.0 in. (14–15 cm)

Range: Field Sparrows are common permanent residents of roadsides, fields, and abandoned pastures in most parts of the Carolinas, but in the higher mountains they tend to be scarce in summer and absent in winter.

Nesting habits: Built by the female, the frail cup of grasses and weed stems may be lined with fine grasses, rootlets, or hair. The nest may be placed directly on the ground in a tuft of grass or a foot (0.3 m) or so above ground in a bush. Sometimes nests are found 10 feet (3 m) high in the topmost tuft of a young pine.

The two to five pale bluish-white eggs are variably spotted with reddish brown. Laying begins in late April in coastal South Carolina and continues well into July. The incubation period averages about 12 days, and two or three broods may be raised. The female usually does all the incubating and brooding, but the male may relieve her occasionally. Both adults feed the young and clean the nest. Offspring are ready for departure when 7 or 8 days old, and the female begins work on her new nest as soon as the male can care for them alone.

Feeding habits: See comments on family. Family parties gather into flocks in autumn, and hundreds of Field Sparrows may be found feeding together in weed-grown fields.

Description: This is our only sparrow with a rusty cap, white eye ring, pink bill, pink legs, and clear breast. The eye ring combined with the absence of prominent facial marks gives the Field Sparrow a blank expression on its face.

Vesper Sparrow
Pooecetes gramineus
5.5–6.5 in. (14.0–16.6 cm)

Vesper Sparrow

Range: The Vesper Sparrow is an uncommon spring and fall transient throughout the Carolinas, with migrants noticeable mostly from mid-October to mid-November and in March and April. The species is uncommon in southeastern South Carolina in winter, but to the north and inland it becomes scarce or locally absent at midwinter. In the North Carolina mountains the species breeds southward to Buncombe and Haywood Counties, and scattered June through August sightings suggest the probability of nesting southward to the Great Smoky Mountains National Park. Vesper Sparrows have also been reported to nest at Greensboro, Rocky Mount, and Wilmington, N.C.

Nesting habits: The Vesper Sparrow nests on grassy mountain balds and in pastures, cultivated fields (hay, wheat, and corn), and abandoned fields, taking frequent recourse to adjacent woodlands. The nest of grasses is built beneath fallen dead weeds or at the base of a bush or weed, usually where vegetation is sparse and low at the time of construction, although it may become dense before the eggs hatch. The four creamy or greenish eggs are variably blotched, dotted, and scrawled with rusty brown. First clutches are laid in April, and the species is double-brooded. Incubation requires about 12 days and is chiefly the work of the female. Both adults feed the young and clean the nest. The young may stay in the nest from 7 to 14 days, and they remain at least partly dependent on the adults until about 30 to 35 days old. As soon as the male can care for the first brood, the female begins a second nest.

Feeding habits: See comments on family. During the nesting season, Vesper Sparrows find their food in or near the habitat chosen as the nesting site. At other seasons, however, they forage in plowed fields, stubble fields, and short-grass habitats.

Description: At first glance a Vesper Sparrow may look like a Song Sparrow that has lost its central breast spot. Watch for the Vesper's narrow eye ring, rusty patch at the bend of the wing, and white outer feathers on a slightly notched tail.

Lark Sparrow
Chondestes grammacus
5.75–6.75 in. (14.5–17.0 cm)

Range: The Lark Sparrow is an uncommon but regular fall migrant along the Carolina coast. Elsewhere in the two states it is a very rare migrant. The species winters sparingly along the coast, arriving in early August and usually departing by mid-April. Fall migrants frequent the edges of brushy thickets and have been known to bathe under the spray from lawn sprinklers. Rarely and erratically, one to several pairs may nest successfully in western or central North Carolina (Avery, Wake, and Richmond Counties).

Nesting habits: In the spring of 1981, Lark Sparrows attempted to nest at two sites near Derby in Richmond County, N.C. One site was an abandoned field and the other was a young pine plantation. The only known successful nest was a scrape in sandy soil at the base of a pine seedling. The scrape was lined with grasses and stems of herbaceous plants. A tuft of pine needles formed a canopy that helped shade and conceal the nest. Both parents fed the young caterpillars and grasshoppers. When flushed, the birds usually flew to nearby large pines.

In the early 1980s, nesting may also have occurred at a drop zone on the Fort Bragg Military Reservation. However, there is no evidence that a Lark Sparrow population has become established in the Carolina

Lark Sparrow

sandhills, even though a few are present most years.

Feeding habits: See comments on family.

Description: This is one of our most distinctively marked sparrows. The head pattern features a crown broadly striped with white, a chestnut ear patch, and a bold black jaw stripe. The breast is white with a central black spot. The long tail is rounded and edged with white; it resembles the tail of the Eastern Towhee. Young birds may have lightly streaked breasts without the central spot, but the tail and face are enough like those of the adult to make identification fairly easy.

Lark Bunting
Calamospiza melanocorys
5.25–7.50 in. (13.5–19.0 cm)

Range: The Lark Bunting is a very rare transient and winter visitor along the Carolina coast from early September to mid-May. The species has been found inland from late April to early May. Although a Lark Bunting was in Cumberland County, N.C., once in July, the species is not known to breed in the region.

Feeding habits: See comments on family.
Description: The male is black with a broad white patch on the leading edge of each wing. The female is streaky brown with a white slur in the wing.

Savannah Sparrow
(Ipswich Sparrow)
Passerculus sandwichensis
4.5–6.5 in. (11.5–16.5 cm)

Range: The Savannah Sparrow is a winter resident of fields and short-grass habitats throughout North and South Carolina, arriving about mid-September and remaining until mid-May. The species is abundant toward the coast and uncommon in the mountains.

A pair lingered into June at North Wilkesboro, Wilkes County, N.C., and a pair appeared to be on territory on June 14, 1983, in ungrazed or slightly grazed pastures at 2,750 to 2,900 feet (840 to 885 m) in Alleghany County, N.C. The species continues to be a very localized summer resident in Ashe and Alleghany Counties.
Feeding habits: See comments on family.
Description: This small, short-tailed sparrow is streaked below, and some individuals look like miniature Song Sparrows. Yellow in the eye stripe, when present, and the notched tail readily separate this species from similar ones.

At least six different races of the Savannah Sparrow occur in the Carolinas. These vary considerably in size and general coloration, but only one, the Ipswich Sparrow (*P. s. princeps*), is readily distinguishable

Savannah Sparrow

in the field. Formerly considered a separate species, this large and pale form of the Savannah Sparrow frequents the sand dunes nearest the ocean from early November through March. The northern end of Pea Island appears to be the best place in North Carolina to look for the rare and elusive Ipswich Sparrow, and Huntington Beach State Park probably is the best spot in South Carolina. However, these birds may visit all of our undeveloped beaches every winter.

Grasshopper Sparrow
Ammodramus savannarum
5.0 in. (12.5 cm)

Range: The Grasshopper Sparrow is a fairly common summer resident in the mountains and piedmont and an uncommon winter resident over most of the coastal plain, becoming fairly common along the South Carolina coast. A few birds frequent

Grasshopper Sparrow

sparrow has a buffy, unstreaked breast. The head is relatively large for the size of the bird. Listen for the song, which is like that of the bird's grasshopper neighbors.

Henslow's Sparrow
Ammodramus henslowii
5.0 in. (12.5 cm)

Range: Henslow's Sparrow is a fairly common but secretive winter resident of coastal South Carolina from mid-October to mid-April. It winters in small numbers north to southeastern North Carolina. As a rare spring and fall transient, the species occurs inland to the mountains. Records indicate that during the 1930s and 1940s the species bred at least locally or erratically from Stumpy Point in Dare County, N.C., westward to Chapel Hill and Statesville and southward to Charlotte, N.C., and Greenville County, S.C.

Today Henslow's Sparrows are known to breed locally at Voice of America transmitter sites in Martin, Beaufort, and Pitt Counties, N.C., and in former pocosin that has been recently clear-cut in Carteret, Edgecombe, Martin, Gates, and Wilson Counties. Henslow's Sparrows show a preference for recently clear-cut areas growing up in weeds and young pine seedlings. They will also nest in very young pine plantations. Those are ephemeral habitats that in a few years become unsuitable nesting sites for the species. The population has been able to remain at the Voice of America sites because they are mowed on a schedule that suits the needs of the birds.

Outside the clear-cut areas,

grassy and weed-grown places such as fields, pastures, neglected meadows, and airports.

Nesting habits: Built in a slight depression in the ground, the flimsy but well-hidden nest of dried grasses usually is arched over on the back and sheltered by a bush, clump of grass, or clod of dirt. Eggs have been found in the Carolinas from late May through mid-September, and two broods are raised each season. The three to five white eggs are variably speckled with reddish brown. Incubation apparently requires about 12 days, and the young remain in the nest 9 days. Although several nests may be found in a suitable meadow, the species is not truly colonial because each male proclaims with a grasshopper-like song his own rather large territory, usually 1 to 3 acres (about 1 hectare).

Feeding habits: Insects, particularly grasshoppers, are a favorite food. Strips of weeds in fences along roads and airport runways seem to be preferred feeding places.

Description: This small, short-tailed

Henslow's Sparrow

Henslow's Sparrow is most likely to be found in low-lying old fields, lush meadows, and the margins of watercourses, where it runs about in the dense vegetation and behaves more like a mouse than a bird.

Nesting habits: During the breeding season, Henslow's Sparrows tend to form loose colonies. The nest and eggs resemble those of the Grasshopper Sparrow. Egg laying begins about mid-May in states to the north of us; so any Henslow's Sparrows present in the Carolinas from early May through August should be nesting locally.

Feeding habits: Although the Henslow's Sparrow is highly insectivorous, it consumes an appreciable number of grass and weed seeds.

Description: This short-tailed and big-billed sparrow has streaked underparts, striped crown, greenish head, and rusty wings. Listen for the territorial male's persistent demands for *"Schlitz!"* Young Henslow's Sparrows resemble Grasshopper Sparrows.

Le Conte's Sparrow
Ammodramus leconteii
4.5–5.5 in. (11.5–14.0 cm)

Range: Le Conte's Sparrow is an elusive, marsh-loving sparrow. It is thought to be a winter resident along most of the South Carolina coast and to some degree inland in the southern counties of the state from late October to late April. Elsewhere in the Carolinas the species is a rare spring transient seen mostly from mid-April to mid-May and a very rare fall transient or winter visitor from late October into February. Some seasons it is fairly common in salt marshes and broom-sedge fields around Charleston, but at other times it is almost impossible to find.

Feeding habits: See comments on family.

Description: Le Conte's is a buffy-breasted sparrow with streaked sides, a rusty nape, and a white median crown stripe. The white crown stripe separates this species from the Nelson's and Saltmarsh Sharp-tailed Sparrows, which are similar in size and shape but have a gray crown. The Saltmarsh Sharp-tailed may show a lighter shade of gray on the median of the crown than laterally, but not normally a pure white stripe. Juvenile sharp-tailed sparrows and many Nelson's adults show a great deal of buffiness and are easily confused with Le Conte's Sparrows.

Nelson's Sharp-tailed Sparrow
Ammodramus nelsoni
4.5–5.5 in. (11.5–14.0 cm)

Range: Nelson's Sharp-tailed Sparrow is a common to abundant winter

Nelson's Sharp-tailed Sparrow

resident of the coastal salt marshes from late September to late May. Many individuals undoubtedly pass over the inland portions of the Carolinas during spring and fall migrations, but those birds are rarely seen unless they collide with a television tower or another tall, lighted obstacle.

Feeding habits: Sharp-tailed sparrows seek food, mostly animal matter, in the densely vegetated salt marshes at low tide. They gather on islands and shorelines at high tide. At first glance a promising marsh may seem deserted, but a few squeaks from the bird-watcher will entice an inquisitive little sparrow to hop upon a stem of marsh grass.

Description: If no two individuals seem alike, do not be surprised. Two species, the Nelson's and the Saltmarsh Sharp-tailed Sparrows, and two different subspecies of the Nelson's occur in the Carolinas. Add to that the necessity for preventing confusion with several other closely related sparrows (Grasshopper, LeConte's, and Henslow's), and the identification problems become too complex for brief written descrip-

tions to suffice. Reference to a well-illustrated, recently published field guide is essential if one hopes to identify sharp-tailed sparrows accurately.

Saltmarsh Sharp-tailed Sparrow
Ammodramus caudacutus
4.5–5.5 in. (11.5–14.0 cm)

Range: The Saltmarsh Sharp-tailed Sparrow is almost identical to the Nelson's Sharp-tailed Sparrow. Until recently they were considered to be one species. The Saltmarsh Sharp-tailed Sparrow breeds along the Atlantic Coast from New England to Virginia and very likely nests in extreme northeastern North Carolina, though no proof of that has been obtained.

Nesting habits: This potential breeder nests in the relatively high and dry portions of the salt marsh. The nest and eggs resemble those of the Seaside Sparrow, but the sharp-tailed's grassy cup tends to be relatively bulky.

Feeding habits: See Nelson's Sharp-tailed Sparrow account.

Description: See Nelson's Sharp-tailed Sparrow account.

Saltmarsh Sharp-tailed Sparrow

Seaside Sparrow

Fox Sparrow

Seaside Sparrow
Ammodramus maritimus
5.75–6.25 in. (13.5–16.0 cm)

Range: The Seaside Sparrow is a common permanent resident of salt marshes throughout the Carolinas.

Nesting habits: Built of dried grasses, the nest is placed very close to the ground and attached to upright stems of marsh plants growing in or near the relatively wet portions of the salt marsh, often in rushes and cordgrasses or in adjacent uplands. Laying takes place in late April or early May, and second broods may be raised. The three or four white eggs are heavily spotted with reddish brown. Incubation takes about 12 days, and young apparently stay in the nest about 10 days.

Feeding habits: Small marine animals are dominant in the diet of the Seaside Sparrow.

Description: This dark, short-tailed, and long-billed sparrow has a yellow spot between the eye and the base of the bill.

Fox Sparrow
Passerella iliaca
6.75–7.50 in. (17–19 cm)

Range: The Fox Sparrow is a fairly common winter resident throughout the Carolinas, usually being more abundant in severely cold winters than in mild ones. In years of major flights, the birds may arrive in late October, and a few sometimes linger into early May. At other times none appear until December, and all have departed before the end of March. Fox Sparrows frequent coniferous woods and woodland thickets, rarely visiting urban bird feeders except when snow covers the ground.

Feeding habits: Scratching with both feet, Fox Sparrows toss aside leaf litter and dig holes in the snow while searching for food. Sparrows of smaller species visit the holes in the snow in search of leftovers.

Description: Noticeably larger than a White-throated Sparrow, the reddish-brown and heavily streaked Fox Sparrow has a central breast spot. In spite of its conical bill, the Fox Sparrow is decidedly thrush-like in its general appearance.

Song Sparrow

Song Sparrow
Melospiza melodia
6.0–6.75 in. (15–17 cm)

Range: The Song Sparrow is a very common winter resident throughout the Carolinas, frequenting weedy and brushy places such as hedgerows, ditches, railroad embankments, edges of woodlands and fields, and the margins of ponds and streams. Song Sparrows visit bird feeders, and they sing in all but the coldest winter weather.

The cutting of woodlands opened new habitat for the adaptable Song Sparrow, which continues to extend its breeding range in the Carolinas. The Mississippi Song Sparrow (*M. m. euphonia*) is a common permanent resident of the southern Appalachians, wintering only in the lowlands but breeding at any elevation where suitable habitat is available. Song Sparrows also breed eastward across the piedmont to Roanoke Rapids, Raleigh, and Charlotte, N.C., and to Greenville, Clemson, and Laurens, S.C. On the North Carolina coast southward at least to Ocracoke and Portsmouth, the relatively pale Atlantic Song Sparrow (*M. m. atlantica*) nests among sand dunes, marshes, and shrubby thickets.

Nesting habits: Typically, the female Song Sparrow builds the nest, using leaves, strips of bark, and weed and grass stems for the bulky outer part of the structure and lining it with fine grasses, rootlets, and hair. Locations of nests range from ground level to a height of 12 feet (4 m) or more in bushes and trees. Ground nests are the most common and usually are concealed under a bush, brush pile, or tuft of grass. Natural cavities and unoccupied buildings are also used. Song Sparrows prefer nesting sites near water, but they will build in dry places. Laying begins in late April or early May except in the higher mountains.

The four or five bluish-white eggs are heavily speckled with reddish brown. Incubation is by the female and requires about 12 to 14 days. Although males sometimes sit on the nest, they do not develop a brood patch. Both parents feed the young, which may leave the nest 7 to 14 days after hatching. At first newly fledged birds remain under plant cover, but they are ready to fly when only 17 days old. Then the female immediately deposits the eggs for her next brood, leaving the care of the previous one entirely to the male.

By the time the second brood hatches, the older offspring can look after themselves, and the male again helps the female with the nestlings. Therefore, as many as three broods can be raised in one season even in the mountains.

Feeding habits: The Song Sparrow eats insects as well as grass and weed seeds.

Description: Although quite variable in color, with the Atlantic race much paler than the Mississippi, all Song Sparrows (except very young birds) have heavy breast streaks that converge to form a central breast spot, which is usually rather irregular in shape. In flight the Song Sparrow pumps its long and slightly rounded tail.

Song Sparrows are admired for their immense repertoire of pleasing musical phrases. A basic song pattern is three clearly whistled notes followed by a trill—*sweet, sweet, sweet sweeeeee.* A longer sequence of notes may sound like "Someone's in the kitchen with Di-*naaah.*"

Lincoln's Sparrow
Melospiza lincolnii
5.25–6.0 in. (13.5–15.0 cm)

Range: During its time in the Carolinas, the Lincoln's Sparrow is a silent, solitary, and rarely seen bird that skulks around brush piles and frequents damp, brushy thickets bordering woods and fields. It is so hard to find and, once found, so hard to identify that we can assume the species is more common as a transient and winter visitor than the few annual reports indicate. Look for it in recent clear-cuts where brush piles and growths of grasses and forbs provide plenty of cover.

Lincoln's Sparrows are most numerous in the Carolinas during fall migration in October and November, when most individuals apparently occur along the immediate coast and near the Appalachian Mountains. Small numbers of this species are found during the winter months, mostly in the upper piedmont and on the coastal plain. The peak of spring migration appears to be in late April and early May. Extreme dates are September 7 and May 11.

Feeding habits: See comments on family.

Description: Song Sparrows are easily mistaken for the slightly smaller Lincoln's Sparrow. When the bird is seen head-on, look for fine, sharply defined blackish streaks in the buffy breast and sides plus a finely streaked white throat bordered on each side by a black lateral throat stripe and a buffy malar stripe. Seen in profile, Lincoln's Sparrow has a buffy eye ring, a broad gray line over the eye (supercilium), and often a peak in its crown. Reference to a well-illustrated field guide is highly recommended.

About its name: Lincoln's Sparrow received its name long before Abraham Lincoln was elected president of the United States. When Thomas Lincoln (1812–1883) was 21 years old, he found a new species of sparrow while on a trip to Labrador with John James Audubon. The bird was subsequently described by Audubon and named for its youthful discoverer.

Swamp Sparrow   White-throated Sparrow

Swamp Sparrow
Melospiza georgiana
5–6 in. (12.5–15.0 cm)

Range: The Swamp Sparrow is a common winter resident throughout the Carolinas from late September to mid-May, especially as one heads toward the coast. This sparrow can be found in wet meadows, marshes, bogs, and wet woodlands bordering streams and ponds, but—in spite of its name—not necessarily in heavily wooded swamps.

Feeding habits: Swamp Sparrows feed on or near the ground, taking insects and seeds in almost equal proportions.

Description: The Swamp Sparrow is larger than a Chipping Sparrow but smaller than a White-throated. Look for its rusty wings, rusty cap, dark streak through the eye, completely black bill, and white throat patch.

White-throated Sparrow
Zonotrichia albicollis
6.5–7.0 in. (16.5–17.5 cm)

Range: The White-throated Sparrow is an abundant winter resident throughout the Carolinas from early October to mid-May. Stragglers have been found in June and July, but there is no evidence of breeding in our region. This species occurs in almost every type of habitat and is common in urban areas as well as in fields, thickets, forests, and swamps.

Feeding habits: Most of the time, the White-throated Sparrow feeds on the ground, scratching with both feet for seeds and insects. However, in fall it consumes many wild berries, and in spring it ascends to the treetops to feast on tender buds and the insects they may attract.

Description: In all plumages this sparrow has a striped crown, a white throat patch, and a yellow spot between the eye and the bill, but in dingy fall birds the yellow spot may be very difficult to see. Listen for the song, two clear whistles followed by three quavering notes. New Englanders render this as "Old Sam Peabody, Peabody, Peabody."

Harris's Sparrow
Zonotrichia querula
7.5 in. (19.0 cm)

Range: Harris's Sparrow is an accidental winter visitor to the Carolinas. Single birds have been seen, usually in mixed flocks with White-crowned and White-throated Sparrows, in piedmont North Carolina, in Buncombe and Polk Counties in the North Carolina mountains, in northwestern South Carolina, and on the coast at Huntington Beach State Park, S.C. Recently, an adult male was near Winnabow, Brunswick County, N.C., April 22–25, 2004, and a Harris's Sparrow was at the Pea Island National Wildlife Refuge, N.C., on the early date of November 1, 2004. The species normally winters west of the Mississippi River.
Feeding habits: See comments on family.
Description: Slightly larger than a White-throated Sparrow, the adult Harris's has a pink bill and a distinctive black crown, face, and bib; its sides are streaked. Immature birds have the pink bill and streaked sides plus a blotchy band across the breast; the buffy cheek and absence of the yellow spot before the eye separate young Harris's from fall White-throated Sparrows.

White-crowned Sparrow
Zonotrichia leucophrys
6.5–7.5 in. (16.5–19.0 cm)

Range: The White-crowned Sparrow is a locally fairly common winter resident found from early October to mid-May in the northern coastal plain of North Carolina, throughout the piedmont of North and South Carolina, and in mountain val-

White-crowned Sparrow (adult)

White-crowned Sparrow (immature)

leys. The species occurs along the coast as a regular and sometimes numerous fall migrant and a rare winter resident, but it is seldom reported from the inner coastal plain south of the Neuse River. Flocks of White-crowned Sparrows winter in hedgerows and brushy areas adjacent to large open fields. The species appears to have become more numerous in the Carolinas during the late 1900s.
Feeding habits: See comments on family.
Description: White-crowned Sparrows have a light bill (pinkish or yellowish), an erect posture, and a

flat-topped look about the crown that readily separate them from the slightly smaller White-throated Sparrow. Head stripes are white in the adult and buffy in the immature, but birds in both plumages have an unmistakably military bearing.

Golden-crowned Sparrow
Zonotrichia atricapilla
7.25 in. (18.5 cm)

Range: This western bird is a very rare straggler in the southeastern United States. It breeds from southern Canada to northwestern Alaska and winters along the Pacific Coast southward to northwestern Mexico. Because the winter range of the Golden-crowned Sparrow overlaps that of the White-crowned, it is plausible that an occasional Golden-crowned might stray eastward with a flock of White-crowneds. The only report from the Carolinas is that of one seen in South Carolina at the Francis Marion National Forest on December 26, 1993.
Feeding habits: See comments on family.
Description: Similar in size and overall appearance to a White-crowned Sparrow, the Golden-crowned, whether an adult or a first-winter bird, has a yellow forecrown. Be sure to note bill color: yellow in White-crowned, gray in first-winter Golden-crowned, and bicolored (dark above, light and perhaps yellowish below) in adult Golden-crowned.

Dark-eyed Junco (Carolina race)

Dark-eyed Junco
(Slate-colored Junco, Oregon Junco)
Junco hyemalis
5.75–6.50 in. (14.5–16.5 cm)

Range: The Dark-eyed (Slate-colored) Junco is an abundant winter resident throughout the Carolinas from early October to mid-April, occasionally to early May. Members of the Carolina race of the Dark-eyed Junco (*J. h. carolinensis*) breed at elevations of about 3,000 feet (900 m) or higher in our mountains south to Sassafras Mountain and Caesar's Head in South Carolina. Permanent residents of various woodland habitats in the southern Appalachians, they are found even in winter to the tops of the highest peaks, although many individuals wander to the lower elevations after the nesting season. Winter-resident Dark-eyed Juncos elsewhere in the Carolinas are mostly from the Slate-colored population that breeds in Canada, *J. h. hyemalis*.
Nesting habits: The female builds the nest of moss, rootlets, and plant stems, usually placing it on an embankment, either in a crevice or

beneath overhanging ferns or grass. Such embankments are often right beside hiking trails or unpaved roads. When juncos nest near human habitations, they may select a site such as a hanging basket of flowers or a convenient nook in a barn.

First clutches are laid in late April or early May, and second or perhaps third clutches may be found well into August. The three to five grayish eggs are variably speckled with reddish brown. Incubation lasts 12 to 13 days and apparently is the duty of the female. She also does the brooding; but both parents feed the young, which leave the nest at about 12 days of age.

Feeding habits: Although nestlings are fed exclusively on animal matter, adults eat mostly grass and weed seeds. Juncos flock for the winter, feeding on roadsides, lawns, and fields, usually adjacent to coniferous woods. Sometimes large numbers of "snowbirds" visit feeders, particularly after a substantial snowfall.

Description: This small, slate-gray bird has a white belly and white outer tail feathers. The *Junco h. carolinensis* is a relatively large junco with a pale gray bill. The influx of winter birds from the north and west sometimes includes a few Oregon juncos (*J. h. oreganus*). Formerly considered a separate species, this well-marked race of the Dark-eyed Junco has been recorded several times in piedmont and coastal North Carolina and at least once in the mountains (a "pale adult" in Transylvania County). The Oregon junco has a black or gray hood that contrasts sharply with its brown back and pinkish-tan sides. The pink sides extend forward approximately to the bend of the folded wing, giving the Oregon Junco the distinctive appearance of a miniature towhee. Some Dark-eyed Juncos may be brownish, but they do not show a sharp line between the dark hood and the tan sides.

A Gray-headed Junco (*J. h. caniceps*) was photographed in Charlotte, N.C., where the bird was present May 25–27, 2004. This pink-billed form has a well-defined rufous mantle and black lores that contrast sharply with the gray head, breast, and wings. Reference to a well-illustrated field guide is recommended if a strange-looking junco is seen. There are several other distinctive *Junco* populations that have not yet been reported from the Carolinas.

Lapland Longspur
Calcarius lapponicus
5.5–7.0 in. (14.0–17.5 cm)

Range: The Lapland Longspur is a rare but apparently regular winter resident in the northern portions of North Carolina. The species occurs southward locally to the Charlotte Motor Speedway at Harrisburg, N.C., and the Maxton-Laurinburg Airport. In South Carolina, Lapland Longspurs have been reported from Huntington Beach State Park and Hilton Head Island westward to Orangeburg and Oconee Counties. Usually longspurs are found amid large flocks of Horned Larks on sand dunes and in fields practically devoid of vegetation. They also occur near jetties and in short-grass habitats such as airports and sod

Lapland Longspur

farms. Extreme dates of sightings are October 5 and April 20, but most known occurrences fall between mid-November and mid-March.

Feeding habits: In winter, Lapland Longspurs eat grain, grass and weed seeds, and a small amount of insect matter.

Description: The Lapland Longspur is easily overlooked by bird students who are unfamiliar with its behavior. Longspurs habitually feed in the bottom of a furrow, and their coloration makes them very hard to see even when they perch on a hummock. When flushing a flock of Horned Larks, watch for the Longspur's more undulating flight and relatively short, notched tail. Listen for its low, staccato, rattling *ticky-ticky-tic* flight call, which is easily separable from the high, sibilant squeaks of the lark. Consult a field guide for help in separating the Lapland Longspur from other longspur species and the Snow Bunting.

Smith's Longspur
Calcarius pictus
5.5–6.5 in. (14.0–16.5 cm)

Range: There are only nine known reports from the Carolinas for this very rare accidental species that usually migrates from Alaska and northern Canada to winter west of the Mississippi River southward to eastern Texas. All Carolina records of Smith's Longspur to date, including two specimens collected in South Carolina during the late 1800s, are of birds found between early November and late March.

From 1999 through 2005, Smith's Longspur was identified at Huntington Beach, S.C., where one remained for more than a month after it was found on January 10, 1999, and another was present January 22–25, 2005. In addition, single birds were reported from Folly Beach, S.C., November 7–11, 2004; Pee Dee National Wildlife Refuge, N.C.; Chatham County, N.C.; and Lumberton, N.C. The first Smith's Longspur found in the mountains of the Carolinas was photographed at Hooper Lane, Henderson County, N.C., on March 26, 2004.

Feeding habits: See Lapland Longspur.

Description: Use of a well-illustrated field guide is essential for accurate identification.

Chestnut-collared Longspur
Calcarius ornatus
6 in. (15 cm)

Range: A bird of the Great Plains, the Chestnut-collared Longspur was first recorded in North Carolina on February 28, 1992, when one, either a female or a male in nonbreeding plumage, was seen and photo-

graphed at the Charlotte Motor
Speedway near Harrisburg, N.C.
Another bird in the same plumage
was found in the southeastern cor-
ner of the Great Smoky Mountains
National Park, Haywood County,
N.C., in mid-May 2001.
Feeding habits: See Lapland Longspur.
Description: Except for the adult
breeding males, Chestnut-sided
Longspurs strongly resemble fe-
male House Sparrows. Use of a well-
illustrated field guide is essential
for accurate identification.

Snow Bunting (in winter plumage)

Snow Bunting
Plectrophenax nivalis
6.0–7.5 in. (15–19 cm)

Range: The Snow Bunting occurs erratically throughout the Carolinas
from late October well into spring.
It is most likely to be found from
early November to late February on
the Outer Banks of North Carolina,
where flocks of 100 or more sometimes are seen, or on the grassy
mountain balds lying on the North
Carolina–Tennessee border. Small
flocks of Snow Buntings apparently
winter on Big Bald Mountain in
Madison County and Round Bald
Mountain in Mitchell County. No
flock of 30 or more birds has yet
been reported from the North
Carolina mountains, any inland locality, or the Carolina coast south of
Carteret County, N.C. Inland sightings, other than those on mountain
balds, tend to occur along the major
river systems and in most cases are
associated with the spring and fall
migrations.
Feeding habits: Snow Buntings glean
grass and weed seeds in barren
habitats, often depending on the

wind to expose food by blowing
away sand or snow.
Description: Large white wing patches
provide a good field mark, but albi-
nistic sparrows are easily mistaken
for Snow Buntings. Reference to a
field guide is recommended.

Family CARDINALIDAE:
Cardinals, Grosbeaks, and Buntings

All members of this family are
equipped with stout conical bills used
for crushing the seeds that constitute
their chief source of food in winter.
Cardinals and their allies also eat
buds and berries in season, and in
spring and summer insects and their
larvae are a major source of food.
Nestlings are fed almost exclusively
on animal matter.

Northern Cardinal
Cardinalis cardinalis
7.50–9.25 in. (19.0–23.5 cm)

Range: The Northern Cardinal is
the state bird of North Carolina,
and the species is a very common
permanent resident throughout the

Carolinas. Found in every conceivable type of wooded habitat, but favoring woodland margins and residential shrubbery, the "redbird" is among the first visitors to a new bird feeder.

Nesting habits: In late March or early April, the male cardinal begins offering his mate tidbits, the tender exchange often taking place right on the feeding tray for all to behold. Soon thereafter the female is busy building her nest, which is usually placed 3 to 15 feet (0.9 to 4.5 m) above ground in a bush, tree, or tangle of vines. Composed of weed stems, twigs, strips of bark, and other pliable fibers, the nest may have leaves or pieces of paper interwoven and a lining of fine grasses.

The three or four eggs are whitish and well spotted with lavender and brown. Laying for first clutches usually begins about mid-April. The day after each egg is laid, the female returns to the nest briefly to turn the egg 180°, so the side originally touching the bottom of the nest is then on top. The egg remains in its original position relative to the rim of the nest and the other eggs in the clutch. Whether egg turning is a one-time event following the laying of each egg or a process that continues during incubation is not known.

Incubation requires 12 or 13 days and normally is the task of the female, although the male may sit on the eggs briefly from time to time. Young usually remain in the nest about 10 days and are fed by both parents. Two or three broods may be raised in a season.

Feeding habits: See comments on family.

Northern Cardinal (female)

Northern Cardinal (male)

Description: Although the Northern Cardinal is not our only red bird, it is our only red bird with a prominent crest. The male is bright red; the female, brownish. Because dark-billed young cardinals have touches of orange-red on the upper breast, eyebrows, and crest, they can be mistaken for the Pyrruloxia, a species not known to occur east of the Mississippi River.

Some people think cardinals are conceited because they frequently say that they are *pretty, pretty, pretty.* Others hear them saying *cheeseburger, cheeseburger, cheeseburger* or simply *cheer, cheer, cheer.*

Rose-breasted Grosbeak
Pheucticus ludovicianus
7.0–8.5 in. (17.5–21.5 cm)

Range: The Rose-breasted Grosbeak breeds commonly in the North Carolina mountains at elevations of 3,200 to 5,000 feet (975 to 1,500 m), but the species is known in the piedmont only as a fairly common spring and fall transient from mid-April to late May and from mid-September to mid-October. In the coastal plain it is an uncommon to rare migrant. Winter stragglers are found occasionally. Rose-breasted Grosbeaks favor mature deciduous forests during migration and on the breeding grounds.

Nesting habits: The nest is a shallow cup of twigs, grass, and other plant fibers placed 3 to 20 feet (1 to 6 m) above ground in a bush or tree. Laid in May, the three to five greenish-blue eggs are heavily spotted with reddish brown. Incubation takes 12 to 14 days, and young remain in the nest 9 to 12 days. The male shares fully with the female in all aspects of family life, including nest building, incubation, and care of young—a notable exception to the usual behavior of the cardinalids.

Feeding habits: See comments on family.

Description: Black above and white below, the male has a prominent patch of rose on the upper breast. The brown-streaked female resembles a female Purple Finch with broad white wing bars and a broadly striped crown. In flight the male flashes rosy wing linings and the female golden ones. During spring migration, listen for

Rose-breasted Grosbeak (male)

Rose-breasted Grosbeak (female)

the sharp, squeaky call note that sounds like a rubber-soled shoe skidding on a hardwood floor. The whistled song is somewhat like that of a robin, but slower and a bit husky.

Black-headed Grosbeak
Pheucticus melanocephalus
7.0–8.5 in. (17.5–21.5 cm)

Range: An accidental from the West, the Black-headed Grosbeak is a very rare fall transient and winter visitor seen mostly at bird feeders in the

Carolinas. The species normally winters south of the United States.
Feeding habits: See comments on family.
Description: The male resembles a male Rose-breasted Grosbeak, but with golden underparts and a streaked back. The female is similar to the female Rose-breasted Grosbeak, but more finely streaked. Both sexes have lemon yellow wing linings.

Blue Grosbeak
Passerina caerulea
6.25–7.50 in. (16–19 cm)

Range: A fairly common to common summer resident of the coastal plain and piedmont, the Blue Grosbeak also breeds locally and sparingly in the mountains at elevations up to about 4,000 feet (1,220 m). The species inhabits brushy open country such as hedgerows, thickets, and abandoned fields. Blue Grosbeaks normally arrive about mid-April and depart by mid-October, but a few individuals sometimes linger into winter.
Nesting habits: Usually placed from 3 to 8 feet (1.0 to 2.5 m) above ground in a fork of a bush or small tree, the rather bulky nest of weed stems, leaves, and grass may contain pieces of cast snakeskin, cotton, rags, or paper. It may be lined with rootlets or horsehair. The three or four unmarked eggs are very pale blue. Laying takes place from late May to mid-July, and two broods may be raised in a season.

The female apparently incubates the eggs about 12 days. Both adults feed the young during their 13 days

Blue Grosbeak (male)

in the nest, but the male tends the first brood after departure while the female builds her second nest.
Feeding habits: Blue Grosbeaks often perch on roadside wires, watching for insects that make up the bulk of their diet. Grain and weed seeds are the chief sources of vegetable matter.
Description: Both the blue male and the brown female are recognized by the very heavy bill and two wide brown wing bars. Blue Grosbeaks are easily confused with the Indigo Bunting, which is a smaller bird with a relatively small bill and no conspicuous wing bars. While perched, Blue Grosbeaks habitually flick their tails sideways. For song, see Indigo Bunting account.

Lazuli Bunting
Passerina amoena
5.5 in. (14.0 cm)

Range: A first-spring male was found at Fort Macon State Park, Carteret County, N.C., on March 22, 1996. It was in a mixed flock with White-throated and Song Sparrows. The

Lazuli Bunting remained at the fort through April 2, 1996. In South Carolina, an adult male was at Westminster, Oconee County, from February 11 to March 7, 1981. An immature male remained at Walterboro, Colleton County, S.C., from March 30 until April 10, 2003. Collectively, the species has been recorded in the Carolinas from February 11 through April 10. Lazuli Buntings breed in the western half of North America and winter mainly from Mexico southward. They are of very rare accidental occurrence in the Southeast.

Indigo Bunting (male)

Indigo Bunting
Passerina cyanea
5.0–5.75 in. (12.5–14.5 cm)

Range: From mid-April to mid-October the Indigo Bunting is a common summer resident of brushy fields, woodland edges, and other clearings in most parts of the Carolinas; but in the mountains the species is not known to breed above 5,200 feet (1,585 m), and in eastern South Carolina its distribution is localized. Winter stragglers are found occasionally.

Nesting habits: The female builds a nest of weed stems, grasses, and leaves 1.5 to 15 feet (0.4 to 4.5 m) above ground in a crotch of a sapling, bush, or stout weed. The three or four pale bluish-white eggs are laid from mid-May to mid-July, and two broods are raised in a season. Incubation is performed by the female and requires 12 or 13 days. The female also appears to be entirely responsible for the feeding and care of the young until they leave the nest at about 10 days of age.

The male remains near the nesting site, singing persistently and defending the nest from intruders. After the young have fledged, he helps provide for them and may even assume complete responsibility for the brood while the female begins renesting.

Feeding habits: See comments on family.

Description: In breeding plumage, the male Indigo Bunting is an iridescent blue bird without wing bars. The female is almost uniformly light brown with the underparts faintly streaked and slightly lighter than the upperparts. Some females are tinged with blue. Young birds resemble the female, but they have faint whitish wing bars and streaks on the back and breast.

After the breeding season, males molt and temporarily resemble females during the winter months. Molting males are blotched with brown and blue until they become predominantly brown. Many males returning to the nesting grounds the following spring have not yet acquired the fully blue breeding plumage.

The song of the Indigo Bunting is given in pairs of musical but sharp, metallic notes: *ti-ti, whee-whee, zerre-zerre,* with the middle pair pitched lower than the first and last. The pairs are sometimes rendered as "fire fire, where where, here here." The Blue Grosbeak begins somewhat the same way, but the song immediately turns into a mumbled jumble of falling and rising notes.

Painted Bunting (male)

WHEN IS BLUE NOT BLUE?
Because Indigo Buntings and Blue Grosbeaks habitually perch on roadside wires, even on cloudy days, they are often seen under light conditions that make them appear to be black. That occurs because there is no blue pigment in the feathers of birds. Their brilliant blue colors are created by the refraction of light, just like the beautiful colors that may appear when sunshine strikes an oil slick. When the sun is covered by a cloud or the bird is perched in deep shade, the same identification problem may be encountered with other birds having a significant amount of blue in their plumage.

Painted Bunting
Passerina ciris
4.25–5.50 in. (10.8–14.0 cm)

Range: Formerly a common summer resident along the coast of the southeastern United States from Carteret County, N.C., southward into Florida, and inland to the fall belt along the floodplains of major rivers in southern South Carolina and northern Georgia, the Painted Bunting is declining throughout its range in the Southeast. The

Painted Bunting (female)

cause appears to be twofold: loss of suitable nesting habitat in the Southeast and capture of birds in Mexico and the West Indies for the lucrative cage-bird trade. Buyers in Europe and Asia will pay as much as $70 for a pair of Painted Buntings. Biologists estimate that more than 5,000 birds are trapped annually in Mexico. More than half of the captive buntings probably die before they reach a potential buyer capable of giving them proper care.

In the Carolinas, Painted Buntings are most numerous in the dense shrub thickets of the barrier islands and adjacent mainland. Males usually arrive on the breeding grounds by mid-April, followed in about a week by females. Most Painted Buntings migrate southward before the end of October, but a few individuals linger into winter. Some have appeared regularly at feeding stations from midwinter until the beginning of the nesting season.

Nesting habits: The male announces his presence by singing from conspicuous perches and defends his territory in fierce battles that may end fatally for the weaker bird.

Usually placed less than 20 feet (6 m) above ground in a bush, tree, or clump of Spanish moss, the nest is a cup of grass, leaves, and weed stems lined with hair or fine grass. First clutches are laid about mid-May, and three broods may be raised in the Charleston area. Northward the number is reduced to two or possibly only one. The three or four eggs are white, spotted and splashed with brown. Incubation takes about 11 days, and young remain in the nest about the same length of time. The female is solely responsible for nest construction, incubation, and care of young in the nest.

Continuing to feed her fledged brood unassisted, the female begins a fresh nest at a new site. When the nest is finished, sometimes in as little as 2 days, the male suddenly begins to court her. On the eve of egg laying, he takes full charge of the first brood, which the female then abandons.

Feeding habits: See comments on family.

Description: Purple head, green back, and red rump and underparts make the fully adult male Painted Bunting unmistakable. The bright greenish-yellow female has a narrow eye ring.

Dickcissel
Spiza americana
5.5–7.0 in. (14.0–17.5 cm)

Range: Primarily a bird of the prairies, the Dickcissel was common in the Atlantic states during most of the nineteenth century, but its numbers declined in the eastern part of its range until it became virtually absent during the first quarter of the twentieth century.

Today the species occurs erratically east of the Appalachians. Small breeding colonies are found from time to time in weedy fields, wheat fields, and other open habitats of the Carolina piedmont and coastal plain. Individuals occasionally appear at bird feeders in late fall and early winter, more often along the coast than inland, but rarely even in the mountains. Although some spring and fall migrants traverse the Carolinas, there is no definitely known time for their passage. The breeding season extends from mid-May through July.

Nesting habits: The female Dickcissel builds her well-concealed nest on or very near the ground. It is a bulky affair of coarse weed and grass stems interwoven with leaves and whatever plant fibers may be convenient, the interior being lined with fine grasses, rootlets, or hair. The three to five pale blue eggs are unmarked. Incubation requires 12 to 13 days, and young leave the nest when about 8 days old. A second brood may be raised. The male takes no part in caring for the eggs or young. Some males depart soon after incubation has begun, but others remain in the vicinity, singing and giving alarm at the approach of an intruder.

Feeding habits: See comments on family.

Description: Dickcissels bear a superficial resemblance to House Sparrows, but the male has a yellow breast marked by a black V that makes him look like a stubby-billed miniature meadowlark. The female has a bluish bill and a touch of yellow on the breast. Both sexes have a reddish-brown patch at the bend of the wing.

Family ICTERIDAE:
Blackbirds and Orioles

Icterids have strong feet and legs and a pointed, conical bill, but otherwise these species show little obvious similarity in appearance or behavior.

Bobolink
Dolichonyx oryzivorus
6.5–7.5 in. (16.5–19.0 cm)

Range: Found throughout the Carolinas during migrations and fairly common to common except in the mountains, flocks of Bobolinks occur from mid-April to late May and from mid-August to mid-October. In spring the males usually arrive a week or more before the females. In fall the species is considerably more numerous along the coast than inland. Look for flocks of Bobolinks in hay meadows, grain fields, and marshes. Bobolinks once nested at North Wilkesboro, N.C., and numerous records from the mountains of North Carolina and adjacent Tennessee indicate a small, erratic, and locally expanding breeding population in that region.

Nesting habits: Male Bobolinks usually reach the breeding grounds a few days ahead of the females and choose a site in a hay, clover, or grain field. Like Red-winged Blackbirds, Bobolinks are colonial, and males sometimes take more than one mate. Arriving females are attracted to the colony by the males' songs and plumage displays, including erection of the buffy patch on the nape.

In a shallow depression in the ground amid dense vegetation, the female builds a scanty cup of coarse grass and weed stems and lines it with finer grasses. In late May or early June the female lays four to seven slightly glossy pale gray or buff eggs, which are irregularly dotted and blotched with various shades of brown. She incubates the eggs for about 13 days, and young remain in the nest about the same length of time. Bobolinks are single-brooded.

Both parents tend the offspring, which hide in the field for several days after they leave the nest and before they learn to fly. Nests are very hard to find because the female runs through the concealing vegetation for a distance when leaving her nest or returning to it.

Feeding habits: Sometimes called "ricebirds," Bobolinks used to inflict heavy damage on the rice crop in the Carolinas during fall migration; but today rice is not a major agricultural crop, and Bobolinks are no longer driven away with guns and torches. On the northern breeding grounds the species feeds mostly on insects and weed seeds, and fall migrants in the Carolinas eat wild rice and various grass and weed seeds.

Description: In spring male Bobolinks are black on the face and underparts, yellowish buff on the nape, and distinctively marked with large white patches on the wings and lower back. Females and fall males are buffy with a boldly striped crown. In all plumages Bobolinks have short and sharply pointed tail feathers that resemble those of a woodpecker.

Red-winged Blackbird (male)

Red-winged Blackbird
Agelaius phoeniceus
7.25–10.0 in. (18.5–25.0 cm)

Range: The Red-winged Blackbird is a common to abundant permanent resident of fields, marshes, lake margins, and other open habitats throughout the Carolinas. An influx of fall migrants from the north causes the species to become locally extremely abundant during winter in the vicinity of roosting places. Roosting blackbirds may become a nuisance. Once Red-winged Blackbirds have dispersed to their nesting grounds, they become good neighbors, breeding in small colonies in marshy places and consuming great quantities of insects as well as grass and weed seeds.

Nesting habits: Built entirely by the female and woven of marsh grasses, the deeply cupped nest is securely attached to the stems or supporting branches of reeds, cattails, or bushes growing in or near water. The nesting season extends from April into June, but the peak of laying is in early May.

The three to five pale bluish eggs are dotted and scrawled with black markings. Incubation, performed by the female, requires about 11 days. Males may help feed the nestlings, but females appear to be primarily responsible for care of the young during their 10 or 11 days in the nest.

Polygamy is not unusual among Red-winged Blackbirds, but pairs frequently are loyal to each other through a nesting season. The species appears to be mostly single-

Red-winged Blackbird (female)

brooded in our region, but replacement clutches are laid if eggs are destroyed. After the nesting season, Red-winged Blackbirds gather into flocks, and the sexes do not associate with each other again until the next spring.

Feeding habits: Red-winged Blackbirds eat insects, grains, and weed seeds.

Description: The shiny black male, with his yellow-bordered red patch at the bend of each wing, can be confused with no other bird that occurs in our region. Females and young males are brownish and heavily streaked above and below. Some females may show yellow or orange patches on the throat, and some first-summer males may have a touch of red and white at the bend of the wing. First-winter males are similar to adult males but have a somewhat mottled appearance.

MIXED-SPECIES BLACKBIRD ROOSTS

Every winter many localities in the Carolinas become roosting sites for large numbers of blackbirds. Mixed-species roosts may be composed of American Robins, European Starlings, Red-winged Blackbirds, Rusty Blackbirds, Common Grackles, and Brown-headed Cowbirds. The density of birds in those roosts has resulted in considerable debate regarding population dynamics of the species involved. Some ornithologists believe that monocultural farming processes and increased acreage under cultivation have contributed to a population explosion among some species. Other researchers maintain that the spreading human population has consistently reduced available roosting habitat. In any case, when birds roost in or near suburban residential areas and shopping centers, local citizens are upset by the noise and droppings.

Numerous control programs have been instituted, ranging from attempts to frighten the birds by making loud noises to killing them with guns or chemicals. Other than achieving very local short-term success, such efforts have been ineffective. Problem roosts should be reported to the state representatives of the U.S. Fish and Wildlife Service, which has employees trained to select and apply the control methods currently considered most effective.

Eastern Meadowlark
Sturnella magna
8.5–11.0 in. (21.5–28.0 cm)

Range: The Eastern Meadowlark is a common permanent resident throughout the Carolinas, frequenting meadows, pastures, large lawns, fields, roadsides, and grasslands while avoiding all kinds of woodlands. Since the mid-1990s, even where suitable habitat is readily available, the species has experienced a noticeable decline in

Eastern Meadowlark

the Carolinas. So far, the underlying cause of the decline is unknown.

Nesting habits: Nests are usually placed in a depression in a wide expanse of grass and concealed by an overhanging tuft of grass. The nest of coarse grasses is lined with finer materials. Egg laying occurs from late April through July. The three to five eggs are white with reddish-brown and purple spots. Incubation requires about 2 weeks and is performed by the female. Normally the male helps care for the young during their 11 or 12 days in the nest and assumes almost full responsibility for the first brood while the female begins building her second nest. Some males, however, may be polygamous.

Feeding habits: Meadowlarks feed mostly on insects.

Description: Meadowlarks are mostly brown above and yellow below with white outer tail feathers and a bold black V across the breast.

Western Meadowlark
Sturnella neglecta
8.5–11.0 in. (21.5–28.0 cm)

Range: During the winter the local meadowlark population is increased by many migrants from the north. These visitors sometimes include a few Western Meadowlarks, which can be separated reliably from Eastern Meadowlarks only by song or by examining the bird in hand. The Western Meadowlark is an accidental found in the Carolinas very rarely between late November and early March. There are three known records for the two states.

Feeding habits: See Eastern Meadowlark.

Description: To facilitate identification, consult a well-illustrated field guide and recordings of meadowlark songs.

Yellow-headed Blackbird
Xanthocephalus xanthocephalus
9–11 in. (22.5–28.0 cm)

Range: The Yellow-headed Blackbird, which breeds and normally winters west of the Mississippi River, occurs accidentally in the Carolinas between early August and mid-May. It is most likely to be found among the vast hordes of Common Grackles, Brown-headed Cowbirds, and Red-winged Blackbirds that winter in the eastern counties.

Feeding habits: Yellow-headed Blackbirds eat insects, including many agricultural pests; grains, with a preference for oats; and weed seeds.

Description: The adult male Yellow-headed Blackbird is completely black except for a white patch at the bend of each wing and bright yel-

Yellow-headed Blackbird

swamps, wet woodlands, fields, and pig pens adjacent to streams and ponds. Flocks may even feed in a conveniently located stable.

Feeding habits: Food items for the Rusty Blackbird are insects, weed seeds, and waste grain.

Description: Adult male Rusty and Brewer's Blackbirds are very difficult to separate in the field. Use of a well-illustrated field guide is recommended. The adult female Rusty Blackbird is distinctive because of her rusty brown head and body. Her pale eye contrasts with a dark patch around her eye. The adult male Rusty Blackbird (January to August) is usually less glossy than the adult male Brewer's Blackbird, both of which have a white eye.

low plumage on the head, neck, and upper breast. First-winter males and brownish females lack the distinct white patch in the wing. The female's yellow plumage is less conspicuous than that of the male. Her larger size and lack of streaking separate the female Yellow-headed from Red-winged Blackbirds with yellow or orange throat patches.

Rusty Blackbird
Euphagus carolinus
8.5–9.5 in. (21.5–24.0 cm)

Range: The Rusty Blackbird is a common winter resident throughout South Carolina from mid-October through April. In North Carolina the species is mostly a spring and fall transient, but it winters erratically throughout the state and sometimes is locally abundant, particularly in the eastern counties. The species frequents freshwater

Brewer's Blackbird
Euphagus cyanocephalus
8.75–10.25 in. (22–26 cm)

Range: Brewer's Blackbird is an irregular but sometimes locally common winter resident in the Carolinas from late November through mid-April. This western species is easily overlooked by those unfamiliar with it. Brewer's Blackbirds visit cattle feed lots and generally avoid fields and marshes where large numbers of other blackbirds congregate.

Feeding habits: Principal foods for Brewer's Blackbirds are insects and seeds.

Description: See Rusty Blackbird. The female Brewer's Blackbird is a dull gray-brown bird; eye color is usually dark, but some females have pale eyes and thus may be mistaken for female Rusty Blackbirds.

Common Grackle
Quiscalus quiscula
10.5–13.0 in. (26.5–33.0 cm)

Range: The Common Grackle is an abundant species found in all sections of the Carolinas during all seasons, but it is not particularly numerous in the mountains and does not breed at the higher elevations. While traveling about the region, one might notice that not all Common Grackles are exactly alike.

The Florida Grackle (*Q. q. quiscula*) breeds throughout South Carolina and northward along the North Carolina coast. Another race, the Purple Grackle (*Q. q. stonei*), extended its breeding range southward into the Carolinas during the 1900s, most rapidly from 1950 to the present. Still a third race, the Bronzed Grackle (*Q. q. versicolor*), is known only as a transient, mostly in the western counties.

Common Grackle

Nesting habits: Although the Florida race usually builds its nests in bushes near fresh water, the Purple race usually nests in small colonies in pines or other conifers. Males engage in elaborate courtship displays, including "peering up" and the "ruff-out squeak." The male helps gather nesting materials, but construction is apparently the work of the female. Made of twigs and grasses, the bulky structures are sometimes reinforced with mud and are frequently lined with grasses and feathers.

The four to six eggs usually are laid in April or early May. They are greenish white, heavily blotched and scrawled with dark brown and gray markings. Incubation requires about 12 to 14 days, and young apparently remain in the nest about 12 to 15 days. Although males help defend nests from predators and help care for the young both in the nest and after departure, they are not known to incubate eggs.

Feeding habits: Feeding mostly in open fields and grassy places, Common Grackles eat a great deal of vegetable matter, including sprouting corn, corn in the ear, and waste grain. They also consume insects, caterpillars, crayfish, mollusks, and minnows.

Description: Larger than a robin but considerably smaller than a crow, the iridescent black Common Grackle has a keel-shaped tail. Females and young of the year have shorter tails than adult males, and the fold, or keel, down the center is less pronounced; but the wedged shape of the tail still is adequate to separate grackles from Rusty and Brewer's Blackbirds.

Boat-tailed Grackle (male)

Boat-tailed Grackle
Quiscalus major
Male 15.0–17.5 in. (38–45 cm)
Female 11.5–13.5 in. (29–34 cm)

Boat-tailed Grackle (female)

Range: The Boat-tailed Grackle is a common permanent resident of coastal Carolina, where it seldom wanders far from salt and brackish waters.

Nesting habits: On the ground or on perches such as bushes or telephone poles, courting males posture grandly, ruffling their feathers, spreading their wings and tails, bowing, jumping about, and vocalizing excitedly. In the midst of this great activity, the birds may point their beaks skyward and remain immobile for a few seconds or even minutes. Suddenly the pose is broken, and active pursuit of mates is resumed.

Boat-tailed Grackles nest in colonies, and males are decidedly polygamous. Nesting sites may be bushes or tall grasses adjacent to marshes or shade trees in towns near salt water. Nests are bulky affairs woven of heavy grasses, deeply cupped, securely fastened to the supporting stems, and reinforced with mud. Eggs are laid mostly in April and May, but sometimes nesting extends into June. The species is single-brooded, laying second clutches only when the first ones are lost.

The three to five eggs are bluish white, scrawled and splashed with dark brown, black, and purple markings. Incubation requires about 2 weeks, and young remain in the nest about 3 weeks. The males do not assist in any manner in the building of the nest, incubation of eggs, or care of offspring. Indeed, males are seldom seen near the nests once the eggs have been laid.

Feeding habits: Boat-tailed Grackles feed chiefly on small aquatic animals, but they also take various other items, including seeds and fruits.

Description: Iridescent black males with their long, keel-shaped tails can be confused only with the much smaller Common Grackle. Female Boat-taileds are decidedly smaller than males and have brown plumage that sometimes appears almost golden on the breast. In flocks composed of both sexes, the contrast in size and color differentiates the Boat-taileds from Common Grackles.

Shiny Cowbird
Molothrus bonariensis
7.5 in. (19.0 cm)

Range: Chiefly a South American species, the Shiny Cowbird is a brood parasite that spread rapidly northward through the West Indies and arrived in Florida by 1985. By 1990 the species was casual as far north as the Carolinas, and it was first reported in Surry County, Va., in August 1996. The species has occurred accidentally northward into New Brunswick, Canada.

A Shiny Cowbird was first found in North Carolina when a male was seen near Aurora in southern Beaufort County on November 16, 1989. A specimen was collected in New Bern, N.C., on October 29, 1990, and four males were seen at a shopping center in Fayetteville, N.C., on October 30, 1991. One was sighted at the Cedar Island Ferry Terminal, Carteret County, on November 8, 2002, and one was at Pea Island, in Dare County, during July 2004.

The species was first reported in South Carolina rather far inland at Lone Star, Calhoun County, on March 25, 1995. During 2003, males and females were seen repeatedly at the Savannah Spoil Site in Jasper County from mid-May to mid-July.

There is understandable concern that Shiny Cowbirds may become established in the southeastern United States and threaten the existence of the Painted Bunting and other passerines that are already having difficulty maintaining their breeding population in the coastal plain. At present there is no evidence that Shiny Cowbirds pose an immediate threat to native species in the Carolinas.

Nesting habits: See Brown-headed Cowbird.

Feeding habits: See Brown-headed Cowbird.

Description: Similar to the Brown-headed Cowbird in size and general appearance, the male Shiny Cowbird is tinged with purple on the head, breast, and back.

Brown-headed Cowbird
Molothrus ater
7–8 in. (17.5–20.0 cm)

Range: First reported breeding in the Carolinas in the mid-1930s, Brown-headed Cowbirds now can be found in all sections of the region throughout the year. They are most abundant in the coastal plain and piedmont in winter, and adults are generally scarce in July and August.

Nesting habits: Cowbirds build no nests of their own but, rather, lay their eggs in the nests of other species. Females lay very early in the morning. An egg of the host species usually is removed the previous day or very early in the morning just prior to laying. Normally the female deposits only one egg per nest, but more than one female may parasitize the same nest.

Brown-headed Cowbird (male) Brown-headed Cowbird (female)

Cowbird eggs are highly variable in size, ground color, and markings; however, they are almost always larger than those of the host species. The incubation period varies from 11 to 14 days, with the cowbird eggs usually hatching before those of the host species. Even if the cowbird hatches later, this large and aggressive nestling usually survives. Brown-headed Cowbird young do not deliberately eject the eggs and young of the hosts. Ejection of the weakest nestling is often a natural consequence of an overcrowded nest.

Fledgling cowbirds normally leave the nest at 10 days of age and soon flock with others of their own species. Females apparently remain in the vicinity of the parasitized nest and lead the young away once they are independent of the foster parents.

The most frequently reported hosts in the Carolinas are the Rufous-sided Towhee, Red-eyed Vireo, and Wood Thrush. Various warblers and finches also make successful hosts. Gray Catbirds and American Robins eject cowbird eggs, and many other species abandon parasitized nests. If the alien egg is accepted, many foster parents manage to fledge one or more of their own young along with the cowbird.

There is no proof that cowbirds have created serious problems for hosts in the Carolinas. Fortunately, females tend to lay in the nests of abundant and multibrooded species. In a given season one female of a host species may lay a total of 10 to 12 eggs deposited in several clutches separated by intervals of a few days to a few weeks. The fledging of young cowbirds in June, July, and August indicates that the eggs are laid by summer-resident birds rather than by northbound migrants.

Feeding habits: Cowbirds eat insects, waste grain, and weed seeds. Their name derives from their habit of feeding in pastures and barnyards about the feet of the livestock. In winter they often occur in mixed flocks with grackles and blackbirds.

Description: Brown-headed Cowbirds have stout conical bills that are much shorter than those of grackles and blackbirds. When cowbirds feed on the ground, their tails tilt upward. Males are greenish black with a brown head, and females are uniformly gray. Immatures are similar to females, but the breast is faintly streaked.

Orchard Oriole (adult male)

Orchard Oriole (immature male; female similar but lacks dark throat)

Orchard Oriole
Icterus spurius
6.0–7.5 in. (15–19 cm)

Range: During the breeding season the Orchard Oriole is a common resident of the coastal plain and a fairly common one in the piedmont and in some mountain valleys. At the higher elevations it is known only as a transient.

True to their name, Orchard Orioles frequent orchards, groves of shade trees, open woodlands, and the edges of fields. They begin arriving in the Carolinas in early April, and most individuals depart in July or August. Winter stragglers are extremely unusual.

Nesting habits: Both members of the pair participate in construction of the nest, which is a bag woven of green grasses that yellow as they dry out. It is suspended by the rim from a fork near the tip of a drooping branch from 7 to 70 feet (2 to 20 m) above ground or water. Evergreens and large deciduous trees such as oaks seem to be preferred nesting sites, but bushes and banners of Spanish moss are also used. Although the male gathers materials, the female apparently does all of the weaving.

Orchard Orioles often nest in close association with Eastern Kingbirds and also, where their breeding ranges overlap, with Baltimore Orioles. Near the South Fork of the New River in northeastern Ashe County, N.C., a pair of Orchard

Orioles nested on a branch of a tree overhanging one side of a narrow unpaved road, and a pair of Baltimore Orioles nested on a branch almost overhanging the opposite side of the road.

The three to five bluish Orchard Oriole eggs are marked with spots and scrawls of brown and lilac. Laying usually takes place in May or June; incubation is by the female and lasts about 12 to 14 days. Young fledge in 11 to 14 days. The male feeds his incubating mate, helps protect the nest, and helps care for the offspring. The species is normally single-brooded.

Feeding habits: Orchard Orioles are highly insectivorous, but they also consume mulberries, pokeberries, and nectar. They obtain nectar from deep-throated flowers, such as those on trumpet creeper vines, by using the long and sharply pointed bill to pierce the nectaries at the base of the flowers.

Description: The fully adult male Orchard Oriole is a black bird with orange-red underparts, rump, and wing patch. The female is greenish yellow with two white wing bars. The first-year male is similar to the female, but he has a black patch surrounding each eye and extending down the throat to a point on the upper breast. People who misjudge the size of the bird sometimes think they have seen a Lawrence's Warbler, a rare hybrid form of the Blue-winged and Golden-winged Warblers. First-year male Orchard Orioles may attract a mate and breed successfully in spite of their subadult plumage.

Bullock's Oriole
Icterus bullockii
9.0 in. (22.5 cm)

Range: Formerly considered a race of the Baltimore Oriole (then called the "Northern Oriole"), Bullock's Oriole is now recognized as a species in its own right. Bullock's is a western oriole that breeds northward into southern Canada and winters from Mexico southward in the tropics. A few migrants and postbreeding wanderers stray east of the Mississippi River and into the Carolinas.

The first published report of Bullock's Oriole in our region was that of a small flock seen at a feeder in Morehead City, N.C., in early December 1959. The birds remained in the vicinity until March 1960. Fifteen years later, one visited a feeder at Southern Pines during the winter of 1974–1975.

The first sighting for South Carolina was a Bullock's Oriole present at Charleston on October 1, 1982; it stayed through the winter. Single birds were found at Raleigh, N.C., on December 18, 1982, and December 19, 1983. One was at Fayetteville on January 14, 1984, and also from March 19 to early May.

By the winter of 1983–1984, Bullock's Oriole appeared to have become an annual, though still very rare, winter visitor in the Carolinas. Since then, sightings have been very erratic. One or more may visit the Carolinas for several consecutive winters, and occasionally males are heard singing in late April or early May. Then the species may be unreported in our region for several consecutive years. To call Bullock's

Oriole a regular winter visitor in the Carolinas would be premature.
Feeding habits: See Baltimore Oriole.
Description: The male Bullock's Oriole is similar to the male Baltimore, but with less black on the head and throat and a large white patch in each wing. The first-winter male looks like a first-winter Orchard Oriole with a white belly. Adult females of the three species can be distinguished by the color of the wing lining: gray in Bullock's, yellow-orange in Baltimore, and mostly white in the Orchard.

Baltimore Oriole
(Northern Oriole)
Icterus galbula
7–8 in. (17.5–20.0 cm)

Baltimore Oriole (in winter plumage)

Range: The Baltimore Oriole is a fairly common summer resident in mature deciduous trees bordering wide streams and fields in the mountain counties north of Asheville, N.C. The species also breeds to an undetermined extent locally and sporadically eastward across the Carolinas. As a migrant throughout the Carolinas, it is generally uncommon, but it becomes common along the coast in fall. From mid-September to late April, Baltimore Orioles are uncommon to locally fairly common winter residents in the eastern and central counties, where they show a preference for towns with abundant broad-leaved evergreen shrubbery and many bird feeders.

Nesting habits: The nest is a 6-inch-deep (15-cm-deep) bag woven of plant fibers, often including string or yarn. Usually it is attached 25 to 30 feet (7.5 to 9.0 m) above ground to the terminal twigs of a drooping branch of a deciduous tree. Although the male may assist her by bringing materials, the female builds the nest.

The four to six eggs are larger than those of the Orchard Oriole but essentially the same in appearance. Laying takes place mostly in May and June; incubation is by the female and requires about 12 to 14 days. Young remain in the nest about 2 weeks. The male stays with his family until the young are strong on the wing, although he usually plays only a minor role in their care and feeding.

Baltimore Oriole nests often last through the winter and are quite conspicuous in leafless trees.

Feeding habits: Baltimore Orioles eat many insects and caterpillars, but they also take grapes and other fruits and berries. In winter they visit holes drilled by Yellow-bellied

Baltimore Oriole (adult male)

Sapsuckers. At bird feeders they are partial to oranges, pound cake, and a paste made of melted suet, peanut butter, and yellow corn meal.

Description: The black-and-orange breeding adult male Baltimore Oriole is a spectacular bird. The female has a mottled back, two white wing bars, and golden yellow underparts. Young males are similar to the female.

Family FRINGILLIDAE:
Brambling and Finches

Members of this family of seedeaters have an undulating flight pattern. Many nest in the far north, and in fall they may move south in large flocks. They often visit bird feeders, where they consume huge quantities of thistle, sunflower, and safflower seeds. Two exceptions are the House Finch and the American Goldfinch, both of which nest widely in the Carolinas.

Subfamily Fringillinae:
Brambling

No member of this subfamily occurs regularly in the Carolinas.

Brambling
Fringilla montifringilla
6.25 in. (16.0 cm)

Range: This Eurasian species is casual in fall and winter in Canada and the northern United States. One was videotaped at a feeder in Brevard, N.C., on October 31, 1998.
Feeding habits: See comments on family.
Description: In all plumages the Brambling has feathers touched with orange at the bend of the wing and on the throat and breast. The rump is white, and the black tail is noticeably notched.

Subfamily Carduelinae: Finches

Many birds in this subfamily visit southern bird feeders in winter but nest mostly in the northern part of North America.

Pine Grosbeak
Pinicola enucleator
9.0–9.75 in. (22.5–24.5 cm)

Range: The Pine Grosbeak is a very rare winter visitor in the Carolinas. This northern finch was first recorded in North Carolina in 1951 and in South Carolina in 1962. The species has been found in our region as early as mid-September and as late as May 30. Sightings usually occur during winters when the influx of Evening Grosbeaks and other northern finches is from moderate to very heavy. Pine Grosbeaks apparently travel in small flocks, five being the largest number seen at once in the Carolinas, and do not visit bird feeders regularly.

There has not been a large influx of Evening Grosbeaks in the Carolinas since about 1980. As should be expected, there has likewise been no reliable report of a Pine Grosbeak since that time.

Feeding habits: As their name implies, Pine Grosbeaks eat the seeds and buds of pines and other conifers, but in winter they also take the fruits and seeds of deciduous trees.

Description: These surprisingly tame finches are about the size of a Northern Cardinal. Superficially resembling male Purple Finches, male Pine Grosbeaks have black bills and prominent white wing bars. Female Pine Grosbeaks are olive gray with white wing bars and black bills. First-year males resemble females; however, they do have touches of red on the upperparts, especially the head and rump.

Purple Finch (male)

Purple Finch (female)

Purple Finch
Carpodacus purpureus
5.5–6.5 in. (14.0–16.5 cm)

Range: Although a few individuals may arrive in August and linger throughout May, Purple Finches are common winter residents in the Carolinas only from about mid-October to late April. Like Evening Grosbeaks, Purple Finches travel in flocks and frequent bird feeders where sunflower seeds are in generous supply. The Purple Finch is a fine singer, and these birds may be heard singing in the Carolinas from the first warm days in February until they migrate northward.

Feeding habits: In fall Purple Finches eat many wild seeds and berries, and in spring they feast on the buds and flowers of maples, sweet gums, tulip trees, cherries, and other deciduous trees.

Description: The adult male Purple Finch looks like a streaky sparrow that has been dipped in raspberry juice. Females and immatures are brown with coarsely streaked breasts. In all plumages the Purple Finch has heavy lateral throat stripes and a white belly. Most individuals have a lyre-shaped tail, prominently notched and flaring outward on both sides at the tip.

House Finches are similar, but they are finely streaked even on the belly, have a straight and slightly notched tail, and lack prominent stripes on the head and throat. First-winter males often have just a touch of red on the forehead, but older males may have nearly as much red as the Purple Finch. Although the two species are about the same length, the House Finch is less robust and thus appears smaller than the Purple Finch.

House Finch
Carpodacus mexicanus
5.5–6.0 in. (14–15 cm)

Range: House Finches being sold illegally in New York were released by the store owner on Long Island in 1940. From those few birds came the vast House Finch population that now occupies virtually all of the United States east of the Rocky Mountains, except the Florida peninsula and the high, unsettled elevations in the Appalachian Mountains.

House Finch (male)

The House Finch first appeared in North Carolina at a bird feeder in Wake County during the winter of 1962–1963; the first positive record for South Carolina came in December 1966. The species rapidly spread across the region as a winter resident, and in less than a decade House Finches were nesting in major cities throughout piedmont North Carolina and southward to Greenville, S.C. Today House Finches are more common in the Carolinas than the once-reviled House Sparrows.

Nesting habits: House Finches will nest almost anywhere: on the ground, in cavities in trees and buildings, among plants in hanging baskets, or in abandoned nests of other birds, particularly orioles and phoebes. The female builds the nest almost without help from her mate.

House Finch (female)

In California, House Finch eggs have been found from late February to early August, with the peak of laying apparently in late April and early May. As many as three broods may be raised in a season, a fact that helps account for the species' rapid range extension in the eastern United States.

Eggs usually number four or five and are bluish white, delicately spotted and streaked with olive, brown, or black. The incubation period varies from 12 to 16 days, and young remain in the nest about 14 to 16 days. The female incubates eggs and broods the young. The male feeds his mate on the nest, and both parents feed the nestlings. The chicks attempt to defecate over the rim, but the nest soon becomes fouled around the edges; the interior, however, remains clean. The House Finch tends to return to the same nest both for the second brood of the season and in subsequent years.

Feeding habits: Food consists chiefly of weed seeds and all seeds available at bird feeders; nevertheless, where House Finches are numerous, fruit crops may be damaged.

Description: This species resembles the Purple Finch but has a finely streaked belly and lacks the heavy stripes on the head or throat. Young males with just a touch of red on the forehead can be mistaken for the Common Redpoll. See Purple Finch for a comparative description.

Red Crossbill
Loxia curvirostra
5.5–6.5 in. (14.0–16.5 cm)

Range: The Red Crossbill probably is the most unpredictable and mysterious bird found in our region. Some winters, flocks of crossbills visit much of North Carolina and northern South Carolina from early November to late spring; but in other winters, the species appears to be absent outside the mountains. The real mystery is when and where the birds breed.

That mystery was compounded by the fact that on May 6, 1964, an immature Red Crossbill about 5 weeks old was collected along with an adult male and an adult female in breeding condition in Wake County, N.C. At Southern Pines,

N.C., a female was seen feeding a recently fledged bird on September 1, 1974.

Over the years from sites ranging in elevation from 3,320 to 5,740 feet (1,006 to 1,750 m), reports accumulated: a female gathering twigs, a pair with juveniles, a pair nest building, and adults carrying food. Finally, from September 5 to October 13, 1981, an active nest was studied at the relatively low elevation of approximately 3,260 feet (977 m) at Boone, Watauga County, N.C. The site was not some remote woodland, but a tree beside a parking lot on the campus of Appalachian State University. In the summer of 1986 an active nest was observed from construction until the feeding of a nestling at Linville Gorge, Burke County, N.C., at an elevation of 3,320 feet (1,006 m). In the summer of 1988, the first Red Crossbill nest for South Carolina was discovered at Caesar's Head State Park at an elevation of only 1,378 feet (376 m).

Obviously, breeding Red Crossbills are not confined to the high-elevation mountains in the Carolinas. Sighting of Red Crossbills as far south as Charleston, S.C., suggests the possibility of widespread nesting outside the mountains during the spring and summer following a major flight of crossbills into the region.

Nesting habits: Red Crossbills usually place their bulky nests from 10 to 40 feet (3 to 12 m) above ground in conifers. The male superintends but apparently does not participate in construction. The three to five eggs are tinged with green or blue and are variably dotted, splotched, and scrawled with brown and black.

The female does all the incubating and brooding, but the male feeds her on the nest and helps her care for the young, which remain in the nest at least 17 days. Bills are still uncrossed when fledglings leave the nest.

Feeding habits: Crossbills feed mostly on conifer and sweet-gum seeds. Although they can and do eat sunflower seeds, they may visit a bird bath and ignore a nearby feeder full of seeds.

Description: Red Crossbills can be identified satisfactorily even if the crossed mandibles cannot be seen. Adult males are dull red above and below with solid black wings and tail. Females are yellowish brown with dark wings and tail, a streaked back, and unstreaked underparts. Immature males are similar to females but mottled with red. Very young birds have uncrossed bills. Adult Red Crossbills are approximately the same length as a Purple Finch, but they are more robust and endowed with a larger bill.

White-winged Crossbill
Loxia leucoptera
6.25 in. (18.0 cm)

Range: White-winged Crossbills appear erratically in the North Carolina piedmont and mountains from late December to early February during major flights of wintering northern finches. Sometimes flocks of 50 to 250 birds are found in spruce-fir forests in the mountains, but most sightings are of single birds or flocks numbering fewer than 20 individuals. Reports from the coastal plain and immediate coast are very rare.

Feeding habits: White-winged Crossbills are partial to seeds of conifers.

Description: Similar to the Red Crossbill, the White-winged in all plumages has two broad white wing bars. The adult male is rosy red. Females are yellowish brown and finely streaked above and below. Immature males are similar to the female but mottled with red. Our only other red bird with broad white wing bars is the Pine Grosbeak, which is about the size of a Northern Cardinal and has uncrossed mandibles.

Common Redpoll
Carduelis flammea
5.25 in. (13.3 cm)

Range: Common Redpolls first appeared in the Carolinas soon after 1900, and a century later they remain rare and erratic winter visitors. Found between late October and early April, redpolls are most likely to be seen during major invasions by winter finches. The term "erratic" is especially appropriate for the major invasion of the Outer Banks that took place in December 2003. Hundreds were seen, and 167 were tallied on the Bodie–Pea Island Christmas Bird Count, a record one-day total for the southeastern United States.

Feeding habits: Although Common Redpolls occasionally visit bird feeders during their sojourn with us, they apparently prefer the natural food supply of forb and grass seeds found in weedy fields. Their feeding behavior is much like that of the American Goldfinch.

Description: Redpolls are small, heavily streaked birds with stout yellow-

Common Redpoll

ish bills. Adult Common Redpolls have the foreparts and rump more or less washed with red. The bright red cap and black chin are diagnostic. Immature male House Finches have the bright red forehead but lack the black chin.

Pine Siskin
Carduelis pinus
4.50–5.25 in. (11.5–13.0 cm)

Range: Like the Evening Grosbeak, the Pine Siskin may be extremely abundant one winter and almost impossible to find the next. In a good northern finch winter, Pine Siskins may occur throughout the Carolinas from late October to early May. In the mountains they can be found in small numbers at elevations above 4,800 feet (1,470 m) throughout the summer and early fall. That the species breeds southward to the Great Smoky Mountains National Park seems certain, though the evidence is far from overwhelming. There are sparse but convincing reports of breeding activity from high-elevation sites such as Mount Mitchell (6,438 feet

[1,962 m]); near the summit of Roan Mountain (6,188 feet [1,875 m]); near the main ridge line of the Plott Balsam Mountains (5,800 feet [1,768 m]), Jackson County, N.C.; and in the Great Smoky Mountains National Park (5,266 feet [1,605 m]). The Plott Balsam sighting of a male feeding noisy young in the nest appears to be the first documented report from the southern Blue Ridge Mountain province of a Pine Siskin nest containing either eggs or young.

A really interesting question is this: How often do Pine Siskins nest in the Carolinas below 3,000 feet (900 m)? In Transylvania County, N.C., at sites ranging from 2,230 feet (669 m) to 2,800 feet (850 m), observers familiar with Pine Siskin breeding behavior noticed pairs chasing each other in April and May 1986. About a month later adults were seen gleaning small insects from the underside of oak leaves, behavior consistent with feeding nestlings. On June 6, immatures began visiting feeders but were unable to open sunflower seeds. Soon thereafter adults and young left the area. On April 12, 1991, an active nest was found in Transylvania County at an elevation of 2,650 feet (808 m).

On June 7, 1982, a preflight fledgling Pine Siskin was under shrubbery near feeders in Asheville, Buncombe County, N.C., at an elevation of about 2,200 feet (ca. 670 m). Even more surprising extralimital nesting activity was noted that same month at Southern Pines in the North Carolina sandhills. The young birds seen at Asheville and Southern Pines hatched in the spring following a major flight of

Pine Siskin

northern finches to the Carolinas. Subsequent breeding activity has not been reported from either city. Because neither the spring of 1986 nor that of 1991 was preceded by a major flight of northern finches, the Pine Siskins found in Transylvania County during the breeding season appear to have been at the lowest elevations in which nesting can be expected to occur in the southern Appalachian Mountains.

Nesting habits: If siskins are seen locally in late winter, watch for breeding behavior. If any are present in April or later, try to confirm breeding. Because confirmation is very difficult, nesting probably is more frequent and widespread than presently documented.

The typical Pine Siskin nest is placed in a conifer at medium height or lower and well out from the main trunk. Concealed by dense foliage on a horizontal limb, the shallow cup of twigs and other plant materials is well lined with soft fibers such as fur and moss. The male is attentive to the female during nest building, but apparently he just superintends the work.

The nest is rather large relative to the size of the builder, a characteristic the Pine Siskin shares with other small birds that begin laying as early as March. The three to six very pale blue or greenish-blue eggs are delicately spotted with light brown and thinly scrawled with black. The incubation period is 13 days, and young may remain in the nest about 15 days. Only the female has a brood patch, but the male brings her food and helps care for the young. Apparently the species is double-brooded in some regions, if not throughout its range.

Feeding habits: See comments on family. In winter, Pine Siskins travel in flocks, often in company with American Goldfinches, and sometimes descend on feeders in droves. Siskins show a definite preference for seeds of pines and sweet gums. The birds reportedly continue feeding in flocks even during the nesting season.

Description: The goldfinch-sized Pine Siskin is finely streaked with brown and has bright yellow patches in the wings and on each side at the base of the tail. The bill is rather long and slender for a finch, and the tail is deeply notched.

Lesser Goldfinch
Carduelis psaltria
4.5 in. (11.5 cm)

Range: A bird having the field marks of the green-backed race of the Lesser Goldfinch was seen in Winston-Salem, N.C., on September 27, 1985. The species breeds in the western United States and Mexico. It withdraws from the northern part of its breeding range and winters southward throughout Mexico. Vagrants are very rare east of the Mississippi River.

Feeding habits: See comments on family.

Description: The adult male of the Texas population is black above and bright yellow below with a large amount of white near the bend of the wing. The adult male of the western population is similar but is greenish on the nape and back. Similar to males of the western population, females are greenish about the head, lack the black cap, and have little white in the wings.

American Goldfinch (male in breeding plumage)

American Goldfinch
Carduelis tristis
4.5–6.0 in. (11.5–15.0 cm)

Range: Most abundant in winter, the American Goldfinch can be found in all sections of the Carolinas throughout the year, but it becomes scarce or locally absent toward the coast in summer. Winter flocks visit weedy fields, thickets, residential areas, and various types of woodlands.

Nesting habits: The nest is built by the female. Usually placed less than 15 feet (4.5 m) above ground in an upright fork of a bush or low tree growing along a stream or the edge of a thicket, the compact nest is woven of grasses, strips of bark, and other plant fibers and lined with down from cattails or thistles.

Goldfinches are late breeders, nests rarely being built before thistles mature in the latter part of June. Thistles provide both food and nesting materials. Some eggs are still being incubated in mid-September. The four to six eggs are

American Goldfinch (nonbreeding plumage)

unmarked bluish white, and incubation requires 12 to 14 days. The female goldfinch sits on the eggs almost constantly, and she is fed by her mate.

Both adults feed the young, which leave the nest at 11 to 15 days of age. Only one brood is raised, and the birds begin flocking soon after the breeding season.

Feeding habits: See comments on family. Goldfinches and some other small finches are partial to thistle seeds.

Description: The breeding male American Goldfinch is unmistakable with his canary-yellow body, black-and-white wings and tail, and jaunty black cap pulled down over his forehead. Breeding females and winter birds of both sexes are dull greenish- or brownish-yellow, but they have the distinctive black-and-white pattern in the wings and tail.

Evening Grosbeak (male)

Evening Grosbeak
Coccothraustes vespertinus
7.0–8.5 in. (17.5–21.5 cm)

Range: First found in North Carolina in 1922 and in South Carolina in 1951, Evening Grosbeaks are erratic winter residents throughout the Carolinas, scarce some seasons and abundant others. The extent of the invasion apparently depends on the availability of natural food supplies in eastern Canada.

Evening Grosbeak (female)

In our region, grosbeaks tend to be most numerous in pine forests and in urban areas having many bird feeders well stocked with sunflower seeds. Although a few birds arrive sooner and depart later, the major flocks generally arrive in November and leave in April. As yet no winter roost has been discovered in the Carolinas, but elsewhere pines and other evergreens appear to be preferred winter roosting sites.

The same conditions that cause many Evening Grosbeaks to move south for the winter often cause unusual numbers of Pine Siskins, Purple Finches, and crossbills to visit the Carolinas. Bird-watchers refer to such seasons as "big northern finch winters." Since the advent of the House Finch as a breeding and wintering species throughout the eastern United States, big northern finch winters have become few and far between. In fact, there has not been a really good one since the mid-1980s.

Feeding habits: See comments on family. Evening Grosbeaks provide much excitement for the backyard birder who is financially able to feed those voracious guests. Many observers have noted that grosbeaks tend to leave feeders before midafternoon, which supports the supposition of a communal roost that may be a good distance from the usual feeding sites.

Description: The male Evening Grosbeak is more colorful than the female, which usually is the case with
our winter finches. He is our only
winter finch with a yellow forehead
and large white wing patches.

Family PASSERIDAE:
Old World Seedeaters

This large Old World family has only
one member introduced to North
America and established in the Carolinas. The House Sparrow spread from
New York throughout the contiguous
United States, moved north well into
Canada, and went south of the border,
spreading throughout Mexico and the
West Indies. In recent years the population of the much-reviled "English
Sparrow" appears to have declined
in the eastern United States, possibly
because of strong competition from
the introduced population of House
Finches.

House Sparrow (male)

House Sparrow
Passer domesticus
6.25 in. (16.0 cm)

House Sparrow (female)

Range: The House Sparrow is an
abundant permanent resident
throughout the Carolinas, being
scarce or absent only in those
habitats well removed from human
settlements. This European species,
which is quite different from our
native sparrows, was introduced in
Brooklyn, New York, in the 1850s.
By the 1870s it had reached Raleigh
and Charleston.
    Although these birds consume
various harmful insects, they are
considered pests because they build
unsightly nests, are frequent hosts
for ectoparasites, and often drive
native species (e.g., Eastern Blue-

birds and Cliff Swallows), from their
nesting chambers.
Nesting habits: House Sparrows
have been found breeding in the
Carolinas during every month of
the year, but the nesting season
generally lasts from March through
September. Bulky nests of grass
and weed stems lined with feathers
may be hung in trees or placed in
crevices of buildings. Both sexes
build the nest. House Sparrows are
multibrooded, but reports of more
than two successful broods per year
are not adequately documented.
    The courting male House Spar-
row struts before the female with

his wings drooped and his tail cocked. She responds by crouching, fluttering her wings, and begging for food like a baby bird. The four to seven eggs are dull white, variably speckled and spotted with purple and gray. Incubation lasts 12 or 13 days and is the duty of the female. Young remain in the nest about 15 days and are cared for by both adults.

Feeding habits: The spread of the House Sparrow was facilitated by its varied diet. It devours grains, fruits, and vegetables as well as insects and garbage. It often forages around stables and feed lots in rural areas, and in cities it favors parking lots at fast-food restaurants.

Description: House Sparrows are brown birds with dingy white underparts. The male has a gray crown, black bill, and black bib. The female has a wide, pale eye line and a light, often yellowish bill. Having no truly distinctive markings, a lone female House Sparrow presents a difficult challenge in bird identification.

Note: Terms used to describe the residence status and relative abundance of birds are defined in the introduction to the species accounts (pp. 30–31).

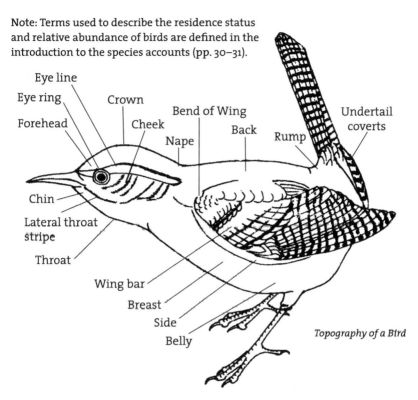

Eye line
Eye ring
Forehead
Crown
Cheek
Nape
Bend of Wing
Back
Rump
Undertail coverts
Chin
Lateral throat stripe
Throat
Wing bar
Breast
Side
Belly

Topography of a Bird

adult. Bird of breeding age, usually with distinctive adult plumage patterns.

air sacs. Outpocketings of the lungs extending into the spaces between organs and in some cases lying just beneath the skin.

albinism. An absence of pigment (color) from skin, eyes, and plumage. May be partial or complete.

altricial young. Birds that are born helpless, with eyes usually closed, and with little or no down.

antarctic. The south polar region.

arboreal. Inhabiting trees.

arctic. The north polar region.

auriculars. The contour feathers on the side of the head, which conceal the external opening for the ear.

aves. The class of animals to which birds belong.

avifauna. All bird species of a designated region.

axillars. The elongated feathers lying beneath the wing and close to the body, a location comparable to the human armpit.

bar. A contrasting mark across a given part of the plumage.

bend of the wing. The outermost

movable joint of a wing, comparable to the human wrist.

brood. The birds resulting from a single nesting effort. Birds may be single-brooded (one brood per year) or multibrooded (two or more broods per year).

cambium. The layer of tissue immediately beneath the bark of some shrubs and trees. The region of lateral growth in plants.

canopy. The uppermost portions of the tree layer of a forest.

carnivorous. Flesh eating.

cere. A soft, swollen, and often brightly colored area at the base of the upper portion of the bill. Occurs in hawks and pigeons.

chin. A small patch of feathers lying between two prong-like projections extending posteriorly from the lower mandible on each side of the jaw.

chin stripe/jaw stripe. Terms used informally in reference to the lateral throat stripes or to the malar stripe.

clutch. The eggs laid by a single bird in one nesting cycle.

community. Characteristic groupings of interacting plants and animals. Each community is usually named for one or more of the dominant plants, as in the pine forest community.

coniferous. Bearing cones, as in pines, firs, spruces, and hemlocks.

contour feather. One of the numerous overlapping feathers (about 1,500 to 3,000 on a typical songbird) that give the bird its overall body shape.

courtship feeding. Ritualized feeding of a female by a male during courtship.

coverts. Feathers covering the bases of the flight feathers of the wing and tail.

crepuscular. Active at dawn and dusk.

crest. A tuft of feathers on the crown of a bird, as in the Northern Cardinal.

crustaceans. Members of a large group of invertebrates including shrimp, crayfish, and crabs.

deciduous. Shedding or losing leaves (of plants) at the end of the growing season.

decurved. Curved downward, as in the bill of a Long-billed Curlew.

distribution. The geographic range of a species.

diurnal. Active during the day.

ear tufts. Paired tufts of elongated feathers on each side of the head, as in the Great Horned Owl. Ear tufts are not actually associated with the ears, which are covered by a patch of contour feathers (auriculars).

ecology. The study of the relationships between organisms and their environments.

environment. The sum total of the biological and physical factors that surround an organism.

exotic. Not native, from another part of the world; an introduced species.

eye ring. A narrow ring of distinctly colored (often white) feathers immediately surrounding the eye of a bird.

facial disk. A feathered area around the eyes of owls that gives them the appearance of having a face. The feathers of the facial disk assist in capturing sound waves and directing them into the ears.

fall line. The zone of intergradation between the coastal plain and the piedmont.

family. A group of closely related genera. Members of a family usually share several important characteristics.

feathers. Highly modified epidermal (skin) scales peculiar to birds, which serve as their principal covering. Feathers may be of several types, including primary, secondary, contour, down, bristle, and powder-down.

fecal sac. A clear mucous membrane containing the partly digested food that has passed rapidly through the digestive system of a newly hatched bird.

fledgling. A young bird that is capable of flight but is still dependent on its parents.

forbs. Herbaceous plants, other than grasses, found growing in fields or meadows.

frontal shield. An elevated portion of the base of the upper mandible.

gape. The open mouth of a bird.

genus (pl. genera). Unit of classification between the family and the species. The name of the genus becomes the first word of the scientific name for all species in a given genus.

gonys. A ridge found along the bottom of a bird's bill on the section at the tip. The red spot on the bill of an adult Herring Gull is above the beginning of the gonys (GO-nis). In some species, there is a noticeable bend in the lower mandible at the beginning of the gonys, a point known as the gonydeal (go-NID-e-al) angle.

gregarious. Occurring in groups.

gular region. A portion of the throat of birds. It corresponds to the large gular (GEW-lar) pouch of pelicans.

habitat. The type of environment in which a plant or animal lives; the place where a bird lives.

hybrid. Generally considered to be an offspring derived from parents of different species.

immature. Not sexually mature.

incubation period. The time between the beginning of incubation and the hatching of the eggs.

insectivorous. Feeding primarily on insects.

invertebrates. Animals without backbones or spinal columns, including insects, worms, and shellfish.

iridescent. Having bright color produced by the selective reflection of light from feathers rather than from the production of pigments. Iridescent colors change with changes in light.

lamellae. Thin plates or scales, as along the margins of the bills of many waterfowl.

larvae. Immature stages of many kinds of organisms. Caterpillars are larvae of moths, butterflies, and various insects; tadpoles are larvae of frogs.

lateral throat stripes. Two dark stripes extending downward from the jaw on each side of the throat. They are sometimes informally referred to as "chin stripes" or "jaw stripes."

length. The total measured straight-line distance in a bird from the tip of the bill to the tip of the longest tail feather.

lobed. Having lobes or flaps, as with the lobed toes of grebes.

lores. The area between the eye and the bill of a bird. May be feathered or unfeathered.

malar stripe. A patch of feathers on the cheek, or malar (MAY-ler) of a bird (e.g., the black "mustache" on the cheek of an adult male Northern (yellow-shafted) Flicker.

mammals. Warm-blooded vertebrates that have hair and produce milk to feed their young.

mandible. Either the upper or the lower part of the beak in birds.

mantle. The upper surface of the back and wings of birds.

melanism. The development of unusually large amounts of black pigment in the color of birds.

migration. The regular movement of a species between one part of its range and another. In the Carolinas, migration is usually associated with a movement southward in fall and a return northward in spring.

mollusks. Members of a large group of invertebrates that generally are encased in shells, such as oysters, clams, and snails.

molt. The periodic shedding of some or all of the feathers. Birds molt at least once each year, and many have a second complete or partial molt.

monogamous. Having a mating system in which a single male and a single female mate. The duration of the pair bond may be for a single nesting, for a single season, or for life.

morph. A color phase, as in red and gray Eastern Screech-Owls.

mustache. A popular term loosely applied to a patch of feathers extending from the bill toward the back of the head; also, the malar stripe.

nictitating membrane. A thin membrane that lies under the eyelids of birds. Although transparent in most species, it is opaque in owls. Its primary function is to protect the eyes from drying out during flight.

nocturnal. Active at night.

omnivorous. Eating both animal and plant materials.

order. A major unit of classification higher than the family.

ornithology. The study of birds.

ovate. Having the shape of the normal egg of a chicken.

passerine. A term used for members of the avian order Passeriformes (the perching birds).

pelagic. Pertaining to the open ocean.

pellet. A mass of undigested food materials regurgitated by some birds.

plumage. The total of all feathers on a bird.

polygamous. Having a mating system whereby a bird may have more than one mate at a time.

powder-down. Specialized feathers that grow in patches on the skin of some birds, notably herons. The tips of the feathers fray, forming a powdery substance that may be used to dress the feathers.

precocial young. Downy chicks capable of locomotion shortly after hatching, as in ducklings.

primaries. The major flight feathers of birds. Primaries are elongated feathers attached along the rear edge of the wing from the bend of the wing to the tip.

recurved. Bent upward, as in the bill of the American Avocet.

regurgitation. The casting out of food from the stomach or mouth.

rictal bristles. Stiff, hairlike feathers surrounding the gape of some birds, as in the Whip-poor-will.

secondaries. A row of elongated feathers attached along the rear of the wing between the bend of the wing and the body.

serrated. Toothed, as in the bill of a merganser.

sibilant. Characterized by a hissing sound.

species. Commonly equated with a kind of organism. The term more properly refers to a group of interbreeding organisms that are generally reproductively isolated from other species.

speculum. A brightly colored area, often iridescent, on the secondaries of some ducks.

subspecies. Geographic races of a species.

subtropical. Characteristic of regions bordering the tropics.

supercilium. A line extending above the eye from the bill to the nape.

temperate zone. A region in the middle latitudes lying between the subtropics and the polar regions. The Carolinas are in the North Temperate Zone.

territory. A defended area. Territory most typically refers to an area defended by a male against entry by other reproductively active males of the same species during the breeding season.

tertial. Any one of the three secondary flight feathers that are closest to the body of a bird, tertials (TER-shels) are different in appearance from the other secondary flight feathers, often being unlike them in shape or color.

tropical. Characteristic of those regions, adjacent to the equator, that have uniform day lengths and constant warm temperatures.

tube-nosed. Having the openings of the nostrils at the end of a pair of tubes extending forward from the base of the upper mandible.

tundra. A major Arctic community that is characterized by low vegetation and poor drainage.

understory. The space beneath the canopy of a forest, often occupied by characteristic tree species such as, in the Carolinas, hollies and dogwoods.

uropygial gland. Lying near the base of the tail in many, but not all, species of birds, the gland, when touched, secretes oil used in dressing the plumage.

vertebrates. Animals having a spinal column, including birds, mammals, fish, reptiles, and amphibians.

wing bar. A light-colored stripe extending across the folded wing of a bird. Usually visible only when the bird is perched.

wing linings. The coverts on the underside of the wing.

wingspan. The total distance between the tips of a bird's outstretched wings.

wing stripe. A contrasting stripe running lengthwise the wing of a bird and often providing a useful field mark for the identification of birds in flight.

Field Guides and Bird-Watching

Baicich, P. J., and C. J. O. Harrison. 1997. *A Guide to the Nests, Eggs, and Nestlings of North American Birds*. Academic Press, San Diego, Calif.

Dunn, J. L., and K. Garrett. 1997. *A Field Guide to Warblers of North America*. Houghton Mifflin, New York.

Harrison, H. H. 1975. *A Field Guide to Birds' Nests*. Houghton Mifflin, Boston.

Harrison, P. 1996. *Seabirds of the World*. Princeton University Press, Princeton, N.J.

Kaufman, K. 2000. *Birds of North America*. Houghton Mifflin, New York.

National Geographic. 1999. *Field Guide to the Birds of North America*. National Geographic Society, Washington, D.C.

Paulson, D. 2005. *Shorebirds of North America: The Photographic Guide*. Princeton University Press, Princeton, N.J.

Peterson, R. T., and V. M. Peterson. 2002. *A Field Guide to the Birds: Birds of Eastern and Central North America*. Fifth edition. Houghton Mifflin, Boston.

Robbins, C. S., B. Bruun, and H. S. Zim. 2001. *Birds of North America*. St. Martin's Press, New York.

Sibley, D. A. 2000. *The Sibley Guide to Birds*. Knopf, New York.

Sibley, D. A. 2002. *Sibley's Birding Basics*. Knopf, New York.

Sibley, D. A. 2003. *Field Guide to Birds of Eastern North America*. Knopf, New York.

Stokes, D. W., and L. Q. Stokes. 1996. *Stokes Field Guide to Birds*. Little, Brown, Boston.

Terres, J. K. 1968. *Songbirds in Your Garden*. Thomas Y. Crowell, New York.

Thompson, B., III. 1997. *Bird Watching for Dummies*. IDG Books Worldwide, Foster City, Calif.

Regional: The Carolinas

Bearden, K., compiler. 2000. *A Birdwatcher's Guide to the Triangle*. Wake Audubon Society, Raleigh.

Bearden, K., editor. 2002. *Birding in North Carolina State Parks*. Wake Audubon Society, Raleigh.

Biggs, W. C., Jr., and J. F. Parnell. 1989. *State Parks of North Carolina*. John F. Blair, Publisher, Winston-Salem. [Out of print.] Rights to the book have been transferred to Friends of State Parks, and a new edition is in preparation at Niche Publishing LLC. For current information on the work, e-mail <bpendergraft@envmedia.com>.

Carter, R. M. 1993. *Finding Birds in South Carolina*. University of South Carolina Press, Columbia.

Fussell, J. O., III. 1994. *A Birder's Guide to Coastal North Carolina*. University of North Carolina Press, Chapel Hill.

Green, C. H. 1993. *Birds of the South: Permanent and Winter Birds*. Republished 1995 with new introduction and appendix by E. F. Potter. University of North Carolina Press, Chapel Hill.

Lee, D. S., and J. F. Parnell. 1990. *Endangered, Threatened, and Rare Fauna of North Carolina. Part*

III. *A Re-evaluation of the Birds.* Occasional Papers of the North Carolina Biological Survey, N.C. State Museum of Natural Sciences, Raleigh.

Parnell, J. F., W. D. Webster, and T. L. Quay. 1992. *Birds and Mammals of the Cape Hatteras National Seashore: Thirty-Five Years of Change.* UNC Sea Grant College Program, UNC-SG-92-01. North Carolina State University, Raleigh.

Pearson, T. G., C. S. Brimley, and H. H. Brimley. 1942. *Birds of North Carolina.* Revised 1959 by D. L. Wray and H. T. Davis. N.C. Department of Agriculture, Raleigh.

Post, W., and S. A. Gauthreaux Jr. 1989. "Status and Distribution of South Carolina Birds." Contributions from the Charleston Museum, XVIII, Charleston.

Simpson, M. B., Jr. 1992. *Birds of the Blue Ridge Mountains: A Guide for the Blue Ridge Parkway, Great Smoky Mountains, Shenandoah National Park, and Neighboring Areas.* University of North Carolina Press, Chapel Hill.

Sprunt, A., Jr., and E. B. Chamberlain. 1949. *South Carolina Bird Life.* Revised 1970 by E. M. Burton. University of South Carolina Press, Columbia.

Thompson, B., III. 2004. *North Carolina Bird Watching.* Cool Springs Press, Nashville, Tenn.

Bird Biology, Habits, and Behavior

Alsop, F. J., III. 2002. *Birds of North America.* D. K. Publishing, New York, in association with the Smithsonian Institution, Washington, D.C.

Audubon, J. J. 1840. *The Birds of America.* 7 volumes. Republished 1967 with introduction by Dean Amadon. Dover Publications, New York.

Baughman, M., editor. 2003. *Reference Atlas to the Birds of North America.* National Geographic Society, Washington, D.C.

Bent, A. C., and others. 1919–1968. *Life Histories of North American Birds.* 24 volumes. Bulletins of the U.S. National Museum. Republished by Dover Publications, New York.

Gill, F. B. 1995. *Ornithology.* Second edition. W. H. Freeman, New York.

Griggs, J. L. 2001. *All the Birds of North America.* Harper Collins, New York.

Kaufman, K. 1996. *Lives of North American Birds.* Peterson Natural History Companions (photo illustrated). Houghton Mifflin, Boston.

Poole, A., and F. Gill, editors. 1992. *The Birds of North America: Life Histories for the 21st Century.* Buteo Books, Shipman, Virginia. Individual species accounts may be ordered by mail (3130 Laurel Rd., Shipman, VA 22971), telephone (800-722-2460), fax (434-263-4842), or e-mail (<allen@buteobooks.com>). Visit <www.buteobooks.com> for further details on prices and ordering instructions. Your local library may be among the numerous institutions that have subscribed to the series.

Sibley, D. A. 2001. *The Sibley Guide to Bird Life and Behavior.* Knopf, New York.

Stokes, D. W., and L. Q. Stokes. 1979–1989. *A Guide to Bird Behavior.* 3 volumes. Little, Brown, Boston.

Terres, J. K. 1996. *The Audubon Society Encyclopedia of North American Birds.* Random House, New York.

Biographies

Odum, E. P., editor. 1949. *A North Carolina Naturalist: H. H. Brimley, Selections from His Writings.* University of North Carolina Press, Chapel Hill.

Orr, O. H., Jr. 1992. *Saving American Birds: T. Gilbert Pearson and the Founding of the Audubon Movement.* University Press of Florida, Gainesville.

Shuler, J. 1991. *Had I the Wings: The Friendship of Bachman and Audubon.* University of Georgia Press, Athens.

Journals

The Auk. Published quarterly by American Ornithologists' Union. Membership information available from Ornithological Societies of North America, c/o Allen Press, P.O. Box 1897, Lawrence, KS 66044-8897.

Birding. Published bimonthly by American Birding Association. Membership and subscription information available from American Birding Association, P.O. Box 6599, Colorado Springs, CO 80904-3624. <www. americanbirding.org>.

The Chat. Published quarterly by Carolina Bird Club, Inc. Mailing address: N.C. State Museum of Natural Sciences, 11 W. Jones Street, Raleigh, NC 27601-1029.

The Condor. Published quarterly by Cooper Ornithological Union. Membership information available from Ornithological Societies of North America, c/o Allen Press, P.O. Box 1897, Lawrence, KS 66044-8897.

Journal of Avian Biology. Distributed by Blackwell Publishing on behalf of the Nordic Society Oikos. Free online trial available at <www. blackwell-synergy.com>.

Journal of Field Ornithology. Published quarterly by the Association of Field Ornithologists, Inc. Membership information available from Ornithological Societies of North America, c/o Allen Press, P.O. Box 1897, Lawrence, KS 66044-8897.

North American Birds. Published quarterly by American Birding Association. Membership and subscription information available from American Birding Association, P.O. Box 6599, Colorado Springs, CO 80904-3624. <www. americanbirding.org>.

The Wilson Bulletin. Published quarterly by Wilson Ornithological Society. Membership information available from Ornithological Societies of North America, c/o Allen Press, P.O. Box 1897, Lawrence, KS 66044-8897.

Popular Magazines

Bird Watcher's Digest. Published bimonthly. P.O. Box 110, Marietta, OH 45750. <www. birdwatchersdigest.com>.

The Living Bird. Published by Cornell Laboratory of Ornithology, 159 Sapsucker Woods Road, Ithaca, NY 14850.

Wildbird. Published bimonthly by Fancy Publications, 3 Burroughs, Irvine, CA 92618-2804. <www. wildbirdmagazine.com>.

Other Resources

Numerous additional helpful resources include books, journals, magazines, tape recordings, CDs, and DVDs not listed above. Many such educational materials are available in local bookstores; in gift shops operated by science museums, state parks, national parks, and wildlife refuges; and by mail order from organizations such as American Birding Association, Cornell Laboratory of Ornithology, National Audubon Society, and the Roger Tory Peterson Institute, Jamestown, N.Y. Those organizations generally offer their members a discount on purchases and on the fee for participation in any guided field trips they may sponsor.

More and more birding information is being dispensed through electronic media. Visit the website for Carolina Bird Club, Inc. (<www.carolinabirdclub.org>), and that of the American Birding Association (<www.americanbirding.org>). Both sites provide information on membership and activities.

Carolina bird-watchers are invited to subscribe to the listserv <carolinabirds@duke.edu>, a forum that deals with a wide array of information and topics concerning the birds of the region. You may subscribe by sending an e-mail to <majordomo@acpub.duke.edu>. Type in the message "subscribe carolinabirds." Put the two words in parentheses without the quotation marks or any other punctuation.

If you are computer savvy and like keeping detailed records, you may enjoy using one of the several software packages that can help you maintain and access your birding records electronically.

The photographs in this book were taken by James F. Parnell, except for those provided by the following photographers and agencies:

William C. Alexander: Canvasback, male; Canvasback, female; Common Eider; Fulvous Whistling-Duck; Gadwall, male; Gadwall, female; Redhead; Ring-necked Duck, male; Ring-necked Duck, female

Reg Daves: Blackpoll Warbler; Glaucous Gull; Gray-cheeked Thrush; Kentucky Warbler; Magnolia Warbler, male; Northern Fulmar; Rose-breasted Grosbeak, female; Ruffed Grouse; Short-eared Owl; Swainson's Thrush

Jack F. Dermid: American Crow; Pileated Woodpecker

Bill Duyck: Alder Flycatcher; Black-billed Cuckoo; Golden Eagle, immature; Least Flycatcher; Ovenbird; Ruby-throated Hummingbird, adult at nest; Rufous Hummingbird; Veery; Willow Flycatcher; Wood Thrush; Yellow-breasted Chat

Walker Golder: Black Skimmer, feeding in flight; Virginia Rail

Gilbert S. Grant: Barn Owl; Black Vulture, perched; Brown-headed Cowbird, female; Chipping Sparrow; Double-crested Cormorant; Great Egret, courting; Masked Booby; Northern Bobwhite; Painted Bunting, male; Red-necked Phalarope; Red-throated Loon; Turkey Vulture, perched; White-throated Sparrow

E. Wayne Irvin: Sabine's Gull; Sharp-shinned Hawk

Jeff Lewis: Common Ground Dove; Magnolia Warbler, female; Northern Gannet

Chris Marsh: Black Vulture, in flight; Pomarine Jaeger, immature on beach; Snowy Owl; Turkey Vulture, in flight

North Carolina Wildlife Resources Commission: Red-eyed Vireo (photographed by Jack F. Dermid)

Brian Patteson: Black-capped Petrel; Black-legged Kittiwake, immature in flight; Common Redpoll; Cooper's Hawk; Cory's Shearwater; Dovekie; Greater Shearwater; Long-tailed Jaeger; Manx Shearwater; Pomarine Jaeger, adult in flight; Sooty Shearwater; White-faced Storm-Petrel; Wilson's Storm-Petrel, in flight

Eloise F. Potter: Baltimore Oriole, male; Carolina Wren; Evening Grosbeak, male; Tufted Titmouse

Hollis J. Rogers: Hooded Warbler, female on nest

Michael P. Schultz: Buff-breasted Sandpiper; Northern Saw-whet Owl

Harry D. Sell: Bald Eagle; Brown Creeper; Common Goldeneye, male; Gadwall, pair in flight; Greater White-fronted Goose; Harlequin Duck; Long-tailed Duck; Marsh Wren; Mississippi Kite; Red-tailed Hawk, in flight; Thick-billed Murre; White-breasted Nuthatch; White-winged Scoter; Wilson's Phalarope

Garland L. Smith Jr.: King Rail; Red-winged Blackbird, female

U.S. Army Corps of Engineers: Figure 8